Reflections
On The Screen

George W. Linden
Southern Illinois University, Edwardsville

Wadsworth Publishing Company, Inc.
Belmont, California

Copyrights & Acknowledgments

Faber and Faber Ltd.—For excerpts from *Films and Feelings* by Raymond Durgnat.

Grove Press, Inc.—For excerpts from *Film Technique and Film Acting* by V. I. Pudovkin. Translated and edited by Ivor Montagu. Published by Grove Press, Inc. All rights reserved.

Holt, Rinehart and Winston, Inc.—Excerpt from "Carpe Diem" from *The Complete Poems of Robert Frost.* Copyright 1942 by Robert Frost. Copyright © 1970 by Lesley Frost Ballantine. Reprinted by permission of Holt, Rinehart and Winston, Inc.

Jonathan Cape Limited, London—Excerpt from "Carpe Diem" from *The Complete Poems of Robert Frost,* published by Jonathan Cape Limited.

Routledge & Kegan Paul Ltd.—Excerpts from *The Phenomenology of Perception* by Maurice Merleau-Ponty and from *Feeling and Form* and *Problems of Art* by Susanne K. Langer.

The University of Chicago Press—For excerpts from *Mind, Self & Society* by George H. Mead. Copyright 1934 by The University of Chicago Press.

The illustrations on the cover and title page are from *Juliet of the Spirits,* courtesy of Rizzoli Film, S.P.A. The illustrations on the chapter opening pages are from stills courtesy of the following sources: The Museum of Modern Art / Film Stills Archive—from *Queen Elizabeth* (Ch. 1), *Occurrence at Owl Creek Bridge* (Ch. 3), *Potemkin* (Ch. 4), and *The Cabinet of Dr. Caligari* (Ch. 7); United Artists Corporation—*Tom Jones* (Ch. 2); Paramount Pictures Corporation—*Hud* (Ch. 5); Janus Films—*Wild Strawberries* (Ch. 6); and Avco Embassy Pictures Corp.—*The Graduate* (Ch. 8). See also credits for stills on the center plates.

To D. W. G.
who exhibited presence

Preface

This book is written in the first person. The reason is simple. At present, that is the only person I have to be in. But there is a deeper reason: The vast, complex, public medium of the film has evolved to a new level in our times. Due to the impact of new media, it is being forced to become an art. Audiences no longer go to the movies to watch anything; they attend films to see something. And the something they see is providing not escape but aesthetic involvement. The reflections in this book are my attempt to understand this experience and its object. The experience is one of participation; its object is the personal film.

Since this book is an attempt to understand, it advances a perspective or a theory of film. The commanding concept of the theory is the essentially dyadic nature of film form. Analogously, it is a theory of the dyadic and ambivalent nature of human life—our ways of being-with-the-world. Hence, the central concept is the interdependence, coexistence, and synthesis of objective/subjective, outer world/inner world, universal/particular relationships. From this central theme, certain aesthetic principles emerge, such as the relationships of sight/insight, vision/envision, purport/import, perception/revelation, theme/plot, visual/aural, and the tensive unity and cumulative development of these relations that constitute the sight/sound monogram we call film. The standard of value is earned immediacy or the coherence of thematic rhythm. The use of these principles forms the framework through which and in which the spectator can participate in film. His participation is described as an experience of excarnation or bi-association.

Every film theory, I suppose, is the erecting of some particular monomania into the status of a conceptual framework. My theory is no exception. I have been particularly taken by the films of Fellini, Bergman, Kurosawa, Ray, Antonioni, Nichols, Kubrick, and others. There is a sense, then, in which this theory is an attempt to articulate my preferences. Nevertheless, it is difficult for me to believe that these attitudes are merely my own, that is, pathological. On the contrary, I believe that they reveal something about the nature of the objects before us: fine films. It is my hope, then, that this book will persuade some others to share my perspective.

The form of the book is the form of the modern film itself. The first four chapters are concerned with an examination of the dimensions of expression, form, materials, and function. These aspects of film are reflected upon from the perspective of particular analogues: drama, the novel, photography, and social messages. The function of the first four chapters is to pose but not to ex-pose the theory as a whole. Chapters 5 and 6 are articulations in depth of the philosophical/psychological assumptions behind the theory. They might be described as a kind of pragmatic existentialism streaked with idealism. Chapter 7 is the statement of the theory (its "plot closure" if you will), and the final chapter consists of further articulation and application of the theory (its thematic enclosure). I do not claim this is *the* theory of film. It is *a* theory—a theory which is internally coherent and which I hope will be experientially fruitful in the sense that it will help the reader to perceive and understand a most complex art form. If it succeeds, then at least you and I will share a community of vision. If it fails, I have at most exposed my weaknesses.

I am indebted to Southern Illinois University for a sabbatical leave, in the fall and winter of 1968, which enabled me to engage in a therapy which turned into a theory. I am also indebted to the Graduate Research Council of the Edwardsville Campus for its continued spiritual and financial support.

My thanks to Professor Irving Deer of the University of South Florida, Professor James F. Scott of St. Louis University, and Professor Richard Weinman of Oregon State University for their cogent criticisms and their valiant aid in trying to make me clarify my concepts and prose. My gratitude also must be expressed to my friends Dr. E. F. Kaelin, Dr. Charles Tenney, Dr. Leo Cohen, Mr. Christopher Brown, and Dr. Gerald Runkle for their continued interest and encouragement. A special word of thanks to my Philosophy of Art class in the spring of 1969 for suffering through much of this and to two excellent typists and ladies: Mrs. Kathryn Kennedy and Miss Patricia Riggins.

Above all, I wish to thank my enduring wife, Jean. It is she who has borne all my obsessions.

George W. Linden
Southern Illinois University
Edwardsville, Illinois

Contents

The Staged World 1

The Storied World 31

"You have shown me a strange image, he said, and a
strange sort of prisoners.
Like ourselves, I replied . . ."

Plato, *Republic,* VI, 515

1

The Staged World

Most good stories begin "Once upon a time." Films do not. They begin "Once upon a now." When discussing adaptations of novels to the screen, Margaret Kennedy summed up this distinction succinctly by stating: "In the case of a novel this means cutting out a great deal of material and turning comment into action. Where the novelist explains, the film must exhibit."[1] This same distinction applies more forcefully, and with a difference, when one regards the relations of theatre and film. In fact, it applies more accurately; for drama is the imitation of an action, whereas the novel and motion pictures tend to take action in a less strict sense and to treat actions as events. Such distinctions might be viewed merely as differences of emphasis or, to rework Wittgenstein's phrase, "family differences"; but they are real dissimilarities all the same. One fundamental difference is that films are visual whereas drama is verbal. Another basic difference is that the space of film is not the space of the staged world.

I take as given D. W. Gotshalk's definition that "fine art is the creation of four-dimensional objects preeminently for aesthetic experience."[2] The four dimensions of which he speaks are expression, form, material, and function. By the word "dimension," I intend the same usage as that of Gotshalk and D. W. Prall. A dimension in art, unlike mathematics, is not an independent variable. It is a value area, which has status of its own but at the same time is mutually implicated with others. Since each value dimension exhibits instrumental as well as intrinsic value, it is enhanced by and enhances the others.

In this chapter, then, I am reflecting upon the expressive dimension of film. It would be bootless, however, for me to bore the reader with an essay on art as expression. The student who is interested in this stance can read those aestheticians who have advanced the theory at much length and with great cogency. Instead, I shall use drama as an instance, or analogical example, of the expressive dimension of film. Such an approach is fitting not only because drama preceded and shaped film but also because my method will be phenomenological and inductive. I shall be concerned with drama and film as perceived objects; therefore, I must examine our differing modes of experiencing them. I hope that such an approach and its resultant reflections will illuminate their identity/difference. Let us turn, then, to some of their family differences.

Drama and film are so close in many ways that their differences are often neglected or ignored. This ignoring of their differences is one reason that most film criticism is so poor, for most film critics are not only theatre trained but also theatre oriented; they naturally tend to evaluate a film as though it were a drama. Yet after contemplating the short history of the film and the many transformations it has undergone during that brief span, one might almost say that the true development of the film has consisted precisely in its attempt to free itself from the stage. The essence of film is its fluidity; whenever the motion picture has been bound to the stage, it has become literally bound, that is, static. This binding has had two historical phases, one spatial and one verbal.

At the beginning of the twentieth century, the two main tendencies of the film as a medium had already been indicated. One direction was that of fantasy, and it was explored by Georges Méliès in such films as *Cinderella* (1900), *Bluebeard* (1901), and *A Trip to the Moon* (1902). The other direction was toward concurrent realism and was exhibited by Edwin S. Porter's *The Great Train Robbery* (1903). It was not long, however, before the pioneering discoveries of Méliès and Porter were ignored, and film suffered a relapse into theatre. Film directors turned to immortalizing great actors and great dramas on celluloid. Arthur Knight tells of one director who was so taken with this possibility that he "immortalized" *Hamlet* by condensing it into ten hectic minutes on the screen.[3]

The first feature-length film to be shown in an American theatre, as opposed to a nickelodeon, was Sarah Bernhardt's *Queen Elizabeth*. No doubt the audiences of 1912 were satisfied that they had their money's worth, even though they had paid the exorbitant sum of one dollar a ticket for the event. But one merely has to view the Museum of Modern Art's version of *Queen Elizabeth* to realize how wonderfully bad it was. It is not because the lighting and the camera work are not up to modern standards that the film is so inept. It is because it is not a film; it is a recording of a preposterously exaggerated stage performance. When Miss Bernhardt staggers awkwardly toward an enormous pile of artlessly disorganized cushions and plops upon them to expire at the end of the "film," one cannot restrain his laughter. What was no doubt done in all sincerity by the actors, and photographed with near reverence by the technicians, turns out to be not tragic but ludicrous. No verbal description would be adequate to portray this grotesquerie. One has to see it to disbelieve it. There is probably no visual example more explicit of the divergence of the stage and film reality than Bernhardt's *Queen Elizabeth*. From her performance alone, we could deduce the principle that whenever the camera is used as a mere recording device, film suffers and cinematic form is violated. Shortly thereafter, through the genius and efforts of D. W. Griffith and others, the film began to extricate itself from the theatre, to move out into the world and into its own. Such masterpieces as *The Birth of a Nation, Broken Blossoms, Intolerance,* and *Greed* demonstrated conclusively that the camera, imaginatively used, could create a new perceptual and intangible world.

The silent film soon developed methods appropriate to its medium and in a very short time, as far as arts go, reached a high point of perfection. This was such a high point that some experts, namely, Dwight Macdonald and Rudolf Arnheim, seem to feel that film, if it has not merely degenerated, has certainly seldom equaled and never surpassed the creations of the 1920s. Then along came another technical disaster: sound. With the release of *The Jazz Singer* in 1927, the camera once more became chained to a fixed position. Not only was it made static but also it was encased in cumbersome soundproofing, for the microphone was completely indiscriminate in the sounds it would record. Actors were forced to occupy an imaginary proscenium whose restrictions were dictated by the limitations of the capacity of the microphone. Movies that had moved became a series of static portraits from which poured a torrent of words. Sight was drowned in sound. Once more, film, the bird that had been born for flight, had fallen to the stage. And it was a primitive stage.

Both the novel and theatre are more essentially verbal than the film. There is a difference, however, between the novel and the theatre insofar as verbal materials are concerned. The novelist uses words to construct a narrative, but words do not function for him in quite the same way as for the dramatist. The dramatist uses words as language; that is, his use of words is the creation of a structure, which has as its primary mode the spoken word. The design of the novel is based on portrayal, and its appeal is primarily to the intellect. The design of drama is based upon parlance, and its appeal is primarily to the will. In fact, drama might be defined as the clash of human will confronted by obstacles. Dialogue thus performs different functions in the novel and in the theatre. In most novels, dialogue is relatively rare and is utilized to climax high points of description. In the theatre, dialogue is continuous, exaggerated, compressed, and loud; description is kept to a minimum. Drama, of course, has scenery and, more importantly, the living actors; and these take the place of description. Almost everything of importance in the theatre is said, and everything that is said is important. The development in the drama is on the stage. While the novelist writes in words, the dramatist speaks in tongues.

Scenery, setting, make-up, gesture, and movement are also important in drama. As James F. Scott of St. Louis University has remarked to me, one can hardly imagine an Ibsen play without the lamps, the windows, the elegantly seedy furniture and bookcases that symbolically exemplify the character of his well-to-do but humanly sterile world. Those film directors whose imaginations move in the realm of theatre emphasize such elements in their films; hence their films tend to be theatrical. Examples are Josef von Sternberg, Erich von Stroheim, Sidney Lumet, and the early Ingmar Bergman. Because all these theatrical elements, or at least their images, are incorporated and absorbed into film, they do not help us in illuminating differences. They can be so used, however; I shall discuss things as necessary as broomsticks and telephones later. Now let me briefly examine pantomime.

Pantomime has a long and honorable tradition on the stage. This, of course, is exactly what the early silent films *were,* though they usually had the addition of written words. The mad comics—Harry Langdon, Mack Swain, Harold Lloyd, Stan Laurel and Oliver Hardy, and the great Charlie Chaplin—soon made film the preeminent pantomime art. But with the coming of sound, most of these actors suffered and so did their films. The wise Harpo Marx remained silent and kept pantomime alive. Perhaps the only genius who was able to fuse gesture and spoken words flawlessly was W. C. Fields. For the most part, however, the birth of words meant the death of gesture. The control of gesture moved to the director, the sound man, and the editor. The actor had words. This diminished the use of his body for the way he would be.

It is not difficult to find films in which gesture and word fail to coalesce and enhance each other. One merely has to look. And when you look, you will usually find that those sections of the film that are wordless are superior to the dramatically spoken phases. *Limelight* and *The Red Shoes* are cases in point. In the latter, one feels a definite letdown during the romantic portions when he has to listen to the actors instead of look at them. A most illuminating case is the fine film *Les Enfants de Paradis.* This film, whose theme plays on the relations of drama to life, includes both pantomime and straight drama. In the pantomime sequences, the male lead, Jean-Louis Barrault, is brilliant. His every gesture is a finely tuned instrument of anguish or joy. But in the rest of the film, he has to act, that is, speak. And in these portions he appears, and hence is, naive and incompetent. His marvelously expressive body and face are reduced to horizon while his voice stumbles through the dialogue. These examples would seem to disclose a basic antagonism between the visual and the verbal and to indicate that great care must be taken that they do not conflict. One such way of taking care is to minimize screen dialogue. In some modern films, such as *Teorema,* dialogue is almost absent. Great theatrical films can be made. A fine example is Jean Renoir's *The Golden Coach,* which is a beautiful synthesis of sight/sound and film/theatre filtered through Renoir's almost invisible style. Nevertheless, film should move out of the proscenium and into its own. And being visual, it should reduce words. I do not ask a film to tell me anything. It should make me see.

The importance of dialogue for the drama, however, cannot be minimized. The play may be the thing, but dialogue is how it does it. If the actors merely address the audience, one has a lecture, a reading, or a sermon but not drama. Drama consists of the interaction of people through the medium of spoken words, and the function of these spoken words is not so much portrayal as revelation. The dialogue must be so constructed that each element in it reveals the characters and the action upon which they are embarked. It is thus necessary that the dramatist have a strong grasp of the basic form of his action, for many different actors should be able to speak his lines and play his parts. The choice of the actor is thus greater in drama than in the film, but it is still limited. It is limited by the commanding form which demands the condensation of all images into the richness of the dialogue.

This may explain why adaptations of Shakespeare's plays from another medium, drama, into film are so frequently unsuccessful. Shakespeare's language is abundantly rich in imagery—ripeness *is* all—but the imagery is often not visual. Hence, when a director comes to the compressed vitality of the soliloquies, he can only wander around with the camera eye into irrelevance. This is what happens in Maurice Evans' *Macbeth*. When Evans launches (and the verb is properly used for he is literally setting out upon a sea of symbols) into a soliloquy, the camera is at its lens end. All it can do is wander around poking at the architecture of the castle, return for a few close-ups of Evans, and then, out of sheer visual desperation, peek out the windows or over parapets at the tranquil countryside. All of Shakespeare is difficult for the screen, though some would by its very nature be more easily adapted than others. *Romeo and Juliet,* for example, is more adaptable to the film than *Hamlet* or *Macbeth* because *Romeo and Juliet* is not so tight a drama. It is too dependent upon accident, chance, and the fortuitous. One has the feeling that if there had been a few telephones about, the young lovers would never have come to such a bad end. Furthermore, the characters, with perhaps the exception of Mercutio, lack depth. But *Hamlet, Macbeth,* and *Lear* contain deeper dramatic characters, and these plays also have the crucial difficulty of the soliloquy.

John Howard Lawson is highly critical of Olivier's *Hamlet* and cites it as an instance of an anti-film; for he believes that, especially in the soliloquies, Olivier goes directly against the grain of cinematic presentation. He sums up his condemnation in these words:

> In Laurence Olivier's film adaptation of *Hamlet,* the actor speaks some of the lines without any movement of his lips, to indicate an interior monologue. At other moments, his lips move to show that the words deal with external reality. The device and the close-ups that accompany it are opposed to cinematic principles. Olivier has assumed that it is the camera's function to bring the stage performance closer to the audience, to enable the actor's eyes and lips to give a more intimate message.[4]

Lawson is partly right, but only partly. It is not the drama or the "stage performance" that Olivier is bringing closer to the audience; it is the image of the actor. And this image, due to its largeness, allows the audience to observe the minute changes of facial expression, the changing strains of the face and eyes which accompany the tone and timbre of the language. The use of sound over image, contrasted with the moving mouth at other moments, adds variety to this unity and clarity to the event. If this is failure, it must be viewed as brilliant failure. Olivier has done better than anyone could expect in attempting to unite the microphysiognomy of the face with interior monologue. In order to realize what a brilliant attempt he has achieved, one merely has to compare his "to be or not to be" sequence with the excessively long and dull close-ups of Ingrid Thulin in *Winter Light,* which are shown while a voice intones the contents of a letter on the audio.

And yet, in the end, it is a failure for all that. Both Miss Thulin and Olivier are incredibly fine and sensitive actors. They are also both very handsome; but, despite these advantages, extended shots even of their attractive faces become dull. There just isn't that much to see. What happens is that, despite these brilliant attempts, the visuals begin to work against the audio. The visuals are drowned in a rich sea of words. There is no visual equivalent available for "take arms against a sea of troubles and by opposing, end them." The defect is not so much in Olivier's brilliant performance or in his ingenious conception of how the scene should be shot. The difficulty comes from the clash of two different media with different demands. Drama is something willed and thought; film is something perceived. The difficulty is due to the difference between the scene and the seen. Drama, through the magic and poetry of its language, incites us to what we can envision; film is concerned with the fission and fusion of vision itself.

Besides the fact that theatre is a "verbal appeal to the imagination" and hence is essentially, not accidentally, dependent upon speech, there is also the difference of centrality of plot. While it is true that some modern plays are almost plotless (for example, the plays of Bertolt Brecht, which emphasize gesture at the expense of dramatic development), it is still the case that drama is the imitation of an action. This is the case, not because Aristotle so defined it or because T. S. Eliot was an oracle of objective correlatives, but because the essence of drama is the portrayal or, more accurately, the revelation of human destiny. Drama, like the novel, is time-bound. But its binding is to the future, not the past. The basic premise of theatre is "What happens *next?*" The basic premise of the novel is "What *has* happened?" The basic premise of film is "What is going on *now?*" This orientation toward the future, and a concern with the pregnancy of the moment as meaningful for an end, is probably why drama is often confused with ritual and religion. Both religion and drama are inherently future oriented, but they differ in that drama presents a closed future. Like religion, the film is open; but unlike religion, the film is concerned with the present, this world, here and—above all—now.

The film and drama, then, differ in their relations to language. One, drama, is directly dependent upon the magic of the spoken word, and the other is relatively independent of that word. This difference can be seen quite clearly in the relative independence enjoyed by the written form of the play. A play may be transferred to an aural medium, radio, with little or no loss to its force or nature. Not so with a film script. Think for example, of the near impossibility of performing *Juliet of the Spirits* as a radio play, as opposed to the comparative ease of thus adapting *Romeo and Juliet.* Furthermore, a play is good reading. But the lack of substance in film scripts, their episodic structure and dependence upon visual accompaniment make them thin reading. The words of the dramatic dialogue carry the cream of the action; the words of the film merely skim the event. In fact, there is an incipient tendency in the words of film to slip into mere sound, sheer auditory accompaniment. This may be one reason why books of plays sell consistently, whereas books of film scripts rarely do well in the marketplace. The script of a film is like a blueprint for a building, but there are many other factors that go into the building of such a mansion. The written play is more like a house that has already been constructed. Granted, it is an empty house without furniture, draperies, or paint; but it is almost ready to inhabit, not merely in the planning stage.

One might note another difference between books of plays and books of film scripts. The book of film scripts is enhanced by and, in fact, almost demands the inclusion of photographs from the film itself. The script is not enough to reconstruct the event for the average reader. It is difficult to imagine, however, how photographs of any stage production of *Hamlet* could really add much to the experiencing of the text, for the reading of the text means a confrontation with Hamlet, not with any specific production of work. This practical necessity for the inclusion of photographs with the text is true even of books about films. The exceptions, perhaps, are those works that are complete theory, such as Rudolf Arnheim's *Film as Art,* or those books, such as Pauline Kael's *I Lost it at the Movies,* that are not theoretical but, then, are not about film either.

The above remark is intended not as a criticism of Miss Kael's thoughtful work but as a description and a warning. It is simply a mistake to think that this work, so beautifully conceived and written, is a book about film. *I Lost it at the Movies* is a series of essays, and, in fact, this is the basic character of Miss Kael's film "criticisms." Like other theatrically oriented critics, she does not invite us to see along with her. What she does invite us to do is to think along with her. Thus she uses film as an occasion for an essay on some topic that may or may not be directly related to the film. In other words, a film provides her the excuse to discuss some topic which the film has initiated in her thought processes. But a film is not thought, it is perceived. Miss Kael's review of *Blow-Up,*[5] for example, says little about the film and much about the gullibility of other critics. Some of them deserve criticism; but then so does Miss Kael, for a dramatic and literary approach to film too often sacrifices feeling and vision to thought. Films are not literature. They are at best image-writing. The literary film critic has a concept where his heart ought to be.

Two instances should suffice to demonstrate Miss Kael's literary and philosophical, as distinct from cinematic, interests. In the case of *Blow-Up,* she misinterprets it as a chi-chi travelogue, then attacks many other critics for their pseudo-intellectualism. While one must agree with her that one problem of intellectuals, especially since the arrival of Bergman, has been a sterile search for meaning in everything and that this hunt is usually an arid and foolish one, *Blow-Up* does have a meaning. It is not a travelogue except in the sense that it records the long distance a photographer, David Hemmings, moves when he shifts from the perspective behind his lens to one in front of it. In so doing, he is rejecting his former alienation from the world and is joining the game of life. The colors, the rhythms, the sound, the visuals all support this transition and make *Blow-Up* the warmest and most human of Michelangelo Antonioni's films.

Another case in point is Miss Kael's complete misunderstanding of another classic, *La Strada.* Her remembrance of it turns on one phrase from the least successful scene in the film, the scene in which the Madman tries to reassure Gelsomina by handing her a pebble and stating that everything in the universe has a purpose.[6] Granted, this assertion is a bit of sophomoric philosophizing, but even within the scene it is negated. Gelsomina asks naively what its purpose is, and the Madman brusquely brushes her naiveté aside. Federico Fellini does have a tendency to verbal statement and is usually at his worst when he falls into the trap; but, in the making of *La Strada,* he was extremely conscious of this failing. Angelo Solmi tells us:

> Bruno Rondi also gives evidence of the director's work before and during the making of the film. "From the beginning Fellini fought against the literary temptations of the theme and against the obstacle created by the picturesque elements inherent in the atmosphere."[7]

That Fellini may have lost this battle a few times in the film is quite true. But to take these losses as the central theme of the movie is a basic error. The theme of *La Strada* is not the delusion that all is well in the world and God's in his heaven but the strength of the female principle. It is thus no accident that the final sequence ends in water, both the ocean and the tears streaming down Zampano's weathered and much older face. The meaning of this film is carried by the visuals, as it is in all of Fellini's work; and at the end we know that even a rock or a brute can be worn down by the most irresistible force in the universe: water. The theme of *La Strada,* then, is the same theme we find put in different pictorial terms in *8½:* the strength of weakness. Even a Zampano can be brought to a minimum of self-consciousness by a simple child-girl and the occasion for the dawning of this self-awareness of his own estrangement is brought by a woman humming a simple tune as she hangs her clean linen in public.

To try to sum up so complex a work as *La Strada* in one theme is perhaps to oversimplify drastically; but to sum it up in one verbal phrase from a minor scene, as Miss Kael does, is even worse. Miss Kael is a brilliant critic; hence, the fact that she went astray should remind us of two things. First, most critics have dramatic and literary training and therefore tend to remember and review films in terms of dialogue. Only rarely do they refer to images or sequences. Consequently, it is relatively easy for a critic to hang a film on words. Second, film makers should be extremely careful of the words they use. Speculative words are misleading in film. Words in film should be kept minimal, expressive, and concrete. Young children show and tell. Directors, like poets, should show.

Drama is, probably, more basically moral than the film. Both morality and drama are teleological, that is, purposive; and both, in spite of what Kant said, are concerned with consequences. Drama is concerned with the unraveling of the pregnant possibilities of the present into a future which will bring it to completion. This is one reason it is so intensely human. But unlike real life. drama is not filled with irrelevancies; it is not a sieve of existence but a clarified form of fulfillment. Loose ends are an anathema to the drama. It is concerned with "untying the knot," as Aristotle put it, but with untying it in a specific direction. Film, because of its complexity and more elastic structure, can absorb more of the accidental than can drama. Both film and drama are temporal arts, yet their relations to time differ. Drama is inherently future oriented, while film condenses into immediacy. Drama is concerned with the destiny of man; film is concerned with the density of the moment. Hence, those films that break with the theatrical tradition and become truly cinematic are directed toward exploiting the visibility of the seen.

Thornton Wilder would not agree. In his essay "Some Thoughts on Playwriting," he claims that the focus of theatre is on the present and, in fact, asserts that one of the essential conditions of drama is that "its action takes place in a perpetual present time," to which he adds "on the stage it is always now."[8] The key word here is "perpetual"; for it tells us not only much about Mr. Wilder's theory (it is false) but also about his practice. If one looks at the Wilder plays *The Skin of Our Teeth* and especially *Our Town,* he will find that they are not written in the dramatic mode at all but are loose forms of narrative. Wilder has transferred to the stage the cinematic technique of soft-focus, which gives his plays the illusion of a "perpetual presence" just as it has kept Doris Day a perpetual virginal bobby-soxer. Wilder's soft-focus lens is the sentimentality of language, which fuzzes the distinctions of the past and the present, to make the present safely past and the past something "veiled in the nostalgic feelings of the present."[9] Thus, as Dwight Macdonald has acidly observed, in Wilder's plays "there is no issue too trivial for him not to take a stand on."[10]

Sentimentality springs from either not having felt something deeply enough or, having felt it with adequate depth, being incapable of its full articulation. *Our Town* suffers from both defects, which is no doubt one reason why it is an extremely successful play. But success is not necessarily a mark of greatness. In fact, one might suspect that the reason *The Skin of Our Teeth* and *Our Town* are so interminably done and never done in by amateur theatricals is not because of spareness of sets but because they are almost impossible to do badly. They are equally impossible to do well. There are an infinite number of ways to fail to achieve *Hamlet.* One can do *Our Town* an infinite number of ways; and each way will be adequate because the structure, the form, of *Our Town* is episodic, a structural weakness that is hidden by folksy asides combined with maudlin speculations on the drift of life. *Our Town* is romantic in the bad sense of the word, that is, it is unclear. It is literally misconceived. Even hamburger looks better by candle-light. But, as Plato said, when these same objects that had been seen by the "fainter luminaries of the night" are exposed to the sun and its light, it is evident that "the same eyes see distinctly" and "that they do contain the power of vision."[11] Wilder's attempt, then, to use the off-focus lens of sentimentality and to collapse drama into a "perpetual present" is successful, not because it is good drama, but because it is so poor. These reflections on structure, however, should warn us of one of the permanent perpetual dangers of film. Film, like *Our Town,* is concerned with the present. And like *Our Town,* its tendency is toward the episodic; hence, one of the great dangers of the film is loss of form and consequent sentimentality. This is the major defect of Fellini's *La Dolce Vita,* though *Dolce Vita* is more flamboyant than sentimental.

These remarks, then, have a direct relevance for principles of construction in the two media. In drama, since it is concerned with destiny, plot is the imaginative projection of that destiny. It is this projection, and not Aristotle's authority, that makes plot so essential to drama. Film is concerned with diversity and, in film, shot follows plot. But plot is determined by theme, for the essence of film is the coherence of thematic rhythm, or, as I have called it, "earned immediacy."[12] The immediacy is earned if there is adequate articulation of the emotional tone through the conflict and cumulative impact of visual and auditory images. Notice that cumulation, though directional, is not necessarily directed toward the future. Thus, one may have a fine film such as Jack Clayton's *The Pumpkin Eater,* which begins in the middle of theme and moves in both directions. Theme is determined by the prior emotional commitment of the director toward the presence that is before his camera's eye. The language of drama is dialogue; the language of film is movement.

These differences in principle of construction may account for the fact that we are often annoyed by the literal transference of techniques from one medium to another. Thus the use of wipes in a film, while acceptable in an old silent, is not acceptable in most modern productions. The wipe is simply a mode of drawing the curtain and violates cinematic form. The wipe is a lazy man's way of changing scene. The same is true of iris-in. While such a device was common in the silent days, it is simply the transference of the stage device of spotlighting. Iris-out is much like turning the house lights up—more accurately, like going from spotlighting to stage lighting. Such devices in contemporary films not only strike us as anachronisms but are irritating, for we know there are more fluid and facile means of transition available in cinema. This does not mean that they should never be used, however. Their very anachronism makes them prime devices for comedy, and they are thus appropriate to such comic constructions as *Tom Jones* or the films of Jean-Luc Godard. When used too frequently, however, they have a tendency to give a film the look of an artsy-craftsy inside joke. One thing is certain: they are direct borrowings from the stage that often fit ill with film form.

The transference of technique may well work the other way, too. Arthur Miller's *Death of a Salesman* incorporates cinematic structure with its flashbacks and its use of the isolated lighting for concurrent fantasy in which the rich uncle appears. These devices, taken from the screen, were fully effective on the stage. When the play was transferred to film, however, these techniques lost their dramatic impact, since they were simply the normal way of going about things. Oddly enough, it was not until the television production that *Death of a Salesman* was given fully cinematic treatment complete with zooming close shots and overhead pans.

Jerome Birdman provided two interesting and contrasting examples of transference of technique in his stage productions of *A Physician in Spite of Himself* and *Agamemnon.* In the Molière comedy, he inserted color film of the actors dressed in their stage costumes romping in an arcadian setting. For added humor, the romp was run backwards. This did bring the audience to laughter; but it violated the dramatic illusion, for while the film was running, all the actors, though hidden in darkness, were uninvolved and the stage was dead. They attempted to segue the transition by chasing each other as soon as the stage lighting returned, but the link was not entirely successful. The failure was due, not to actor inadequacy, but to the mixture of the flatly concrete with the three-dimensional dramatic progression.

An even more striking example of incongruence was exhibited in the *Ice Capades* of 1968, which had a travel theme and even some individual action sequences, such as Indians chasing cowboys, in which the screen image and the actual skaters were interchanged. The device used was a strip screen through which the actors could skate as the cut from film to embodiment. Though the technique was clever, the two levels of abstraction did not coalesce; they clashed. One had the immediate feeling: The skaters *look so small.* In the continuous viewing of a film, the eye tends to collapse into the screen and we forget the enormous size of the images. We forget that movies are bigger than life. But when the two media are juxtaposed—large image and man alive—we are aware of the contrast, and the illusion is shattered. Lived space and scene space differ in kind.

In his production of *Agamemnon,* Birdman used two devices that were much more effective. One technique was to tape-record the chorus and play the lines in stereo around the audience, thus eliminating the chorus as a visual go-between and giving it an aural, spiritual existence. This technique is an analogue of the use of music in the cinema to reinforce emotional impact. In its lack of music, by the way, drama again differs from film, since the "music" of drama is carried only in the poetry of the language; actual music would normally interfere with the dramatic illusion. In the stage musical, of course, the songs take the place of soliloquy in drama, and the actor usually steps out of his part in the action to carry on a musical colloquy with the audience. In *Agamemnon,* the intellectual meaning of the words —which consist of narrative of past events and editorial comment on the present proceedings—was not lost, and its choral meanings were enhanced by having them treated as if they were music. When the chorus was needed as a visual element, it was introduced by spotlighting at the foot of the stage in the orchestra pit—a place perfectly suited to the technique in use.

The other device used in *Agamemnon* was a novel treatment of the palace doors. During most of the action, they were darkened and acted as background for the play. At certain critical points, however, they were lit and became a screen. By back projection, color wipes of abstract designs reminiscent of blood, daggers, nets, and vengeance were cast upon the door-screens while the action proceeded on the stage in front of the changing color patterns. In this instance, there was no need to segue the film technique into the stage action, since it was acting as a fluid horizon to the action itself in the same way that back projection has been used in many films. This use of technique was extremely effective; for here what was utilized was not concrete images but abstract patterns, which provided background rhythm and depth symbolism for the abstract dialogue of the Greek drama.

Since there can be effective transference from one medium to another, it would be a mistake to conclude that a given device should never be taken from film and used in theatre, or vice versa. Nevertheless, it is true that certain techniques are not completely neutral and that they lean toward or are more appropriate to one medium than the other. That the ordinary audience is aware of this distinction was demonstrated in the recent radio advertising for a showing of the film version of the ballet *Romeo and Juliet*. The announcer assured the listeners that this was not merely the recording of a stage production but a film that used fourteen different cameras to transform the action. Whether this mode of advertising brought more people to the theatre is unknown, but it is recognition of the fact that the general film audience has become fairly sophisticated and demands that films utilize their own techniques. Those devices that tend to establish a static perspective and a fixed point of view go against the general thrust of the medium. If we move from the characteristics of the object to the qualities of the experience, these observations seem to be validated.

Pauline Kael entitles one of her clever essays—in this case, a justified attack on academia for its inherent capacity to turn the living into the safely dead—"It's Only a Movie." The significant word in the title is the "only," which reveals her theme: the casualness of the motion-picture experience. The informality of the motion-picture experience means, among other things, that it is one of the few refuges left to a child where he can indulge his fantasies in relative public without worrying about adult disapproval. Miss Kael describes the difference between this experience and other aesthetic experiences in these words:

> No cultural glow suffuses the Saturday afternoon movie audience; they are still free to react as *they* feel like reacting, with derision or excitement or disappointment or whatever. Nobody says you have to like a movie (not, that is, until you get to the art-house age) and, as it isn't an occasion, there's no aftermath for you to fear. Going to a movie doesn't wind up with the horrors of reprimands for your restlessness, with nervous reactions, tears and family disappointments that you weren't up to it. It's only a movie. What beautiful words. At the movies, you're left gloriously alone. You can say it stinks and nobody's shocked. That's something you can't do with a Dickens novel or a Beethoven symphony or even a poem by Browning, and because you can't, because they're all preselected and prejudged and graded for greatness, you don't talk about them with the other kids the way you do about movies.[13]

This absence of the concept of status from the Saturday matinee is shriekingly obvious to any adult who has the temerity to attend. And it is, we must admit, a lost value. I can recall being a member of an audience of restrained professors at Princeton who were being slowly bored into stupor by Godard's *Band of Outsiders*. Nobody shouted, "It stinks!" And only a few females had the courage and the intelligence to walk out.

The absence of status is a relative matter, of course. As teen-agers, we go to the films more to explore each other than the film medium. As adults, most of us become serious filmgoers—at least our prime purpose in going is to see the film. And while it is true that the cost of attending the movies has risen dramatically and that the neighborhood movie house is dying a quick death, it is still not the same thing to go to a movie and to go to a drama. The splitting of motion-picture exhibition into more specialized houses catering to more specialized audiences tends to make it more like going to the theatre. But there is still a difference—we call it the *legitimate* theatre. Certainly the Cinerama outlets try their utmost to ape the theatre crowd, complete with plush establishments, high prices, and advanced reservations. But they still sell popcorn. Even for an adult in modern times, when movie exhibition is being forced by the economics of television to become more of a snob occasion, there is still more casualness and less seriousness about taking in a movie as distinguished from attending a drama or a symphony performance. One can be a movie fan or a baseball fan, but it sounds odd to talk of a drama fan. The basic reason for the difference, I suppose, is that one goes to the theatre not only to see the play but also to be seen, which is one of the justifications for intermission. On the other hand, though one may be seen at a film or a baseball game, one does not go there for that purpose.

The practice of introducing the intermission in film presentations is simply out of place. Though most film producers cannot distinguish between quantity and anything else and insist on the blockbuster spectacle, it is difficult to think of any of the "spectaculars" that could not safely be cut. In fact, every so-called superproduction I can think of could well be cut mercilessly, with the exception of von Stroheim's *Greed,* and even it, I understand, underwent radical editing. No doubt the break in *Lawrence of Arabia* sold a lot of soft drinks after people suffered through so much heat and sand. Perhaps the break in John Huston's *The Bible* helped, in that one could forget the everlastingness, as opposed to eternity, of the turgid film. But the intermission is simply pretentious, a theatrical device used to "enhance" films of excessive longevity. One might as well show advertising in the middle of a crucial scene. Such breaks are alien to the film. The breath of film is continuity.

Attending a baseball game is a much more intellectual experience than watching a film. After all, nothing at all, or practically nothing at all, happens during a baseball game. One sits for a couple of hours in order to see five or six minutes of action. But the actual running and hitting are merely devices to draw up the vast amount of information concerning batting averages, lame legs, pitchers' weaknesses and strengths, the condition of the field, innumerable past performances and the like, which the spectator reads into the so-called action. He can't simply see a man on first base; what he must see is a man who steals well against left-handers but who twisted his ankle three games previously and is matching wits and muscle against a catcher with a strong arm and a second baseman who is slow in getting to the bag, *ad infinitum*. The movement in baseball is an excuse for highly involved intellectual speculations on possibilities and for the excitement of finding whether this peculiar form of detective work mixed with history will be confirmed by fact. The film is much more immediate and concrete; motion is constantly present and carries its meanings with it in the form of visage, word, and music. Yet the baseball fan and the movie fan are alike in one important respect: Each is part of the mass. And the mass is a lonely crowd. Each sits in a theatre of his own. One might better call it a collection than an audience. But the people in the theatre form an audience, not a mere collection externally connected to each other. This difference, I believe, is one reason for the status involved in theatre-going. The difference reflects the difference of space in film and in theatre. The baseball fan, of course, differs from both in sometimes sharing the space of the spectacle directly. He throws bottles.

The differences between a film audience and the audience in the legitimate theatre may be only matters of degree, but that does not make them any less real. First of all, there is a felt difference between being in a theatre audience and being in a movie audience. One feels as though he is a member of a theatre audience, and the very use of the word "member" conveys the organic sense of relationships involved. One feels as though he is an individual in a mass when watching a film. When this felt difference is moved to the intellectual level, that is, reflected upon, one realizes that the stage experience tends toward cohesion and conjunctive relationships, while the film audience is basically disjunctive. There can be no doubt that these felt differences are due to the characteristic objects before us, for it is the function of all art to shape and direct experience so that the experience of art differs from other events. The experience one has in the legitimate theatre is not experience in general but experience of drama. The experience one has in a motion-picture house is not experience in general but experience of film. In order to understand these differences, we must articulate this "of" with a phenomenological description and reflection upon the differing experiences. We may then take the signal qualities of the experience as telling us something about the objects involved.

As has already been remarked, going to a drama is a much more formal experience than going to the movies. One must make reservations in advance for an assigned seat, the seats themselves vary in price according to their spatial location and social value, the ushers put you in your proper place, and, of course, you are wearing your best clothes. The house lights are high, not merely to facilitate the work of the ushers, but so that, as in church, you can show off your best clothes. After all, you wore them for that purpose. You have gone to the theatre to see the drama, but you have also gone to see and be seen by others. Going to the legitimate theatre is a *social* occasion. The house lights dim, a hush falls over the crowd as the mantle of shadow surrounds it. One feels irritation at the few errant coughs of anticipation. The curtain opens, stage lights go up, and the play begins. The movement of light from the status of a surrounding ambience to a focal space, that elevated real space between the arches of the framing proscenium, draws the eyes to the stage and your attention follows, combined with a mixture of anticipation. The drama begins, and your attention follows the gestures and words of the actors. In drama, as in film, attention follows sound and vision. In our everyday experience, vision follows attention.

Compare these initial experiences with those of attending a motion picture. Again you enter a theatre, but you are probably more casually dressed than you would be at the drama. It is not likely that you will even note the others who are already seated or those who are entering. In any case, observing others would be more difficult, for the house lighting is not so high, particularly if it is a second or third feature of a continuously running film. As a rule, you stumble through this dimness to a seat on your own; or, if it is a larger movie house, the usher leads you with a small flashlight. You take a seat—not *your* seat, for here things are less organized—and whichever seat you appropriate becomes your perspective. Unless this is a road-show performance, you are not assigned any seat in particular, nor do the prices vary according to location and social importance. During this stumble into primary appropriation, you are surrounded by music, for the manager has provided some ambience for the crowd, if only an aural one. The curtains may part, though it is more likely that the screen hangs before you in a dim grey; and, as the music stops, the shadows on the screen begin, while you hear the whir of the projector high up and behind you. Usually the feature does not start first, but instead you are "treated" with ads urging you to buy popcorn and pickles, teasers from the coming attractions, perhaps a cartoon—though this is becoming less frequent—and, if it is an art house, an insipid travelogue on the wonders of Angola, the New Hebrides, or some other unlikely spot. The photography of the travelogue is slick and sometimes superb, but the running commentary over the visuals sounds as though it were written by nursery school dropouts. Once the manager or the projectionist (and in small theatres they are usually the same) has decided that the majority of the patrons have stumbled to some seats—any seats—the movie begins. Or does it? No, usually what *begins* is the title and then innumerable credits for the various people who have had a hand in the construction of the film. Once the credits have been run, the motion picture finally begins. And when it begins, you are presented with a space, usually a rectangle, which is framed and which is a fluid, ever-changing not-quite-three dimensions. As Rudolf Arnheim has remarked, the space on the screen is not really two-dimensional and not really three but hovers "somewhere in between."[14] It is a kind of two-and-a-half dimensional space, but its basic characteristic is its variability.

But notice that the informality of attending the movie comes in right at the very beginning. Searching in the dim dark for your own seat is quite a different experience from being ushered to a reserved seat in the theatre. Attending the movies is a kind of bearable democracy. It is individualistic from the start. If the motion picture is at a drive-in, the individuality, the disjunctive character of the "audience" is even more marked, for here each couple or group is wrapped in its own steel and chromium cocoon. In these circumstances, one does not even share the sound directly. Sound is usually focal in the drama and comes entirely from the stage. In the average motion-picture house, one is wrapped by the sound of the loudspeakers. In the drive-in, each pupa is linked to its own electronic umbilical cord. Another difference at the drive-in, of course, is that, like being at home watching a film on television, you are surrounded by a lived and familiar space instead of being, as you are at either type of theatre, a spectator in an unfamiliar, strange space huddled together with the others in a closed dark.

The initial impression one has in drama is that one is looking into a box, not, as in the movies, looking at a fairly flat projection. It is a box, or room, with only three sides, and the lighting is deceptive. Because the stage lights appear to be much brighter than they actually are, almost all photographers, when they try to take pictures of stage actions, fail to set the apertures of their cameras wide enough. The lighting of objects, actors, and settings in drama appears to be brighter than that of the motion-picture image, perhaps because the lighting in drama is three-dimensional and displays greater qualitative continuity, thus the illusion of greater intensity. Or it may be because the light that forms the image on the screen is being fragmented by the film strips in the projector and hence is thrown on the screen in varying shades of light and shadow. At any rate, the lighting on stage appears brighter, and in art, unlike life, what appears to be the case is the case. The illusion of looking into a box soon disappears, for the actors by their actions begin to transform this highlighted space into a place. In theatre, space precedes place; in film place precedes space. This is true not merely because the scenery is infinitely more variable in film but because the theatre actor is initially inhabiting a space which, though separated by the stage, by lighting, and by other distancing devices, is still continuous with that of the audience. Thus the actors must explain such things as where they are, what their costumes signify, and what the scenery entails. In film there is a much greater tendency to take these as given; and explanations, at least verbal ones, tend to be boring rather than illuminating.

Here we come, then, to a basic difference between the experience of drama and the experience of cinema. In drama, we experience a space that is, from the audience point of view, distinct but continuous; in film, we experience a space that may or may not be distinct but is discontinuous. Cinematic space is discontinuous in the sense that the audience cannot inhabit it. It is discontinuous in that it is not truly three-dimensional. It is discontinuous in the sense that it is constantly variable, and the variations are due to the shifting perspectives of the camera angles and movements. Furthermore, the shifts of scene are rapid and fluid; they are much less obtrusive than shifts of scene on the stage, which normally involve the lowering of lights or the closing of the curtain. The noncongruence of lived space and dramatic space establishes psychic distance. This noncongruence is even more distinct in film, and it not only establishes psychic distance but also conditions the nature of the art object experienced.

The discontinuity of space in film tends to make it more disparate, whereas the space in drama is condensed. Ralf Stephenson and J. R. Debrix state this difference admirably: "A play will generally include far less space than a film, but by means of its dialogue it can cram far more action into the space at its disposal; it makes space work harder."[15] And they carry this contrast further: "A film will normally be shorter than a play, but by means of its visual range will get more action into a given time: it makes time work harder."[16] A vivid example of this last assertion occurs in the film *Charly*. The motorcycle-pot-wild sequence is projected in quick alternating and concurrent images. By fragmenting space, the director intensifies time. Combining the disjunctive character of the experience of the movie spectator with the discontinuity between his real body and motion-picture space and adding to this the natural identification of his eyes with the viewpoint of the camera, one comes to the essential nature of the motion-picture experience. The motion-picture experience is an experience of excarnation.

In the theatre, which is a form of incarnation, there is a complicity of rhythm established between the audience and the actors. The actors literally weld the theatre group into an audience, and in a sense, make them co-participants in the action. The actor is a person possessed, not a poseur, and this possession flows from the stage to incorporate the audience. This is possible since the audience inhabits the theatre much as the actor inhabits the stage. Hence, the audience in the theatre is at least tangentially a part of and not apart from the action being expressed. John Howard Lawson has described this complicity, this interaction between the audience and the actors.

> We have all seen the colloquies that take place at the circus between a clown and children in the front row. A similar bond is created in more subtle ways between the stage actors and the adult audience. Nothing of the sort can happen in film, and our response to motion-picture actors is affected by the knowledge that it cannot happen. The audience can be within a foot of a screen actor's face, but it cannot make contact with him.[17]

Of course, Lawson's language is a bit inexact. It is not the actor's face that is a mere foot away but an image of the actor's face. Nevertheless, his main point is well taken and means that the audience reaction to the film can have no effect on the changing phenomenon before it. For this reason, the film must be considered as an invariant gesture, since the images on the screen, their direction, pace, and flow, remain supremely indifferent to audience response. Not so in the drama, for here the actors, by establishing a reciprocal bond with the audience, incorporate the audience into the action; and the actors change the emphasis of lines, speed the action or slow it, in terms of audience response. The stage actor is constantly taking "cues" from the audience; and he is acting in relation to the responsive, inhabited space, not merely of the stage, but of the entire theatre.

Our relation to the stage actor is distant due to our fixed perspective, the elevated stage, the costumes, the lighting, the make-up, and all the various devices used to establish psychic distance. But though distant, it is personal, for the persona he is creating reacts and is implicated with our persona. Our relation to the film figure is intimate and impersonal. We may have a close-up of the actor's image so intimate that we may perceive the very pores of his skin (complete with blackheads, no doubt, if it is a film of the alienation of modern youth in the mode of *angst*—the nobody-understands-me-and-we-cannot-communicate syndrome) and yet not be distressed, as we would be if this were a living body. Being an image, it is an imaginary presence. In fact, due to the magnitude of the image, we may perceive facets of the face that we could never see under any circumstances in normal experience. There are occasions, of course, when such blow-ups can be a bit disconcerting. When a living parody such as Anita Ekberg, for example, is expanded to occupy an entire screen of cinemascope, as her image does in *La Dolce Vita* or *The Temptation of Dr. Antonio,* one does have a slight feeling of being smothered. In some instances, one must suppose, enough is simply too much. But generally, such reactions are not the case, for we are quite aware that it is an image we are perceiving.

When speaking of the screen actor, Lawson states: "The close-up tends to deprive him of illusion; it exposes every artifice in his make-up and every pretense in his gesture or speech. He is less real as an actor because he is more real as a person."[18] Lawson is correct in this assertion, but again he is speaking loosely. The camera does not deprive the screen actor of illusion, but it does deprive him of *theatrical* illusion. It is true that screen action differs radically from stage acting, but the difference is not that one involves illusion and one not. Both consist in the creation of illusions, but they are illusions of different types with different centers of control. The actor on the stage has control of the image he is creating. He uses his real body as an instrument to embody an unreal character. Thus Hamlet becomes incarnate and the stage actor may use his own depression to portray the unreal moodiness of Hamlet. The screen actor, on the other hand, is concerned, not with projection, but with introjection. He does not act so much as react. His real body must be used to express the proper image for a sequence of shots, but the center of control and of the space to be used is not with the screen actor; it is with the camera. This is why most stage actors usually overplay in motion pictures. The stage actor is accustomed to adjusting his tone, rhythm, and gesture to a given theatre and moving in its total space. When he acts before the camera, his tendency is to act to the total space of the set and not to the limited space of the camera frame. Some actors, such as Laurence Olivier, seem to move with ease in either kind of spatial situation. Others, such as Fredric March, never seem able to reduce themselves to the camera space and consequently always seem stagy on the screen. Still others seem to have a natural presence before the camera; and, with the addition of clever make-up and editing, they become more than mere people—they become superpeople. No doubt Marilyn Monroe was beautiful in real life; but, like the *Playboy* girl of the month, she was transformed into a smooth, powdered image that was much more perfect than any given lady could be.

The differences between theatrical illusion and film illusion can be seen quite clearly in Olivier's production of *Henry V. Henry V* is no doubt the best adaptation of Shakespeare's various plays to appear on the screen; yet even it had disconcerting elements. The beginning reconstruction of the excitement and presence of the Globe Theatre is very compelling. We are then asked to move in imagination to the plains of Agincourt; but Shakespeare's language, as beautiful as it is, is simply irrelevant at this point. We do not have to *imagine* France; a camera cut takes us there. After the byplay of Pistol and Bardolph and the night brooding of the former prince who has now become king, we have the call to arms. Who can, after that stirring battle call, forget Saint Crispin's Day? The actual battle scenes, with the crosscutting from the French noblemen to the ungentlemanly English longbowmen and their rain of arrows, are highly "realistic" and exciting. Here film is doing one thing that it can do best: it presents us with a panorama of action but with a unity and coherence that no one involved in the actual battle could hope to match, let alone actors on a stage. This is followed by a shock. Henry goes to woo the fair Katharine. Their courting scene is magnificent, but he woos in a phony castle. The plains, the flying banners, the rain of arrows, the falling warriors have all given us a strong illusion of reality and three dimensions; suddenly we are confronted by cardboard castles and the screen image falls flat. Olivier has mistakenly mixed theatrical props with film reality, and they don't fit. This does not mean that only real castles must be used in film; but it does mean that they must appear to be real, otherwise one has a clash of cinematic and dramatic illusion. Film demands *authentic* illusion.

Why is it that when we see an actor prancing around the stage with a broomstick attached to him, we accept this phenomenon as a man riding a horse and yet if we were to see the same actor in a film we would be shocked and disturbed? In the film, we would demand that the actor be actually riding a real horse. Think, for example, how absurd it would be for Olivier to be riding a broomstick in the film *Richard III*. The answer that film is more "realistic," though given by some—particularly by Siegfried Kracauer, who believed that reality could somehow be "redeemed"—does not seem to help. The reason is that "more realistic" is not very precise; and, at any rate, it begs the question. The fact is that we are willing to and do accept more make-believe on the stage than on the screen. The question is "Why is this the case?" The answer, I believe, goes back to the concept of bodily displacement, which is a basic distinction between the two media. Let us examine first the phenomenon of bodily displacement in ordinary experience, then note some of the differences in displacement between the two media.

One may often experience, when riding a train, the peculiar sensation produced by the illusion that the mountains are moving while the self is stationary. The same sensation may be experienced when riding in a car. One's practical awareness may be temporarily suspended; and he may perceive the car as eating up the pavement or, looking out the rear window, may see the pavement falling away from the car. Such an experience is admittedly unusual, but it is not uncommon. It is probably the basis of much motion sickness. If one reflects upon his state of consciousness during such a phenomenon and asks himself where he feels himself to be, the answer is immediate: nowhere. Or rather, one feels himself to be in the immediate, nontemporal *now,* while things are still enmeshed in space and time; hence *they* are moving. The experience strikes us as odd; and, since it strikes us as odd, we say that it is not normal. We know perfectly well, however, that it is normal in the sense that the experience is common and accessible to all. We also feel this sense of displacement, though usually as bi-presence, in dreams. I suggest that this is exactly what happens in the motion-picture theatre but not in the legitimate theatre. In the motion-picture theatre, the distinction between things and people is either obscured or erased; in the legitimate theatre, things are things and people are people.

The telephone is a device written in the imperative mode. There is probably no other common instrument that is so irritatingly insistent and imperious. It *demands* that we answer its call. Now, a telephone on stage is very much like one in everyday life. It has the same stridency, the same urgency, and the audience is tense until the actor actually picks up the phone. A telephone in a motion picture, even when there is brilliant editing to try to enhance its "performance" as in *Dial M for Murder,* simply does not have the same ringing intensity. One does not feel the same tension building within himself until the actor picks up the receiver. It is not merely because we are aware that what we are seeing is an image, though this is certainly the case; but it is because the screen telephone and the screen actor are on the same plane: they are *both* images. Hence, the demandingness of an instrument determining human behavior is diminished. The same is true of fittingness. Clothes on the stage are used to reveal character, setting, time, and the like, as well as to provide psychic distance. But, as Fellini has correctly observed, the clothes that screen actors wear are absolutely essential to the revelation of character. The reason is that screen clothes share the same status as screen people. They become, as McLuhan rightly observes, extensions of the skin; but, unlike extensions in ordinary life, they are not on a different plane. The incipient tendency of the camera to turn people into things is one of the dangers of cinema. In some films, such as *Last Year at Marienbad,* the things—that is, the images of the architecture and abstract gardens—display more motion and life and become much more fascinating than the actors, who have been diminished to the status of formal automata.

Strictly speaking, people are not *in* space. Things are *in* space; people *inhabit* space. The actor, in the theatre, inhabits a particular delimited portion of space; and, with his bodily movements, his gestures, he shapes that space. The actor incorporates the stage place; he infects it with human significance so that it ceases to be a simple "here" and becomes *this place.* The area between two chairs on the stage is length; the area between two actors is distance, for measure has become humanized. No matter how lovely or lively or exciting the scenery may be in a play, it is still only a possibility, that is, a potential place for action; it is a situation. It is up to the actor to realize the being of the situation through action. Here we have the reverse of painting. In a painting, action is revealed through being; in drama, being is revealed through action. Since the cinema is also a form of visual composition of images, it also, like painting, centers more on being than on doing.

The actor transforms the space of the stage by his bodily presence. The more he is able by his bodily presence and gesture to transform the space of the stage, the more "at home" he will be on the stage and the greater will be his grace. We refer to this grace when we say that an actor has a strong presence. Grace is the outward expression of inner flexibility, the revelation of power through style; and grace demands that the center of control be in the person. It radiates from him. Insofar as the actor is capable of embodying himself within and hence transforming his spatial environment, he exists on the stage and the dramatic illusion is complete. If, on the other hand, he is constantly referring to himself as an other and fails to embody the character and its space, we say he is awkward, hammy, or lacks stage presence. He is anxious. Such anxiety is perfectly understandable. Some people have a low tolerance for the massed stare of the other. And as children, all of us were first brought to self-conscious laughter by this method; the first game we learned was peek-a-boo.

The poor actor, like the child, is immature, and his anxiety about the self as an other becomes evident in his exaggeration of lines and gestures. The exaggeration takes the form of misplaced emphasis. It is unstable and exhibits lack of control. Thus, the exaggeration of the incompetent actor is symptomatic of his inner lack of self-confidence and his inability to believe that he can communicate effectively. In his efforts to overcome this felt lack, he contributes to its enhancement and projection. The more he strives, the worse he gets; and his performance takes on the quality of bad faith. He appears phony. The more the audience responds in restlessness and coughing to his inadequacy, the more he is unable to forget himself as an other and the more self-conscious he becomes. The intensifying self-consciousness leads to greater and greater attempts to communicate; and the more he tries, the more he fails. Hence, he does not communicate and verifies his own hypothesis. Those who are confident can afford to be subtle.

Exaggeration, of course, is a basic necessity for the stage actor vis-à-vis the film actor. Since the audience is seated in a specific place with a fixed perspective, it cannot alter its situation; it cannot move in for the near view. The stage actor knows this; and he knows that consequently he must play for the last seats in the balcony, not merely the first row. Not only are his movements, gestures, and volume of voice pitched with greater intensity than the motion-picture actor's, but his make-up is also altered by the fixed perspective of space. Make-up in the theatre is heavy and must be used to work with the given space and the stage lighting. But it must also be constructed so that it exaggerates the eyes and the mouth and those other portions of the face which emphasize their expression. With make-up, the stage actor must literally underline the expressive portions of his face. This difference in make-up is immediately evident in film and can be used for specific purposes. Ingmar Bergman's *Ansiktet* (in the United States, *The Magician*) means literally "The Face," and the whole comedy revolves on differences of costume and make-up and on the play between stage character and "real" character. A more successful mixing of the two media in terms of make-up occurs in Fellini's *8½* and *The Nights of Cabiria*. The flat pancake make-up used on the telepathist in *8½* gives him an unearthly, almost demonic, appearance which is perfectly suited to his situation. The same is true in the hypnotic sequence of *Cabiria*. Here the exaggerated stage make-up not only conveys a charismatic kind of demonism but also works as a counterpoint to the tender expressions of Cabiria as she drops her normal cynicism and goes into a romantic dream about her imaginary lover. The make-up of the old magician perfectly counterpoints the seedy little theatre and the shoddy environment in which Cabiria finds illusory happiness with an imaginary Oscar.[19] This biting "realism" of setting and make-up saves the scene from collapsing into sentimentality. The sentiment is real, but it is held in a tight grip of decayed visual circumstance. The use of stage make-up for normal film acting, of course, would be not only inappropriate but also offensive, for here the camera can provide the illusion and bring the spectator to "the near view."

In the film, then, the center of control is not in the actor but in the camera. Therefore, the film demands that a character constantly underexpress. A close-up magnifies a pout or a change in the light of the eye into an expressive gesture that would demand a whole bodily movement on the stage. In this situation, Mies van der Rohe's dictum concerning architecture applies literally: in film acting, less is more. Perhaps this is why one of the great film actresses, Simone Signoret, claims that she has never acted. It is certainly why Fredric March kept saying to himself during one filming: "I keep forgetting. I'm not supposed to act." Furthermore, the camera itself can be an actor, and it often is. Gesture on stage belongs to the actor; gesture in film belongs to the camera.

When a camera tracks through a room or dollies down a street, the room or the street becomes an actor on the screen; and the changing, sometimes swinging, direction of the camera also becomes an invisible actor shaping the visual space. The spectator is literally nowhere in relation to this movement. For it is not the same thing to watch a street move and to walk down a street. This is true of any street, and certainly the street where you live. But the moving street on the screen is nobody's environment—or everybody's. The sensation is analogous to the one experienced when we see the mountains move from the train or see the car eating up the road. Things, through the agility of the camera, may become as active and certainly as significant as people. The camera thus erases the distinctions between agent and patient, between person and thing. Probably for this reason, most stage actors detest working in films, for in film they have lost the ability to incorporate space, to embody themselves. They cannot *shape* the way they will *appear*. And having lost their control of appearance, they have lost control of their performance. Furthermore, they are working in an area of improvisational ignorance. They do not know how they will look or how they have acted until the film is released. They become open and vulnerable. The way they will appear, and hence be, is determined by the camera, the director, and the editor, not by the actor. The stage is an actor's medium; film is a director's medium.

Due to the identification of his eyes with the camera viewpoint, the film viewer is subject to an experience of bi-sociation. Though he is literally in a seat, he negates that perspective and identifies with screen perspective. Thus, the viewer of the film is subject to bodily displacement, while the member of the audience at a play is not. The appreciator of the play inhabits, tangentially, the same space that is being shaped by the actor. This is even more forceful in theatre-in-the-round, where the normal distancing device of the proscenium has been abandoned. It no doubt also helps to account for the fact that the soliloquy works very well on the stage but is difficult to handle on film. The stage actor in soliloquy is unlike Gertrude Stein or children who talk to themselves in front of others. The actor is talking to himself in the presence of others, that is, with the purpose to be heard and to have his inner monologue shared. Hence, the actor steps out of his situation and speaks with the audience, but he cannot step out of their common space which facilitates the communication. Nor can he step out of his character, or the dramatic illusion will be destroyed. The stage actor, after all, is living an unreal life in a real way, but the film actor is confined to living a real life in a reel way. The fragile bond of soliloquy, then, is broken in film, for the swirl of images works against the words; they become competing, not complementing, gestures.

Cinerama and the short-lived three-D processes are attempts to overcome this difference. But the wrap-around screen has so far been a failure. It has been a failure for two reasons. In the first place, the spectator still has no real relation to the space on the screen; and, more importantly, the screen space becomes too vast for a visual grasp of the whole. Since the eye cannot compose it into unity but strives to do so, attention tends to lapse. In fact, lapse in the sense of laxness is a characteristic quality of the extended screen. The smaller the space to be traversed, the more rapid a movement appears. Consequently, when the screen is extended and becomes a wrap-around, the movements on it appear slow and soft. They appear "not normal." This may be compensated for by increasing the speed at which the film is shot or projected, but, so far, these compensations have not been entirely effective. Nor has distortion been completely eliminated, in spite of refined lenses and new processes. The one thing the expanded screen can give us success- fully is not human action but open countrysides. This was quite successful in *Hud* and in *Lawrence of Arabia.* But when one becomes too fascinated with scenery, the movement of the film itself tends to suffer. In *Lawrence,* it often took a supreme effort of attention to return to the acting and the story line when there was all that horizon to contemplate. One would almost think that the wide screen was the invention of John Ford who has long been the master of the horizon. But Ford at his best does not allow the expansion of visual space to interfere with and slow down his cinematic time. In *Lawrence of Arabia,* David Lean does. This can be seen particularly in his constant use of the pan. Consequently, one has a feeling that *Lawrence* is a movie that does not so much move as dwell.

The film actor can "step out of" film space, of course, but this technique, as all technique in art, must have a purpose. In *Tom Jones,* when Tom holds his hat over the camera lens to exclude the voyeurism of the audience or when he turns to speak to them directly asking if they have seen his money, the result is one of delighted shock. In the film, Tony Richardson uses almost every cinematic trick, including stop motion and speeded chases, but none of them has the impact of these direct confrontations. Certainly the delighted shock is partly a result of the audience not being used to such a technique, although it is an old cinematic device and goes back to the first bit of narrative realism. Edwin S. Porter's *The Great Train Robbery* ends with a gun being pointed directly at the audience and being fired. No doubt one can find other examples, particularly in the various three-D experiments. No, I think that the delighted shock rests on a reason deeper than lack of familiarity. There is shock because the viewers have forgotten that they are watch- ing a film and that the viewpoint is the camera's. Hence, Tom is holding his hat, temporarily, over the eye of the spectator. Or when he turns to the audience in search of the money, he is using this gesture as if he were on stage. In so acting, he wrests control of the visual space from the camera and enhances his own appear- ance. More importantly, he forces us to locate ourselves with respect to his image, something we are seldom forced to do when viewing a film. He is literally putting us in our place, for this gesture jolts us out of our bodily displacement and forces us back into our seats. At the level of sensation, we had been momentarily inhabiting the same space. It is this dislocation, or rather, sudden location, that occurs and that engenders the amusing sense of shock we feel. Once our self-consciousness and laughter subside, we identify once more with the camera viewpoint and forget where we are.

These differences in spatial habitation, then, help to explain why we will accept a broomstick as a horse in a drama but not in a film. In drama, the actor has control over the space he shapes. Furthermore, we are implicated in this shaping; we are tangential to this re-creation. Thus stage space ceases to be mere space and becomes place, a place that is centered upon the radiating influence of the forces generated by the actor. Our attention is riveted upon *him,* and we accept his use of the broomstick because it is an expression of his embodiment. On the screen, the broomstick has as much presence as the actor. They are both images and, in that sense, are co-equal. There is thus a tendency for them to become co-agents, co-competitors for our attention. The "thinginess" of the thing is dissolved as is the persona of the actor. But distance is essential to art. Not only must there be psychic distance established between the viewer and the object, but also there must be appropriate distance between the elements within the object. Hence, on film we demand a real kingdom and a real horse. Film requires authentic illusion.

Notes

1. Margaret Kennedy, "The Mechanized Muse," in *Film: An Anthology,* ed. by Daniel Talbot (New York: Simon and Schuster, 1959), p. 106.
2. This is the basic definition of fine art articulated in D. W. Gotshalk's book *Art and the Social Order* (Chicago: University of Chicago Press, 1947).
3. Arthur Knight, *The Liveliest Art* (New York: Macmillan, 1957), p. 29.
4. John H. Lawson, *Film: The Creative Process* (New York: Hill & Wang, 1967), p. 194.
5. Pauline Kael, "Antonioni's *Blow-Up,"* *New Republic* (February 11, 1967), pp. 30–35.
6. Pauline Kael, *I Lost it at the Movies* (Boston: Atlantic–Little, Brown, 1965), pp. 191–192.
7. Angelo Solmi, *Fellini,* (London: Merlin Press, 1967), p. 110.
8. Thornton Wilder, *On the Intent of the Artist,* p. 83, as quoted in Susanne Langer, *Feeling and Form* (New York: Scribner's, 1953), p. 307.
9. Dwight Macdonald, *Against the American Grain* (New York: Vintage, 1962), p. 49.
10. Macdonald, p. 50.
11. Plato, *Republic,* VI, trans. by Francis Cornford (Fair Lawn, N.J.: Oxford University Press, 1968), p. 508ff.

12. George W. Linden, "The Film: Remembrances of Things Present," *Bucknell Review,* Vol. 13, No. 2 (1965), pp. 58–70.

13. Pauline Kael, "It's Only a Movie," in *Film Study in Higher Education,* ed. by David C. Stewart (Washington, D.C.: American Council on Education, 1966), p. 133.

14. Rudolf Arnheim, *Film as Art* (Berkeley: University of California Press, 1960), p. 12.

15. Ralf Stephenson and J. R. Debrix, *The Cinema as Art* (Baltimore: Penguin Books, 1965), p. 70.

16. Stephenson and Debrix, p. 70.

17. Lawson, *Film,* p. 191.

18. Lawson, p. 191.

19. We must not overlook the irony that Miss Masina won a real Oscar for this performance.

2

The Storied World

Most novels do not begin "Once upon a now." Most films do. Novels are almost invariably written in the past; films are delibly shot in the present. Novels are tied to the past because narrative is the form of fictional prose, and the essence of narrative form is the past remembered as history. Thus, Henry James was quite right when he defined the novel as art and as history. He was mistaken, however, as Susanne K. Langer points out,[1] in not seeing that art and history fail to coincide. James consequently confused the novel with actual history or at least conceived it as a history of the actual. It is neither. A novel is a history of a possible world. A novel is a history of an illusion.

Film, like the novel or the heart of Columbus, is also concerned with the possible. It provides us with an illusion, an illusion that could be true. It provides us with a possible world, which we feel we might inhabit. In doing so, film follows the heart's surmise, penetrates to meanings hidden in the illusion, and reveals to us hitherto undisclosed aspects of the world and of ourselves. In film, aspects emerge from visibility to feeling to awareness that we would not ordinarily have perceived, had we merely remained at the level of the natural standpoint. All art transcends the natural standpoint to create an illusory world of emotional depth. It then negates itself as illusion and leaves us with altered eyes to view our everyday world. Film, being an art, and a public one at that, participates in this dialectical movement. Unlike the novel, however, film does not so much pose a world as ex-pose one. It takes us, transports us, into a land of "Once upon a time," then returns us to our common world. But because of the peculiar nature of time and space in film, because it collapses all its elements into a fluid present, film's "Once upon a time" is *now*. A novel is a remembrance of things past; a film is a remembrance of things present.

While the novel is a narrative that deploys past events moving toward a present, a film directly displays the present. It presents the present. Even though a novel may be concerned with the present almost exclusively, it is still written and experienced in the reflective mode and hence never quite reaches the present. A film, on the other hand, never quite reaches the past. Hence, where the novelist describes, a director shoots; where a novelist is forced to explain, a director exhibits. Thus, while the novelist constructs the present as past, the director presents the past as present. Although film may borrow certain devices from drama to establish distance (such as scenery, costumes, and archaic language) or may use certain techniques of its own (such as a dissolve into a monologue or a flashback to evoke the past), it never quite succeeds in coinciding with or establishing the past as past. The essence of film is its immediacy, and this immediacy is grounded in its tenselessness. In fact, a film might be defined as a tension without tense.

Moving pictures are composed of pictures, and pictures have no tenses. Béla Balázs states:

> They show only the present—they cannot express either a past or a future tense. In a picture itself there is nothing that would compellingly and precisely indicate the reasons for the picture being what it is. In a film scene we see only what is happening before our eyes.[2]

One may at first be conscious of the fact that Olivier is portraying Henry the Fifth; but, once the soliloquy is over and the battle of Agincourt begins, one sees the battle taking shape before his eyes, and the conviction carried by the images, this immediacy of the present, later leads the spectator to reject the painted castles as props and as phony. The fact that these pictures are moving also adds to their condensation into the present. Through motion there is a kind of spatializing of time and it becomes difficult, if not impossible, to say "then" on film. Condensation also changes the status of relation; thus, relations in the novel tend to be causal, whereas relations in film tend to be casual.

The novel can be much more precise in its treatment of time than can the film. Being more abstract, it can be more exact. Hence the novelist can write: *"Before* John and Mary were married . . . *After* the second anniversary . . . *In November* they discovered she was pregnant . . . *June 12th,* the baby was born . . . *In August* he was baptized. . . ."* But, as Stephenson and Debrix point out,

> Film has no words like these; film has no tenses—past, present, or future. When we watch a film, it is just something that is happening—*now*. . . . The immediacy of what film shows us consequently surpasses anything in other arts, and it can have a terseness and a pace that literature cannot match.[3]

One can, of course, always find borderline cases. Ernest Hemingway's style, for example, by its short punching quality, comes close to the terseness of film. The spatialization of time in James Joyce's *Ulysses* or the shifting "camera angles," "zooms," "pans," and "set-ups" in William Faulkner's *As I Lay Dying* also come close to film, not merely through similarity of technique but through the movement toward emotional intensity in a fluid present. Nevertheless, the basic orientation of the novel is to what has happened. Film *is* what's happening.

Just as the novel and film are alike and different in their relations to time, so they are also alike and different in their relations to space. Unlike drama, both the novel and film utilize a space that is intangible and nontangential to the standpoint of the spectator-participant. The space of the novel is a construct of words; it is a space that is engendered by the imagination of the reader, once he has become moved by description to envision. The space of film, however, is immediately given to the eye by the flickering visual image. Both the novel and the film tell stories, but one tells by saying and the other by presenting. Hence, the reader of the novel must conjure up the author's posed world through his own active imagination. But the moviegoer is presented a story already given in image. In this sense, his imagination is more passive, for the film presents its own pace and space; and the shifts in either are controlled, not by his imagination, but by the camera. It is probably fair to conclude, then, that the novel is primarily a representational medium, whereas film is primarily a presentational medium.

Perhaps it should be obvious that moving pictures are not novels. Certainly this is what I have been arguing in emphasizing the immediate presence of the film and the basic mnemonic character of novels. But this is not obvious to everyone. To the layman, the relation between the novel and the film appears to be one of absolute identity. Or rather, one might call it moral identity, since the average man insists that though the film and novel may not be the same, they *ought* to be. To the respected critic Brendan Gill, the relation seems to be one of substance and attribute, though it is quite arbitrary which one picks as substance and which as attribute. To Marshall McLuhan, the relation is one of formal or structural identity. Let us examine these three specific points of view before returning to a general discussion of the relations of films and novels.

Most surveys reveal that the useful fiction, the average layman, simply does not buy many books. If he does, few of them are novels; and, of those, even fewer are ever read. It is probably safe to assume that most people buy books for the look of their living rooms rather than to add new furniture to the mansions of their minds. The motto seems to be "Buy the book if you must, but see the movie." And, perhaps, for sound pragmatic reasons. It takes less time to see the film. Furthermore, it often takes much less effort. One does not have to think as much to experience the film and, besides, it is continuous. As far as the average man is concerned, the novel and the film are practically identical. But practical identity for him means identity. Hence, if he has not read the novel, he will consider himself to have read it after watching the film. If he has previously read the novel, he will either criticize the film for not being faithful to the book or praise it for being a fine rendering of the original. It takes someone more subtle—say, a professional critic —to condemn a film for being too faithful to a novel. This, of course, is exactly what many critics do, although it is far more common even for the professionals to condemn a film for violating the novel. The basic assumption of the ordinary layman, then, and of some critics, is that for a motion picture to be faithful to a novel it must simply be the novel.

One contemporary critic, Brendan Gill, has the distinction of downgrading two films in the same review for contradictory reasons. He rejects the film *Reflections in a Golden Eye* on the basis that John Huston did not follow the novel with greater fidelity and made the film realistic, whereas the terrain of the novel is a purely fictional land. Huston, he claims, has been unfaithful to Carson McCullers' intention and to her work. At the same time, Gill rejects *Far from the Madding Crowd* because it too slavishly follows Thomas Hardy's novel. Not only the director but also the producer, writers, and actors are condemned for excessive reverence.[4] Huston is accused, therefore, either of good faith that has been misplaced or of bad faith, and John Schlesinger is condemned for having displayed good faith with too much fidelity.

If one takes Mr. Gill's critiques literally, he appears to be contradicting himself or at least to be outlining an almost impossible task for a director. He is also overlooking the fact that both the novel and the film are types of fiction. They simply happen to be different kinds of fiction. Huston's film is not more real than the novel on which it is based. Though it may give the illusion of greater reality, the film is also an illusion, a visual instead of a verbal one. That there is a sense in which the film and the novel exist on somewhat the same plane is evidenced by the fact that we speak of the film *version* of the book or we say "the novel on which the film is *based*." But the idea of "basing" and the word "version" also connote differences. There must be some sense, then, in asserting that a film can be a translation or, even more accurately, a transformation of a novel. The question is still open, however, as to what should be kept, what should be thrown out, what should be transformed, and how.

Gill explicitly rejects the theory that films should be judged strictly as films without regard to their novelistic antecedents when he states: "This is an old and not very intelligent theory, and, significantly, is nearly always employed as a device for defending a movie that has failed, rather than for paying tribute to one that has succeeded."[5] Not because of but in spite of Mr. Gill's dogmatism and pejorative language, there is some truth in what he says. But there is also some truth in asserting that it is more fruitful to compare films with films than to compare films with novels. Because of the intimate organic relations of form and content, no matter how faithful the film, it can never express the content of the novel as the novel expresses it. Different materials demand different modes of expression. The novel, after all, projects a world from words; the film presents one in images.

Some forms of expression, Mr. Gill seems to feel, such as Hardy's, should stay safely ensconced between dead covers and should never be resurrected by adaptation. Presumably what he means is that it is most difficult, if not impossible, to transform Hardy's pessimistic value world into visual terms. In assuming that it is the value world of the novel, not the characters, events, or plot, that is of central importance for film, Mr. Gill is essentially correct. A motion picture should make us see the world the author has envisioned.

Another novel champion, Marshall McLuhan, is convinced that film is linear and print oriented and that television images are nonlinear—in fact, antilinear. Thus, he attempts to prove that the decline in the popularity of baseball is due to television because baseball is a game of specialists who play a game that proceeds one-thing-at-a-time, whereas television demands generalists with everything happening at once. This evidence is simply not evidence. Football has as great an amount of, perhaps more, specialization than baseball, and it has been enhanced by TV. In recent years, no sport has made more dramatic strides in popularity than golf, and this rise in popularity is due almost entirely to television coverage. It would be difficult to imagine a more linear game than golf, either in the literal or the figurative sense. Baseball is declining probably because it is a highly intellectual game in which most of the time nothing is going on; and, unlike golf, it is difficult if not impossible to edit. Hence, long lapses exist and they cannot be compressed. But this is not due to its linearity, as opposed to the nonlinearity of football.

McLuhan is attempting, via TV, to assimilate the film to the novel, not only in the sense of its supposed print orientation (why he missed the pun that filmstrips are printed is a puzzle), but also in the sense of narrative. He does not look to see whether films are in fact linear and ABCED-minded; he assumes that they must be, then attempts to prove his point. He first attempts to collapse film into literature by asserting that both the film maker and the writer try to transfer the "reader or viewer from one world, his *own,* to another, the world created by typography and film."[6] This is, of course, true, but it does not show that print and film are therefore identifiable in some specific and significant manner. It is the function of all art—whether film, painting, sculpture, or drama—to transport the viewer to another world, to give him another temporary world to live in. McLuhan's assertion that movies are a form of "statement without syntax"[7] is slipshod and false. Film images may be tenseless, but they are not without syntax. In fact, the Russian school has long held that film is little else but syntax, a formalist point of view, which McLuhan ought logically to hold if he were consistent with his assertion that the "medium is the message"—an assertion that puts the entire emphasis and value on form and declares that content is irrelevant at best and pernicious at worst. One can attempt to assimilate film to literature; but, in order to make the attempt, one should be more accurate and more subtle than McLuhan—one must be a Jean Cocteau, a Robert Bresson, or an Alexandre Astruc. Even then, one should remember that what he is doing is describing analogies, not reducing one art to the other.

Thus, while McLuhan tries to draw sharp distinctions between the film and television, he attempts to blur the distinctions between the film and the novel. He claims that the viewing of film demands a high degree of and training in literacy. This is merely a half-truth. The film experience does demand a definite amount of visual literacy but does not necessarily demand verbal literacy. This can be observed quite clearly in children, who can grasp the flow of images and the reference of one to another even though they have not as yet learned to read. A little reflection will show that the following McLuhan assertion is false: "The close relation, then, between the reel world of film and the private fantasy experience of the printed word is indispensable to our Western acceptance of the film form."[8] In fact, a slight knowledge of history will show it false. The audiences who were shocked by D. W. Griffith's first use of the close-up and fled from the theatre when the first face filled the entire screen were *verbally* literate. Newspapers and books, after all, were not invented after the Griffith films. The difficulty was that the audiences were *visually* illiterate in a new form: film.

But McLuhan continues: "Film, both in its reel form and in its scenario or script form, is completely involved with book culture. All one need do is to imagine for a moment a film based on newspaper form in order to see how close film is to the book."[9] One does not need to imagine, one has simply to see. Look at Jean-Luc Godard's *Breathless* or Richard Lester's *A Hard Day's Night,* and you will see films based, not on newspaper content, but on newspaper form. Or look at the verbal version of Federico Fellini's *Juliet of the Spirits.* The printed version consists of a long interview and two scripts: the original script and the shooting script. The film itself differs from both written scripts.

It may be that McLuhan is correct, though he does not identify his authorities and grandly personifies the film industry in general, when he states that "even the film industry regards all of its greatest achievements as derived from novels, nor is this unreasonable."[10] It may not be unreasonable, but it is doubtful. If one reflects for a few moments on some of the great films, he will find that they can be classified into three categories with respect to the novel: fine films not based on novels, fine films based on poor novels, and fine films based on fine novels. The same categories, of course, could hold for poor films. But if one confines himself to the set which McLuhan pinpoints as "the greatest achievements" of film, he will find that either McLuhan or "the industry" or both are probably wrong. In fact, it is highly doubtful that the greatest films are derived from novels. There even seems to be a kind of basic antagonism or inverse relationship between the novel and the film. It seems almost as though the greater the novel, the less likely that the resulting film will be great.

It is difficult to think of a truly revolutionary film that was derived from a novel. The word "revolutionary" here is intended to refer to both those films that changed the course of the development of film art and also those films that stand as examples, *par excellence,* of the medium. *The Great Train Robbery, The Birth of a Nation, Intolerance, The Cabinet of Doctor Caligari, Grand Illusion, Citizen Kane, La Strada, The Bicycle Thief, Potemkin, Zero for Conduct, Alexander Nevsky, Children of Paradise, Shoeshine, Umberto D, Hiroshima Mon Amour, Wild Straw-berries, Last Year at Marienbad, The Four Hundred Blows, L'Avventura, The Young and the Damned, The Seven Samurai, On the Waterfront*—one could go on almost indefinitely naming films that were written specifically for the screen, insofar as writing was involved. Many of the great directors have avoided making any films based on novels but have preferred, as Bergman and Fellini have, either to collaborate on scripts or to do all their own writing.

Fine films made from poor or at least mediocre literary works are not difficult to list, either. Such films as *Treasure of the Sierra Madre, The Postman Always Rings Twice, Gone with the Wind, The Informer, Double Indemnity, The African Queen, Rashomon, The Ox-Bow Incident, Greed, The Maltese Falcon, The Graduate* are all cases in point. But it is much more difficult to list fine films made from fine novels. There are a few, such as *Tom Jones, Ulysses, The Grapes of Wrath, Lolita, The Red Badge of Courage;* and it should be noted that these films often deviate drastically from the novels on which they were based. *The Grapes of Wrath,* for example, contains as a film none of the mystic uncertainty of the novel and completely changes the ending of the novel in order that the film may be upbeat and may end on a note of optimism, not despair. It is not difficult at all, of course, to remember poor films made from fine novels. Almost any film version of *Crime and Punishment* is hardly worth watching, and the same may be said for *The Red and the Black, The Brothers Karamazov, Moby Dick, Huckleberry Finn,* and many other screen disasters. Some cases that are moot come to mind. For example, *The Old Man and the Sea* is not a great novel nor is the film a great film. One could no doubt draw up innumerable lists of this type; and it must be granted that no matter how many films might be listed, such inventories would probably prove little.

Nevertheless, it is worth noting that many films considered the high points of the various genres in the history of the motion picture were not adaptations of novels nor did they depend primarily upon novelistic technique. The American discoveries of film possibilities made by Griffith and exploited in the silent comedies, the Russian films of socialist realism and non-heroes, the German cinema of expressionism, and Italian neo-realism all avoided dependence upon the novel. The same can be said for most of the great creators of personal films, whether from primarily silent times, such as Chaplin, or from the new age of alienation, such as Bergman, Fellini, and Antonioni. At the very least, then, we must conclude that McLuhan's attempt to identify film with the novel, like the attempt of the layman, is suspect. In all probability, it is false.

These reflections should make it evident that the relations between the quality of novels and the resulting quality of the film are not simple. No doubt the film companies pay enormous funds for famous novels; whether they happen to be fine novels is irrelevant. It is the fame, after all, that is important, for the motive behind such purchases is not artistic but commercial. It is the producer who usually "buys" the novel, and, once bought, it ceases to be a novel and becomes a property. It may well be that those films based on novels with reputations, notorious or otherwise, do in fact make more money. This may have been what McLuhan meant, but it was far from what he said. And even then, few would accuse Chaplin or Fellini of having become poverty-stricken by the film. It would appear, then, that films are not so easily identified with the novel as both the ordinary layman and Marshall McLuhan assume. As Professor Baumbach has remarked, many college students can barely read or write, but they are filmically literate.[11]

What the camera can provide is the richness of immediate presence, and this very complexity of quality makes film "the most difficult of all arts both to practice and appreciate."[12] This richness of presence must be unified by taste and sensitivity, by an awareness of the emotional rightness of visual images, and it cannot be reduced to verbal rules. René Clair was quite aware that—although, from the viewpoint of intellect, one could set up a strict metre of shot structure on the basis of shot length, scene alternation, and internal movement—from a practical point of view, it would not work. " 'I am resigned,' he concluded, 'to find neither rules nor logic in this world of images. The primitive wonder of this art enchants me.' "[13] Had Marshall McLuhan been as sensitive as René Clair to the differences that lie at the base of every analogy, he might not have mistaken presence for sequence and tried to reduce film to a linear succession of static parts.

The theory of aesthetics resulting from McLuhan's prior positions is one of sheer formalism and rests upon a constant confusion of the verbal and the visual. It is summed up in his most famous phrase: "The medium is the message." What this means, if it is taken to be meaningful, is that meaning is purely a function of syntax and is completely independent of content. Hence, it is the sheer how of things and not their why that is important. It must be admitted that McLuhan tries to base the reduction of film to words on the structural similarities of shot sequence and verbal construction. He has to depend upon sequence, of course, since he has already claimed that a shot is without syntax. That such an analogy does not appear applicable has already been noted. It is difficult for McLuhan himself to avoid depending upon content. His belief in the importance of plot brings him to the posture that film is a closed medium.

The arguments in *Understanding Media* that film is medieval are false in one sense and true in another. They are false insofar as they argue that film is composed of static essences and true when they claim that a film is a kind of two-hour cathedral. The assertions of stability are McLuhan's attempt to express a belief in a set universe of clear categories and Thomistic essences. This same attitude brings him to utilize Henri Bergson's contrast of the living and the static to misinterpret the nature of film. While it is true that in one frame a camera captures only the static, it is untrue that what the human eye perceives on the screen is a series of changes of states and essences. What one perceives is the flow and patterning of images. This patterning is in part done by the spectator. During a ninety-minute film, about forty minutes is composed of a black screen; yet the persistence of vision negates the darkness and allows us to perceive a continuously flowing phenomenon. McLuhan's analogy of the building of cathedrals and the construction of film, however, is a medievalism that bears some truth. The truth it carries, however, negates his attempt to assimilate film to the novel.

McLuhan is quite right in stating that the creation of film is a corporate activity. The creation of a film, like the building of a cathedral, depends upon the coordinated interplay of activities among a large group of specialists. The products of the activities of each particular group of specialists must be governed with a view to the whole, and the quality of the part must be so constructed as to enhance the unity and the impact of the whole. Thus, the sculptor who worked on the cathedral did not create free-standing works but elements that were designed to enhance and enliven the architecture. In the same way, the costume designer or the make-up man who works in films contributes elements that should help constitute the revelation of character and situation, only a part of which is contributed by the written script. Like the construction of the cathedral, the film demands a hierarchy of coordinated activity and one overriding authority in charge, usually the producer or, more effectively, the director. Both the film and the cathedral are incredibly expensive and depend upon complex economic relationships. Both provide a temporary haven for those seeking communion and temporary escape from the real evils of the world. But, of course, they differ greatly as to time. It may take centuries to build a cathedral, and it is designed to last for centuries more. No film could afford to take so long to shoot, it rarely lasts more than a few years, and the solace it is designed to provide is usually confined within the span of two hours, not an eternity. It is precisely the corporate character of film production, of course, that has been such a painful reality for most writers.

The task of a writer is an exercise in loneliness; in fact, writing is almost narcissistic in its singularity. Everything the writer creates, everything he includes or fails to include in his novel, must, one way or another, come out of the depths of his own experience and being. The agonizing solitude of the writer provides him with a control over his work that is perhaps as absolute. as anything can be in this life. This means that the viewpoint of the author is basic, and his perspective determines the theme, the style, the form, the tone, and the content of his work. Whether the narrator is a character in the story, as he usually is, or the author himself, the point of view of the narrator and his rendition of past events lie at the heart of the novel. He is not subject to the revisions of the continuity director, the cameraman, the sound technicians, or the prop man. Ultimately, in the novel, the author and the author alone is responsible for the characters and the scene. But the film is not primarily scene but something immediately seen. Hence, even if it is a highly personal film, stamped with the style and characteristics of the director, even this viewpoint is submerged by what is immediately seen and heard. If the writer has simply been hired to work on a film, his impact on the end result will be even less, and it is not at all unusual to find a film that has had many scriptwriters. It is most unusual to find a novel with more than one author, and it would be a rare publisher indeed who would hire several authors to write and revise the same work. This process, of course, is quite normal in the film. And it is often successful. Films are not composed of words. A motion picture is composed of images. And the images move.

The altered relation to words is one reason that the motion-picture experience exists on a lower level of imagination than that of the novel. The author of the novel uses the bulge and nuzzle of language to move the reader onto an imaginary plane. And what is imagination except seeing as if present that which is not present? The world the novelist describes may be enchanting or enchanted, but it is not now actually present in sensation. A novel is something thought, not something seen. The world the motion-picture director displays, on the other hand, is one which appears present in the visibility and urgency of immediacy. Through the rhythmic tension of images and depth, the director elicits the visibility of the actual and projects it, both literally and figuratively, into an immediate possible present, not an imaginary past. Worlds, not words, are important in film. Without words, the novel could not manifest itself, it could not be. But film can and does exist without words. Admittedly, it is better with them (if one excludes the avalanche of excessively talky films that succeeded the technical breakthrough of *The Jazz Singer*). But the true function of words in film is not to portray but to punctuate vision.

Usually an author writes his novel in sequential order; he writes the first chapter followed by the second, and so on. Sometimes, he may write a climactic scene, and then write up to and away from it. If he is writing a mystery novel, he may well write the ending first, then plan the rest of the book and write it to meet the final revelation. It is a rare author, however, such as James Joyce, who works on three or four different chapters at the same time or in alternate sequences. Such a mode of shooting is the normal procedure in film; and if one ever watches a film being shot, the one overwhelming feeling he has is that it will be a miracle if all of this chaos is ever brought into any semblance of order. The order of composition of the film is from the outside in; the order of composition of a novel is from the inside out. Very few significant films are shot in sequence, and the resulting cut product, of course, is always much, much less than the amount of film used. This will vary with the director and his character. During the first thematic phase of Akira Kurosawa's *High and Low,* the spectator is conscious of the careful composition and the extended length of the scenes. These takes last about ten minutes on the screen, yet each was edited from one hour's shooting. The shot/film ratio of this sequence is thus six to one. My guess would be that Fellini's shot/finished film ratio is probably three or four times that of Ingmar Bergman for the simple reason that Fellini is more emotional, more flamboyant, more in love with happy accidents, whereas Bergman is more theatrical, more intellectual, and more controlled.

The status and functions of the writer, then, differ considerably with respect to the film and the novel. In some films, such as *8½,* the writer may serve as an intellectual foil and as an alter ego for the main character. Sometimes he may be a disembodied narrator, as in *Tom Jones,* or an embodied one, as in the framing device of *Quartet.* Usually, however, the writer is not in the film in any form at all, though he is almost always in the novel in one form or another. The main difference in the relations of the writer to film and to the novel is the element of control. With respect to the novel, the writer is a mortal and singular god; whatever is there, he created. In film, he is merely one worker among many. For his novel to become a film, it must undergo "treatment" and become a shooting script. And a film script, as we said in Chapter 1, is merely the skeleton for an aural-visual world and not a full-fleshed creature. Since the skills needed to transform a novel into a shooting script differ from those of the novelist proper, few novelists become successful screenwriters. Some, such as Faulkner, have made their bread and butter by screenwriting, but we remember them for their novels, not for their sharp shooting scripts.

If we turn to the experience of the reading of the novel, we find that the reader's experience is analogous to that of the writer: he has much more control. We have already described the bearable democracy of attending the movies. When one reads a novel, he usually reads it in familiar surroundings, that is, in his own home. Since one's lived environment is familiar and known, it is seldom an object of sensation. It is simply assumed; and being assumed, it can much more easily slip into a surrounding ambience and become an unperceived, or at least dimly perceived, horizon of the self. Hence, when one takes up the novel and begins reading in his easy chair, the surrounding room soon begins to slip away. One becomes unaware of the place and ground of his own body and imaginatively becomes excarnate, inhabiting—omnisciently, of course—the world of the novel. This easy slip into externalized subjectivity is evidence that McLuhan is right in asserting that the founder of modern thought was not Descartes but Gutenberg. At any rate, as soon as one is imaginatively engaged in the novel, he feels himself to be nowhere and nowhen in relation to the actual world. But he has much more control over the pace and direction of his experience than he has in film. He can dwell on this situation or that, this character or that, and he can thumb his way back to a previous passage to confirm an image or impression. The reader's vision and ability to envision consequently follow his attention, whereas in film our attention follows our vision. We cannot stop the flow of the film, reverse its order, or dwell on a scene since its directionality is forced upon us. We can be and are selective, but the degree of control the movie spectator can exert is much less than that of the novel reader.

One has the feeling when reading the novel that he is in direct communion with the author. The novel reader's experience, then, is like that of the moviegoer and unlike that of the member of the audience in the stage play in that his own persona, his self as a generalized other, is bypassed. It is the function of all media, whether the motion picture, radio, television, the novel, or the telephone, to bypass the self-as-other and to negate the natural standpoint. For this reason, films and novels can be both intimate and impersonal, for the persona of the individual is not involved. This, I take it, is why children with speech defects usually become avid readers, and why children who stutter seldom do so on the telephone. It also explains why my teen-aged daughters are so addicted to the telephone; it allows them to reach the aural being of the other without having to suffer from his gaze. Media provide the possibility for immediate participation without the concomitant defect of embarrassment. They provide us with another way to be. And that other way to be is an experience of excarnation.

The experience of the reader of the novel is analogous to the activity of the director of the film in the sense that the reader's contact with the world depicted in the novel is usually over an extended period of time. It takes longer to read a novel than to watch a film. No doubt this is one reason why the lazy say, "I won't read the book. I'll wait to see the film." Of course, being lazy, they overlook the fact that what they are seeing is not a novel on celluloid but a different object: a moving picture. It may be the novel in shadow but not in substance.

The experience of the reader is analogous to that of the director in another sense: it is intermittent. One usually reads a novel, then puts the book aside for the press of everyday life before once again resuming the illusory world. But the illusory world of experiencing the film is continuously present. One reason that it is possible for the reader to experience the novel intermittently is because the novel is a narrative. It is something he must think together in imagination. The verbal symbols are constant and fairly simple to resume. The task of the director is much more difficult. He is working, not primarily with thoughts or with the verbal, but with the aural and visual; hence, he must be able to draw these disparate elements together on the basis of emotional rhythm. The necessity for emotional unity varies according to the type of film involved, of course. Hence, a documentary tends to be thought, while a fictional film is much more dependent upon feeling. In the novel, feeling is a precipitate of thought. In film, thought is a precipitate of feeling engendered by vision. In the novel, we see because we remember; in film, we remember because we see.

The experience of the reader of the novel is much more singular than that of the spectator of the film. The word "singular" is used here in various senses. The experience is singular in the sense that it is more rare and less frequent. At least in the modern world more people view films more often than read the novels on which those films are based, however loosely. The experience is also singular in the sense that one usually reads a novel alone. Rarely is novel reading a group experience; and, although in a very real sense each individual watching a film is in a theatre of his own, films are nevertheless a group experience. The reading of a novel is singular in the still further meaning that only one sense is usually involved: vision. One rarely reads a novel aloud; hence, the written symbols must carry the force to create the entire imaginary world. But it is precisely the counterpoint and fusion of sight and sound that are basic to the impact of film.

While the film and the novel are alike in that they are not primarily concerned with the imitation of an action, as is drama, but with the development of events, their approaches to the events differ due to their different demands and emphases. The novelist tends to reveal what people do through what they are; the director, to reveal what they are through what they do. What the novelist deploys, the director must display. It is exactly here that the film based on the novel usually fails. For a film to be an adequate rendition of a novel, it must not only present the actions and events of the novel but also capture the subjective tones and attitudes toward those events. This the novelist can do quite freely by using description and point of view. It is much more difficult for the director, since he must either discover or create visual equivalents for the narrator's evaluations. Let us examine two failures to find images of equal valency. One, *Hud,* was merely a limited failure, while the other, *Lord of the Flies,* was almost a total failure.

Hud is a good film, which has many brilliant moments in it. One must admire James Wong Howe's truly beautiful photography. He captures not only the clarity of the Western setting and its expansive nature but also the emotional urgency and desperation of the destruction of the cattle due to foot-and-mouth disease. By shooting the burial scene of the cattle from a low angle, he made the audience feel as though it were being buried, and this greatly enhanced the desperation of the situation presented. One also must admire the fine acting of Paul Newman and Brandon de Wilde and the beautiful strength and subtlety with which Patricia Neal made an ordinary, middle-aged female into a woman. Hers was probably one of the healthiest portrayals of the sexuality of a real human being since Simone Signoret's performance in *Room at the Top.* Alma (not Halmira) is forthrightly sexual, and she frankly wants Hud; but she refuses to be subjected to physical or psychological rape. She insists on being treated as what she is—a person and hence a center of value. Martin Ritt should be praised not only for how he handled these actors and the shooting but also for the way in which he utilized the vast expanse of the wide screen to emphasize the open loneliness of the West. But, being the director, he must also shoulder the blame.

Not only was he to blame for casting a man too old and weak, Melvyn Douglas, for the part of the grandfather so that the main point of the novel was lost, but he also violated the tone of the novel. The theme of *Horseman, Pass By* is not really the growth of a young man, Lonnie, to adulthood. After all, that is the subtheme of most novels, and it was Hemingway's stock in trade. The theme is the dying of the old ways and the conflict between the values of the past, as embodied in the grandfather, and the new don't-give-a-damn self-aggrandizement of the operator, the rich bum, Hud. Changing Halmira from Negro to white makes Hud a bit less opportunistic and the film more commercial but does not seriously damage the main theme. The weakness of the grandfather does. The film thus becomes a story of two strong people, Hud versus Alma, and of a boy's transition to disillusion, sex, and adulthood. But the main failing was not being able to translate the basic tone of the novel. The haunting and engaging quality of the book is the lyrical love of the land and the tender regret at its despoiling. It is a land that was won and held by hard men, but hard men of a new breed are destroying its values and in the process are destroying themselves. The meaning of the tone is this: Home is no longer a place. The home place is deliberately negated, and everyone becomes a tumbleweed. Hud Bannon, once he has destroyed, belongs no place and is going no whither; he simply moves. In spite of the fine acting and the luminous photography, the film lacked this sadness at the loss, not of innocence and childhood ways, but of a real and tangible world of value, at the destruction of place and the substitution of space.

As an attempt to translate the novel into film form, *Lord of the Flies* was almost a total failure. Some critics praised it, of course; but even assuming that they had good taste and understood film form (two vast assumptions), it is clear that they were praising their remembrances of an admired novel and not what they were actually seeing on the screen. It is highly doubtful that anyone who had not previously read the book could even have found the film intelligible. I attended the film with two educated and sensitive adults, neither of whom could figure out what the film was about or, most of the time, what was happening. Once I had briefly outlined the book for them, they were able to reconstruct some of the film and to view it as partially intelligible. But both agreed that the film was negligible, that is, a waste of time. Yet William Golding's novel is not only very popular, particularly with the young,[14] but also well written and powerful. Why, then, was the motion picture such a disaster? The answer, I believe, is partly technical and partly methodological, but mostly the disaster resulted from a failure to translate ideas and descriptive events into appropriate visual analogues and to capture their human meaning.

Technically, the film was poor in quality. The editing was jumpy and erratic, and the camera work was murky and obscure. The visual quality of the film was thus inept enough to class it as amateur in the bad sense of the word "amateur." Had *Lord of the Flies* pretended to be an underground film, it would no doubt have won prizes for its incoherency. Certainly, it was superior to *The Do It Yourself Happening Kit, Prelude: Dog Star Man,* and other such "masterpieces" of episodic murk. But it was not designed nor was it intended to be an exercise in incoherent subjectivity. It was intended to be a feature film that expressed the novel. The examples of unclear camera work that concealed instead of revealing the thematic sense of the original are numerous. A few instances might suffice. There is a long build-up, in both the novel and in the film, of the importance of the monster. Golding's techniques are both narrative and dramatic; in the film, they are almost totally dramatic. But when the climactic scene comes in the film, the shots of the decayed parachutist are so unclear and so dim that the frantic reaction of the boys is not merely unjustified, it is unintelligible. One has to strain to look to see what is being shown. Golding's main point, irony, is totally lost. One may say the same thing for the chase of Ralph. Not only does the camera work detract from the event, but also the rhythm of the sequence does not build to the appropriate terror of the book. And the closing scene with the sailors loses the impact of the novel. The camera is in so tight that we fail to realize that the sailors are from a battleship—a man-of-war that is actually fighting in the adult world—and, again, the profound irony touched with hopelessness, which is a distinguishing quality of the novel, is lost. What has been lost is the *human meaning* of the events, the art of the novel.

The film itself is episodic. It lacks the internal unity and coherence of the novel. But internal unity is the prime condition of quality, whether in art, practical objects, or life. That which has internal unity is the least affected by external accident and idiosyncrasy. Lacking such qualitative coherence, the film was subject to manifold interpretations—many of which were not relevant to its theme—and to plain obscurity and puzzlement. It did not speak with one voice nor did it speak clearly. This disjointedness and the resultant working of the episodes to cross-purposes and irrelevancies were probably partly due to the lack of a script. I am told that the boys were merely given the book to read and then asked to improvise. Even accomplished actors have difficulty doing this. As Trevor Howard has remarked, the second *Mutiny on the Bounty* might not have been quite the disaster it was if the actors had known what they were doing and where they were going. As he said dryly, "It helps, at least, to have a script." When there is no script from the outset, the director and the actors have no narrative skeleton around which they may improvise. Without a skeleton, nothing holds; everything becomes an amorphous mess. Golding's novel is highly structured, and his techniques are masterfully utilized to enhance and to reveal the structural development of plot and theme. The lack of structure in the film, however, renders it so weak that no viable tension is developed between the foreground action of the plot and the thematic horizon. The two become confused, and the possibilities of contrast, complementation, reinforcement, cumulation, and revelation are lost.

The decision to use amateur actors and to shoot the film as a semidocumentary in the neo-realist tradition was a proper decision. The novel, after all, is almost a philosophical tract as well as a fictional narrative. Since the element of thought is so heavy and so meaningful in the novel, the methodological choice of documentary was correct. The documentary film does establish greater emotional distance and does move in a more intellectual context than does the straight dramatic or personal film, which has a unity of emotional quality as its core with concepts in the background. But the boys tried to act and not to react. These young actors were not handled as Vittorio De Sica could have handled them. The result is that the film is dead. The only scene that comes alive at all and has the ring of authenticity is the one in which Piggy is explaining the reason for town names. This boy is so remarkable that he becomes carried away by his own inspiration, and the camera captures that living time. The other scenes are flat, however. They are awkward, stiff, and stagy. There is nothing more awkward than the deliberately natural.

Most of these failures must be attributed to the director. A fine director does not need professional actors if he has control of his editing. Obviously, this presupposes that he has control of the shooting. If he can design visual analogues for the novel's descriptive events, he can, even with complete amateurs, turn out an impressive film. Robert Flaherty's work, with the exception of *Louisiana Story,* is a case in point. The director needs to be able to translate ideas into sights and sounds. He must be able to present us with what we would normally visualize or envision. It is precisely here that the film version of *Lord of the Flies* was such a dismal failure. We are not given visual equivalents of the narrative representations. Again, the failures are many. If I but mention the failure of a critical scene, however, that may suffice.

A crucial scene in the novel is Peter's mystic experience of the Lord. Peter is young and impressionable, but he is old enough to be torn by conflicting loyalties. The tension that builds in him reaches its climax in his mystic fascination with the decayed pig's head and the swarm of flies. This is a crucial scene in the novel, since without it one cannot understand Peter's character, his behavior and choices, or his death. The ironic choice of his name is enhanced by this scene, for his later death on the rocks is a bitter reversal of the Catholic claim. Golding's scene is powerful and profound. What do we see in the film? What we see is a young and very frail boy staring at a pig's head with flies buzzing around it. The camera draws in tight for extreme close-ups, but all we can get out of it is the image of a confused boy. There are many filmic ways this could have been handled, such as montage or flashback, but the scene is shot with straight realism. Such straight realism is the least appropriate tool for revealing the mystic depth of this scene. In some cases, such as this, it is necessary to be surreal in order to capture the human meaning of a reality. Remember, for a moment, the grisly scene of the mother carrying a slab of fetid meat in the dream episode of *Los Olvidados.* The master, Luis Buñuel, knows full well that in some cases the only way to capture the human depth meaning of reality is to enhance it with relevant fantasy.

From the viewpoint of the creator or the spectator, a film such as *Lord of the Flies* must be viewed as a disaster. Like the scientist, the aesthetician can learn as much from failures as he can from successes; usually, he can learn more. For reflection on different kinds of badnesses reveals the necessary conditions for art much more clearly than do the triumphs. One reason that the high points of an art are less revealing in this respect is simply because they *are* triumphs. Therefore, the hard work, the sweat, the brutal decisions, the agonizing technique, are usually hidden—the art of the artist is normally suppressed, and the values are centered, as is the spectator's attention, in the work. The fine work, consequently, often appears easy and artless. Certain inferior novelists, like inferior directors, constantly move themselves into the center of the picture and distract from their works. Such showboating detracts from the work at hand or at mind or at eye and ear. The artist who is sure of his voice lets his object speak.

What, then, can we conclude from reflecting upon the film *Lord of the Flies?* One thing we can conclude is that a director can change the plot of a novel, he can eliminate certain characters and scenes, and he can include scenes not included in the novel without violating it. But he cannot seriously violate the theme of the novel, and the one thing he must be able to translate into his new medium is its tone. If the tone of a work is lost, the work is lost; but the tone of the novel must be rendered in an aural/visual patterning instead of by the use of descriptive dialogue or other narrative device. The author's intellectual viewpoint must become the director's emotional standpoint. If this happens, the camera will capture the relevant visual analogues. If not, the meanings of the novel are lost. Of course, if the director succeeds in his effort, he will have produced not a copy of the novel, but a new object: an art film that aims at close targets in a different way.

Professor Battestin has come to many of the same conclusions we have by discussing a success, *Tom Jones,* instead of a failure, *Lord of the Flies.* He admits that the film does not have the moral earnestness of the novel nor does it express the belief in overriding Providence. Such a difference is inevitable, for John Osborne and Tony Richardson do not inhabit Henry Fielding's world. Nor do their audiences. We live in a time when such orderly beliefs as Fielding's seem naive and irrelevant. We may be wrong, but this is our milieu. Hence, Osborne and Richardson cannot speak as Fielding spoke; and, if they did, they would not be understood. Nevertheless, as Battestin points out, the film is a successful rendition of the novel, and to say "that the film *Tom Jones* is a successful adaptation of the novel is not to equate the two works in purpose or effect." Each has its own purpose and its own effect, yet they are analogically identical.

As I have insisted, so has Battestin: analogy is the key.

Analogy is the key. To judge whether or not a film is a successful adaptation of a novel is to evaluate the skill of its makers in striking analogous attitudes and in finding analogous rhetorical techniques. From this point of view Osborne and Richardson produced in *Tom Jones* one of the most successful and imaginative adaptations in the brief history of film. This, as we have seen, is less true with regard to the authorial attitudes and ultimate thematic intentions of the two works. The real genius of the film as adaptation is in its brilliantly imaginative imitation of the *art* of the novel. Those "gimmicks" that so much surprised and delighted audiences may be seen as technical analogues of Fielding's own most distinctive devices.[15]

I could not agree more, although I feel, and hence I think, that Professor Battestin puts entirely too much emphasis upon technique. He thus runs the risk of implying that art is reducible or equivalent to technique; and, although the mastery of technique is a necessary condition for art, it is not sufficient. What more is needed is expressive power, and such power is supplied by tone and voice. Since the manner of speaking of the novelist and director differ, what the novelist bespeaks, the director should behold. Once he has beheld it, he must present it. Battestin seems to see this when he states that "Richardson has managed to communicate in a few frames skillfully juxtaposed the way it feels to fall in love." More accurately, Richardson has felt what it feels like, thought what it feels like, and has presented what it feels like, for this particular Tom to fall in love with this particular Sophie. For the director, as for the novelist or poet, feeling comes first. The rest is articulation.

The film, then, must capture the feeling-tone of the novel and translate this basic quality into its appropriate medium. Sometimes the director follows the novelist with extreme exactitude as, for example, Richardson does in the eating scene with Tom and Mrs. Waters. At other times, he includes scenes which are not in the novel at all but are implied by its characters and descriptive structure; for example, the brutal stag chase. At other times, he concretizes visually the implied analogues of the author; for example, the dull grey shots of the prison scenes, which render in immediate visual quality the analogues to Hogarth's *The Rake's Progress* implied by Fielding. Once the director has a firm grasp of the central emotional quality of the novel, he has the end in view. He must then discover or create the means appropriate both to his medium and to his message.

If a film is to be an adaptation of a novel, then, the film director has a more difficult task before him than if the film script is an original. He must learn to walk a fine line between excess reverence for the author's work (see Luchino Visconti's *The Stranger*) and disregard (*The Long Hot Summer*). Sometimes a film may deviate radically from the book and still be an engaging and interesting film; for example, *To Have and Have Not*. Usually such deviations, however, since they are due to commercial, patriotic, or other such nonartistic reasons, end in disaster. The narrative line of the novel can be incorporated into the film script and will emerge as plot and incident. But the tone, the stance, the voice of the author may be much more difficult to translate. A successful film adaptation of a novel should not *be* the book. Nor should it be a substitute for the book. If it is truly successful, it should be a work of art in its own right, which excites the reader to go reexperience that world in another medium: the novel. *Ulysses*[16] and *Tom Jones* were such films.

The novel, like the film and unlike the drama, is intimate and impersonal. Whereas the impersonality of film is grounded in its intangible space and variant pace, the impersonality of the novel is due to its reflective mode and its emergence at the imaginative level. This may be one reason why nudity and sexual activity of various types have been able to make quick appearances in both the film and the novel but are only slowly becoming accommodated on the stage. It is one thing to have such images objectively in nontangential shadows or in the imagination of a reader and another to have them become a part of the same incorporate situation. Nudity in dance and drama will probably continue to be merely a device whose primary purpose is to shock. Were it to become thematic substance, the psychic distance of these arts would probably be destroyed. Art should be human, but it risks its own death when it becomes all too human.

The dehumanization of art in our time was perceived a long time ago by José Ortega y Gasset. This trend in art is still evident, particularly in music and the novel. Whether the thinness of the modern novel can be accounted for by a continuing trend to dehumanization or whether it is due to the death of the Gutenberg culture and the arrival of the electronic society as McLuhan argues, one thing is certain: We are witnessing the decline of the novel as an art form. This expiration apparently takes four general directions: the movement toward facticity, the emphasis upon the consequential, the cataloging of the inconsequential, and the sketch. All these directions may be at least in part due to the impact of film and film form on the sensibilities of the author and his resultant novels.

The movement toward facticity is best exemplified by the so-called journalistic novel or novel of pseudo-history. Truman Capote goes so far as to claim that this is a new art form, but the only evidence we have for this is his declaration. Such works as *In Cold Blood* and *The Confessions of Nat Turner* are examples of this genre. While they retain the love of language and vivid description common to the novel and even include imaginative constructions of what might or could have been the case, their main aim is at a factual ground. Hence, they become elaborations upon "actual" occurrences. The quotation marks around the "actual" is a reservation since it is questionable whether history as we have it or as we re-form it is ever actual. In any case, such works, like film, move within the ambience of supposed presentational fact; hence, their horizon and often their aim are toward facticity as distinguished from the purely fictive. They might thus be looked upon as types of third-person biographies. It may well be that the concreteness of the film has influenced some writers to move in this direction, a direction that is beyond the fictive realism of the American novel of the 1920s and 1930s and might well be called by a motion-picture label: neo-realism.

Another direction in the decline of the novel is the emphasis on the consequential. This movement is perhaps best exemplified by the work of John Barth, whose *Giles Goat-Boy* is a prime instance of this trend. Here depth development of character and fictional projection of circumstance are suppressed. The world of the novel is reduced to events, and the emphasis is upon intricately contrived plot. Plot thus comes to the foreground, and all other elements either sink to the horizon or are sacrificed to the exigencies of intricacy. The desperate love of language and the soaring lyrical descriptions of the imaged world which one finds, for example, in the works of Vladimir Nabokov or, occasionally, in those of J. D. Salinger, are absent. Perhaps the overlong short stories that Irwin Shaw terms novels could also be placed in this category. It may be that the trickily plotted film, such pseudo-detective stories as *In the Heat of the Night,* may have given an impetus to the creation of the heavily plotted (and often plodded) novel. Irwin Shaw—one of our most brilliant short-story writers—perhaps does not really belong in the same class with Barth, however, since he does still place emphasis upon the human values of a lived world. In spite of its vivid events and acerbic asides, *Giles Goat-Boy* is a peculiarly aseptic novel.

A third direction is what Nathan A. Scott, Jr., has termed "The New Mystique of *L'Actuelle.*"[17] This movement I have termed the emphasis upon the inconsequential. It would seem at first that this is contradictory to the direction taken by Barth, but actually it is merely a contrary. Both share a de-emphasis upon human meaning. Barth develops this by playing with plot, and Alain Robbe-Grillet, by attempting to eliminate it. Scott discusses this trend in terms of all the arts; for example, painting (Pablo Picasso), music (John Cage), the novel (Robbe-Grillet), drama (Samuel Beckett). Since I am concerned here only with the novel vis-à-vis film, I shall confine my remarks to the work of Robbe-Grillet. One of his novels, of course, is the film script of the logical puzzle seen on film: *Last Year at Marienbad.* The main goal of the artist in this genre seems to be to try to attain objective anonymity. His cry (taken from philosophy) is "To the things themselves!" This means that the art of the novel must eliminate, insofar as possible, emphasis upon plot, character, and eloquence. This attempt to create *le roman objectif* means that the author must negate his human stance and must try to present things in their simple thereness. One must, insists Robbe-Grillet, renounce and abandon "the cult of the human" and "look at the world which surrounds us with unprejudiced eyes." That such unprejudiced vision is a fiction itself will be discovered in Chapter 6, concerning perception. Nevertheless, the thrust of this movement is clear: The author should be an impartial mirror, not even a connoisseur[18] of things. The peculiar marking quality of the novels that result from this method is their depth-lessness. Hence, like the avant-garde film of sheer design, they strive for presentational patterning apart from human meaning.

Such artists desire (although perhaps "desire" is too human a word) that their novels, like MacLeish's poem, not mean but *be*. But there is a significant and important difference between the stance of Alain Robbe-Grillet and Archibald MacLeish. MacLeish is insisting upon the fusion of value in the object; Robbe-Grillet is insisting on its excision. Hence, Scott's use of Wallace Stevens' goal to walk "barefoot into reality"[19] as the destination of Robbe-Grillet is an inept metaphor. Robbe-Grillet obviously demands to walk forth, not barefoot, but on plastic soles (or souls, as the case may be). He wishes neither to contaminate nor to be contaminated by any human reality. This faith in a split world that is value-free is an interesting one to find advocated by the artist, since it is a posture that even the scientist has abandoned as illusory. Robbe-Grillet is nothing if not consistent (though the former is a possible alternative). By demanding that his art become nonsignificant, he is running the danger that men will regard it merely as insignificant. Novels, after all, are created for the delectation of the descendents of *Pithecanthropus erectus,* not for the contemplation of computers; and there are probably few human beings who will find themselves attracted by such a desert of words. We may take the abdication of the artist seriously, but it is doubtful that we will so regard his resultant works. Even so, we will feel a human sense of loss.

The last direction in the current decline of the novel is the reduction to the sketch. These novels read (and sound) as if they were not written or, to use Capote's phrase, even typed. They have the look of being dictated. Such works tend to be shallow and slipshod; and their appeal rests, if it rests at all, on vivid or salacious content. This form of the novel, then, is akin to what we describe in Chapter 8 as the avant-garde episodic when we are speaking of film. *Candy, Myra Breckinridge,* and *Last Exit to Brooklyn* are instances of this genre. They de-emphasize character, eloquence, and narrative sequence, though they do have a kind of plot. Such works read not like novels but as if they were hastily dictated film scripts. In spite of their emphasis upon erotic fleshly incident, the novels themselves have the form of incomplete skeletons. Granted that such things may be in our common family closet, one must still remember that a skeleton is dead; it is merely what was once a living being. Though not novels, such sketches might, however, make indecent shooting scripts. They display a spareness that could allow a film director great latitude for imagistic improvisation.

This last conclusion leads us to the thought that perhaps the best basis for adaptation of literature to film might well be the short story or the poem and not the novel. Both the poem and the short story have compression of image and incident and are hence internally thicker than the novel. Like film, they normally deal with a less extensive time span. That many fine films have been based on short stories is obvious. *Occurrence at Owl Creek Bridge* and *The Killers* are cases in point. Few, however, have been based upon poems, although some poems[20] have been based on films. The lyric poem is probably too compressed to provide more than a scene for a film or perhaps a sequence. The narrative poem, on the other hand, would appear to be a very fertile ground which has as yet been hardly touched. William Wordsworth's "Michael" or Robert Frost's "The Death of the Hired Man" or "Mending Wall" or even "Grape Picking" could well become impressive short films or even full-length features. The combination of a disembodied narrator on the audio with visual geography is also a powerful possibility, as has been shown by the films done on and with Dylan Thomas.

Of course, a director must be able to think; but, like a poet, he should be able to get the feel of things first. Once he has the feeling, he can think it into visual form and presentation. The novel is more abstract than the film. Being visual, the film is vivid. Hence, the film is limited to the concrete instance. All art is concerned with the concrete instance, but it differs as to the kind of instance and the way in which that instance embodies the universal. The force of the novel comes from the clash of ideas and emotions on an intellectual level. In film, such clashes must be developments of the immediate visual and auditory elements. Thus, although it is not impossible, it is quite difficult to display and indicate thought on film. Russian directors are very fond of attempting this and have evolved a whole series of visual clichés—for example, the train roaring forward with its red star on its front is the pioneering spirit of the progressive socialist society (try to think of a Russian film without a train in it somewhere); the peasant girl or mother in babushka silhouetted against the waving wands of grain is health, Mother Russia, Ceres, and so on. The commitment to the dogma of montage as the essence of film, montage as conceived by Sergei Eisenstein and V. I. Pudovkin, is the reason for these recurring motifs. Sometimes they are effective; but usually they are not, for the connection between the visuals is purely intellectual and external. When this externality is combined with an overriding moralistic tone, one feels that most Russian films are simpleminded.

It would be difficult, perhaps next to impossible, for a film to present the girl E. E. Cummings sings of when he writes: "Harun Omar and Master Hafiz/ keep your dead beautiful ladies./ Mine is a little lovelier."[21] How could a film director capture this girl? Such a task would be next to impossible. The best most directors would be able to do in attempting to capture this "Mine" would be to show the picture of some particularly ravishing woman, say Elizabeth Taylor or Sophia Loren or Vanessa Redgrave. But it is the very facelessness of the literary image upon which its forcefulness rests. Since we cannot see Cummings' beautiful lady, we are forced to imagine her. Since we can neither hold nor behold her, we are forced to create her; and this abstract lady can often be more forceful, more enchanting, more striking, and certainly more perfect than any real lady could ever hope to be. The imagination is not prone to incorporate defects. The direct appeal to the imagination first is a weapon that the film director has difficulty in wresting from the novelist.

Both the novel and the film usually have plots, though plot is not so important in film as in the novel. Both normally develop by the principle of cumulative progression, though the tendency of the novel is to be linear and of the film, mosaic. In some especially cinematic novels such as *Ulysses* or *The Sound and the Fury,* there may be elastic time and interweaving of memory, dream, hallucination, and the present. There may also be a fairly constant shifting of perspectives or "camera angles." In spite of these techniques, the medium of the novel is words; and words provide at the outset a greater psychic distance, or at least a greater sensitive distance, than do moving visual images. Thus we are brought back once more to the concepts of the present and presence. The novel is basically representational and the film, presentational. John Howard Lawson states it in this way: "Film is not concerned with memory or contemplation. It has no narrator to create a bond between the past action and the present telling of it. Film can place events in any time order, but it emphasizes their immediate impact; it treats the past, and even the future, as if they were in the present tense."[22]

One can think of both clumsy and brilliant exceptions to Lawson's statement. A clumsy example would be the opening and closing of the film *The Sun Also Rises,* in which a standard device is used to try to throw the work into a novelistic mode. The film begins with the camera wandering around Paris in a fairly aimless fashion, while a narrator's voice carries over the visuals telling us (as if we could not see) that this is Paris. He then informs us that things were different in an older Paris, the one shortly after the first World War. The camera holds on the address of a specific building, then there is a dissolve into the past. The altered dress, the old cars, the horse-drawn buggies now tell us that we have moved to a novelistic situation.

Everything becomes present in costume. At the end of the film, the camera pans up to hold on the sun while the narrator's voice once again intones lines from the King James Version via Hemingway. It is a fine voice, but the framing development was irrelevant. The unknown narrator cannot transform the film into a novel.

A more brilliant instance would be the scene in *8½* in which Guido has his first audience with the cardinal. While the cardinal speaks piously of the sacred nature of the family, Guido sees a slattern descending a hill. Part of his past is woven into the present scene, and there is a double narrative comment. The cardinal unwittingly comments by referring to the call of an albatross, and we know that Guido is bearing the burden of his past. Furthermore, Guido himself comments on the image by saying, sotto voce, "Memories have no respect." Fellini, whose unconscious is always near the surface, is, of course, also giving us a pun by having the cardinal speak of other birds. Another brilliant example is the continual punctuation of the visuals in *Hiroshima Mon Amour* by the phrase "You have seen nothing of Hiroshima, nothing." These examples do not invalidate Lawson's point, however. They merely show that great skill is needed to overcome the basic emphases which differ in the two media. As Béla Balázs says, the "sound film demands a style of weightless words,"[23] and his use of the word "sound" can be taken in both senses, in the sense of an auditory film and in the sense of a solid or well-constructed object. It may be that film is a kind of writing, as Astruc has claimed; but, if so, it is not a kind of word writing or thought writing but, as Stephenson and Debrix state, "a picture writing."

One might assume that, since each reader must re-create the world of the novel on the basis of verbal clues, there is greater variation in the worlds created than in those presented by the film. This assumption overlooks the fact that the viewing of film, as the viewing of anything, is not a passive process of simple assimilation. Being human, we approach everything with prejudiced eyes. While it is true that the film exhibits itself at a lower level of abstraction than the novel, even in the film, what is given on the screen is an occasion for vision and not merely that which is forced upon it. Several years ago, when running a commercial film series, I showed Jules Dassin's *He Who Must Die,* a film based upon Nikos Kazantzakis' novel *The Greek Passion*. I asked my various friends what they thought of the film. One, a sociologist, said, "I'm tired of poor Greeks"; and another, a historian, replied, "It was great. The most antireligious film I have ever seen. The Church will never recover from this." The next day the Methodist minister reserved an entire section for his Sunday school class on the basis that it was the "most profound religious experience" he had ever had with a film. Presumably, the same shadows were passing on the screen before each viewer, but there was a real sense in which each was in a theatre of his own and was watching a film that was not quite the same as his neighbor's.

The film, then, may be a novel shadow; the question remains whether it is the shadow of the novel. That we do in fact so judge films is quite evident. During the credits, we are reminded that certain films are based upon the novel or taken from the novel. This taking may be so loose and inept as to bear little resemblance to the original. For example, *The Long Hot Summer* was a painful exercise dubiously attributed to Faulkner but in fact only tangentially related to his book *The Hamlet*. Or a film may follow a book with both fidelity and integrity. *Ulysses* does. We not only do judge the worth of a film on how faithful it is to the book, we are in fact encouraged by most directors to do so. The question still remains, however, whether such judgments are legitimate.

Such judgments can be legitimate if one keeps in mind how complex they really are. It is not enough to say that the film *Moby Dick* is a failure because it changes the plot of the novel. As a matter of fact, it changes the plot little. What it fails to do is to provide visual equivalents for the great theme of the ultimate failure of values in the given world and the consequent desperation of dedicated idealism. It fails to give us Herman Melville's intense emotional commitment and the great tragic rhythm of the novel. All the facts are there. And much of the action, such as the harpooning of the whales and the death of Ahab, are presented vividly. But it is only in the short scene of the meeting of Ishmael and Queequeg or the sermon of the whaling minister that the film truly comes alive. What was description, analysis, thought, and ambiguity in the novel is absent from the screen. No doubt, basing a film on a novel will increase the box-office take, but in judgment we must remember that we are comparing two different works of different orders, which touch each other at various points but nevertheless have different internal purposes and hence different forms and techniques.

In this chapter, I have been reflecting upon some of the family differences between novel and film. I have used the novel as an analogical example of the structural or formal dimension of film. What these reflections reveal is that film incorporates characters and narrative line from the novel. Because of the inevitable differences of the two media, however, the narrative line of the novel becomes transformed by film into plot. But plot is merely a subplan in movies. Plot in film is but an element in theme. Thus, the director must be able to translate the novelist's verbal value system—his tone or stance—into a visual theme if he is to capture the novel. Theme expresses the artist's view of the nature of existence.

Akira Kurosawa's film *High and Low* was mentioned earlier in the chapter. An analysis of his films would show the thematic, as distinguished from plotted, nature of film. Kurosawa's films have the following phases of form: (1) thematic statement, (2) bridge, (3) dominant theme, (4) development of dominant theme, (5) secondary theme, (6) development of secondary theme and articulation of dominant, (7) coda for reflection. In *High and Low,* of course, the secondary theme—a business struggle—is introduced first. Still, this analysis would fit almost all his films. It will also fit the films of many other modern directors. The reason is simple. Novels begin in imagination. Films end in it.

Notes

1. Susanne K. Langer, *Feeling and Form* (New York: Scribner's, 1953), pp. 289–290.
2. Béla Balázs, *Theory of the Film* (New York: Roy Publishers, 1952), pp. 120–121.
3. Ralf Stephenson and J. R. Debrix, *The Cinema as Art* (Baltimore: Penguin Books, 1965), pp. 100–101.
4. Brendan Gill, in *The New Yorker* (October 28, 1967), pp. 165–167.
5. Gill, p. 165.
6. Marshall McLuhan, *Understanding Media: The Extensions of Man* (New York: McGraw-Hill, 1964), p. 285.
7. McLuhan, p. 285.
8. McLuhan, p. 286.
9. McLuhan, p. 286.
10. McLuhan, p. 286.
11. Jonathan Baumbach, "From A to Antonioni: Hallucinations of a Movie Addict," in *Man and the Movies,* ed. by W. R. Robinson (Baton Rouge: Louisiana State University Press, 1967), p. 170.
12. Stephenson and Debrix, *The Cinema as Art,* p. 115.
13. René Clair, "Rythme," in "Les Cahiers du mois," *Cinéma* (1925), quoted in Stephenson and Debrix, *The Cinema as Art,* p. 115.
14. The popularity of the novel with the young is no doubt because they see it as a sustained attack on adult hypocrisy. This attitude could as easily be termed the intolerance of youth.
15. Martin C. Battestin, "Osborne's *Tom Jones:* Adapting a Classic," in *Man and the Movies,* p. 37.
16. The film version of *Ulysses* refutes George Bluestone's assertion that "Proust and Joyce would seem as absurd on film as Chaplin would be in print." Thus does time destroy us all. Bluestone's book is the best analysis of the relations of film and novel. See George Bluestone, *Novels into Film* (Baltimore: Johns Hopkins Press, 1957), esp. pp. 1–64.
17. Nathan A. Scott, Jr., "The New Mystique of *L'Actuelle:* A View of Cinema in Its Relation to Our Period-Style," in *Man and the Movies,* p. 200ff.
18. Scott calls such writers *chosistes,* connoisseurs of things. But such names

connote the human elements of desire, interest, valuation, and so forth—all of which seem inappropriate when applied to those who wish to efface the human and leave things to their "thinghood."

19. Scott, in *Man and the Movies,* p. 208. The line is from Stevens' "Large Red Man Reading."

20. Richard Wilbur's "The Undead" is based on *Frankenstein Meets the Wolf Man* and Bela Lugosi's *Dracula.* It is not a translation of either film but a work of art in its own right, since it has taken elements from these films and transformed them into the images of poetry.

21. E. E. Cummings, *Poems 1923–1954* (New York: Harcourt, Brace & World, 1954), p. 14.

22. John H. Lawson, *Film: The Creative Process* (New York: Hill & Wang, 1967), p. 212.

23. Balázs, *Theory of the Film,* p. 229.

3

The Scene World

In the preceding chapters, we have seen that film differs in many ways from both the novel and the drama. Yet, though it differs from them in the sense of essential direction, mode, emphasis, and form, it at the same time shares some of their techniques and elements. Film is capable of taking some of their aspects, transforming them, and incorporating them into its own medium. This omnivorous quality—the ability to incorporate and transform—makes film both a powerful mode of expression and one difficult to discuss. To those who appreciate film, the very complexity of its facets renders it fascinating. This very complexity rules out the validity of any simple *auteur* theory of film; for, although the director is often the most important person in determining the over-all form of the film and film is more essentially a director's rather than an actor's or writer's medium, the director is not always the most important person involved. He may be. But he may not. It depends on the film. More precisely, it depends on the source of unity, for it is the cumulative unity of theme that makes a film valuable. Not mere structure but qualitied structure distinguishes fine film from hack work. If style is the controlled expression of power, then one of its meanings is the ability to fuse expressive quality with structure. If the style of a film is the function of the visual-aural value system and editorial rhythm, if these provide the necessary unity of theme, then the *auteur* is the director. If, on the other hand, the tautness of narrative line provides the cumulative unity, then one must look to the writer, for he is the *auteur* not merely of the script but of the film. Granted that the director, "as *integrator* of everybody's work, has more 'stylistic' problems than anyone else" and that "hence his 'style' usually flavours the film,"[1] it is still the case that a fine script can rescue a mediocre director. James Agee's *The Night of the Hunter* would be a case in point. Or it may be that while the script is shallow and the direction muddled, the film still attains a modicum of thematic unity because the actors provide such strong performances. *A Man and a Woman* is an example of such a film. The script is banal, a *Ladies' Home Journal* story as interpreted by *Life*. The editing is sloppy (for example, during the first long sequence in the car, the shots from the inside out establish the regular rhythm of windshield wipers, for it is raining; but the shots from the outside in show no rain on the windshield and the wipers are at rest). Sometimes the editing is too self-consciously exotic, as, for example, the cuts from the racing to the camels to the racing. These scenes are visually striking, but they lack depth meaning. There is no reason for the camels other than that a motion picture is being made. Nevertheless, the sensitive acting of Anouk Aimée and her husband almost rescue *A Man and a Woman*. In such an instance, one might say that the actors are the *auteurs*. Or it may even be the cameraman who is the *auteur*. Both *Champion* and *Hud* bear the unmistakable mark of James Wong Howe's brilliant camera work. If one wishes to play the *auteur* game, then, one has simply to ask the question "Where is the center of control?"

Perhaps the most important center of control that the film incorporates from the novel is the narrative line. Events by themselves quickly degenerate into the sprawl of everyday living, but in film the narrative line functions to unify the various scenes into the ongoing event. Certainly, one of the most important elements that film absorbs from drama is depth. From drama, the film incorporates the deep concern with human life and its meaning. It transforms projected destiny into thematic density. This concern is the basis in film for the transformation of the seen into the scene. For film, like drama, is not concerned with reality per se, *an sich,* or *en soi;* it is concerned with *human* reality. Film is concerned with the lived world.

The intuition that film is concerned with the lived world is the premise upon which the documentary dimension of film is built. In its most extreme form, the documentary argument rules out the possibility of film art and demands that film become merely the recording of reality. The documentarist thus argues that the true standard for film must be its reality, and by "reality" he means "photographic reality." If the novel may be said to contribute the element of structure and the drama the depth of expression, the photograph may be considered as the material dimension of a film aesthetic. Hence, those theories that emphasize the photographic, recording basis of film may be said to be theories that advance the values of the materials. It is one thing, however, to talk about the importance, value, and integrity of the materials and another to claim that the material dimension is the only proper intrinsic goal of an art. The materials are admittedly one goal but by no means the only one. While it is true that a motion picture should be authentic, authenticity is not necessarily an external standard. A motion picture, being a composite image, may quite legitimately portray and be a world of its own.

Perhaps the most forceful, though one must admit the most turgid and garbled, statement of the argument that the materials are the only proper end of film is found in Siegfried Kracauer's book *A Theory of Film: The Redemption of Physical Reality.*[2] Kracauer uses the concept of "end" in the sense of "proper or appropriate goal." He argues that the true goal of film is primarily to record unstaged reality and, in doing so, somehow to redeem it. Pauline Kael has acidly remarked that no one can redeem the reality that he experiences. She states: "If it's good, marvelous; if it isn't, we can weep or booze, or try to change it. Redemption, like sublimation, is a dear, sweet thought."[3] One need not be this caustic with Professor Kracauer. Presumably, what he meant by "redemption" was eliciting the visibility of the seen, that is, forcing the eye to attend to that which it would normally overlook. He also intended a deeper meaning, at least in his book *From Caligari to Hitler,*[4] in which redemption seems to consist in capturing the inner essences of both people and things; the inner essence of people being their subconscious and unacknowledged drives, the inner essence of things, their emotional import. As Kracauer's theory develops, however, he de-emphasizes this revelatory or redemptive character of film and finally not only comes to the position that it should be abandoned but also contradicts his main thesis: the recording of unstaged reality. Thus the word "end" begins to take on another meaning: "demise." Strict adherence to Kracauer's later theory would be the death of film as an art, for Kracauer's argument ends by sacrificing revelation to recording.

When some people see the word "revelation," they become uncertain. The belief seems to be that the word should be reserved exclusively for some function of religious anxiety. Or, it is held, the word should be used for more positive experiences, such as an encounter with the holy or the numinous. But religion does not have an exclusive hold on either the word or its meanings. There is nothing necessarily mystical in talking about revelation in art or in everyday life. Intellectual and egoistic prejudice makes us feel that we know, think, and then act; life is neither that clear nor that certain. All knowledge, even sensation, is a revelation through action. I respond to the color, the shape, the fuzziness, the weight, and the scent of the peach; then I bite into it. In the biting, the peach reveals its ripeness (which had been but a promise of the nose and eye) to me. An analogous kind of experience happens in film. I yield to the flow of images, dialogue, and music and, by moving with the rhythm of the phenomenon before me, find myself responding (*re spondere:* "speaking back"). The moving qualities before me force me into this extorted response and through the responding reveal further nuances and meanings of the object to me. Perhaps the most moving element in this extortion is the felt rhythm of time, the illusory time, which the motion picture presents to me. Such experience is possible because movies move.

A motion picture is a moving structure of coherent rhythms. It is a moving structure of occurring sensuous content. This content may be more voracious than veracious, yet it should be consistent within itself: an authentic illusion. A film should not merely have but should display an organic form, which is an illusion—a projection—of what life is like in the living of it. To say that it is organic is to demand that it incorporate semi-independent centers of mutually enhancing quality and activity, that these active qualities exhibit a thematic permanence through patterned change, that the whole be articulated by rhythmic progression, and that this cumulative progression through interacting growth reveal the thematic end. Such a film cannot avoid being personal. Personal—not in the sense that the writer or director or producer literally puts himself into the film, but in the sense that, through his improvisations and hard choices, he *invests* the film with his value responses. What we mean by "personality" in the individual is an analogous instance: the functional identity of patterned changes exhibited through growth.

A film is a synthetic unity of sound and composed shots. The previous chapters have shown that most film criticism is reductive; that is, most film critics suffer from verbal asceticism, and they tend to ignore, to disregard, the visual and aural elements and form of film in order to concentrate on only one aspect: the verbal. Those critics and theorists who hold that film is primarily a recording are often equally reductive. They attempt to reduce film to merely one of its elements: the photograph. However, the photograph is only the material basis of film. Film is primarily made out of it but is not totally constituted by it. This is what I meant by saying that film, if we put sound aside for the moment, is a synthetic unity of *composed* images. The word "composed" is used with precise ambiguity and means that the shot, the photograph, the still, is *internally* composed. To say this is to indicate that its internal structure is not mere accident. It means *also* that the shot is *externally* composed; that is, it is fit into, edited, fused with a larger ongoing whole. Furthermore, it means that the internal structure and external sequence must, if it is a fine film, be mutually relevant. The study of photography can tell us much about film. But it cannot tell the whole story. A film can.

As I said, the theorist who most consistently argued that the photograph was the essence of film was Siegfried Kracauer. In spite of the length of his argument, the principles of his theory may be stated quite simply. There are four such principles:

> First, photography has an outspoken affinity for unstaged reality. Pictures which strike us as intrinsically photographic seem intended to render nature in the raw, nature as it exists independently of us. . . .[5]
>
> Second, through this concern with unstaged reality, photography tends to stress the fortuitous. Random events are the very meat of snapshots. . . .[6]
>
> Third, photography tends to suggest endlessness. This follows from its emphasis on fortuitous complexes which represent fragments rather than wholes. A photograph, whether portrait or action picture, is in character only if it precludes the notion of completeness. . . .[7]
>
> Fourth and finally, the medium has an affinity for the indeterminate of which Proust was keenly aware. . . . Photographs, implies Proust, transmit raw material without defining it.[8]

At first sight, these four conditions for a film aesthetic seem both cogent and true. I accept the concern with the outdoor world, the inclusion of chance, and the tendency toward endlessness. But I seriously question whether film can or ought to transmit "nature in the raw" as it "exists independently of us."

The first principle, which is later converted to become a quality of the medium, is that photography has "an outspoken affinity for unstaged reality" and renders "nature in the raw" as "it exists independently of us." We have already discovered in our previous reflections that film is concerned with creating an analogue, not of an independent reality, but of the lived world. We have also discovered that such an analogue must have the character of authenticity, that is, that it be an illusion that is consistent within itself. While it is true that film is very close to life, it does not follow that it *is* life. It would appear, then, that Kracauer is confusing the authentic and the real. Furthermore, we have discovered that we are human; and, being human, we approach the world with prejudiced eyes. It is thus unlikely that we ever can or do experience reality as it "exists independently of us." Were such an experience possible, it is doubtful that it would be intelligible. Were it intelligible, it would probably not be communicable. What we can and do know is the world as experienced. But that is quite different from some supposed transcendent reality which exists in itself.

Kracauer seems to believe that there is *a* reality. This unitary reality is independent of man, although accessible to knowledge. Hence, if all men would only perceive and talk correctly, they could agree on the objective, common reality. Futhermore, in Kracauer's view, this reality is static and unchanging. It makes no difference whether it is matter or form; it is self-identical and given. This accessible, eternal, unchanging, objective, unitary reality should be the true touchstone for aesthetics, at least the aesthetics of the film. Kracauer seems to intimate that the other arts (film, remember, he denies being an art) have no concern with truth nor need they be concerned with it. But he insists that film is inherently concerned with truth. His reasons are probably political. He wants to rule out propaganda and make it alien to film. As far as the individual person is concerned, this metaphysical position would entail that the self is not merely transcendental, but transcendent. It is a self-beyond-phenomena that is certain and settled.

As I have indicated, it is not immediately obvious that metaphysics need come into a theory of film at all or even into an aesthetic theory. One could well write an aesthetic theory and do his best to eliminate any metaphysical references, as has been done by Eugene Kaelin.[9] But it is not what Kracauer has done, and such an approach would go deeply against his temper. If we assume Kracauer's stance—that is, that we must talk metaphysics—it is still not obvious that we are obligated to talk his kind of metaphysics. Were I forced to choose, I would rather side with our Eastern cousins and take the position that all things are non-*svabhava;* all things are without self-nature, and forms have no own-being. This would mean that the very concept of "thing" is an abstraction of a sort, for a thing is a relational energy system. The difference between function and substance in this view would simply be lapse. The same would be true of the self. Its inner nature would be a patterned flow, a rhythmic, synergic energy system. Someone has said that "every organism is a melody singing itself," and what we take as the self for conceptual purposes is this melody. But just as a symphony includes by embodying and transcending a melody and thus is much greater than a melody, so the self also goes beyond its patterned rhythms.

I see no necessity or obligation to talk in this way. But if we did, we would come out with a theory of film quite different from that of Kracauer. Instead of taking the single shot as the basis of film, one would turn to the flow of rhythm. What would be important would not be that which is captured in the static print, but that which happens between the prints. Were film to try to be the redemption of such a reality, its attempt would be to capture motion in all of its accelerations, decelerations, changes, and rhythms. Reality would not necessarily be singular but would be multifaceted, and it would certainly not be merely given. It would be reality-in-the-making. Since it would be relational, with everything implicated with everything else, literally complicated (that is, folded together), distinctions would be a matter of convenience or of taste. This everything-happening-all-at-once kind of universe is intuited by Marshall McLuhan, though the political implication he draws from it, tribalism, does not follow. Were I forced to choose, I would rather side with McLuhan and Lord Gautama than with Kracauer.

Allied to his substance metaphysics, Kracauer has an inadequate theory of perception. His view is that man is a detached viewer of the universe; therefore, he mistakenly identifies the human eye with the alienation and simple recording of an abstracted camera lens. Kracauer believes perception is something that happens; it is, for him, essentially passive. One merely records what is presented or impinges on the eye, and this sets the complex mechanism of the body reacting to its circumstance. Had Kracauer really read Kant seriously, he would have realized that the whole point of the critiques is that the experienced world is the only one we can know and that that experienced world is partly shaped by the percipient. For anything to attain the status of a perception, it must first be filtered, analyzed, abstracted, and transformed. Perception doesn't happen to anyone. Perceiving is something we *do,* and knowledge and awareness are the precipitates of action. Action itself is a precipitate of tension. Every organism acts on its environment before it reacts to it. Hence, perception is not built up out of "simples" but is carved out of wholes. By analogy, films are not made of stringing together simple shots but are the articulation of vision in both senses of that term.

A few words about the best known of all Japanese films, Kurosawa's *Rashomon,* may clarify my point. *Rashomon* is a film in which the plot is de-emphasized—in fact, it is left unresolved—and theme is brought to the foreground. The structure is a series of interwoven flashbacks with the same story told from four different perspectives, no two of which are completely compatible. Those viewers who are incurable realists and have an intellectual bent thus play the logical game of attempting to deduce which version is the truth and what was the reality being presented. In fact, some spectators play this game so fiercely that it ceases to be a game and degenerates into a wrangle. But even as a game, it is not worth the candle. Why? The difficulty, I believe, is with the word "the." Kurosawa is attempting to present not *the* truth but truths. All of the flashbacks are both true and false. To those who live their lives instead of merely thinking them, this is immediately obvious. If you are ever involved in intensely personal relationships and hear different people relate their versions of the same story, you will discover that no two stories are alike, yet each person is convinced he is telling the true version. And he is. But because it is *his* version, it is also false. Fortunately, the lived world is not as simple as those of us who try to reduce it to concepts.

The instability of reality and its almost total illusiveness is a constant theme in Kurosawa's films. Donald Richie perceived quite clearly that *Rashomon* was the film that presents Kurosawa's basic and recurrent theme.

> The world is illusion, you yourself make reality, but this reality undoes you if you submit to being limited by what you have made. The important corollary—you are not, however, truly subject to this reality, you can break free from it, can live even closer to the nature you are continually creating—this occurs only in the later films.[10]

This does not mean that life is but a dream and that man cannot know anything. What it does mean is that we can never have the whole truth. Truth is always partial, as Saint Paul told us; and known reality is relative. What *Rashomon* is demonstrating is not that men lie, although we all do, but that we *cannot* do anything else because our finite perspectives are limited. Being limited, they are in that sense false. Kurosawa's basic theme, then, is not only that we but know in part but also that there is no other way that man can know as long as he is a living being. Even these partial truths are revealed to us only through the illusions we have helped to create.

Now, it is not a question of whether man has illusions or doesn't have them. Kurosawa's argument is that illusions are necessary for the condition of man. In *The Seven Samurai,* the plea is for the Stoic acceptance of necessary illusions.

There is no doubt that the illusions are necessary as long as one is dealing with man alive, yet there is choice. We can always choose which illusions we try to make coherent. Thus, in his later films, *Ikiru, The Seven Samurai,* and *High and Low,* Kurosawa is concerned with the moral problem: how man relates himself to his illusions. The moral problem, as he sees it, is the *fixation* of illusion. A man is false if his illusion *has him.* The imminence of death forces Watanabe (in *Ikiru*) to give up his fixed idea of himself and to learn to become. A business crisis, a kidnapping, and a murder force the same realization on Gondo in *High and Low.* Both men learn that they must relinquish the false assumption that a man is and cannot become. Each learns that he is not the kind of man he had assumed himself to be because no man is a kind—he is a living being. Thus, the central virtue for Kurosawa's characters is courage. Man must have the courage to accept uncertainty; he must have the courage to become, to grow. Man, the possible being, lives through self-transcendence. But self-transcendence is never absolute. It is never "once and for all time."

These reflections on the films of Kurosawa demonstrate why I reject part of Kracauer's first principle that film presents "nature as it exists independently of us." Life, whether on screen or off, is not a static whole. Life is a perpetual process of transition and, if it is lived well, a squandering of finite values. Life is not a pumpkin pie no matter how you slice it, even if with a sense of thanksgiving. Life is in the living of it, in the nuance of rhythm. Even if the self or the living world were as static and substantial as Kracauer assumes it is, it would not follow that the photograph is the true recording of it. The camera can and does lie. In fact, Durgnat goes so far as to exclaim: "The camera is a born liar."[11] It is not the given world, if indeed there is a given world, that the camera records but a world filtered through the emotional bias and value system, the *selectivity,* of the photographer. Every shot involves selectivity by the man who positions the camera and adjusts the lens. Hence, even the most realistic photographs already have human meaning given with them, for they reveal the selective eye and the deciding hand that controlled what they were to record and how.

Permit me to shift to an analogy from everyday life. My friend has a camera. Let us assume that it is a Polaroid, so that the results can be swiftly known. He asks me to stand still or even to pose, and he snaps my picture. We wait a few seconds, and he shows me the print in obvious triumph. Triumph because he wishes to marvel— and especially wishes me to marvel—at the accuracy of his possession, for he hopes that this will reflect on his value as a person. And I protest: "But it doesn't look at all like me!" My friend is shocked. He is hurt, and he argues that the snapshot looks exactly like me. Or, if he is a metaphysician, he argues not only that it does in fact look like me but also that it is impossible for it *not* to look like me. If he is a true friend, he may concede that the snapshot does not flatter me, but he will still insist that it does look like me. Is this a situation in which one of us is right and the other is demonstrably wrong? Does a person necessarily talk nonsense when he states, "That photograph doesn't look a bit like me"?

Let us put aside minor quibbles, such as the fact that pictures don't look, people do. There still remain some difficult puzzles with the words "look like" and "me." Let us take the relation of resemblance first. When my friend says that the photograph looks like me, he evidently intends that his camera has faithfully recorded my features in a two-dimensional way. Hence, his meaning of "look like" is Kracauer's basic meaning: "record." When I protest that the snapshot doesn't look like me, the meaning I intend is "express." I may assert this by saying that the shot does not capture me; or, if I am truly agitated, that it does not capture the *real* me. Obviously, all of us have an idealized version of how we appear. But I intend more than that. The meaning I intend by "look like" is "reveal." When it comes to "resembling" or "looking like," my friend and I are in the same ambiguity in which Kracauer found himself; the ambiguity of recording/revealing. When one recognizes the ambiguity, he can see that both my friend and I are right, since we are talking about different things; and both of us are wrong, if we are intending to assert the same thing.

Perhaps some of John Howard Lawson's basic premises can help us here. He states: "The camera is *not* the human eye; it sees more than the eye can see; it sees it differently."[12] Lawson then proceeds to amplify each of these assertions. In the first place, he points out that the camera is much quicker than the eye. The camera can provide us with an instantaneous record. But the eye is subject to lapse; hence, there is the phenomenon of persistence of vision. If there were not a slight delay between the recognition of one image and the constitution of the next, the motion picture would not be possible. The function of a projector is to delay images, to hold them just long enough to exploit the persistence of vision and to adjust the film to the human eye. Lawson also points out that the camera can record much more than even the most attentive eye can see, a point proved by Eadweard Muybridge in 1877 when he disclosed that the four feet of a horse did in fact all leave the ground during a gallop. The eye is defective not merely in speed but also in definition. The photograph can define things with greater accuracy, and it captures everything in its purview. The human eye, however, is guided by attention.

The camera is an indifferent eye. It can constitute a foreground and a background through its focus, filters, position, or movement. It can also constitute the emotional tone of a scene by the same means. These means may be further affected by the setup prior to the shot and the editing that follows. Lighting is also an important element—so important that Lawson calls a photograph a way of "painting with light." Now, the camera cannot do all this alone. The camera *doesn't care* what it sees; it merely records what it is set to do. If a photograph is essentially a "process of painting with light," the Polaroid is not the painter; my friend is. Thus, it is my friend who chooses the setup, perhaps even the props, the perspective, the lighting, the focus; and it is my friend's intention toward me that is expressed when the camera records his shot. As I have stated before, and as Grierson agrees, shot is dependent on the prior emotional commitment of the director and, in this case, the photographer. Hence, the photograph does look like one aspect of me as filtered through the vision of my friend.

From my point of view, this is still not adequate. Aside from the narcissistic or romantic notions I may have about myself, I still have the feeling that the photograph does not look like me and that perhaps there may be some ambiguity in this me. Certainly I am not conscious of myself as an aspect. Nor am I conscious of myself as a series or even a sum of aspects. I am aware of myself, insofar as I am aware, as a living being engaged in a world. The me I live is not the me of an aspect or any sum of such aspects. In fact, I seldom see aspects of myself at all since I seldom look at myself except when I am engaged in momentary narcissism or, perhaps, some practical urgency such as shaving. In short, I am hardly ever an object to myself because I am myself. I am normally much too engaged in being myself to abstract some aspect of myself for contemplation or perception and certainly not for aesthetic contemplation. This may be why Douglas Morgan has remarked that most men would rather hold a woman than behold her. Certainly I rarely behold myself. And this myself which I am busy *being* is just the expressive rhythm of living which, from my point of view, is *between* the shots.

Now, if my friend knows me well and also is an expert cameraman, he may be able to capture some of this lost betweenness that is the living me. If so, we do not argue about whether the photo looks like me or not or even whether it flatters me or not. We will agree that it looks like me because his view of me-as-an-other will coincide with my view of me-as-an-other, and both views will be grounded in or will point to the expressive rhythm that is the living me. We will agree and will say that the photograph is authentic. And this, as Susanne Langer remarks, is all that we ask of a photo—or perhaps everything that we ask of a photo, for it is a great deal. We do not ask that a photograph be real but that it be authentic.[13] By "authenticity," Professor Langer means "givenness," a primary abstraction of the immediacy of experience.

Professor Langer's short note on the film is perhaps the most perceptive theoretical approach to film that has as yet been written. But I believe we can get a bit closer to what is meant by the concept of "authenticity." One way might be to look at its opposite. I presume that the opposite of the authentic is the phony. Of persons, objects, situations, we say that something is phony when we sense that it is not what it appears to be. The authentic, conversely, would then be what it appears to be. It would be the genuine. The authentic carries, or rather shows on the face of it, what it is. Its comportment reveals its being. But perhaps this is using too metaphysical a language. Taking an analogy from music, we could say that the authentic is that which displays the proper overtones. It is that which is true, not in the sense that a sentence is true, but in the sense that a pitch is true. The authentic is that which echoes itself through various circumstances just as a melody may echo itself even though it may be transposed into different keys. The authentic is that qualitied instance of circumstance which vibrates according to its own unique pattern.

Film is so close to our being-in-the-world that we tend to forget that it is an abstraction. But a film is a created object. And it is an abstraction. Were this not so, it would be impossible for film to be a *significant* appearance, a shaped apparition. Were it not shaped, there could be no tension between texture and depth, hence no form and, without form, no art. Film is an art, for it has its own appropriate forms. But shaping and form demand selectivity, for form itself is the feeling-forth through content by chance and by brutal choice to eventual and emergent meaning. In film, this feeling-forth begins with theme. If plot follows shot, form follows theme. Even the most realistic film, as Durgnat has remarked, includes "impossibilities of many kinds"; and he adds, "The camera's quick changes of viewpoint within the scene, the cut, the flashback and crosscutting all outrage simple 'literalism.'"[14] Only film-society addicts would sit like mute fish or reverent Quakers to watch silent films. Music and selected natural sound are also outrages against literal realism.

Even the apparent simple situation with my friend and the Polaroid was not simple. There was a sense in which we were both right. He was right in asserting that the camera correctly recorded the aspect of me that he had selected. I was right in asserting that *that* aspect of me was not the one with which I was most familiar. I was further right in insisting that no aspect by itself could capture the totality of the living me. Even from exclusively my point of view, not his, there is complexity which appears to approach a paradox. The paradox would come from which me *I* meant—the me that he constitutes as my other, the me that I perceive (rightly or wrongly) as my other, or the me that I am continually being but not seeing. And we were both wrong. For the camera recorded what struck its sensitivity at the very instantaneous flutter of its shutter.

What all this means is this: If the director of a film is an artist, he will try to realize the expressive form of his theme, and he will realize, being an artist, that the expressiveness of the film must be articulated and not his own private feelings. This error vitiates most of Mr. Durgnat's book. He neither does nor can, on his theory, draw any distinction between expression and self-expression. This same excessive subjectivity, I might add, is both the content and the ruin of most experimental films. Kracauer was right in intuiting the hidden connection between subjectivity and formalism. The greater the internal subjectivity, the more this will be expressed objectively in formalistic patterns. But Kracauer's dislike of the avant-garde film led him to a drastic negation of the formalistic property of all film and hence to the denial that film can be an art at all.

If the director is an artist, he will strive to capture in his expressive form that betweenness of shots which is an analogue of the actor's actual being-in-the-world. He will also try to elicit from the actor appropriate gestures, expressions, postures, and intonations that are revelatory of that betweenness. This means, of course, that film actors *do* act. Their acting, however, is on a diminished scale due to their bodily position; they cannot be as grand. Another way of saying this is that, although the actor has lost his absolute control (relatively—no one has absolute control) of space and can no longer inhabit it, he has not lost total control. Hence, there is illusion still, but it is not as obviously illusory; it is not the illusion of theatre but the illusion of film. The actor is striving to express himself through the part; he is not living the part in an unreal way as he would on stage. This, I suppose, is what we mean when we say that a film performance should be genuine or firm. This seems to me merely to be saying once again that we demand that film be authentic.

Confusing the authentic with the real often leads one to a further step: the confusion of literal and metaphorical truth. Thus, one might argue that film and photographs in general should depict what they portray, and "depiction" is usually meant in its most literal sense: "record." Thus, one is led to insist on using the word "truth" in its propositional sense, as when we say that the sentence "Snow is white" is true if and only if there is some white fluffy stuff coming out of the sky and false otherwise. Of the various levels of meaning of words, Saint Thomas Aquinas long ago warned us that the literal was the lowest common meaning. In fact, in reading the *Summa Theologica,* I have the feeling that whenever I read a passage merely literally, I can be sure that the meaning is false. This same distinction might well apply to the "readings" of films or of any art.

Literal truth has nothing to do with art. A work of art is a nondiscursive symbol and as such does not fall into the category of a propositional assertion. If one must apply the word "truth" at all to art works, then the meaning should be a metaphorical one. Thus, we may say that a film or other work of art is honest or true if we mean truth in the sense in which the carpenter says that the wall is true or in the sense that we say an instrument rings true. "True" here is close to the concept of the "authentic," for the voice with true pitch is the one that not only is right on the proper note but also has the appropriate reinforcing overtones. All authentic art, and this includes film, is metaphor.

Oscar Wilde has said that all art is at once "surface and symbol." I take this to mean that not only is the individuality of a work the tensions between its surface and its depth but also that art is a folding together of two different realms. It is metaphor. Robert Frost gave us a working definition of metaphor when he said that it was "saying one thing and meaning another." But that was Robert Frost the kindly old New England cracker speaking; it was not Robert Frost the nasty genius. Had it been Frost the poet, he would have said that metaphor is saying one thing and meaning them *both*. Because art is a metaphor, it can bridge the chasms between feeling and form, for the function of expressive form is to present feeling to the understanding in the mode of articulation.

While words carry or express the metaphors in Frost's poetry or Wilde's, it is not primarily words that carry the metaphors in film. In fact, we often find a direct verbal metaphor disturbing in film. Why? Because films are not composed of words; they are created of composed images. Hence, the projected image may function as a metaphor; and in films that are works of art, one may find many such visual metaphors. Whether such metaphors are effective depends on whether they are affective, and this will be a function of how they are used. If we examine the use of visual metaphors in film, we find that there are at least three ways in which they are used: the fixed image, the composed image, and the moving image.

The held shot, or fixed image, is used quite often in film and can be a powerful expressive tool. Since the film itself is a moving phenomenon, the energy of its rhythmic progression seems to drain into the still shot. A fixed image can be literally and figuratively arresting. The spectator's attention is following his vision and when the vision is stopped, attention is stopped. How it is stopped will make a difference in response. If the stop shot is sudden, unexpected, and part of a fast rhythm, the result will normally be laughter. Our eyes shock us into laughter in *Tom Jones* when his pratfall into the pond is suddenly stopped. If, however, the stop shot comes at the end of a long slow rhythm, the effect is one of inducing contemplation in the spectator. The last, long, lingering photograph of Jean-Pierre Léaud's face in *The Four Hundred Blows* seems to absorb the preceding rhythms and theme of the film. It forces the spectator to reflect upon the tragedy of this boy's life.

The word "composed" may also mean "at rest." The shot that is at rest in a moving context often has about it an uncanny sense of intensified meaning, perhaps because the spectator who has been watching is suddenly forced to look. Or perhaps it is intensified because his look is forced. The magic world that had been posing before him is disrupted; it is *ex-posed*. He is unexpectedly compelled to attend to the appearance of what he had been seeing only in the loose sense of watching. Because of the inaccuracy, slowness, and expectancy of the human eye, even this arresting may be deceptive. For example, the fusing of the images of the actress and the nurse in *Persona* and the fusing of the industrialist's image and that of the kidnapper in *High and Low* actually involve cuts. But those fused images seem to hang in the memory because of the metaphorical forcefulness of identity through difference. Affective forcefulness in these two instances brings effective contemplation, and the mind grasps them as still. Nevertheless, genuine uncut stills are inserted into motion pictures and such shots may be rational, irrational, or a mixture of both.

We have already discussed some of the rational uses of the arrested image in our reflections on the soliloquy; and we came to the conclusion that if the shot is held too long, as are some in *Hamlet, Winter Light,* and *The Passion of Joan of Arc,* the film tends to become turgid and dead. The arrested shot should be used sparingly and for a specific purpose. If not, the spectator's eye and attention become restless, and the film illusion tends to dissipate. Another possible result of holding too long is that the image may become a visual cliché. A further difficulty is underlining. If a shot is used metaphorically, then is underlined verbally, it tends to lose its visual force and to become merely a bore. The director most effectively uses the held shot by including it, but merely by "throwing it away." This technique is used with great frequency in the films of Kurosawa and Antonioni and is an integral part of their styles. Let us examine some specific visual metaphors.

Mike Nichols revealed a true brilliance for film directing in his first venture, the film version of *Who's Afraid of Virginia Woolf?* He took an excessively talky play and, without cutting the dialogue, drastically transformed it into a moving film. His fine achievement in many ways improves on the stage production. Nichols, for example, brings out the allusions to Tennessee Williams and *A Streetcar Named Desire* during the snapdragon scene with an emphasis that was not present on the stage. But it was a first effort, and there are flaws even in a fine job. Two flaws appear in *Virginia Woolf* in almost the same place. After the roadhouse blow-up, Nichols takes his camera up high into the night, and we have a long-shot of the station wagon parked askew with its right taillight blinking. He holds the shot and holds it and holds it. Then he slowly, much too slowly, dollies in on it. After the first few seconds of the original shot, we had the point: She returned home in a hurry, parked the car erratically, left the door open and the turn signal going. But while one's nerves are screaming: "O.K., Nichols, I got the point," he continues to hold, then to add insult by the slow dolly. The same thing occurs shortly afterward when we have the marvelous effect, over the visuals, of the sound of tinkling ice in a glass. This is very effective. But then Nichols has Miss Taylor stagger out on the porch and sing about ice, that is, tell us about it. This verbal underlining was unnecessary. Here it detracted from the intense night and its visuals.

A similar mistake occurs in the fine film *Occurrence at Owl Creek Bridge*. The film begins with a long high shot through some rib-racked leafless trees, then slowly moves in on the dismal frost and the "execution." Suddenly we are thrown into the world of life with images of the man in the swirling water, dewdrops on grass blades, swirling foam, bursting water bubbles, insects moving on tentative legs, and trees budding in the joy of spring. All these images are scrupulously shot and edited and feel perfectly right. Then a country song comes from nowhere over the audio, and the spectator is *told* about the joys of life. The visual images are so powerful that they carry in spite of the song. But the mooning about life and its marvels is distracting, for we have already seen the marvels of life and the resurgence of hope through the brilliantly edited sequence. The disembodied singer and his guitar are irrelevant at best; at worst, they tend to conflict with the force of the visual metaphors. In a rare lapse, Antonioni commits the same error in *Blow-Up* when he has Hemmings pick up his radiophone and *tell* the audience that the queers and poodles are moving into the neighborhood of the antique shop. He had already shown us this was the case.

Blow-Up abounds in visual metaphors. In the antique shop sequence, Antonioni has Hemmings buy a propeller. He has a desultory discussion about its delivery, then insists on stuffing it into his Rolls convertible. The girls insist that it be delivered. Later we see it lying on the floor of the studio. What is its meaning? There are several possible meanings. One is that it was just an excuse for Hemmings to leave the shop. The shop scene was necessary, otherwise he could not have delivered his cynical advice on the ineffectiveness of travel and how dull things are in Morocco and Nepal. Since it is a prop without a motor, it could be a metaphor of his advice to the girl. He realizes that there is no escape from the self. Or it could be a severed phallus acting as a symbol of the photographer's own alienation. It could also be a pun: It is a prop to be used in tableaux. It could be a simple absurdity: finding a symbol of the air age in a dilapidated antique shop that Hemmings wants to buy for its props. It could be a symbol of simple whim, as is the guitar neck, which he later abandons and which is kicked aside but which he wants at the moment because everyone else is after it. It could be a prop for the plot that disrupts the theme. The theme of *Blow-Up* is depth involvement in a disposable society, and the propeller is delivered precisely when Hemmings and Redgrave are beginning to become involved in depth. It thus breaks up their romance. It could be all these things. Or it could be none of them. Yet somehow it seems both rationally and irrationally "right"—perhaps because this unexpected object is tied to a human story, and its meaning is a function of its context.

Two more images in *Blow-Up* might be mentioned: one a thrown-away image and one a pun. The castaway image is the strange neon sign, which hangs in an abstract horizon to the park. Antonioni had that sign especially constructed for the film, then tore it down. It is strangely reminiscent of an airline ad—a kind of half-arrow or half-flight—yet we cannot rationally say exactly what it means. It appears absolutely right. Antonioni does not comment on it or explain it. He uses it and throws it away. A pun also occurs in the park. Hemmings meets a fat brown-suited trash man who turns out to be a white-haired woman stabbing paper. She waddles across the screen. In retrospect, we realize she could be a takeoff on Hitchcock and his celebrated inclusions of himself in his films. This image shortly precedes the fluttering pigeons and the beginning of the murder mystery. *Blow-Up* has a surfeit of literal and figurative birds. The fact that many such images can also be puns is not surprising. A pun is, after all, a low-grade metaphor.

As Goethe used to insist: Context, context, context—everything depends upon context! And in film this is certainly true. What I mean by the sense of rightness is the appropriateness of a shot or element to its functional context. How it works. What it does. If too much attention is drawn to the shot, it ceases to work. The first shot of the soaring bird in *Crime and Punishment U.S.A.* is effective, for it expresses the young student's sense of desperate yearning. Then the directors repeat the shot, and the second use detracts from the first. The image of the soaring bird degenerates into a cliché and takes on the same status as the dreary "poster shots"— mother against the wheat, the tractor against the sky—which the mind and eye are forced to suffer in so many Russian films.

Young directors often make such mistakes. Fortunately, they learn from experience. Hence, we hope that another new director, Paul Newman, goes back to examine some of the elements in *Rachel, Rachel*. *Rachel, Rachel* is a remarkable first effort in film and not only because the acting is so powerful. There are many things in it that are right, but the use of color throughout the first sequences is all wrong. Newman is trying to convey to us the hysterical claustrophobia of Rachel's small-town world, but the eye is constantly hit with the joy of yellow. It is not that yellow cannot be menacing. It can. A more experienced director, Roman Polanski, makes the yellow wallpaper in *Rosemary's Baby* literally crawl with menace. Again, the meaning of an element is a function of its use.

Time and again, what we remember from films are some small gestures, some images or "bits" that seem to carry more import than they could possibly have in isolation. The pig hanging in the window just prior to the Fool walking the tightrope in *La Strada,* the images of the retarded boy in the same film, the shattered bamboo screen in La Saraghina's window or the bicycle in the bathroom in *8½,* the sudden juxtapositions of the tenderness of flowers and the brutality of violence in Kurosawa's films, the trapped bee in *Viridiana,* the killer pilot reading *Playboy* in *Dr. Strangelove*—these and similar images literally haunt the memory. Sometimes their meanings are obvious. Yet sometimes we cannot say for certain exactly what they mean. Still they continue to haunt us as enigmatic images that were, for some inexplicable reason, exactly right for their contexts. It is totally absurd for W. C. Fields to insist upon donning his mittens to play the zither in *A Fatal Glass of Beer,* and it is equally absurd for him to dip a loaf of French bread in his soup or go out to "milk the yak." Yet, somehow, these images have a kind of unconscious rightness about them, a striking and irrational sense of appropriateness. Even though we may not be able to *say* what they mean, we immediately feel them as somehow intelligible when we see them in their contexts.

The shot that is simply held may induce tedium. We saw this with the taillight sequence from *Virginia Woolf.* The most extreme examples of this would probably be Andy Warhol's *Sleep* or *Empire State.* Yet the held shot, or the hesitant one, can be a most powerful element. Perhaps the most notorious of such shots in recent films is the famous blasphemy of *Viridiana.* Luis Buñuel is a visual director. Consequently, his films also are rich with visual metaphors. Many of them are shocking, but they are economical and they work. The hesitancy of Viridiana's hand as she reaches for the teat of the cow and then cannot milk it is an image that cannot be misread in the context of the film. Nor can one misread the image of the dog being dragged by the rope which is then freed only to be followed by another dog being dragged by another rope. But the image that raised cries of "blasphemy, perfidy, infamy!" was the image of the bums gathered around the table in the pose of Leonardo da Vinci's *Last Supper.* Here the visual metaphor works not so much because it is held but because of its composition. Its metaphorical meaning is fully intended by its structure and place; Buñuel underlines it with Handel.

The visual metaphor that is arresting because of its rational, irrational, or mixed content usually strikes us immediately. Unless it is strongly underlined by the aurals, however, as the Last Supper image was, we are not normally immediately struck by the compositional metaphor. We usually become aware of such metaphors after the fact, yet films are rich in compositional metaphors also. The long introductory sequence of Kurosawa's *High and Low* is filled with visual underlining, most of it done in terms of composition. Nor is it inappropriate that the compositional metaphors are mostly Christian. The original title of the film was *Heaven and Hell;* and the first half takes place in "heaven," in the rich manufacturer's apartment overlooking Yokohama. Of course, Kurosawa's practical problem was to fill up a wide screen with visual content, but the way he uses this content structurally serves as a metaphor for the situation. Perhaps a few examples will suffice.

During the second telephone call from the kidnapper, Kurosawa has his actors inhabiting the whole screen; but they are so arranged that their forms drain from right to left down into the telephone, which is anchored by the main character, Gondo, and a small group to the left. The composition of this scene with its strong sweep down to a central point of interest is the same evolutionary drain of structure that one has in Giotto's *Mourning the Dead Christ,* although it must be admitted that Giotto's angels with their exaggerated grief are absent from the top of the screen. The takes in this sequence are quite long, and the emphasis is repeatedly upon composition. The film almost stops, but Kurosawa is, as always, inventive and does not let things come to a dead standstill. Thus, he has Gondo taking a shower when the third phone call comes (his baptism? washing away his past?); and there is a frantic scurry of activity, complete with the detectives having to dive under a coffee table so the kidnapper can't decipher their presence. When Gondo finally decides to go along with the ransom—he doesn't really decide until the existential moment on the train—Kurosawa again uses composition forcefully. In the foreground, we see two detectives talking of the situation. Off to the right are two more policemen marking the ransom money. Both these groups are in the light. Back in the left center of the screen sits the victim/hero Gondo in deep shadows. The composition is eloquent: This is Gondo's Gethsemane. Camera angles in this film, by the way, are also used as metaphors. In "heaven," the shots are high; in "hell" (the slums), the shots are low.

More common than the compositional metaphor is the moving metaphor. This is appropriately so, for, as we shall repeat again and again, movies move. This, of course, is a function of the way in which things are shot but, most importantly, of the way in which they are edited. The nervous energy of the cutting in *Breathless* reflects not only its title but also the madcap pace of the characters and theme. The famous woodchopper's run in *Rashomon* is sheer cinematic impressionism and conveys the frantic nature of his flight. The hand-held camera work and fast cutting of the intense train sequence in *High and Low* also express the high anxiety of the plot/theme situation. On the other hand, the slow rhythms and the smooth transitions of Satyajit Ray's *The World of Apu* express the gradual deepening and growth of the love between the man and wife.

Ingmar Bergman uses guns as a visual metaphor for sexual excitement in one of the most painful sequences ever put on film: the beach romp in *The Naked Night* (also titled *Sawdust and Tinsel*). While the cannon boom and the soldiers laugh, the clown's wife cavorts in the surf. The crosscutting is increasingly rapid, and this building excitement enhances the slow painful passage that follows as the Christ-like clown carries his nude wife past the soldiers. The close-ups of his anguished, twisted face and his bleeding bare feet stumbling over the hot stones are almost unbearable. Were it not for the clown's fantastic make-up and the fact that the close-ups exaggerate his grotesque face, we would cry.

In what is one of his most brilliant films, and almost his best, *Smiles of a Summer Night,* Bergman uses cannon again, but by his camera use and editing comes out with quite the opposite meaning. After the opening that establishes the lawyer's position, Bergman has him leave the office and amble home. Bergman uses a long dolly to the left and the camera "walks along" with the lawyer as he strolls home to the young wife whom the dialogue has already mentioned. As the camera moves along with the lawyer, it picks up in the foreground a series of cannon with all of their ends firmly stopped. Bergman does not have to comment verbally on the message. We already know that the relationship between the lawyer and his teen-age wife is one of unbearable, pristine purity and innocence—the kind of innocence which, as Durgnat remarks in another context, is so pleasantly relievable that it is hardly worth discussing. But here it is worth discussing, for by camera work and editing alone Bergman has made us *see* the theme.

Not only things and structure may function as symbols and metaphors then, but camera position, camera focus and movement, editing, and visual tempo—all these can and do appeal directly to the spectator's unconscious. By their allusions, they conjure up images that fuse with the illusions before the eye. These allusions are more powerful than any direct statement could be. What they bring forth in the mind's eye (as distinguished from the body's) is what Kracauer called the subversive image. Such subversive images bridge the gap between subject and object. By fusion they create the scene world. One of the great masters of this technique was Leni Riefenstahl, whose documentaries were literally attempts and, perhaps regrettably, extremely successful ones, to *create* reality. Not only did her brilliant editing re-do so-called historical fact to make the Nazis appear as the most noble saviors of the world, they also became part of the feeling-content of the German people and hence one of the emotive forces used to try to conquer the world. In this sense, then, her films *were* historical fact, for they reveal quite clearly what a large number of people, the Germans and their sympathizers in many countries, believed to be the case.

Before Hitler's rise to power in Germany, Leni Riefenstahl was an actress of undistinguished talents. She appeared mostly in a series of ski and mountain pictures dedicated to extolling the concept of duty. But what she did or failed to do as an actress is not important. What is important is that once she abandoned the attempt to become an actress and began directing cameras, she became one of the world's most polished documentary-film creators. The word "creator" is used advisedly, since, in the first place, her greatest strength was not in her directing but in her scissors; she was a superb editor. In the second place, her films were not attempts at straight documentary that tried to capture and thus reveal reality as it was in everyday experience, as were the films of the early Flaherty and Grierson. Even so, if one admires film, he must admire her brilliance.

There can be no doubt that the Nazi movement was one of the greatest barbarisms of mankind. Nor can there be any doubt that Leni Riefenstahl's evil genius was a perfect tool for the propaganda machine of Herr Goebbels. Granted all this, one must still admire her technical grasp and film proficiency, especially her sense of sequence and of the right image. Had she done nothing else, two films which were the result of her creative cutting, *Olympiad* and *Triumph of the Will,* would assign her a place of respect, if not honor, among the world's finest editors. Technique, after all, as Plato argued, is neither moral nor immoral. Only the use of technique is properly the sphere of moral judgment.

Of course, *Triumph of the Will* is not a newsreel. It is a carefully arranged and scrupulously cut work of art that does not record reality but stages the drama of the Nazi party convention in Nuremberg in 1934. Hitler had personally ordered that this filmic record of the first party congress be made. Riefenstahl created it. In its original version, *Triumph of the Will* lasted three hours. Even though the Museum of Modern Art's print is a cut version, one cannot miss the passion and the intense fervor that this film must have aroused in the German people, because it can through the sheer immediacy of its visual symbols arouse some of the same feelings in us. And we, thank the Lord, live in a different time and space. Yet we are also moved.

Poets, drunkards, and saints all agree that the greatest ideas somehow come out of the clear blue. It would seem that this is where the gods come from, too. Hence, playing on this image, Riefenstahl has the opening sequences of *Triumph of the Will* show a small plane moving like an angry gnat through a sky of enormous cumulous clouds. Slowly the plane comes into close-up, then it lands at Nuremberg, rewarding the upturned, expectant faces of the crowd. The arrival of the plane is intercut with shots of the ancient town and of cathedral spires, thus heightening the feelings of aspiration while at the same time tying the event to the solidity of the past. Hitler descends like a god among men to share his power with the willing faithful. This brilliant opening sequence is followed by equally fascinating track shots of the crowd: pudgy little kinder held aloft by beaming parents to view the deity in the flesh; miles of young brown-shirts, much like boy scouts with their youthful faces and their staffs and drums and flags; and the interminable faces of the cheering multitudes intercut by delegations in regional dress. Hitler and his staff are shown paying their respects to the past dead. There is a coda of horseplay and endless tables of food to show that the people are really enjoying this "country fair." This sequence not only establishes that the Germans are just boisterous, blond idealists but also emphasizes the plenty that has replaced the starvation of the period before the Hitler regime. We are then shown the hysterical mass rally in the huge stadium. Thousands on thousands of arms and voices unite in "Sieg Heils" as the Führer reminds his people of past atrocities and promises them future glories. There is constant intercutting of such Nazi symbols as the swastika and the eagle, and intercuts of the solidity of the concrete stadium emphasize the permanency of Hitler's promises. Leni Riefenstahl, with the aid of thirty photographers and her scissors, took "historical" fact and transformed (twisted, if you wish) it into a mystic, pagan religion. The national state is one of the many modern forms of idolatry and is not a characteristic unique to Germany, but this form has seldom been portrayed with more impact than in *Triumph of the Will*.

This is not an entertaining film—certainly not a comedy. But it is a compelling motion picture. The rhythm of the cuts and the playing on subconscious imagery create a cumulative power, which reaches its climax at the indoor rally and Hitler's final speech. The very force of this film should give us some pause. For one thing, it makes patently clear to all of us how easily "history" can be created on film. For another, it should make us a bit wary. If, after all this time, and coming from a different world of experience, we can be moved by the vitality of a film that has nothing to do with our conscious heritage, would it not be possible for us to become hysterical over one created for that very purpose? Viewing *Triumph of the Will* can help us to understand something of the mind of the German people in 1934. And since, even now, we find ourselves sharing some of the same emotions, it should make us realize what a fine basis for fear we have within ourselves. It is no accident, then, that many people detested this film, but their hatred was not based on its failures: it was based on its success.

Triumph of the Will may be taken as an instance of Oscar Wilde's epigram that nature imitates art. Another instance of this principle was Balázs' filming of the construction of the Turk-Siberian railroad. The workers who saw the film were so inspired by their own images that they finished their job ahead of time, and the film had to be recalled in order to move the completion date of the railroad forward on the prints. It would be a misuse of a Renoir painting to use it as an umbrella, but it is not so obvious that it would be a misuse of a film designed for emotional nationalism to produce patriotic fervor. In fact, it is not obvious at all. *Triumph of the Will* was carefully designed to promote Germanic pride. It fulfilled its design.

All documentary is dependent upon selectivity. No one would claim that the old *March of Time* newsreels were simply the objective recording of the facts. Even television newscasts, which are composed under much greater pressures of immediacy, involve a great deal of editing and interpretive arrangement before they are put on the tube. Perhaps one may be emotionally justified in calling *Triumph of the Will* "bastard reality"; but one could say the same, and with much more justification, of Flaherty's *Louisiana Story,* which is hardly comparable to his *Man of Aran* or *Nanook of the North*. Like Wordsworth, he did too much, and Flaherty's films consistently go downhill toward "bastard reality."

Perhaps because film is this strange objective/subjective phenomenon, it can have such a strong hold on us. By fusing the subversive image with the visual one, it brings the illusion of the world as it is lived directly into our hearts. The relation of the spectator to the film thus becomes not so much one of communication but rather of communion—a common being-with and a vicarious participation in projected mystery. The tension between the unconscious and the consciousness of the spectator imbues his percepts with more than ordinary meaning. The moving images take on extraordinary meaning. Hence, they often exhibit the aspect or aura of revelations. The revelatory power of film performs three functions: It provides a record of past rhythms, it elicits the visibility of the seen, and it articulates the expressive quality of the nuance.

Siegfried Kracauer expresses this first function of revelation in an uncharacteristic style, almost a poetic outburst, in his book *From Caligari to Hitler*. He says, "To meet actors familiar to contemporary moviegoers in a past that has become history is an uncanny experience; what was once our life is now stored away, and we have somehow unknowingly moved on."[15] And he is right. It *is* an uncanny experience. Look at your old home movies and you are struck with the wonder about what happened to that young child first teetering on unsteady legs; she is now as dead as Napoleon. Yet there is a sense in which she still lives in the now young woman, for the beginning rhythms are fully articulated today in an adult walk. This fixing of the appearances of the past is no doubt one reason why the movies of the 1940s and 1950s often seem funny to us. We are immediately struck by the odd clothing styles ("odd" meaning merely that they have changed) and by some of the awkward techniques. The invariant gesture of the motion picture, like other people's children, reminds us that we have grown older without knowing it. The ability of the camera to capture the rhythms and the milieu of the past, its unintentional time-binding, is one aspect of its power of revelation. No doubt it is sensitivity to this quality of time-binding that leads some theorists to become extravagant in their praise of neo-realism, the non-actor, and so on, for there is a sense in which each film is a revelation of its circumstance.

The second function of the revelatory power of film is that it elicits the visibility of the seen. The familiar objects in our everyday milieu become extensions of our being; we react to them as wholes. This means that the more familiar things are and the more embodied circumstances become from our living perspective, the less we attend to them as visual objects. Since they constitute a part of our horizon and, in a real sense, a part of us, we do not abstract ourselves from them. We do not view them as apart from us; hence, *we do not see them*. Their visibility becomes hidden for us. It is this hidden visibility that the camera can elicit. For a concrete example: The last time I shaved off my moustache, my wife did not notice for three weeks; my students noticed the first day. I am not a visible object to my wife; I am to my students. I have become a part of her living world and consequently am not abstract enough to be seen. To my students I am abstract.

It is this ex-posing of the familiar, putting it into a frame and rendering it an object of perception, bringing it before us from the realm of feeling into the realm of the eye and ear, which, I believe, Siegfried Kracauer hoped to intend by his concept of "redemption." In a poetic and beautifully expressed sentence he says, "Intimate faces, streets we walk day by day, the house we live in—all these things are part of us like our skin, and because we know them by heart we do not know them with the eye."[16] Such is the function of habit. The house I live in becomes an extension of my skin.

What our body has learned to inhabit becomes our lived world. Our way of meeting that world, how we cope or contend with it, becomes our impalpable body of habit, our acquired stance. This acquired stance I shall refer to as our posture, our lived perspective, our natural standpoint. The familiar becomes habitual; the habitual becomes invisible. The function of habit, as the pragmatists have pointed out, is to erase thought. It also erases perception. Thus, our familiar world becomes all too familiar. Our senses repose in it, see from it, take it for granted; and it becomes the constant here from which we engage the rest of the world. That from which we see, that from which we hear, that from which we touch, that in which our senses repose can become *re-posed*—made problematic—and thus ex-posed by the camera.

Our familiar living is a constant forgetting. We become literally blind to our surroundings, to "our relation to this earth which is our habitat," as Gabriel Marcel puts it. By defamiliarizing us with our surroundings, by converting the seen into the scene and forcing us really to see it anew, the camera can shock us into an awareness of our perpetual forgetting and our assumed stance. In fact, it is this power of the camera to re-present in a new context and thus elicit the visibility of the seen, which Marcel claims is the revelatory function, the redeeming character of film.

> And I will say that to me who has always had a propensity to get tired of what I have the habit of seeing—what in reality, that is, I do not see anymore—this power peculiar to the cinema seems to be literally redeeming [*salvatrice.*][17]

But this revelation, this salvation, is not entirely pleasant, for it calls into question and puts strain on our habits. It disrupts our presuppositions. And, as anyone who has moved the furniture of his mind knows, the experience can be unsettling. It doesn't seem like home anymore.

It is this shaking of our presuppositions, this earthquake of assumed concepts, which I take to be the moral theme of Kurosawa's films. The crisis of cancer forces Watanabe to review his position and to learn to "burn before the dying of the light." The final sacrifice, not of his future, but of his "settled past" forces Gondo to the revelation that he is not the person he conceived himself to be. In reconceiving himself, he becomes reborn. He comes alive from the shell of his habit. This does not mean that all his habits are discarded. On the contrary, he falls back on the learned trade of his body. He leaves the complacency of "heaven," sits down on the floor, tears open the ransom cases, hides the smoke powder in them, and restitches the casings. As he does so, he remarks: "In my day, shoemakers made briefcases too. I never thought my days as an apprentice would be so valuable. Yet here I am, starting from scratch again." From this point on, Gondo begins to grow. At the end of *High and Low,* he has learned not only to accept his own actions but also the irrational actions of the kidnapper. He has become an older, a wiser, and yet a more gentle and more childlike man. His tired eyes see anew and he has called his world into question. Kurosawa leaves the audience and Gondo with the question reverberating: "Why are you so convinced that it is right that we hate each other?" Although Akira Kurosawa does not profess any given philosophy, analysis of his films shows him to be one of the most existential of all directors.

As fallible men, the course of our lives is normally one of progressive closure.

Thus, our past is often molded to become a settled horizon strewn with the relics of our forgotten freedom—all the things or, more accurately, people we might have been. As our past becomes increasingly abstract, settled, and fixated, we foreclose the options of our destiny. We cease to be open to the future. We ignore the true options of our futures and regard them as unreal. Like mollusks, we drag our calcified past with us and find ourselves worn and breathless facing a future in which "tout est donné." But what film can show is that our past is not settled, not necessarily concretized and determinative. It can demonstrate that the past of the film character, like Gondo's, is merely another construct, a fictional demand of the ego and its surroundings. By "sounding the depths," as Marcel puts it, film can reveal to us the underlying current of our possibility. By eliciting the visibility of the seen, it can force us to *re*-view and thus reveal the living that we are. It is no accident that the title for Watanabe's ordeal is not a settled noun, "life," but instead is a process verb. *Ikiru* means "living"! The exclamation point at the end of that sentence is purely intentional. It is like the *kana* at the end of one of Basho's poems about an insignificant flower. It means not just living and not just alive, but *so* alive!

The presentational immediacy of film, then, not only can provide us the pure blind joy that Santayana called beauty but also can open our eyes. Because of its peculiar abilities to warp space and time, it can reshuffle our past and can renew the game of life. This may be and often is painful. Nevertheless, even a card game must begin from such relative chaos. If not, the deck is stacked. But besides forcing us to look again, *really* look, film can also reveal the subtlety of expressive gesture. It can articulate the nuance.

Gabriel Marcel discusses the possibility of including in a film a professor—a historian of philosophy—lecturing on Kant at the Sorbonne. If the scene were merely to record the professor's lecture, such a sequence would be illegitimate in film. Why? ". . . because the spectator does not go to the cinema in order to hear explications; they would not be legitimate except in a lecture, not even in a play."[18] I take this to be an accurate insight. Conceptual content should not be in the forefront of film, and the verbalization of arguments, straight explications, are contrary to film's possibilities. One finds the ending of *Psycho* patently offensive when the "psychologist" lectures the audience in a most elementary manner on what they have already seen. The same thing may be said for what is otherwise a fairly fine film, Harry Brown's *Intruder in the Dust*. At the end of this film also, we are subjected to a simpleminded lecture (the lawyer explaining to the boy) that Negroes have dignity and that we all ought to love one another. In both these instances, the film died before it ended. As I have said previously, we do not go to movies to be told. We go to movies to see.

But, as Marcel continues, a philosophy professor could appear in a film if his appearance were handled in the proper way.

> Most assuredly a historian of philosophy can be a film character, but [only] under [certain] conditions or under a very rigorously controlled aspect. What must be accentuated and thrown into full relief is his comportment in the behaviorist sense of character, his manner of walking, of sitting down, and with regard to his speech, his intonations and perhaps his facial contractions—by no means and to no degree the content of what he says.[19]

The key word here is "comportment." Marcel is indicating that the technological apparatus of the camera can bypass the body as other and can reveal the nuances of gesture and rhythm that are the very being of the professor, his way of being-with-the-world. It is his *way* of saying that is all important, for it reveals how he meets his lived world. It reveals him to himself and to others not merely as he would like to appear but as he is. We referred to this bypassing of the self-as-other to capture the expressive meaning of nuance when we said that the film actor was less real as an actor because he was more real as a person. The camera can and often does capture the fugitive gesture, the small intonation, the quick change in the light of the eye—what Balázs called the "microphysiognomy" of the face and body. Like the telephone, it bypasses the body as other.

Insofar as the camera does this, it bypasses the self of the actor-as-other and reveals his depth meanings, meanings which the actor himself may be unaware that he is expressing but which a creative editor can structure and articulate. What is important in this case is that self-expression become objective expression, that what Collingwood called "psychic expression" be transformed (by editing) to the level of aesthetic expression. We are not interested in Humphrey Bogart as such; but we are interested in the way he reveals Bogart, uses Bogart's depth rhythms, to articulate the world of Fred C. Dobbs. The director can tell the actor how he wants the scene played, but in his editing primarily he can articulate the value system and rhythm of his characters. One of the most amazing aspects of *Treasure of the Sierra Madre* was how John Huston consistently could articulate the full import of a small gesture, a torn sombrero, a changed intonation, a gold tooth. Such a film achieves emotional wholeness and unity, and as spectators we are stunned by its power.

I have been pushing the analogy between the actor and the spectator because I believe that film provides a strong ground for this analogue. Just as the actor has his concept of himself bypassed by the camera, so the spectator has his self-as-other bypassed by the same means. The spectator does not *see* himself on the screen. He is not *in* the picture. He may expect, suspect, or inspect; but he is still a spectator.

Yet there is a forgetting of the everyday self while watching film and a feeling of exhilaration, which accompanies this release from our habitual selves. The spectator identifies with the perspective of the camera and his normal bodily image is negated. He is no longer his natural standpoint. Like the actor, he is undergoing an experience of excarnation, an experience of bi-presence. And this disembodied state for the spectator diminishes his self-consciousness. Through the magic lantern he becomes a temporary other.

Although the critical awareness is often lowered when watching film, the spectator does not necessarily go into a somnambulistic or, rather, static trance. This can be demonstrated simply by watching a motion-picture audience. Some will be in a trance, some will be distracted (often by each other), and some will be perched on the edges of their seats watching with full critical awareness. Those who have disciplined, as distinguished from naive, perception are working at watching the film totally. Like the camera, they are trying to take it all in. But this partially lowered sense of self does have a significant effect: It increases the tendency to believe. One feels an overwhelming urge to believe the flow of images before him. Film might be called an unwilling suspension of disbelief.

This naive faith that film elicits in us is sometimes an acquiescent and sometimes a creative fidelity. And because it can engender this attitude of trust and openness, I regard film as basically humanistic. As Marcel says, it is "the best means we have at our disposal today in order to bring man into the presence of a certain image of himself, an image which ought to surpass the limits of purely anecdotal realism."[20] Film, as Leni Riefenstahl dramatically demonstrated,[21] can utilize allusion to sound another aspect of bi-presence. Film can elicit the subversive unconscious image and fuse it through movement with the shadows on the screen. This is what Marcel has called "onirisme"—a visual hallucination that resembles a dream. Such images might be illegitimate in the theatre or might be impossible to achieve in literature, but they are the common currency of fine film. This is what film does well, it is what it can do best, and according to Marcel what it *ought* to do.

> I believe profoundly that the film in its highest expression owes it to itself to arrive at a synthesis or perhaps a fusion of dream and reality, and everything seems to demonstrate above all that this distinction or this division is relative to a certain state of development of the creature and that metaphysically it ought to be surpassed.[22]

Man is both subject *and* object. So is film. Because of this affinity, film can be a most potent teacher—an experience that teaches, as Pudovkin put it, "not only through the brain, but through the whole body."

From these reflections and concrete examples it follows that gestures, postures, things in film are sometimes memorable. They are not memorable because they are mere snapshots. They are not memorable because of their thinghood or their merely "being there." On the contrary, they are meaningful when they are used as metaphors of the human condition presented in the film. Or they may be meaningful because they are unsolved intellectual puzzles, which somehow strike the depths of our emotions. At any rate, things in film are meaningful because of their significance for the humans involved or for ideological and emotional content that surrounds them. Things are not meaningful in themselves, a mistake that Joseph Losey began to make in *The Servant,* then intensified to the point of boredom in *Accident.* The interminable shots of houses and walls and doors in *Accident*—the camera literally caresses them—are presumably to allow contemplation of the events, but they simply induce disinterest. The empty facades, the strange, enigmatic stupa-like building in *L'Eclisse,* on the other hand, haunt the memory, for they reveal the shifting human relations of the two lovers. The technical moral is this: A director should *use* his shots.

The camera does have a tendency to erase the distinctions between people and things, since it turns them both into images and they exist on the same plane. This is not a virtue but a potential defect. If it is used to humanize things, it is a virtue. If it is used to turn people into mere objects, it can be a defect. The pious pornography of *Private Property* is not the fact that it involves two fools in an attempted rape but that the director by his shots and editing turns the woman into a mere thing, a phony mannequin. This is often the result of the "glamour treatment," so that the so-called supersexy star actually turns out to have about as much sex appeal as a stainless steel knife lying in a snowbank. One assumption of this book is very simple: People are more important than things. Objects and photographs should be so handled that their human meanings are brought forth and articulated. Films should expose the emotional import of things.

Notes

1. Raymond Durgnat, *Films and Feelings* (Cambridge, Mass.: The M.I.T. Press, 1967), p. 24.
2. Siegfried Kracauer, *Theory of Film: The Redemption of Physical Reality* (Fair Lawn, N.J.: Oxford University Press, 1960).
3. Pauline Kael, *I Lost it at the Movies* (Boston: Atlantic–Little, Brown, 1965), p. 270.
4. Siegfried Kracauer, *From Caligari to Hitler* (Princeton, N.J.: Princeton University Press, 1947).

5. Kracauer, *Theory of Film,* p. 18.

6. Kracauer, *Theory of Film,* p. 18.

7. Kracauer, *Theory of Film,* p. 19.

8. Kracauer, *Theory of Film,* p. 20.

9. Eugene Kaelin, *An Existentialist Aesthetic* (Madison, Wis.: University of Wisconsin Press, 1962).

10. Donald Richie, *The Films of Kurosawa* (Berkeley: University of California Press, 1965), p. 76.

11. Durgnat, *Films and Feelings,* p. 100.

12. John H. Lawson, *Film: The Creative Process* (New York: Hill & Wang, 1967), p. 176.

13. Robert W. Sowers as cited in Susanne Langer, *Feeling and Form* (New York: Scribner's, 1953), p. 411.

14. Durgnat, *Films and Feelings,* p. 31.

15. Kracauer, *From Caligari to Hitler,* p. 25.

16. Kracauer, *Theory of Film,* p. 55.

17. Gabriel Marcel, "Possibilités et Limites de l'Art Cinématographique," *Revue Internationale de Filmologie,* Vol. 5, Nos. 18–19 (July–December 1954), p. 164. Marcel's words are: "Et je dirai que pour moi qui ai toujours eu une propension à me lasser de ce que j'ai l'habitude de voir, c'est-à-dire en réalité de ce que je ne vois plus, cette puissance qui appartient en propre au cinéma me semble littéralement salvatrice."

18. Marcel, p. 168. "Mais du point de vue de l'esthétique cohérente du film, ce sera là un abus ridicule: pourquoi? parce que le spectateur ne vient pas au cinéma pour écouter des explications; elles ne seraient licites que dans une conférence, non pas même dans une pièce de théâtre."

19. Marcel, pp. 168–169. "Certes un historien de la philosophie peut être un personnage de film, mais dans des conditions ou sous un angle très rigoureusement déterminé. Il faudra que soit accentué et mis en plein relief le comportement au sens béhavioristique du personnage, sa façon de marcher, de s'asseoir, et en ce qui concerne le langage, ses intonations, peut-être ses contractions faciales, non point à aucun degré le contenu de ce qu'il dit."

20. Marcel, p. 176. "Si je dis que la fonction essentielle du film est humanisante, je veux dire par là qu'il possède, à n'en pas douter, les moyens les plus efficaces dont nous disposons aujourd'hui pour mettre l'homme en présence d'une certaine image de lui-même, d'une image qui doit dépasser les limites d'un réalisme purement anecdotique."

21. It is interesting to note how emphatically Miss Riefenstahl is ignored by both Kracauer and Lawson. This silence indicates how heavily politics influences some film theorists.

22. Marcel, in *Revue Internationale,* p. 176. "Comme je l'avais dit à Varèse, je crois profondément que le film dans ses plus hautes expressions se doit de parvenir à une synthèse ou peut-être à une fusion du rêve et de la réalité, et tout semble démontrer d'ailleurs que cette distinction ou cette répartition est relative à un certain stade du développement de la créature et que métaphysiquement elle doit être dépassée."

4

The Social World

Though historians may argue over dates and whether the film was born in France or America, there can be little doubt that America first nurtured, then helped bring the infant art to its maturity. Like everything else in America, once started on its own, it became an industry. But if one looks at the short years of its growth and the coexistent conditions of American society, he will find that the years of development and the social conditions have striking lines of interaction. Film, being a popular art, was both a precipitate and a cause of social change and reconstruction.

The rapid period of social reconstruction in America had a profound influence on all the arts. Government subsidization turned out masses of poor post office murals but also helped to develop such painters as Thomas Hart Benton, Grant Wood, and Ben Shahn. One can see the results in such short stories as Vardis Fisher's "The Scarecrow" or Clifford Odets' play *Waiting for Lefty* and in the plethora of socialist-realist novels from Upton Sinclair to John Dos Passos and John Steinbeck. Not only the artists but also the critics were imbued with the ideal of social significance for the arts. Sometimes this had deleterious effects, as, for example, the attempt to persuade Ernest Hemingway that he *ought* to be more socially conscious. The immediate result of that pressure brought *For Whom the Bell Tolls,* one of his less successful works. But the results were often salutary also. Albert Maltz's short story "The Man on the Road" had such an impact that it resulted in legislative action for the protection of miners. This interplay between social change and the arts was even more evident in that most popular of the arts: the film.

Various genres of film were thus born. The gangster film from *Little Caesar* on argued for the reconstruction of society as well as for the excessive self-aggrandizement of the gangster. The political reform film, the economic reform film, the let's-help-the-nation-fight-its-enemies film, the integration film, all became standard types of film fare. The mass audience and the infectiousness of film lent themselves quite well to the transmission of the message of social reform and social solidarity. Sometimes the industry had to do a quick reversal, since political alignments also shifted rapidly. The pro-Russian film, for example, was quickly replaced by the nervously anxious anti-Russian film, and America went through the excessive jitters of blacklisting and congressional investigations of the film industry. In spite of that irrational episode, the social-message film still survives. One must admit, however, that in our day it is usually considerably more conservative than in the past and that sometimes it degenerates to the level of supplying background visuals for foreground music.

The effects in the realm of thought have been as far-reaching as those in the arts.

America may not have an official philosophy, but at least it does have an indigenous one: Pragmatism. Pragmatism, like America itself, is a sprawl more than a system, yet the general direction of its import is clear. A conjunction of German Idealism and Scientific Naturalism, Pragmatism is firmly bound to the ideal of the experimental reconstruction of society. Its impact on our educational institutions has been tremendous, as has its influence on psychology. Though it must be admitted that the movement in psychology now seems to be away from group to grope therapy, one still finds such writers as Erich Fromm arguing that not the individual but society as a whole must be reordered. Since both in immediate circumstance and in horizon, then, we have been surrounded by the social bias, it is not surprising that Americans tend to be sociologists at heart.

Americans are not alone. That other colossus of the modern power state, the USSR, has also specialized in films of social consciousness and has utilized film as a most effective weapon for social reconstruction. There is a significant difference, however. While America has permitted the message film and has often rewarded its birth quite handsomely, the Russians have permitted nothing else. In fact, they have demanded that the movies be subject to the social cause. Any films that tended to neglect or to defame the imposed social ideals were and are labeled "bourgeois," "reactionary," "hooliganistic," "revisionistic," and other such tiresome but frightening terms. Perhaps the book on film theory that argues this position in the most humane and eloquent fashion is John Howard Lawson's *Film: The Creative Process*.[1] Lawson's book is well written, perceptive, and intelligent; but it is so warped by his russophilia that he tends to misinterpret many modern films. Hence, he downgrades the values of the works of Bergman, Antonioni, Fellini, Kurosawa, and most of the directors who are the leaders in the new art of the personal film.

While the primary function of any work of art is to provide vivid aesthetic experience, some works also refer beyond their own qualitied structure. In some arts, such as music or painting, this external functional dimension appears to be slight. In others, such as architecture and film, the dimension of function is of foreground importance. In this chapter, then, I shall be reflecting on the functional dimension of film. I shall use the genre of socialist realism as my analogue. The socially engaged film is a strong and legitimate form. Its best examples are found in humanistic Marxism and semidocumentary realism. Such works not only provide powerful aesthetic experiences but can also be vivid arguments for social change. The danger of the message film, however, is that it may degenerate into abstraction, in which case the message takes precedence over the medium. In such situations, film becomes sloganistic propaganda. Since it is my belief that the functional dimension of film should be incorporated by thematic development, emotional intensity, and personal involvement, I shall be using examples of personal films that also express the social dimension. I will contrast such films to the thin Marxism of the Russian cinema.

The argument that art does and must or does not and must not serve a social function is a very long one. It is stated in its most extreme forms by both Plato and Benedetto Croce, although it must be admitted that Plato, being a greater genius, is not at all consistent in his point of view. The doctrine of the artist as subject to a kind of social king's X can be found in Plato's theory of the artist as an inspired lover of sights and sounds who is stung by the anguish of love. This genius theory is to be found in the *Ion,* the *Phaedrus,* and the *Hippias Major.* But it is not this theory for which Plato is usually castigated in aesthetics. Rather, it is his insistence in the *Republic,* and especially in Book X, that the artist, as any other citizen, should be subject to and can realize himself only in the good of the whole. Hence, if the artist cannot create works in the accepted modes, one that promotes peace and one that promotes courage and resolve, he will be ushered safely to the gates of the city by the guardians and told to practice elsewhere. Art, like everything else in the *Republic,* is subject to moral judgment and evaluation. It must be admitted that Plato is not entirely humorless in this moralistic stance. He has much fun pointing to the Pythagoreans, who torture strings to try to find proper harmonies. In spite of these asides, however, Plato's general attitude toward the enterprise of art is, in the *Republic,* grimly moralistic and authoritarian. This general point of view has often been revived and embodied historically. It is expressed most notably in the views of the Roman Catholic Church and in the artistic theory, as distinguished from the practice, of Leo Tolstoy. Tolstoy's *What Is Art?* might well be viewed as a moralistic Christian theory with a proletarian backbone.

At the other end of the spectrum, one may find the view that art transcends social structures and hence is not subject to their conditions or demands. This is the theory of art for art's sake. This line of thought may also spring from Plato, that is, from his genius theory, which later finds embodiment in Kant, Schelling, Hegel, and Croce. It reaches its clearest formulation in Croce's argument that art is the creation of an intuition and that intuitions, being images, are no more subject to moral judgments than mathematics. It makes as much sense, Croce would say, to talk about an immoral movie as it does to talk about an obscene tetrahedron. Art, being pure transcendent imagination, should be subject only to its own creative rules and should be neither praised nor condemned on the basis of its utilitarian aspects. Arguments in the same spirit may be found in Roger Fry's and Clive Bell's writings concerning "significant form." Both claim that art and painting in particular are to be judged according to their own internal characteristics and that a social dimension or representational element in art is, if not downright pernicious, at least always irrelevant.

The argument for the social obligation and responsibility of art does not spring from this latter tradition but from the tradition of Plato's *Republic*. The reason for this short history was simply to show that, when it comes to matters of principle, there is usually little change through time. The language may change and the emphases may shift from one point to another; but, when it comes to basic principle, there is no great difference between the *Republic,* the writings of Jacques Maritain, and those of John Howard Lawson. When it comes to applying moralistic strictures on works of art, the language of the Catholic Legion of Decency and that of the Communist Party may differ. One will talk about moral decay and the other about bourgeois decadence; but the fervor is at the same high pitch of intensity, and the moral and philosophic perspectives are often indistinguishable one from the other.

The general horizon of the perspective of socialist realism is not difficult to describe. It consists in a firm belief in classes of society. This means not only that the masses exist but also that there is a spirit or mind of the mass, a given entity called "class consciousness." The relationship between classes is disjunctive and inherently antagonistic so that the basic condition is one of conflict. This means that society must be viewed as revolutionary and its conditions as causal and explanatory, the ultimate principle of explanation being one particular type of institutional relation: the economic. The key explanatory principle, then, is viewed as history, and history is the grinding and necessary (thus called by socialist realists "scientific") record of the class struggle of the oppressed and the oppressors. Along with this rather gray and external view of things goes a specific value structure.

The value structure is that the good is to be created in this world by man. Furthermore, the best values are those found in the lower classes. This belief Bertrand Russell has somewhere called the erroneous faith in "the superior virtue of the oppressed." That there is no empirical proof that those at the bottom of society are any more courageous, honest, or psychologically stable is beside the point. In fact, the surveys that show greater psychological breakdown at the lower economic and educational levels are carefully ignored. The reason being, of course, that what one is dealing with in socialist realism is not a scientific theory at all, but a faith. One dogma of the faith is the nobility of labor and the superiority of those who earn their bread by the sweat of their brow. The Puerto Ricans have a saying that if labor were good, the rich would have monopolized it long ago. But such jaundiced observations are no part of socialist realism. On the contrary, the more back-breaking the labor, the more noble it is deemed to be; and one displays virtue by conformity to the group. Hence, self-sacrifice in the name of the masses is considered the proper approach to sainthood.

In aesthetics, the theory is anti-individual and anti-hero. The emphasis is on the heroic, as distinguished from the hero. The hero should be not some man but some group or, better yet, the undistinguished and indistinguishable masses. That which is unique, peculiar, individual, or eccentric should be de-emphasized; and the emphasis should fall upon common characteristics. Since man is viewed abstractly —that is, not as an individual but as a social product constituted by external relations such as causality and economics—the hero should be a type. This gravitation toward the group and the type is often accompanied by sentimentality and poster art, along with a strong sense of universality, which, oddly enough, is easily converted into a kind of earthy nationalism. The socialist-realist artist, of course, sides with all these values, which he considers the "good" ones, although he often, because of his own creativity, is brought into conflict with them. Hence, we find him demanding special dispensation for the artist, as though for him there were a special king's X. Everyone else is one of the masses and he loves them, but the artist would like to view himself as different. In its most brutal form, this is expressed in such tragic situations as the last years of Boris Pasternak, who was hounded to his death for such sins as "revisionist tendencies," "bourgeois decadence," and "hooliganism in the arts."

Of course, one must agree that there is some truth in this point of view. No philosophic perspective could long hold sway or inspire dedication in men if it did not include some truth, for it must not only sway their hearts but also persuade their intellects. One cannot dispute that in this finite world, the rich do have it better. Furthermore, there is no doubt that a completely unfettered capitalism can be as painful and exploitative as a despotic socialist mode of organization. Nor are the socialists wrong in insisting that, although man does not live by bread alone, he cannot live without it. It is foolish to talk about concern for man's spiritual welfare and to have no regard for his social welfare. The spirit must dwell in the body, and it will dwell in the only body it has. Even the churches are slowly beginning to learn some of this truth.

Perhaps the two most attractive characteristics of this doctrine are its basic dynamic outlook and its avowed, though not always realized, compassion. That these ideals are often distorted in practice is often a function of basic institutional rigidity combined with the necessity for bureaucracy when one is attempting to provide order for enormous masses of people. Yet the ideals are basically generous, humane, and life-affirming, whether one finds them stated by Karl Marx, Thomas Jefferson, or Confucius. Though there may always be privilege and discrimination as long as there are institutional structures for the order of society, it is good to attempt to make them flexible and accessible to change. Compassion for humanity may be one of the basic values, since though one may claim a king's X for status in any given society, there is no king's X in life. The one thing all men have in common is suffering. One may well agree with the enthymeme: He is human; therefore, have compassion.

The socialist-realist emphasis on the group at the expense of the individual deprives art of its subtlety and depth. No man is a type. We live from the inside out; and, though it is true that without any externality we could not exist, it is equally true that from our subjectivity springs all that is eccentric, fugitive, mean, or noble. The reduction of the individual to himself-as-other does violence to his individuality. It also fosters a false romanticism for such nonexistent entities as the common man or the people. This romantic movement toward externality is usually accompanied by an inverted puritanism, which takes a rigid and punitive attitude toward human failure. But failure is part of the human condition. The assumption of a totality of meaning, whether God or History, will neither eradicate nor explain it. To place the ultimate principle of explanation in a transcendent, rigid realm is to deprive man of his freedom. And one of man's freedoms is the freedom to fail.

That the film has been more subject to social judgment than have the other arts is an obvious fact. There is no country that does not censor films in some way. The standards of censorship vary greatly, of course, from country to country. Hence, Americans seem most anxious concerning sexual relations, whereas the Swedes are concerned about broken crockery. There are some obvious bases for this concern. One is that film does capture the milieu of a society, not in the sense of reality so much as in the sense of authenticity. Furthermore, film is a popular art and as such is of concern to the established political order. Perhaps as importantly, film is incredibly vivid and infectious. Hence, its very power is a source of anxiety to those who either wish or are obligated to exercise social control. Being a money-making industry, film is as subject to political and social pressures as any other corporate enterprise. Thus, the film industry is often solicited or forced to participate in political causes. The most striking examples would be the thousands of films ground out during wars to bolster the emotional bias of the country and to provide solidarity of purpose and resolve. But such cases, as important as they may be from a political point of view, are not what socialist realism has in mind, since they are basically uses that intensify and consolidate the status quo. The goal of socialist realism is social change through conflict by the exposure of defect in the status quo.

The socialist-realist film is a definite type or genre, and it has as its function not merely the reflection of social distress but also the instigation of social change. One can thus trace its expression from one country to another, as the rigidity or chaos of social conditions brings intellectuals to use film form to argue for reform. During the late 1930s, America was the home for a series of such films, ranging from the semihumorous melodrama, such as *Mr. Deeds Goes to Washington,* to the biting insights of *The Grapes of Wrath.* After the second World War, there was a brief flurry of social films, which dealt with postwar or racial problems fairly honestly. Such films as *The Men, Champion, Home of the Brave, Intruder in the Dust, The Best Years of Our Lives* are all of this type. Some of the more honest films such as *The Southerner* caused little impact, and some sheer potboilers of the inauthentic like *Pinky* were very well received. The furor of excessive patriotism and the sad history of blacklisting turned the American film from the protest concerning economic problems more onto the social plane and tended to force those films that were made into weak statement or emotional cop-out—a leading characteristic of Stanley Kramer's later films. Success may have had something to do with this also, for the more successful one becomes in Hollywood, the more he tends to play it safe. Still, this genre of film has not disappeared in America. It is still made, as it was in the 1940s and 1950s, although at that time it was done in different form as in the comedies of Preston Sturges or in a Western setting as in *High Noon* or *The Ox-Bow Incident.*

The fame of the modern Italian motion picture began with the socialist-realist films that sprang from the disorganization following the second World War, and this movement produced many masterpieces. *Open City* and *Paisan* were the beginnings, but the genre reached its high points in more structured films such as *Shoeshine, The Bicycle Thief, Il Grido,* and *I Vitelloni.* Besides the superb *Umberto D,* it also fostered potboilers such as *Bitter Rice* or incredibly dull Marxian essays such as *La Terra Trema.* Another outcome was the excess melodrama of *Rocco and His Brothers* and the small honesty of *Il Posto.* The Italian neo-realist movement has followed the American pattern and fled into the excellent black humor of *Divorce, Italian Style* or the overblown baroque of *La Dolce Vita.* Again, political and church pressure had something to do with this change of course, but one has the feeling that the fervor of social commitment runs a bit deeper in Italy and that it will spring forth once again.

Outside of individual countries, there are certain directors who excel in this mode regardless of where their films are produced or directed. Luis Buñuel is the most striking example of this group. It can be said that Jean Renoir might also fit into this category, particularly if one regards such films as *The Southerner, The River, The Rules of the Game* and *Grand Illusion.* While one can point to certain films such as *The Four Hundred Blows, Zero for Conduct,* and *The Wages of Fear,* nevertheless, France has not been especially strong in socialist realism. The same may be said of Germany. The young film makers of Poland and Czechoslovakia, however, have excelled in this genre with such films as *Ashes and Diamonds, Knife in the Water, Closely Watched Trains,* and *The Shop on Main Street.* Sweden, true to its tradition, has stuck to the moods of internality.

The British socialist-realist films were born after the second World War by a conjunction of the documentary tradition and protest against the Establishment. In this sense, they were a product not of social chaos but of the rigidity of an outmoded order, and they have been used as a tool to try to render institutional structure more flexible. The British films have a hardness and a coolness that are not so characteristic of their Italian and American counterparts. It is not that the British film makers cared any less, it was merely that they possessed better technique than the Italians and more objectivity than the Americans. Hence, they produced such fine films as *Saturday Night and Sunday Morning, This Sporting Life, The Loneliness of the Long Distance Runner, Room at the Top, A Taste of Honey, Sparrows Can't Sing, King and Country,* and the flawed but nevertheless moving *The Entertainer* and *Look Back in Anger.* There were also the less impressively mounted but moving films such as *The War Lover, The Man Upstairs,* and *Hand in Hand.* One of these films, *The Angry Silence,* was so direct and forceful that it brought immediate political and social pressure. In general, the British films were more bleak and pessimistic than those of other countries, though they were not immune from the emotional cop-out either, as is evidenced by *The Key.* The same might be said for the ending of the fine film *Bridge on the River Kwai.* Realism with the function of social criticism and reconstruction has been the driving force of much of modern British film. Most of the rest of production has been dedicated to bright and brittle comedy with a strong fey streak. But whether in comedy or social criticism, the British films are notable for their lack of sentimentality. The British, like the Americans and unlike the Italians, tended to use actors with previous experience either from film or theatre or both. Hence, their films placed more emphasis upon story and upon personal relationships than upon the social circumstance.

The perpetual rebirth of the social-message film and its emergence in country after country establish it as a viable and legitimate film genre with a history and development of its own. Furthermore, the fact that these films not only gained critical success but that many of them made tidy profits shows that the motion-picture public does not always prefer to go to Western Union for its messages. The Soviet Union was the one country that began its film industry in this vein and never changed. The first explosion of the Russian film was a magnificent outpouring of fine work by Sergei Eisenstein, V. I. Pudovkin, Alexander Dovzhenko, and others. But the socialist-realist doctrine soon became a dogma in the Soviet Union, and Russian films have done little but become weaker since the explosion of the 1920s. One cannot honestly compare *The Forty-ninth, The Cranes Are Flying,* or *Ballad of a Soldier* favorably with such films as *Potemkin.*

Potemkin was originally entitled *1905,* and the revolt of the sailors was conceived as a minor incident in a large panoramic film (à la Griffith's *The Birth of a Nation*), which would attempt to cover the entire Russian revolution. Fortunately, Eisenstein became carried away by his own theme and in particular by the Odessa Steps sequence, so that the result was a highly condensed work of art. In a sense, then, *Potemkin* is a happy accident; and, as all art, it succeeds in converting chance into overwhelming necessity on its own terms. *Potemkin* may well be one of the most admired and most analyzed films ever made. Eisenstein uses it as the paradigm example in most of his writing, and it has been exhaustively written about by many others. Even Joseph Goebbels referred to it as the standard of excellence when he was urging Nazi film makers to produce higher quality films. Everyone seems to agree that *Potemkin* is a masterpiece. Why is it a masterpiece?

It is a masterpiece of film because it is a deliberate construction that succeeds in transmitting the emotional intensity of immediacy. Eisenstein discovered a truth that holds in art but not in logic: The parts must cease to be parts and become elements. The function of elements is to retain their own weight and at the same time to express the whole. Eisenstein achieved the transformation of the parts into elements and the elements into expressive modes of the whole by the use of concentration. The essence of *Potemkin* is cumulative impact built through the conflict of images that are condensed into the tension of theme. This film is closer to an orchestration than it is to a drama. It has the appearance of a documentary, the appearance of history happening, but it is neither. It is an imaginative interpretation of documentary content with careful selection of the weight, rhythm, and force of the elements so that they combine into one rhythmic, unified whole. It has a slight story element, but the theme predominates. In short, *Potemkin* is a visual poem.

In his analysis of the film, Eisenstein tells us that it consists of five main parts: (1) Men and Maggots, (2) Drama on the Quarter Deck, (3) The Dead Cries Out, (4) The Odessa Steps, (5) The Meeting of the Squadron. This structure is composed of deliberate progressions and reversals with a caesura between Parts 1 and 2. At the same time, there are two progressive lines of movement, that of the people in the city and that of the men on the ship. These lines are unified at various points, for example, by the dead sailor and by the small boats carrying food to the sailors. Eisenstein does not attempt to expand the action beyond the meeting of the fleet and thus holds the concentration of tension within a limited form, making the dual revolt a symbol of the revolution as whole. The much praised Odessa Steps sequence is the heart of the film, for it embodies both the suspense of the personal destiny of the individuals and the thematic tension of the crowd. The emphasis is upon the interplay of these two elements. Eisenstein here abandons natural time and expands the Steps sequence by montage in order to concentrate its emotional intensity. This cumulative tension and release is no accident; it is a deliberate construction created by editing. The rhythms of close-shot–long-shot and the upward and downward surges of the people on the steps are controlled in the order of increasing intensity. And the shots of the elements included—the glasses, the boots, the carriage, the baby, the mother, the guns, the movements and counter-movements —are all selected for their emotional impact as well as for their visual urgency.

Eisenstein was a master of montage: the deliberate selecting and intercutting of film shots to create one cumulative emotional impact. It is a method designed to bring out the visibility of actuality once it has ceased to be possibility, hence one has the feeling of necessity. *Potemkin* is an extension and intensification of the immediate and unforeseen. It begins with the sailors complaining about their food, and the total episode becomes expressive of the whole revolution. Eisenstein tends to overemphasize environment, but he is the master of transmitting a single emotional quality through organized impact, thus making us see what we would not see were we actual members of the revolt. Yet we *feel* as though we were members, not witnesses. The Odessa Steps sequence reverses the horizon and foreground and we no longer feel that this is a picture about a revolt, but that it *is* the revolt itself. This seeming-to-be is its authenticity and indicates eloquently that Eisenstein was a master of illusions.

Potemkin is thus not so much a story as a symphony, not so much an episode as a variation on a theme. Although it includes the allusive indeterminacy of reality as experienced, it transforms that indeterminacy into clarity through style. Eisenstein later became enchanted by his own discoveries of cumulation, expansion, condensation, and montage to the extent that the formalistic elements of his later films, and particularly their emphasis upon the mass with the neglect of the personal elements, vitiated his power. Once he deserted the affective balance of *Potemkin,* his films also lost their effective impact on the audience. Ironically, this strange genius of socialist realism became a cinematic formalist.

Motion pictures today have moved away from Eisenstein's method and have become more personal, more concerned with individual destiny, more subjective, and more idiosyncratic. Yet the influence of Eisenstein has not been lost. I do not mean by this that the critics who still advocate montage as the only true essence of films are correct. Montage in Eisenstein's sense is merely one of many techniques. What I mean is that Eisenstein moved the film from the impersonal panoramic technicalities of Griffith to a more personal and intense plane and that his techniques of editing, counterpoint, fusion, and rhythm still exert much influence today. One may find these elements in the films of Fellini, Kurosawa, Ray, and many others. Think, for example, of the water-bug ballet that is used as a coda in *Pather Panchali* or the dissolve and montage of lights in the transition from the motion-picture theatre to the intensely tender scene inside the carriage in *The World of Apu.* Such uses of rhythms and their arrangements of dominant and overtone shots show that Ray and the other directors, like the Eisenstein of *Potemkin,* shoot not merely with their heads but also with their hearts.

Now, it is important to try to grasp how Eisenstein went astray in his later films; for, if we can understand this, we will then be able to see the meaning of the running argument between Eisenstein and Pudovkin. We shall also be able to understand some of the weaknesses that appear later in Lawson's theory, for his theory is basically a synthesis of the concepts of Eisenstein and Marx. We must put aside Eisenstein's personal problems in life and the political pressures on him. Undoubtedly, the political pressures specifically affected his work, most notably in terms of content. But to claim that Stalinist pressure dictated not merely the choice of subject matter but the form, style, and tone of his later motion pictures is to claim too much and to provide too easy an explanation. Even though these pressures may have had great effect on him, they still do not explain the direction of his practice or the practice of his direction following *Potemkin.*

The key to this development, I believe, can be found in the phrase I used when I said that Eisenstein's films progressively lost *affective* balance. The mark of an artist is simply this: He is a person who refuses to separate the look from the feel of things. Eisenstein became progressively enchanted with the look of things at the expense of their feel, and he then became absorbed in playing with the arrangements possible by shifting the appearances around. His films thus show a progressive movement away from the human, a progressive movement toward the visually abstract. In short, his films become external portrayals, and the actors find themselves not engaged in a world but simply thrown into a world where everything merely happens around them. Milieu is turned into environment, the horizon becomes the foreground, and man is lost.

This movement toward externality and away from the individual as the concrete person, let alone the individualized expression of the internal meaning of external circumstance, is evident when Eisenstein comments on the storm scene in *King Lear* and contrasts two methods of presenting emotion.

The simplest method is to present on the screen a human being in a state of ecstasy, that is, a character who is gripped by some emotion, who is "beside himself." A more complicated and more effective method is the realization of the main condition of a work of pathos—constant qualitative changes in the action—not through the medium of one character but through the entire environment. . . . A classical example of this method is the storm raging in the breast of King Lear and everywhere around him in nature.[2]

What Eisenstein fails to see is that these methods are not exhaustive, nor are they necessarily exclusive. One of the strengths of film as a medium is that it can reveal the inner as outer and the outer as inner. Antonioni's sure sense of how to use external circumstance to express the inner state of his actors is the great strength of his films. The problem is not to depersonalize man but to personalize things. When this general direction of thought toward the impersonal is conjoined with Eisenstein's inveterate belief in novel quality produced by the conflict of images, one can see how he came to turn more and more toward the formalistic arrangement of the image and away from the human world. He began to substitute the visual clash for emotional unity. He separated the feel of things from their look and became intellectual, that is, combined things according to their external relations. Thus was poetry lost. But quality can also be emergent. It need not depend on clash.

Both Pudovkin and Eisenstein were advocates of montage. Both were convinced that film was *par excellence* a director's medium, since the director was the center of control and specifically the center of editing. Pudovkin stated the importance of editing with characteristic bluntness in the first sentence of his introduction to the German edition of *Film Technique:* "The foundation of film art is *editing.*"[3] Where they diverged was on the point of what montage should be and how editing should be used. Eisenstein insisted that the essence of montage was conflict and that the purpose of editing was to extend this conflict into external circumstance. Pudovkin, however, insisted that it was not the collision of images that was important but their linkage, and that this linkage should be an emotional one. Hence, for him, montage was to be properly used when it converted external appearance into a symbol of the inner consciousness of man. Thus, he argued that the film actor can be more personal and more subtle in his acting, for he does not need to use the heightened voice and intensified gestures of the stage actor. Though the theatre actor has various advantages, such as rehearsals and the continuity of the play, to enhance maximum linkage of himself with the part, such linkage is possible also in film and is the essence of every art. Pudovkin said, "A concrete feeling of connection between the individuality and the image to be created is normal and essential for the creative process in every art."[4]

Pudovkin viewed the photograph as merely the raw material of film but film itself as a concrete and moving phenomenon; hence, he insisted that "every object must, by editing, be brought upon the screen so that it shall have not *photographic,* but *cinematographic* essence."[5] The writings which claimed that the images of people should be treated as mere images and composed as one might compose a sequence of photographs of trees or cars, Pudovkin referred to as pure theory. The word "theory" for the practical Pudovkin was simply a swear word; hence, he insisted that the true function of the image is to reveal the inner state and particularly the inner states of men. The image must not be seen as a *property* of a person but as an expression of and enhancement of his being. Thus, Pudovkin stated that the "living person must not only not be eliminated in the process" of editing, "must not only be preserved, but must be brought out; and if this bringing out be not realistic, that is, not unified and alive, in the end the man in the film will be a great deal more lifeless than the aeroplane."[6] Pudovkin thus viewed the goal of film and one of its strongest characteristics as the ability to unify the external and the internal circumstance of man. This, he believed, reveals the superiority of cinema.

> On the stage the actor will tell of a flight, in literature the author will add to the tale a description of the circumstances exterior to the inward emotions of the person flying, but only the cinema can unite for the benefit of the spectator the direct and fullest sensation of both.[7]

In this running argument between the two great Russian directors, I must side with Pudovkin. He has eloquently stated the principle of revelation. The problem is not how to dehumanize man but how to personalize things. But Pudovkin does not go far enough.

Let us examine a Pudovkin quote, and perhaps the point I am attempting to make will become clear.

> In my earlier film, *Mother,* I tried to affect the spectators, not by the psychological performances of an actor, but by plastic synthesis through editing. The son sits in prison. Suddenly, passed in to him surreptitiously, he receives a note that next day he is to be set free. The problem was the expression, filmically, of his joy. The photographing of a face lighting up with joy would have been flat and void of effect. I show, therefore, the nervous play of his hands and a big close-up of the lower half of his face, the corners of the smile. These shots I cut in with other and varied material—shots of a brook, swollen with the rapid flow of spring, of the play of sunlight broken on the water, birds splashing in the village pond, and finally the laughing child. By the

junction of these components our expression of "prisoner's joy" takes shape. I do not know how the spectators reacted to my experiment—I myself have always been deeply convinced of its force.[8]

Now, it is not surprising that Pudovkin was moved by his own creation; this is true of all creators whether they be parents or painters. After all, it was Pudovkin who conceived this sequence. The problem with it is just that: It was *conceived,* that is, thought. But it was not thought through clearly enough for its emotional overtones or in terms of the relevance of the various shots to the circumstance of the actor. What has an unknown child to do with the prisoner? Had it been *his* child or a member of his family or even a member of his village, it would have been more relevant and would have carried more emotional weight. But merely being "some child in general smiling" it is bound to the main character merely externally to try to portray, but not to reveal, his inner state.

One has the same reaction to this sequence that one does to the sudden pan up to the bird (mentioned in the last chapter) which Terry and Denis Sanders use in *Crime and Punishment U.S.A.* to try to express the hope in their hero. The feeling is that the image is trite. The triteness comes not from the fact that birds are bad symbols but because the relationship between the man and the bird is not made relevant enough. When Joseph Losey cuts from the trial scene in *King and Country* to a concurrent trial in the mud with soldiers "trying" the rats they have just flushed forth from some bloated horse, the ironic mock trial enhances the human one. Losey has previously established the malcreant rat by having one drop on a soldier's bunk. He had previously established the mud and the boredom of the soldiers and had tied their situation in with that of the man on trial. Hence, the cut seems natural and does not appear forced. The sequence serves as a bitter and ironic commentary as well as an extension in depth of the trial of the man. The intercutting of such shots as the spider in its web, the dew on the grass, and the joyous sunlight in the montage sequence of *Occurrence at Owl Creek Bridge* expresses the joy of the prisoner's imagined escape, because, had he escaped, these things would have been part of his world, and he is escaping into them and with them in the split-second of imagination. Had Pudovkin's prisoner, on the other hand, imaged this sequence as *his* sequence, his future release, it would have been more effective. But since his given condition, imprisonment, is static, the images do not fit his rocklike situation. Such montage can be highly effective when the psychological performance of the actor is not ignored but is on the contrary elicited and then this performance is fused with montage elements that are relevant to either the actor's actual or imagined circumstance. But images-in-general fail to carry the emotional core of unity that is necessary in spite of their presumed objectivity. Pudovkin's difficulty is that he has tried to think in terms of images of what might be felt by a man; but what we demand as spectators is not merely that the director has thought of images but that he has felt them through to their artistic relevance. We demand images that are expressive of *this* man and this man's world, whether lived or imagined.

In the horrible but beautiful dream sequence in *Los Olvidados,* the images carry the immediacy of conviction and the vividness of revelation. We see the excessive slow motion of the mother bounding forward in the boy's dream carrying a large slab of cut meat. We do not raise the question of the objectivity of the images, for we sense their rightness with respect to the psychological experience of this boy. We do not need to translate these images into an intellectual context ("the boy feels that his mother is a whore") but simply accept them as revelatory of the world into which the boy has been thrown and with which he is engaged. The same may be said of the beautifully photographed and edited Nevers sequences in *Hiroshima Mon Amour.* We are not concerned one way or another about their *objectivity* but about their rightness to context. In fact, we know that the woman is objectively in Japan, not in France, and it is precisely this objective knowledge which adds poignancy to the fact that she is carrying Nevers with her. What we are struck by is the fact that these images are so right for this woman. They add the emotional depth of the theme of the film, which is not the intellectual meaning of war or Hiroshima or death. The theme of this film is the problem of how this particular, individual woman can come to terms with her brutal memories and try to cope with her given world. The rest is background. What Buñuel and Resnais have done in these instances is not to present a world, but to allow us—nay, force us—through vision, to enter into *the* lived world of their main characters. That lived world, like the lived world of us all, is a mixture of both the imaginative and objective planes. In art, it is more than a mixture; it is a synthesis.

John Howard Lawson's book *Film: The Creative Process* is, as I have said, so right on so many things that it does not seem proper to criticize it. Lawson is correct in insisting that the essence of film is motion. He is sound in maintaining that film, unlike theatre, demands that plot be secondary to theme. He is right in his general description of film form as cumulative development, usually as conflict-in-motion. He is correct in identifying one of the basic problems of film as defining the relations of the individual to the group and to the world. But Lawson's basic perspective is a mixture of the theories of Marx and Eisenstein with a movement toward those of Pudovkin; and this mixture commits him to a theoretical strait-jacket of objectivity and, when it comes to the human world, abstraction. Furthermore, this prior commitment renders the tone of his concepts literally and figuratively too red, that is, too forceful. Thus, when Lawson has a choice between progression and suspense, between development and conflict, between articulation and clash, he invariably chooses the most revolutionary mode of description. It must be admitted that many films can be adequately described in his terms. But there are quiet films. To talk of such quiet films, with their slow rhythms of articulation, as composed of clashes or revolutionary jumps in quality, is literally to do violence to their rhythms.

It is quite clear what Lawson is attempting to do both on the political and on the aesthetic level. In both cases, he is trying to move theory away from the abstraction of the type and to the concrete person. Thus, he quotes Marx as stating:

> It is not the consciousness of human beings that determines their existence, but, conversely, it is their social existence that determines their consciousness.[9]

He immediately follows this with a more concrete quote from Engels:

> Men make their own history, whatever its outcome may be, in that each person follows his consciously desired end, and it is precisely the resultant of these many wills operating in different directions and of their manifold effects upon the outer world that constitute history . . . What are the historical causes which transform themselves into these motives in the brains of the actors?[10]

But it is equally relevant to ask, "What are the motives that are transformed into historical causes and external circumstance through the medium of behavior?" It is quite true that we all live on the outside. It is also true that man's behavior is dependent on and often sharply conditioned by external circumstance. But behavior is also a function of man's wishes, hopes, dreams, aspirations, and choices. A man reduced merely to a system of external relations is a thing, not a man. Like Pudovkin, Lawson believes that the function of film art is to condense external circumstance into the personal situation. But, also like Pudovkin, he does not go far enough. The problem is not to condense circumstance into "the human" or man-in-general, but to condense it into the lived world of this specific individual.

The relationships between an individual and his embodiment, that is, his lived world, are particular and are peculiarly intimate. The individual personifies his world. Through his behavior he flows out into his world, and it, in turn, permeates and constitutes him. To a great extent, the relations are casual. One defect of the

Marxist perspective is that the casual must be hypostatized into the causal. Hence, the Marxist does not see the individual in his intimacy with his world but sees a semiabstraction, the man, opposed to another semiabstraction, the environment. Since the Marxist has two entities constituted by a kind of external self-containment, he must then describe their relation. The relation becomes causal, and the causality is usually described as unidirectional. Hence, the problem for him is not how do people world, but how "human personality is shaped by human history." This commitment to the abstract relation of causation and externality weakens Lawson's film theory and brings him to misunderstand the meanings of *L'Avventura, Hiroshima Mon Amour,* and *Wild Strawberries.* It also brings him to place a film that is only fairly successful, *Ballad of a Soldier,* in a position superior to the much more successful *Wild Strawberries.* Let us examine these films, both from Lawson's point of view and ours.

By almost any standards, *L'Avventura* must be regarded as a masterpiece of film making, at least by the standards of unity, rhythm, visual beauty, and sensitivity. Yet, though he is very sensitive to the film, Lawson downgrades it, for it does not fit his standards of socialist realism. Hence, he cites *Il Grido* as Antonioni's "most lucid film," not because it has the best construction or the greatest inventiveness and sensitivity, but because it deals with the problems of the working class. But surely this is to misunderstand and foreclose any grasp of the subtle movements that have been taking place in Antonioni's work. Viewing his works as a whole, one can see that they move away from the abstraction of socialist realism into the realm of personal feeling, with a gradual turn toward the redemptive possibility of behavior. *Il Grido* is an external statement of socialist realism. The next three films, *L'Avventura, La Notte,* and *L'Eclisse,* are adventures into the personal psyche of women, as is *Red Desert.* With *Blow-Up,* a man emerges as the central person, and the shift, which has been subtle but evident in the preceding films, is away from sheer pity as a foundation for the human relationship of behavior.

Lawson feels that the message of the modern film is a sustained attack on society and the revelation of the collapse of bourgeois values. Thus, he picks the films of Luis Buñuel as superior to those of Antonioni and specifically praises *Los Olvidados* and *Viridiana* for their vivid attacks on society and the church. Buñuel is a great director; there can be no doubt about that. He never throws anything away. But the difference between his films and those of Antonioni is the difference between dogmatism and searching. Buñuel has attained a dogmatic social position and a self-confident atheism, which allow him to speak with less vengeance and stridency in his later films. He has become, if one can ever say this of such a revolutionary, more relaxed; and his films have improved, for they have greater sureness of tone and less overt propaganda. Both *Los Olvidados* and *Viridiana* are exceptional films. No one else could have made them or have made them as well. But unless one is committed to a Marxist position and hence to a common faith in the efficacy and ultimate truth of atheism, it is not at all clear that one must choose settled self-confidence as a value superior to the agonizing search. A search can be as moving and as meaningful as a solution. In fact, it may be more meaningful, since it shows that the mind is still open and all the conclusions are not forgone. Buñuel is explicitly attacking bourgeois values, but it is not so apparent that this is Antonioni's goal or method in the films following *Il Grido*.

It is not apparent for two reasons. One is that all art, since it is the creation of a value system on its own terms, is a deviation from and hence often viewed as a criticism of the status quo. Antonioni's films are a criticism of the aridity of modern society and the attendant psychological frustration for the individual, but his solution is not one of the "holy" working-class values. In fact, his later films deal almost entirely with the educated and often wearily wealthy elite, and it is only Hemmings' short sojourn in the poorhouse that brings a working-class element into *Blow-Up*. The second reason it is not apparent is this: The differences between most so-called bourgeois values and socialist values are negligible. Both emphasize the reconstruction of the world as the salvation of the individual. Both view work as holy and self-sacrifice as noble, and, most importantly, both view man as though he were a thing, externally. Hence, it would be as valid to say that Antonioni's films are a criticism of socialist values as of bourgeois values. Antonioni is trying to work toward a personal statement of values, which will differ from both. The problems of personal meaning are not confined to the NATO countries. Antonioni could as well have had his background that of Kazakhstan as of an extinct volcanic island.

Lawson is quite right in seeing that Antonioni is presenting in *L'Avventura* a world in which a universe of feeling has been diminished and almost extinguished. But he is misleading when he interprets this to mean that "guilt is inherent in the bourgeois social condition" and that Sandro and Claudia are finally forced to face the "guilt of their alienation from life." What they are forced to face is the *fact* of their alienation from life and their alienation from each other. They are forced to face the shallowness of their relationship, and there is a slight hope in that last scene that through the recognition of their finite limitations they may be able to overcome their separation through a sense of mutual pity. This final scene is not sentimental; but it does indicate that Claudia may, through her energy and openness, be able to break down Sandro's self-frustrating barriers.

Lawson objects that the compassion is entirely on the woman's side, but for these people, it is the way it should be. If Sandro could deliberately and with malice "accidentally" overturn the ink pot of the young artist who personifies his own self-rejection of his ability to come to terms with his world, obviously the ability to attain self-awareness and regeneration must come from the other person. Furthermore, it is right that the woman should be the one who comes to this insight, for she is more emotionally sensitive and the only one capable of changing the situation, not by dynamite but by the gentle wearing of the waters of compassion on the rock of indifference. Lawson even quotes Guido Aristarco approvingly:

> It has been suggested that Antonioni's emphasis on the woman's deeper consciousness of moral values may be related to her more "independent" position in bourgeois society. She is less entangled in the production process, and may be less directly affected by corrupting influences.[11]

That is sheer balderdash. It is not washing machines, automobiles, wigs, false eyelashes, or even things as "necessary as neckties and taxicabs" that are at stake in *L'Avventura*. *L'Avventura* is not a diatribe against the beautiful "dollar bringing virgins" from Cincinnati or the sweet, "nujol-needing Americans." What is at stake is the possibility of the attainment by these two particular people of the goods of the spirit, not the goods of objective society.

Though Lawson has himself been trying to move film theory and practice away from the excessive objectivity of Marx and Eisenstein to the more personal level of Pudovkin and, he claims but I do not, Chukhrai, it is the true movement into the personal world that he finally calls *the* flaw in Antonioni's films:

> . . . it also points to the flaw in the design: these people are concerned *only* with emotional fulfillment. Their sickness is social, but they are trying to cure it in personal terms. In this sense, women enjoy a greater "freedom" than men.[12]

With his precommitment to a fixed socialist-bourgeois value system and moralistic externality, Lawson probably could not have said otherwise.

Of course these people are concerned with emotional fulfillment, since, being members of the semielite, they already have the external goods of life. It does not follow, however, that this is all they are or are capable of being concerned with. Nor does it follow that their sickness is therefore external and social. In fact, if we are to believe J. S. Mill, it is quite the opposite. One deals with personal problems in personal terms; and, if these can be resolved even tenuously, then one may be able to express them outward. Sandro and Claudia would not be "cured" by joining the Peace Corps. But if they can establish, through openness and compassion to one another, a true, even if transient, human relation of permeability, they then might or might not take up some social cause. One thing is certain. Unless and until they can become even halfway honest with each other and therefore to themselves, they cannot be honest with their world on any terms, regardless of the idealism of their external relations. Persons, even alienated ones, come before causes. And causes have meaning only in terms of persons. Recenter the casual world, and the causal one can be engaged and transformed.

It is true that if one worries about plot in the accepted sense and continues to moon over what happened to Anna, *L'Avventura* will make no sense as a film. But this does not prove, as Lawson believes it does, that its characters are therefore weak and are cut off from reality. On the contrary, their incidents and situations are articulations of the theme of the film: the search for the being of an other, how to be-with in this given, personal world. The way in which Antonioni uses the most objective reality, a mountain and a brick wall, to reveal the inner states of his individuals shows precisely and adequately in *visual terms* who, where, and what these people are and are to each other. There is even hope in the transvestism or transwiggism of the scene between Claudia and Anna, for we have the hope that the less capricious and more well-grounded Claudia will be able to break through her exterior and that of Sandro. Lawson's objection that her response is passive and hence "forbids any larger extension of her experience"[13] is particularly inept. Her passivity is the whole point. It is through the weakness of her strength that she will be able to extend both her experience and that of Sandro, and only through it. It was not our better angels that built a wall, nor did they know what they were walling in or out. As Lao-tzu said: Nothing can withstand the force of water.

Antonioni has made what is perhaps one of the most lucid statements of what his films and, by extension, many modern films are about. Lawson quotes him:

> The truth of our daily lives is neither mechanical, conventional nor artificial, as stories generally are, and if films are made that way they will show it. The rhythm of life is not made up of one steady beat; it is, instead, a rhythm that is sometimes fast, sometimes slow: it remains motionless for awhile, then at the next moment it starts spinning round. . . . The important thing is this: that our acts, our gestures, our words are nothing more than the consequences of our own personal situation in relation to the world around us.[14]

But since Lawson hears only one rhythm, the "International" in full beat, he misinterprets the meaning of this quote and says that Antonioni is showing us merely feeling "atrophied when it is cut off from its source and meaning—outside ourselves."[15] Antonioni is showing us man and woman alone, but he is at the same time searching for how they can come together, truly together with each other and then their world. *Blow-Up* shows that he believes this to be possible by reorientation within the self. Today myself, tomorrow my world, and the tomorrow and tomorrow afterward: the world.

Lawson complains of the lack of plot and story in modern times, but it is merely his conception of plot or story that is at fault. By definition, for him, plot and story must be external to the person and cannot be revelatory of the inner rhythms of the individual. But this is to miss the basic meaning of many modern films and to miss one of the things that film can do and that other media have difficulty doing: use technology to bypass the bodily other and to reveal the inner relations of beings. The modern film is not, as he says, "concerned with the description of states of feeling rather than the sights and sounds of the visible world."[16] On the contrary, it is concerned with *presenting* the movements of feeling in their very surge by using the visible world as a symbol. Painting and sculpture are concerned with capturing the moment of revelation; film is presenting the movement of revelation.

This insistence on externality brings Lawson to miss the point of *Hiroshima Mon Amour*. In this case, he mistakes location for reality. Hence, he claims that "the connection between the lovers and the bombing of Hiroshima is real, because they are in the city where the destruction took place and the emotion which bridges the gap in time is a response to their environment."[17] But there is no "gap in time" for the Japanese lover. Nevers is no less real *in time* than Hiroshima for being geographically remote. It may be that Hiroshima has intensified the woman's anxieties, but it is not what triggers them. What sends her to her problem—and this is what the film is about, *her* problem—is her viewing of her sleeping lover. This brings the quick cut to Nevers and the lover of the past. She cannot come to terms with the one before her on the bed until she has buried the dead. In this sense, she uses her Japanese lover for some direct and indirect therapy. Of course the cut "portrays her inability to accept present reality, her sense of loss, her intense alienation. This is the explosive element *between* the shots. The external drama, the real problems of the living woman and the living man, are drowned in a flood of inner feeling"[18] because that is what the film is *about;* that's *her* problem. Not until she can come to terms with her memory can she can come to terms with her lover or her world. The outer world precipitates a movement to an inner world, which is culminated in a return to and transformation of the relation to the outer world. That is plot, though it is not plot in the way Lawson wants to define it. In fact, it is the very irreversibility of objective time that intensifies the urgency of the woman's decision. The tension between external and internal time is the major theme of Alain Resnais and Marguerite Duras.

This insistence that progression in a film must be objective and not merely emotional (as though there were some magical surgical tool by which they could be so easily separated) brings Lawson to misinterpret the ending of *Hiroshima.*

> In *Hiroshima,* the denouement shows the lovers separating as the woman leaves for France. There are many practical, prosaic reasons for this separation. [It is not clear what Lawson means by this, but presumably adultery should have a better excuse from his point of view.] But the preceding progression tries to provide an unconvincing and abstract barrier to their passion. It attempts to extend the love story to include a lifetime of thwarted and "pure" emotion, but each closeup of the man and woman in the tearoom testify to the failure of the effort.[19]

They separate, not because of a blockage of "pure" emotions by vivid past memories, but because the woman *has grown up.* She no longer needs the man as a sounding board for her own emotions; and, having buried her memories, she is capable once more of making her own decisions. The barrier is not "that she knows nothing of Hiroshima" or that her love for the German was so "pure" that it cannot be matched. The barrier is that now she has learned to walk on her own, and she can discard her crutch—made in Japan. Once she has decided in the bathroom scene in the hotel *not* to commit suicide, she is on her way, wherever that way may go. This same bias toward things brings Lawson to rank an interesting but in many ways inferior film, *Ballad of a Soldier,* as superior to Ingmar Bergman's best: *Wild Strawberries.*

Lawson believes that *Wild Strawberries* is seriously flawed for two basic reasons: (1) it lacks the "tough substance of real experience" and (2) it misuses time. Let us let Lawson speak and then we will examine what he says:

> (1) *Wild Strawberries* is weakened by its concentration on the professor's dreams and reveries, which lack the tough substance of real experience; the film never touches the causes or effects of his failure, which remains self-contained and self-defeating.[20]

Here again we see Lawson's commitment to abstract externality leading him to immediate misconception. The whole point of the articulation of Isak Borg's situation is that the causes are effects, and the effects are in turn causes; and the dream mode, by its very fluidity, establishes this at the outset. The film appears self-contained and self-defeating precisely because it is an articulation of Borg's being, and his very being is self-contained and hence self-defeating. That's his problem. And that's the "cause." But the film as a whole is not so negative as this. Borg finally does rise to a higher level of consciousness and, more importantly, emotional commitment. He engages himself between his son and daughter; he advises against an abortion and tries to affect their lives. Though there is an ironic twist with the maid, he realizes that, as long as he has breath left, he can do something. He has escaped death before he dies.

As to the usage of time, Lawson again:

> (2) In *Wild Strawberries,* there are moments when the gap between past and present is visualized on the screen. The professor sits eating wild strawberries near the house where he lived as a young man, and it is suddenly transformed; the sun glitters on the windows and curtains sway in a gentle breeze. Isak sees his cousin as a girl; he calls, "Sara . . . It's me, your cousin Isak . . ." But she cannot hear him across the years . . . his emotion as an old man looking back is made more poignant by the passage of years.
>
> However, in the film as a whole, the insistence on Isak's inability to feel or communicate with others makes the time pattern repetitious and static. The imminence of death is the theme of the film, expressed at the beginning in Isak's dream of his own funeral. Isak searches the past to justify his life before it ends, but there can be no justification because there is not energizing passion in his life. . . . The idea that his spirit (his real self) is dead negates the past movement of time and reduces the tension concerning his approaching death.[21]

But the theme of the film is not the imminence of death, the theme is the *presence* of death. Isak is already dead in dream, dead in his emotions, dead in his external relations to others, dead and empty in the center of his being. His body moves through the world; his superego still holds tightly to his consciousness; but his personality is dead. The problem of the film is whether he can be resurrected as a human being before his total demise. Hence, again, the inevitability, the irreversibility, the urgency of "objective time" in tension with his internal time on several levels intensify the conflict of times and build the pressure of the form. It is, in fact, "the idea that his spirit (his real self) is dead" that negates past movement, for the past is past and, because it is so, intensifies the urgency of the present. Since the past is irretrievably gone yet currently functional and the future is pressingly evident, the tensions build over the present; they cumulate and collapse into the present; and the spectator is gripped by the inescapable question: "Will Professor Borg live, if only for a brief moment, before he dies? *Can* he choose, can he become engaged, can he open up?"

What Lawson cites as weaknesses are truly the strengths of the film. Bergman succeeds beyond hope, and that is why this is probably his greatest film. It is a film in which all things count, and they count because they are interwoven on several levels to intensify and articulate not merely the aspects but the crisis of Borg's present. Furthermore, it is a film that is essentially suited to the temperaments of Bergman and his protagonist, for, in spite of its alleged subjectivity, its tone is cool, cold, and objective. Bergman is a poet. But he is a poet of ice, not of fire. He is an intellectual film maker, and he speaks through the eye to the mind and then to the heart. He does not speak through the heart to the mind.

Though the particular and intense problem of this film is whether this individual, the honored professor—and he is honored as an other by the ceremony at the end, by the young people's serenade, and by the gas station attendant—will come to life before there is no longer any chance and hence no choice, the more general theme is a prevalent one in both modern literature and film: current man's incapacity to make emotional commitments. This theme is keyed on two levels: the level of illusion and the level of reality. Another way of saying it is on the level of memory/dream and the level of the present. Bergman uses all his cinematic tricks —including flashbacks, dissolves, sudden conjunctions of the past-present, double printing—to move between the two levels and to use them for mutual intensification. Furthermore, he interchanges both things (the handless, timeless clock of the first dream and Borg's father's watch when they make their third stop) and people (Bibi Andersson is the long-lost love of the strawberry patch who preferred his brother Siegfried and the pipe-smoking tease of the present; the venomous psychologist of the second stop is the interrogator in the "final exam" sequence). All Bergman's usual symbols are here—the narcissism of mirrors, the ghostly clopping of horses' hooves, the creaking of carriages (this time hung up on a lamp post), young love in the tender strawberries, the blazing but strangely cold noonday sun, the brooding forests, and the lazy lapping of the water on the immaculate shore.[22] But they are not as obtrusive or as awkward as in his other films. Here they are assimilated into the form and become true elements.

It is the form, not the symbolism, that makes *Wild Strawberries* a significant film. The form is a dual spiral that returns on itself again and again, with each level bringing us to a deeper and finer insight into the origin and nature of impotence. This is an internal film in the sense that its target is the individual mind of Professor Borg; but the tone of the examination is clinical—more than clinical, for it is not only objective but also ironic. One may contrast this to the simple, intense arc of *The Virgin Spring* and *The Seventh Seal* or the incompletely fused dual form of *Dreams*. Besides this, there is movement of and within the form, for we do not know whether Borg will come alive before he completes his journey in either sense of the word "journey." Hence, we do not have the static portraits of *Winter Light* or *The*

Silence. Bergman brings all this together—symbolism, character, dialogue, criss-crossing situations, past-present—into one rhythmic, vibrating, spiral whole.

Wild Strawberries begins like a much different and in some ways strangely alike film, *8½*, in illusion. It begins inside the dream of Professor Borg, who is brilliantly played by one of Sweden's great directors: Victor Sjöström. The spectator is as disoriented and confused as the doctor. What kind of man is he, what does this strange dream mean? Slowly we begin to realize that he is a cold, distant man. We are participants in his revelation to himself. He is a man whose function is to bring life into being and to care for it by profession but who is incapable of life himself. A hollow man who has yet to live. A closed man. A man who cannot give. To put it in Freudian terms, just as *The Naked Night* is concerned with an excess of id, so is *Wild Strawberries* concerned with an excess of superego; and we know that as long as Borg insists on control, he will have none.

Gradually, we begin to view the articulations of Borg's impotence and its causes-effects-causes (the broken love affair, sibling rivalry, the unfaithful wife, the distant mother, the father who could not touch). And Borg sees them along with us. He comes to the awareness as we do that his son (Gunnar Björnstrand) is the same kind of prig that he is and that he has helped to constitute him as well as bring him into the world. Though he had rejected her before, Borg now comes to take an interest in and to extend compassion to his daughter-in-law (Ingrid Thulin). He urges this masculine woman to be a female and, in the end, sides with her against his son. Borg has come to an awareness of who, how, and where he is; and he desperately wants to change, to get out. But he can't. In the last, beautifully ironic scene, he attempts to break the ancient barrier with the housekeeper by addressing her in familiar terms, but she puts him back in his place as cool as a dust mop and reminds him of his status. So Borg is able to open some, but not all the way. Surely this final scene should satisfy even Lawson's demand for the hardness of "reality." There is a note of optimism here, but it is not total. Bergman is asking, "How far can a turtle get out of his shell?" His answer: "Not far."

As in his other films, Bergman's men are much weaker than the women, and he looks upon sex as an act of desperation (that is, if we put *Smiles of a Summer Night* aside). Though he is not openly preaching at us, Bergman is speaking to us and giving us a theory of life. He is saying that to live is to learn the limits of our despair. But once we have the knowledge, knowledge is not enough. For habit is too hard, too binding, too mortal a thing to be changed by knowledge alone. Once you have learned the limits of your despair, *lean* on them, and there may be a slight glimmer of hope. If the knowledge is not merely intellectual and rational, if it also becomes emotional knowledge (as it finally does with Professor Borg), then there is an outside chance that we can change a little. It is but a little, but it is still change—a change that Bergman feels is for the better. It is fitting, then, that at the conclusion of the film, Borg should wear a crown of laurel and not of thorns.

The young people with their beautiful, touching (and cruel), carefree ways are a brilliant contrast to Borg and Marianne taking their honored and fated trip. The portrayal of the psychologist biting at his wife is a truly vicious one and tells us not only about these two people but also what Borg and Bergman think of them. This couple also give us an allusive understanding of what it may have been like with Borg's wife and that there may be a true sense in which she was driven, not enticed, into infidelity. We do not know whether Bergman intends that Bibi, when her carefree and golden days are gone, will meet the same cold fate of Marianne, the mother, or the psychologist's wife. Nor does that matter, for that depends on which boy she chooses and would be quite another film. Both Bibi and Borg are moving toward the sun, by the way—one toward the warmth of Italy, the other toward cool Nordic understanding. But this film is about Borg and his world. Bergman has here done a remarkable thing. He has made a cool film about a man who cannot touch anyone, and he has touched us with him.

Just as Lawson downgrades *L'Avventura, Hiroshima Mon Amour,* and *Wild Strawberries* for the wrong reasons (namely, because he does not feel the intense pressure created by the tensions between real and imagined time), so he overvalues *Ballad of a Soldier* because "it does not attempt to go beyond the lyric statement of the theme, and the war background gives emotional depth to the action."[23] But there is very little action in any real sense in *Ballad,* and the emotional effect is not dependent upon a plot, as Lawson himself admits. Upon what is its thin emotional effect dependent? Sentimentality mixed with a distaste for war. Granted it is a ballad, but the simplicity of the film, which Lawson takes for its purity, is also simple in the poor sense: it is puerile, shallow, and naive. Lawson attempts to transform these qualities into virtues:

> The growing love between Alyosha and the girl offers no dramatic confrontation with a "problem" because both are aware of the larger obligation imposed on them by the war, and this immense social fact gives order and meaning to every moment of the boy's existence.[24]

However, the striving to attain "immense social facts" reduces the boy, his situations, his relations to the people he encounters, and the other people themselves into mere stereotypes. Chukhrai's film could have had depth and could still have retained its lyric qualities; *Nothing but a Man* does. *Elvira Madigan* is also a romantic ballad, but it never degenerates into false sentimentality or reduces its characters to types. It remains powerful because it is personal. But *Ballad of a Soldier* is shallow, not in technique or structure so much as in character and in its projected value system.

Now, it must be admitted that there are some fine things in *Ballad of a Soldier*. From the very beginning, director Grigori Chukhrai indicates that he is not going to tell us a story but to make us see. Thus, the most important "character" in this film has no lines and is never seen on the screen; the most important character is the camera. The film begins with the gruesome close-up of the advancing tanks and the frantic fleeing of the young boy. The camera wheels, darts, sneaks toward the wheels, falls under the tracks, slithers away, and darts into sudden sky like a frightened bird. From the opening sequence, we are aware that we should watch the camera (though we can't see it), not the people. But Chukhrai is also telling us to watch the people. He wants us to be concerned, and concerned in depth, about the boy. So he does want to tell a story after all. But the attempt to tell the story, to tell it as "it really is or ten times better" as Hemingway would say, is frittered away in technique and romance.

The camera work is often touching, imaginative, and bold. Vladimar Ivashov and Shanna Prokhovenko are responsible for the fine camera work. They are also responsible for the subtle play of light, the dark brooding look of the trees outlined against the boxcar, the white steam reaching out to envelop the railroad bridge, the joy of water and light on a sun-washed face, and the reflections of a lonely girl in an isolated mud puddle (an image, by the way, also used by Kurosawa in *The Seven Samurai* but used there for a less romantic and more feminine purpose: she combs her hair). These techniques are often dazzling and help to constitute the film. A ballad is a romance; and the beautiful montages, the double printings, add to the feeling-tone. This type of montage is essentially romantic and is used to collapse time and space into the immediacy of feeling. Hence, the camera techniques ask us to care about the boy; but we can't care about him because we never get to know him. We always remain on the outside, and the film is sheer presentational surface. Were there a tension between this surface technique and depth content, the film could be a masterpiece. But the content is negligible, and what is there is naive.

The first attempt at content is the bad scene when the young soldier is given his leave. This ultrademocratic army is simply not to be believed, whether it is the Red army or any other. We are then treated to noble Slavs posed against rippling fields of wheat or simple skyline, or mother at work at home, and one keeps awaiting the alabaster mountainsides. The relationship between the young boy and the girl is so simperingly sweet and shallow as to transform them into cardboard figures. The encounter with the wounded veteran is fairly effective; but then we are treated to the incredible puritanical fury of the boy, his self-righteous fervor and messianic intolerance of the adulterous wife. The least he could have done was to have given her the hard soap. It's the best thing for cleaning.

Now, the Russians are not the only romantics in the world. Nor are they the only practicing Puritans. After all, America has given the world a Bronx butcher as Romeo (*Marty*) and a Puerto Rican punk as Mercutio (*West Side Story*) among nameless others. If it is the case that we learn about people from their behavior, it is equally the case that we learn about people from their projected idealizations: how they dream themselves to be. Films, more than any other art, are peculiarly equipped to present this facet of a people and of individuals.

When we examine *Ballad of a Soldier,* we find out a great deal about the Russians. Not as they *are* (though we may infer some politics from the thinness of the film) but as they would like to be or conceive themselves to be. They conceive themselves to be kindly, generous, sentimental, romantic, earthy (but with no real dirt), democratic to a fault, and adherents to and cherishers of the simple, patriotic virtues. And they conceive themselves to be pioneers building a brave new world through sacrifice. The long train sequence is no accident. The train is essentially a romantic symbol of a past age. It is powerful, majestic, masculine, adventurous and yet solid in its iron massiveness. Its long lonely whistle appeals directly to the heart, and its clanging wheels bang the energy of progress toward virgin lands. Trains are sacred; cars are profane. Even *The Idiot* has an interminable train sequence. All these romantic elements fit with the romantic techniques. But Chukhrai also wants us to take the story seriously and to feel grieved at the boy's inevitable death, which is given in the opening frames. This we cannot do, for no matter how much one piles one external circumstance on another, we never really know the boy except as a self-righteous prig who has all the aspects of a cardboard hero. And we cannot feel grief at the loss of soggy cardboard. Since we do not and cannot know him from the inside, the poignancy of his inability to visit his mother and his fleeting glimpse of her loses its urgency. We are left with a handful of fluff fabricated by technical virtuosity. In the end, *Ballad of a Soldier* is a three-phase antiwar poster. Even paper tigers can't take posters seriously.

Lawson admits that there was weakness in the Soviet film following the heyday of Eisenstein, Pudovkin, Dovzhenko, and others. He admits that the Soviet film was debased into a series of "idealized replicas." This admission is true, and it would also be a true description of *Ballad of a Soldier*. It also is an "idealized replica," as is so much of the dreary Soviet working-class art. But Lawson presents peculiar reasons for this insipidity, and he draws odd conclusions from it. The reasons he gives are the rise of Stalinism, which brought the debasement of film and "the extraordinary rate of social expansion" in the Soviet Union. Neither chaos nor social expansion has seemed to affect the Italian, Japanese, or American film industries or, for that matter, those of Poland and other satellite countries. The true difficulty is the forcing of a naive value system on the arts by an all-powerful political bureaucracy. The Russian film will not undergo the rebirth that Lawson hopes for until it is freed from so much arbitrary and capricious precensorship. If one regards history, the hope for this is slim indeed. Russian politics has traditionally been Oriental and despotic, and there is little sign that it will allow the arts to speak on their own. But when any one institution totally dominates a society, whether it be a puritan church or a puritan government, the other institutions, and in particular the arts, are in fetters. For a man addicted to objective reality, it is remarkable how mystically romantic Lawson can be. No matter how enchanted one may become by the concept of "the people," one still should not overlook the hard facts of institutional structure.

In art and in life, one can often relevantly ask the same question: "What is the man's staying power?" For one mark of fine art is that it does not settle for easy choices. If the horizontal dimension of film is composed of its objective movement and narrative line, its vertical dimension is constituted by the depth of the individual human problems to be resolved. The expressive value, if any, that emerges from the film is a function of the shaped tensions between the horizontal and vertical planes or between the surface and the depth. Both Grigori Chukhrai in his film and Lawson in his evaluation stay entirely on the horizontal plane, that is, on the surface. And while one may admire linoleum patterns for their charm, one realizes that they are really fit only for kitchen floors. Old-fashioned floors, at that.

Lawson's theory correctly isolates the relation of the individual to the group as one of the main problems of film. But then he comes down on the abstract side of the slide: the group. This choice, combined with his political presuppositions and his tender yearning for the masses, brings him to develop a theory which, for all its clarity and brilliance, still stays on the surface. The consequence is that he is confined to an external view of film, a causal view, and to a theory that emphasizes clash and conflict as the essence of film. He fails to see that clash, conflict, and contrast are merely modes of tension and that it is quite possible for a film to be evolutionary as well as revolutionary in its structure and import. The key passage in Lawson's book is probably the following:

The difference between the use of montage in the Soviet film of the twenties and its use in the work of certain contemporary directors is of crucial importance in understanding the nature of film communication. When cutting is used to convey subjective states of feeling or irrational relationships, it is in conflict with the method developed by both Eisenstein and Pudovkin. Pudovkin is more concerned with psychological experience, but it is always conceived as a response to reality and an expression of human decisions.[25]

Lawson then goes on to praise the films of the 1920s and to downgrade the more modern movements in film, all the while exalting montage, Russian montage, as the true essence of film. Surely he is correct in asserting that the modern film has moved away from the theories and practice of Eisenstein and Pudovkin and that movement within a scene and tension have come to replace external juxtaposition and the clash of images. This is true. But it does not therefore mean that Bergman, Fellini, Resnais, De Sica, Kubrick, and others are therefore wrong. What it means is that they are different. It may also mean that film form and film technique have evolved to a newer and higher stage of development, in which Russian montage is seen as one, but only one, device, which may be used within the entire tense complex of a film if it is appropriate to the situation. But there are many films in which it is not appropriate.

Lawson's film theory, then, seems unnecessarily aesthetically exclusive, and some of his other philosophical presuppositions appear further suspect. It is not a priori obvious that feeling should be immediately conjoined with the irrational. Nor is it obvious that feeling should be considered as wholly, completely, and irretrievably subjective. In fact, if the relations between man and his lived world are ones of direct assimilation, transformation, and return, that is, a relation of personifying his world or worlding his person, then an abstract causal description is inadequate and the feeling-quality, tone, shape, and rhythm of things in the lived world cannot be ruled as simple subjective projections of the individual. One may feel sadness when looking at a weeping willow; but it is not the self, it is the willow that weeps. The lassitude of its branches, the shagginess of its over-all mass combined with the delicacy of the leaves and the drooping quality of its fragile limbs all constitute its weepingness. One does not feel sorry for the willow. He simply perceives the emergent quality of its expressive structure.

Nor can we forget the fact that Lawson's straitjacket of externality has forced him to use concepts that are partially accurate but much too vivid. Thus, he sees the essence of film form as conflict-in-motion instead of also realizing that there can be cumulative tension. When he comes to his final statement of film form, the three phases of its movement are described as premise, progression, and climax. "Premise" is much too external and intellectual a concept and sounds as though it had accidentally wandered from logic into aesthetics. "Progression" is a much better choice and carries the meaning of movement plus some of the feel of cumulation, a quality so necessary in any fine film. "Climax" is, aside from its sexual overtones, much too vivid a word and much too dramatic. Were one to take it seriously, there would be a constant confusion between theatre and film. Therefore, though I will follow some of the main movements of Lawson's theory, for his theory does helpfully describe some films, I will not use his concepts of "premise," "progression," and "climax." Instead, I will use the words "situation," "articulation," and "revelation." And that will make a difference. All the difference, at least in theory. And, I hope, in film.

Notes

1. John H. Lawson, *Film: The Creative Process* (New York: Hill & Wang, 1967).
2. Sergei Eisenstein, *Notes of a Film Director,* pp. 59–60, as quoted in Lawson, *Film,* p. 279.
3. V. I. Pudovkin, *Film Technique and Film Acting,* trans. and ed. by Ivor Montagu (New York: Grove Press, 1960), p. 23.
4. Pudovkin, p. 247.
5. Pudovkin, p. 25.
6. Pudovkin, p. 255.
7. Pudovkin, p. 261.
8. Pudovkin, p. 27.
9. This passage is from Marx's preface to *A Contribution to the Critique of Political Economy,* as quoted in Lawson, *Film,* p. 272.
10. Lawson, *Film,* p. 273.
11. Lawson, pp. 249–250.
12. Lawson, p. 250.
13. Lawson, p. 341.
14. Lawson, p. 342.
15. Lawson, p. 342.
16. Lawson, p. 285.
17. Lawson, pp. 320–321.
18. Lawson, p. 284.
19. Lawson, p. 340.
20. Lawson, p. 303.
21. Lawson, p. 321.
22. A brilliant analysis of Bergman's growing vocabulary can be found in James F. Scott, "The Achievement of Ingmar Bergman," *The Journal of Aesthetics and Art Criticism,* Vol. 24, No. 2 (Winter 1965), pp. 63–72.
23. Lawson, *Film,* p. 303.
24. Lawson, p. 289.
25. Lawson, p. 282.

5

The Lived World

Were one to follow through the implications of the McLuhan-technologist position, the Kracauer-objectivist position or the Lawson-Marxist position, the world would become measured and safe and known. It would be a *known* world. But a world of knowledge is not a real world in any fundamental sense, for it is stable and scrubbed clean of all mystery. And a world scrubbed clean of all opacity would be a world without man, too. As Alfred North Whitehead has remarked somewhere, men cannot live by bread alone, but they can't live on disinfectants either. The rational ideal is a fine one, and it is the best one we have; but it is still an ideal. Reason itself is an abstraction from concrete circumstance. So if the Medium were the Message or if the camera were the Redemption of Physical Reality or if the individual were Reducible to the Collective, there would be no guilt, no joy, no eccentricity, no uncertainty, and nothing left worth living for. And if someone were suddenly to bang open the henhouse door, we could reply blandly, "There ain't nothin' but us objects here." Fortunately, the millennium has not arrived. There is still a living world, and it is inhabited by man alive.

In the first four chapters, I have reflected upon film from the perspectives of expression, form, materials, and function. Each of these perspectives is valuable in itself; but the reflections have revealed to me that reducing film to any one dimension may unduly restrict our capacity to appreciate, understand, and evaluate something as complex as film. Though film can be forced into a theatrical, structural, technical, or ideological straitjacket, it seems that a broader, more humanistic stance is required. In the tracing of the "family differences" between film and theatre, film and novels, film and photographs, film and social messages, such a new perspective has emerged. This new perspective is one of existential humanism. If film is an analogue of a broader stance—man's ways of being-with-the-world—then it has a natural affinity for the subjective/objective approach of phenomenology. To grasp the appropriateness of this approach, however, presupposes some knowledge of the analogue. This chapter and the next are therefore concerned with an existential analysis of man's behavior. They are concerned with some of the ways man engages his world.

To be or not to be is not the question. We already are. The question is, then, "How do we are?" That is, "How do we exist?" And "exist," "am," "be," "are" should be taken as active verbs, not as passive states or as given properties. Insofar as I exist, existence is something I do. The way that I do it is through my expressive body. I order and am ordered by my world. I become informed, I perform, and the world is transformed. Notice how the word "form" keeps coming in there. But form, as I have remarked previously, has no own-being, nor is it to be thought of as clear and distinct. Form is the displacement of the background, or part of the horizon, into the foreground. Hence, form is emergent pattern that is never completely defined but becomes individuated enough that it may serve as a ground of action. It both selects itself and is selected by me. Perhaps it would be more accurate to say that it selects itself through me. The drawings of children and chimpanzees show that line precedes outline; but, though the child goes beyond the simple circle to the outline of representations, the chimpanzee remains arrested.[1] The child, however, progresses and is thus able to constitute objects as apart from him and to regard them as other than mere extensions of his primitive being. This process of abstraction continues into the adult, and the tragedy is that as adults we seem almost condemned to identify with the abstract. As adults, our life is a perpetual forgetting. We are perpetually forgetting that the outline of the self is at the same time the inline of the world.

"Existence is indeterminate in itself, by reason of its fundamental structure,"[2] not because nuclear physics has established such a principle or because some trickster God in his divine humor has so designed things for man, but because to exist is the process of eliciting meaning from that which had been meaningless and then incorporating that meaning into the self and its world. This necessary contingency, this ambivalent being, man, exists by transcendence. Man is a going-beyond. "Human existence . . . is the transformation of contingency into necessity by the act of carrying forward."[3] Insofar as I exist, then, I must have vision in both senses of the word "vision." I must perceive the actual once it has ceased to be possible. I must then be able to envision it as capable of supporting a future, that is, as a further possibility. Genesis tells us that man was condemned to live by the sweat of his brow, that is, to work. The very concept of work implies the negation of the given and that things may be other. Work demands possibility, perception reveals possibility, action embodies possibility. Man is the animal with the capacity for an awareness of possibility. There can be constituted objects for man, and these objects are both a challenge and an opportunity. Because of this, man's basic orientation is toward transcendence.

The very word "exist" reveals this meaning of movement toward the world and its possible transformation. I have said before that we all live outside. Marcel puts it in this way:

> The prefix *ex* in exist, has a primary significance because it conveys the meaning of a movement towards the external world, a centrifugal tendency. I exist: that means I have something by which I can be known or identified, either by another person or by myself insofar as I assume for myself a borrowed otherness; none of these characteristics are separable from the fact that "there is my body."[4]

On the basis of a possible, but never fully known, future, man acts and, in acting, changes himself and his world. To exist, then, is to manifest oneself or to be manifested. As Marcel points out, it is really irrelevant whether we say, "I experience" (*Ich erlebe*) or "It lives in me" (*Es erlebt in mir*).[5] Both are ways of expressing man's fundamental presence to the world, a presence "without which the fact of existing would not have the density it has for me."[6] In the beginning, there is a primary presence, and this presence manifests itself. In this sense, man may be said to be an expressive animal, for he not only expresses himself through action but the "things" express themselves through him. I believe film is peculiarly equipped to reveal this primary presence manifesting itself.

Existence is not a state but a dynamic process involving action and its precipitation into habit and institution. Existence is a dialectic involving the phases of presence, incarnation, incorporation, and excarnation. But the dialectic between and within the self-world has a third term: the body. Without the body, there could be no access to the world. Existence, then, is that ambiguous situation in and through which the body worlds. In order to grasp what this means, we must begin with what it means to have and to be a body, for existence is "perpetual incarnation."[7]

We are turning here, of course, to the mind/body problem—a problem that has an ancient and not altogether honorable reputation in the history of philosophy. From an Eastern mystic point of view, from the point of view of modern philosophy, or from lived common sense, one might say that the mind/body problem is no problem. Another way of putting this is that it is a problem only if you think it is a problem. But reflective common sense is really old philosophy; hence, we tend to regard the mind/body as a problem. Whether one studies the metaphysicians of modern times, such as Whitehead, the language analysts who are trying to exorcise with syntax "the ghost in the machine," or the existentialists, one finds all of them hitting the same theme: The terms of the mind/body problem must be recast. As long as they are formulated in the old ways, there will appear to be a problem. It may be that the solutions offered by these three different trends of thought are not complete and have not thoroughly dissolved the problem. One thing is certain: If philosophy in the twentieth century is meaningful, its value will be its rediscovery of the body.

Put in its most simple terms, it would seem that one has two alternatives. Either he can say, "I am my body," or he can say, "I am other than my body." If one states, "I am my body," he is committed to the abolition of mind and to the reduction of the world to a materialistic hypothesis. Descartes, the father of contemporary common sense, came perilously close to this choice, though he did reserve a small place in the universe for the priority of thought, the "I think." British philosophy is only now recovering from Descartes, and this is why the language analysts are so anxious to bury him. If one says, "I am other than my body," he is committed to an idealistic position such as that of Berkeley, and then the difficulty is in explaining the persistence or even reality of things. One can, of course, argue a middle position, and this is exactly what Kant attempts when he claims that we must be empirical realists but transcendental idealists. But Kant's philosophy, as valuable as it is as a forward step, is still not adequate, for he ultimately withdraws mind from matter by insisting that it consists of a priori structures. At this point, the "solution" to the "problem" seems to be impossible. But the dissolution of the problem is quite evident, if we merely admit that all these men were right and that all of them were wrong.

Hobbes and, to a great extent, Descartes are right in insisting that the body is a mechanism. The sciences, particularly physics, chemistry, and physiology, are continually coming up with new evidence of this position. Electrical impulses can change the behavior patterns of animals, rats can be conditioned to the abstract situation of stimulus-response learning, and chemicals can affect not only memory and attention span but also the entire shape of awareness. The body is a chemical mass that constitutes a field of interaction. But what is overlooked in this mechanistic perspective is that there are types of fields and that each field can differ from others. While it is true that certain chemicals alter the retention and attention functions of rats, recent experiments at Stanford University also show that the milieu, the situation of the rat, accelerates or retards his production of those very chemicals. Hence, a rat with an exciting and challenging environment will not only learn more quickly but will produce a chemical base by which such learning can take place. A rat in a dull environment will be not merely mentally retarded but also chemically retarded. It would appear, then, that the chemical mass that is the body is not merely a thing but a field with its own form and imminent meaning and that, furthermore, it is not a field that is indifferent to its interaction with other modes of order.

Berkeley and, to a great extent, Bergson are right in insisting that the body is animated by goals. The study of organisms shows that they strive for homeostasis and equilibrium in the world-as-tasks and that many of these tasks are not merely actual demands but are also virtual. An organism reveals a set of aptitudes toward its world and characteristic ways of coming to terms with it.[8] The world of organisms is a vital order, but there is no reason to assume that meaning is anything other than imminent in the vital situation. To say that there therefore must be a soul and then to argue that this soul is another type of thing would simply put us back into the mind/body problem. The exchange between instinctive reaction and the vital situation, a situation much of which the organism itself brings into being, can best be described as another order of behavior. This would put aside the problem of a separable soul and the hypostatizing of the mind. It would allow one to regard this type of order as the interaction of the organism and its biological milieu.

Kant is correct in maintaining that there are only objects *for* consciousness. The difficulty is that he then removes mind from experience so that it becomes a set of a priori forms, which, though they help to constitute experience, are indifferent to it. This also leads him to assert not merely the universality of such structures but also the universality of their type. But comparative anthropology and linguistics show that while most people have some concepts of causality, quantity, and so on, and intuitions of space and time, the kinds of concepts and the way they are used are quite different. Time does not have the same content or form for an Australian aborigine as it does for a European or an American. The human order, then, is not a system founded on objective knowledge but one that is based in perception, a perception that is sometimes an immediate interaction with the world, that is, lived, and sometimes attentive, clear, and known. Studies of young infants show that they will smile at a mask with eyes but no mouth. They react to centers of expression first and only later to defined qualities. Such behavior is also subject to the system of society and the group and individual habits that are precipitated. Human existence is a function of social structures and institutions, which bring man into being at the human level but which also constrict him. His meaning consists in transcending these conditions. Hence, man's situation is ambiguous, for consciousness constitutes phenomenal objects by importing meaning into them but at the same time refuses to be identified with them. It then returns to itself in order to attempt a transcendence of the structures it has created. Mind, then, is a rhythm of synthesis, a system of integration, which is inseparable from that which it synthesizes. It is a higher form of behavior or order, but it is not a thing.

This approach to the body in terms of behavior is the one taken by Merleau-Ponty. As one moves through the various orders of behavior, from the fixed responses of the syncretic behavior of ants through the amovable behavior of chickens to the symbolic behavior of man, three things become evident. One is that man is never merely an animal. As Merleau-Ponty states it:

> Man can never be an animal: his life is always more or less integrated than that of an animal. But if the alleged instincts of man do not exist apart from the mental dialectic, correlatively, this dialectic is not conceivable outside the concrete situations in which it is embodied. One does not act with mind alone.

> Either mind is nothing, or it constitutes a real and not an ideal transformation of man. Because it is not a new sort of being but a new form of unity, it cannot stand by itself.[9]

Even Adam had to see the animals before he named them; and, once he had named them, they could be known. One thing that is evident, then, is man's inherence in his body. Existentialism idealizes the body, but it also incarnates the soul.

The second thing evident is that, though there are various levels of behavior, behavior itself is neither a thought nor a thing but is expression. Behavior is the mode whereby the organism expresses itself in and through its world. The third evident thing is that as one moves to the higher orders of behavior, they are characterized by greater and greater flexibility. It is not merely that man's behavior is more complex and unified than that of other organisms; it is also more adaptable. Adaptability depends upon both the ability to order and to be open. Hence, those organisms that cannot be permeable to their experience are unable to synthesize, and their behavior is simplistic. The analogue of simplistic behavior in film is the rigid type design. The personal film with its phases of situation, articulation, and revelation is an analogue of permeable behavior. Those organisms that are permeable and can synthesize are those with the greatest symbolic and actual power and are able to attain full humanity.

The characteristics of permeability and presence are emphasized in Marcel's philosophy, for he is really more concerned with ethical and religious questions than with the problems of the theory of knowledge. It is interesting to note, by the way, that the word *presence* displays more "presence" when it is said in French than in English. Its sound has greater depth and stability, perhaps because it becomes a heavily stressed iamb (pun intended). Aside from the difference of emphasis, however, Marcel agrees that the world is not just some great documentary film, which has nothing to do with me. It is not something merely present before my indifferent eyes. On the contrary, it is a phenomenal world to which I have access precisely because I am incarnate.

> To be incarnated is to appear to oneself as a body, as this particular body, without being identified with it nor distinguished from it—identification and distinction being correlative operations which are significant only in the realm of objects.[10]

If I regard my body as an object, then I must disregard my subjectivity; and it is no longer my body. On the other hand, if I attempt an escape into pure subjectivity, there is no body and there is no "my" possible. It is neither adequate nor accurate, then, to say simply I *am* my body unless we understand the "am" to mean "The mind is the expression of the body, or the mind is the way the body means."

Though there is a sense in which my body does not belong to me (for example, in some states I legally have no right to have my burial wishes carried out, for my body belongs to my heirs), the body is not, strictly speaking, an object. It is that by which objects come to be. It is the unperceived given perspective that is the ground for all phenomenal objects in my world. My body is my perpetual, unperceived "here" upon which I am able to establish objects as "there." Not only is the presence of my body the ground for any objects appearing at all, but my body is permanent and is with me in a sense in which they are not.[11] George Mead came close to eliminating the subjectivity of the body altogether in his *Mind, Self and Society*. He viewed his body as if it were a table. But that the body is a subject is shown not only by its presence, permanence, and so forth but also by the experiences of it as an affective object. Pain immediately expresses itself noncausally through my body. Furthermore, my body is self-reflective in the sense that it is capable of double sensations, that is, the hand can touch the hand. The body, like the film experience, is thus ambiguous. It is a subject/object. The system of levels of behavior expressed through the body reveals its subjectivity in such experiences as embarrassment. But we use the body as object when we flee into it for refuge, as in organ speech or other disabilities in which we claim we are not responsible for our symptoms. This is the use of the body as excuse. Since we relate ourselves to our bodies in different modes of synthesis, the body is both direct and indirect.

Insofar as my experience becomes integrated, I create for myself an impalpable body: habit. This impalpable body is a restriction in the sense that it establishes my style and my address to the world, and it tends to perpetuate itself in future action. But it is also a freedom, for it is the ground for my being able to experience anything at all. Habit gives me the room to see. Man must both be committed to the world and at the same time be able to synthesize, to dominate, that commitment. Hence, growth, like perception, is the growing into differentiation and greater subtlety, the reintegration and reinforcement of style. The ability to restructure and dominate one's commitment is what I have called the "moral theme" of Kurosawa's films. An address is not merely an abstract number. One can tell a great deal about man as both a golfer and a man by the way he addresses the ball and the way he moves in his world. The same may be said of gesture in general. My gestures express my way of being-in-the-world.

This complex ambiguity of the body, I shall refer to as its "withness." There are several ways in which withness has the precise ambiguities that I intend. In the first place, it denotes the perpetual, imperceptible perspective, the unperceived "here," that is my body. In the second place, it suggests the pun on "witness" and hence implies the cognitive objectivity of the body. That is, insofar as my consciousness recedes from my body, I disregard its myness and view it as a body among other bodies. It therefore becomes abstract or is related to them. But in the third place, "withness" intends a fundamental difference of emphasis from the objective point of view. It also carries the meaning of subjectivity. Hence, while objects may be next to objects, people can be with things, more importantly, they can be with other subjects—people. Intentional consciousness, situated consciousness, thus can become consciousness-in-the-world. There is an immediacy of access here that is below the level of knowledge. As Marcel says, it cannot be called a "relation" or a "communication," but must more properly be termed a "participation." This direct participation in the world might be called "feeling," if by "feeling" is understood not a passive receptivity but an active presence, that is, feeling as an opening unto the world, as a yielding-to-become-one-with.

Marcel analyzes this withness in terms of one's feeling at home and the reception of a friend. As to feeling at home, he states:

> I cannot refer to my *feeling at home* unless I grant or imply that the self does or can seem to itself to impregnate its environment with its own quality, thereby recognizing itself in its surroundings and entering into an intimate relationship with it.[12]

As for the reception of the friend, he continues:

> If this is the case, it must be maintained that to receive is to introduce the other person, the stranger, into a region which has these qualities, and to admit him in to participate with it.[13]

One of the vivid complaints in an otherwise unremarkable film, *No Exit,* is made by the lesbian when she sees in imagination that her room has been rented and is now occupied by a couple unknown to her. She protests that they can't make love, it isn't right because it is *her* room. These are all cases of the extension of the subjective spatiality of the body.

Perhaps the most common extensions of the subjective spatiality of the body are extensions of the self through tools. Hence, when one uses a hammer, the hammer soon becomes incorporated as part of the body schema. One does not then attend to the smack of the hammer on the palm of the hand but, having incorporated the hammer into one's being-in-the-world, perceives the strike of the hammer head on the nail. The same may be said of other tools such as the automobile. McLuhan is undoubtedly right when he claims that the success of the Volkswagen is due not to its deliberate stylelessness but to the fact that it provides wrap-around space. Hence, it becomes a personal extension. The advertising is used to enhance such concepts by stressing that the VW is a toy or is a womb substitute. But other cars provide the same phenomena of bodily extension. When one drives a new or a strange car, he keeps looking to see where his fenders are, how much clearance he has, and so on. Once the car has become familiar, that is, the subjective spatiality of the body is extended, one no longer looks at the fenders at all but knows their locations.

The same may be said of space as well as tools. One feels at a loss in a foreign city or after having moved to a different town. Such simple tasks as going to the grocery store become almost insurmountable; and one feels depressed, for he has traded a familiar space for an unfamiliar one. Everyone needs a home base. In the same way, the home becomes the extension of personality of the woman; it is her corporate way of expressing herself. Thus, if her house is disorganized or dirty, *she* feels disorganized or dirty. The function of the architect is to be able to convert sheer space (which has nothing to do with his client) into place. If he is successful, he transforms it into this place and no other. Negatively, this personalization of space expresses itself in restriction, and one claims that this is not ground but private property. Thus arise conflicts over territory and litigation over rights. Another negative indication is to be found in our misnamed vital statistics. By far the largest number of accidents and deaths in automobiles occur within twenty miles of home. As one comes closer to personalized space, his foot increases its pressure on the accelerator.[14]

A recent experiment with airline pilots throws light on both space and time and on the relevance of their subjectivity. It was discovered that when pilots flew jets from Oklahoma City to Rome their physiological systems were thrown off by the time schedules. Not only were their physical processes disrupted, but also their mental abilities, such as adding simple columns of figures, were impaired. The same phenomena occurred when they flew from Rome to their home base in Oklahoma, but the recovery times for both the physical and mental functions after the return trip were one half those of the outgoing trip. This demonstrates not only a disruption of the relations of subjective and objective time but also that when one is returning home and escaping into the familiar, recovery is much faster. Man, then, is not just in the world, he inhabits it. By inhabiting the world, he shapes that world, even to the extent of space and time, into a personal world according to his intentions.

This does not mean that man shapes the world as he wishes it to be. On the contrary, objects themselves are never completely given and always escape man's horizons. Furthermore, those of us who share the same milieu shape things according to the same symbolic structures and in approximately the same ways. This is why we can communicate; we share the same worlds. In fact, it is only when one can throw off the natural weight of the actual, can negate his social and individual habits, that he can become open and permeable to new possibilities. Without our individual, impalpable, and social bodies, we would not be able to see at all; and, when we do see, we can go on to further integration. Unfortunately, the self as so constituted is both an opportunity and a prison. The Negro is currently rebelling against the social body we have created for him. Some people become fixated, cut off from virtuality; hence, they become rigid and perverse. They treat themselves and the world as objects and merely repeat or retreat into past patterns of simplified synthesis. In other words, they become impersonal, which is another way of saying that they become spiritually dead. But, as Whitehead has said, "It is the business of the future to be dangerous," and life is adventure.

Thus we are incarnate beings; and, through assimilation, participation, and appropriation, we can extend ourselves and incorporate our world. We can extend ourselves even farther into the realms of others, society, and things. This is particularly true in relation to the arts, for we can here become excarnate and can inhabit new and unfamiliar worlds. Dream and imagination are both ways of literally and metaphorically becoming beside ourselves and becoming able to participate in different worlds. Thought also has this power; and, when it travels out from the self, it modifies the behavior of the body. When students are thinking, their bodies withdraw into themselves, their hands hold up their heads, and they act as though their skulls had suddenly become very heavy. Thought involves an escape from the body, which is written on the surface of their bodily posture. They have withdrawn from the world of action and entered the realm of contemplation. And it does not really make a great deal of difference what subject one studies when he enters that realm. What the student is trying to understand ultimately is his world. And the reason we wish to know about our world is that we want to know who we are.

The artist is in an especially fortunate circumstance in this regard, for he works with materials that are shaped to his expressive purposes. Though he may not and usually does not have a clear intention of what the end product will be, the relationship between himself and his work is particularly intimate. Thus, as he proceeds in his work he must choose here, reject there, articulate this and suppress that tendency of the materials. In so doing, he increases their expressive power, for compression intensifies impression, that is, the image he is creating. And in the process of creating, rearranging, and reworking, it becomes more and more clear to him what he is saying and, by implication, what he has the capacity to say. In this sense, also, he is painting because he wants to know who he is. For he knows that he is a who and not a that.

These reflections on the primacy of the withness of the body make it evident that the hand, the ear, the nose, the eye, and so forth, cannot be reduced to the simple status of organs, which are then externally—that is, merely causally—related to indifferent objects. The eye is that through which I can see; it is the instrument of my vision. While I have an awareness of my bodily schema as a whole, my body as a whole is not a perceptual, but merely a virtual, object for me. I can perceive certain parts of my body and regard them as objects. In fact, I may regard them as entirely other at times and thus look at my feet and wonder what they are doing "way out there." When someone steps on my toes, however, my consciousness immediately collapses into my body; and the stomped toe becomes the temporary center of the universe. In spite of the fact that I can experience this reflective otherness from my body, the bruised toes dramatically demonstrate that I "am" my body. There is an odd corollary here: The things we are most often embarrassed about are our bodily functions, such as stomach rumbling and excretion. John Huston included a humorous example of this in his film *The African Queen* when he had Bogart's stomach rumble at tea. Yet these are the least personal aspects of our being. While it may have been a godsend to the selling of books, the "discovery" made by the "realistic" novel that man has functions below the belt does not reveal anything particularly human. These functions we share with other animals. They are meaningful only if transformed by a higher symbolic context.

It should be evident that this short description of incarnation and its movements toward embodiment bear some close analogies to the situation of the film. The film director, through the agency of the cameraman, expresses his intentions toward a world through the camera. He selects what the setup will be, what angle will be chosen, what lighting will be used, what speed will be appropriate, what gestures will be expressed and retained, and how the whole will be eventually synthesized. In a sense, then, the director is a powerful finite god, for he is creating a world in accordance with his intentions and embodying in that world the rhythms of his taste and value structure. He sees through his camera much as he sees through his eyes. For the spectator of the finished film, the situation is analogous. He identifies with the viewpoint of the camera, and its perspective becomes his access to the film world before him. Like his own body, the camera is an unperceived but perpetual "here." In the experience of film, the camera becomes our virtual body.

But the camera by itself with no human intervention is an indifferent eye. Hence, it does not see things in the same way as a human being unless there is the insertion of the human into its recording process. Let us go back to looking at my feet. When I look at my feet, they appear to be the proper size. If I hold my two hands at unequal distances in front of me, one appears identical in size to the other. If I look into a mirror, the image appears to be about the same size as my head and facial structure. All these perceptions are in one sense incorrect. The camera would show my feet as very large compared to the rest of me if the shot were from below; it would record one hand as larger than the other if shot from the position of my eyes; and would record the image on the mirror as extremely small, about the size of an orange. Due to its literalness, the camera not merely foreshortens and records the discrepancies in space, but, in fact, it exaggerates them. My eye does not do so. My adult eye is in no sense indifferent to its world. My concepts are interfering with my perceptions. It may be that with children seeing is believing, but with adults believing is seeing. I anticipate that the structures before me will be of the same, or proper, size, and I see them so. Our conceptual presuppositions demand constancy, and our eyes work in accordance with that demand. In order to understand how this occurs, we must briefly trace what it means to grow up. We shall then return to the perceptual and precognitive processes themselves.

Before I begin a short discussion of me, myself, and I, let me mention—in order to put aside—the theory of instincts. There are fashions in human thought just as there are fashions in clothing. Thus, while we move from one type of threads to another to clothe our bodies, we move from one group of concepts to another to clothe our thoughts. These movements of fashion tend to recur. When Freud first began to use the word "instinct," it became the fashion. With the rise of behavioristic and stimulus-response psychology, "instinct" became a dirty word, which was not to be used under any conditions. But the basic concept of instincts began to reappear in other phrasings. Hence, investigators now talk about "original imprinting" or perhaps "IRMs" (Innate Release Mechanisms). Some of the more popular writers in biology and anthropology, such as Robert Ardrey and Desmond Morris, while avoiding these terms, still are utilizing the same type of concept when they talk about "genetic determinants." It must be admitted that they do stay on a more behavioral plane than their predecessors; but they have a tendency to reduce certain patterns of relationships of behavior (for example, territoriality, status competition, and the pair-bond relationship) to a prebehavioral base. Thus, they argue that man's overt behavior is founded on his genetic inheritance and that society is really the means whereby man rationalizes his genetic drives. This then becomes a genetic theory in both senses of the term: (1) that human behavior is explained by its antecedents and (2) that the antecedents are reducible to genetic arrangements. This seems to be merely a more sophisticated form of Lamarckism, the theory of acquired characteristics as future determinants. If I am misinterpreting these theories, I apologize. Even so, the entire genetic approach, in the sense of historical approach, would still suffer from the danger of reductionism. Such descriptions run the danger of saying that man is nothing but whatever the antecedent conditions are described to be. But the fascinating thing about man is not his mereness; it is his moreness. He is not reducible to any given bundle of explanations, whether genetic or psychic. Even if it could be proven (which is highly unlikely) that there is a set group of instincts, this would not help much to explain human behavior. For the course and development of human life does not depend on what one has but on what one does with it.

The same may be said of Freud's theory of innate instincts, for example, the incest prohibition. It is doubtful that any psychic phenomena are sufficiently differentiated to be regarded as "facts" at all, and, if they were, it would still have to be proved that they exhibited causal relations to each other. Now, it must be admitted that Freud was a genius. He discovered many of the processes that we actually use in behavior modifications, particularly the devices of repression, regression, sublimation, and transference. But it must be admitted also that Freud himself exhibited toward his theories an understandable, but nevertheless excessive, narcissism. Granted, he did not become as rigid as his followers; and yet we find him at the end still holding strongly to certain preferred fictional forms (Oedipus), certain self-created fictions (penis envy in women), and unenumerated bundles of inborn instincts (taboos on cannibalism and incest). If one puts aside Freud's rigid symbolism and also his belief in inborn psychic determinants, one in no way reduces his stature. It is still apparent that Freud was a genius, and, as his main achievement, he erased the usual distinctions between the mind and the body. He put the mind back into the body, the only place where it could be and the only place it can belong.

The romantic desire to embrace a simple genetic or simple psychoanalytic reductionism of behavior to a given pattern of causative factors is perfectly understandable. After all, human behavior is extremely complex, and there may well be no system that will ever describe it adequately. From an existential point of view, life is the struggle to embody and to institute finite values. We sometimes succeed; we sometimes fail. But there are no excuses. Man alone and together makes himself what he is and is to become. If one merely regards the human infant in comparison to the young of other species, one thing is immediately evident: Man is born at least a year too soon. The human child is characterized above all by openness, helplessness, flexibility, and indeterminateness. He has no set of stock responses, and his process of growth is the process of taking on definition.

This empirical fact, no doubt, led Mead to assert that the self *"is not initially there,* at birth" and to describe children as "these various vague beings." Unfortunately, Mead slides from one meaning to another of the word "whole." "Whole" may mean a unity, or it may mean an articulated unity. The latter meaning is the one Mead intends when he describes children. Thus, he is quite right in insisting that the functions of institutions, such as the family, kindergarten, and games, are to introduce "organization . . . in the child's experience," for here he is describing the continuing patterning of definition and articulation. Mead is misleading, however, when he says that the child "is not an organized whole," "he is not a whole self," and "you cannot count on a child." But you can count on a child. You can always count on him not to be an adult; and, almost from the beginning, you can count on him to express his own characteristic rhythm and way of being-with-the-world. If one watches a group of newborn infants, he will discover that each has his own sleep pattern and volume of crying. If one takes societies as an analogue, the notable difference between an advanced society and a primitive one (for example, aborigines or "civilized" extremist groups) is that the primitive groups exhibit maximum unity, but this is unity as uniformity not as individuation or articulation. Hence, members of such societies tend to think and act in terms of stereotypes—although the word is misused since such images are not in "stereo" but are merely typic. They lack depth or subtlety. Such shallow simplicity is charming in a child.

There are certain difficulties with Mead's general point of view. One has already been mentioned: a tendency to confuse articulation with unity. Another difficulty is his tendency to reduce consciousness to self-consciousness and to ignore preconscious modes of awareness; hence, he misunderstands the importance of the body and views it merely objectively.[15] Another difficulty is that he calls some gestures significant and others nonsignificant, when he really should say that some are intended to be symbolic and others are simply expressive. All gesture is significant and, as we shall see, often those very gestures that are not deliberately intentional are the most significant. It is these gestures which Marcel emphasized and to which I referred in my discussion of the articulation of nuance.

The two philosophic principles upon which Mead bases his analysis of the development of human consciousness are emergence and relativity. In fact, he defines consciousness in terms of these principles.

If we accept those two concepts of emergence and relativity, all I want to point out is that they do answer to what we term "consciousness," namely, a certain environment that exists in its relationship to the organism, and in which new characters can arise in virtue of the organism.[16]

By "relativity," he merely means that the patterning of the organism is a determining factor in the environment which it inhabits. By "emergence," he does not mean the interference of some divine fiat or mysterious "life-force" or other obscure element. All he means is that structural differentiation can, and often does, bring about a different qualitative whole. He uses the most simple example, water:

> Water, for example, arises out of a combination of hydrogen and oxygen; it is something over and above the atoms that make it up. When we speak, then, of such characters as sensation arising, emerging, we are really asking no more than when we ask the character of an organic compound. Anything that as a whole is more than the mere form of its parts has a nature that belongs to it that is not to be found in the elements out of which it is made.[17]

The principle that a whole is not reducible to its parts, but that the parts are transformed into elements of the whole and thus enhance and are mutually enhanced by it, is a fundamental concept in aesthetics. As for the principle of relativity, one might say that the entire range of Goethe's reflections on art could be summed up in one phrase: look to the context.

Mead, of course, is not arguing a theory of aesthetics, but he is using principles familiar in aesthetics in order to describe the ways in which human consciousness comes to be. Consciousness can come to be, according to him, because man is a symbolic animal. The ability to symbolize is itself an emergent from a more primitive mode of activity: gesture. Thus, out of unconscious gesture emerges conscious gesture, out of conscious gesture emerges language, out of language emerge imagination, self-reinforcement, self-consciousness, reflection, and, in short, thought. Meaning also is an emergent from the social act and emerges prior to conscious contrivance through the medium of adjustive responses to gesture. Such interaction produces the ground for symbolization, and the symbolic process changes the world of the symbolizing organism.

> Symbolization constitutes objects not constituted before, objects which would not exist except for the context of social relationships wherein symbolization occurs. Language does not simply symbolize a situation or object which is already there in advance; it makes possible the existence or the appearance of that situation or object, for it is a part of the mechanism whereby that situation or object is created.[18]

This means that man's world is never simply and barely *there* in its naked actuality, except perhaps when consciousness is slowly coming to itself as one bumbles around early in the morning. Man alive faces a hypothetical world, not a rigid environment: "The environment is in a very real sense determined by the character of the form."[19] While it may be that the hand precedes the eye in dealing with the world, the world even it deals with is not merely a given target but one that permits and supports the consummation of acts. The bare fact that man exists, then, has direct implication to the structure of the world. This world is the kind of a world in which a man *can* exist.

Of course, it is also the kind of a world in which other animals can exist, but their way of existing is of a different order. The animal is given aspects-in-profile as is man, but his behavior remains for the most part on a signal, not a symbolic, level. Man, however, through his synergic ability to synthesize and his symbolic system, can and does convert aspects-in-profile into objects. In this sense, there are, strictly speaking, no objects in the world of an animal, nor do animals have personalities. Functional differentiation for animals is translated into their bodily structures (for example, the drone has weak wings, the worker bee is sterile, the queen is incredibly fertile), whereas with man there is very little physical distinction in accord with functional articulation. Functional differentiation for man resides in the social body. Another distinction from the other animals is that man is subject to self-reinforcement. The dog can be taught to stand on its hind legs at a given signal, but it cannot give itself the signal. The dog's language is not self-reflexive. But it is the very characteristic of speech that "this process of self-conditioning is going on all the time." The self-reflexive nature of man's symbolizing processes is much more important in determining behavior structure than is mere imitation. It is through and by means of symbols that we are able to communicate and to put ourselves in the place of the other. But even as we speak to the other, we are also speaking to ourselves.

> I want to simply isolate the general mechanism here, because it is of very fundamental importance in the development of what we call self-consciousness and the appearance of a self. We are, especially through the use of the vocal gestures, continually arousing in ourselves those responses which we call out in other persons, so that we are taking the attitudes of the other persons in our own conduct. The critical importance of language in the development of human experience lies in this fact that the stimulus is one that can react upon the speaking individual as it reacts upon the other.[20]

Man, then, is a symbolic animal that not merely lives in but helps to constitute a selective environment through the processes of social interaction. This determination of the character of the environment is the constitution of the relevant, and it takes place at the most elementary levels of functional interaction.

This means that the meaning of the organism is embodied and distributed throughout the organism and throughout his environment, but it does not entail that this elementary meaning-giving is a conscious or even a specifically psychic process. It is a function of behavior, of action upon and reaction to both the environment as selected and the response to action itself. When Marlon Brando (in *The Wild One*) took on the look of a stricken ox and mumbled, "Man, you just go," he was, even at this inarticulate and animal level, attempting to confer meaning on his environment. In so doing, he was constituting it as *his* environment, one that came in direct conflict with that of the townspeople.

What I have termed "selection of relevance," Mead calls "putting oneself in relation to"; and this putting into relation is at the most elementary level, for example, the emergence of color as perceived quality. Hence, Mead says:

> Our constructive selection of an environment—colors, emotional values, and the like—in terms of our physiological sensitivities, is essentially what we mean by consciousness. This consciousness we have tended historically to locate in the mind or in the brain. The eye and related processes endow objects with color in exactly the same sense that an ox endows grass with the character of food, that is, not in the sense of projecting sensations into objects, but rather of putting itself into a relation with the object which makes the appearance and existence of the color possible, as a quality of the object. Colors inhere in objects only by virtue of the relations to given percipient organisms. The physiological or sensory structure of the percipient organism determines the experienced content of the object.[21]

The only additions I will make to this later are attention and expectation. One attends to the aspects, expects red, and perceives it. I agree with Mead that an organism is, in a sense, responsible for its environment, and there would be no food-edible object if there were no organisms that could digest it. The reservation I have is that Mead's ingrained pragmatism tends to make such a selective process highly dependent on utility alone. Such a description may well be adequate for other animals; but, when it comes to man, other factors come into play, both literally and figuratively. Man is a utilitarian. There is no doubt about it. But he is also more than that. Sometimes, he just likes to mess around. And it is more likely that utility is a precipitate of play than play is of utility.

At the higher level of the relations of organisms to organisms, this process of selective interaction and symbolization becomes increasingly more complex and subtle. It is at this level that the self as a self emerges. And the self that is an object to itself is "essentially a social structure," which "provides for itself its social experiences." Hence, one may imagine a solitary individual cut off from all society, but even the man in isolation would retain his personality only by talking to himself or thinking in terms of the social symbol system. The complexity of the social relations of the nonisolated character ensures that the self so constituted is not simple. Hence, due to the various roles we play with different people in the social game, we have multiple personalities. One has a personality as a father, as a husband, as a wage earner, as a teacher, and so on; and this co-existence of multiple personality is quite normal. Thus, it would be quite correct, once one adds the principle of self-reflection, to rewrite Elizabeth Barrett Browning's poem: "How do I know me, let me count your ways." For we know ourselves in great part by reflecting upon the reactions of the others to us. This again differentiates man from the other animals, for it places him in the realm of reason and foresight as well as in the realm of hindsight. Even at this objective level, however, two things hold these multiple personalities in unity. One is the internal awareness of the self as a living process, and the other is the concept of the generalized other.

Concepts by their very nature are universal; and, when one attains the reflective level, the interaction of the individual's thought processes and his social relations precipitates a new concept, the concept of the generalized other. Mead states:

> The very universality and impersonality of thought and reason is from the behavioristic standpoint the result of the given individual taking the attitudes of others toward himself, and of his finally crystallizing all these particular attitudes into a single attitude or standpoint which may be called that of the "generalized other."[22]

This process of condensation of reflective self-aspects into a settled self-concept, however, is not merely an internal process of synthesizing but is also a function of the social milieu of the individual. What happens to Gondo (*High and Low*) is that by accident he is thrown into a new and disorganized community. When this unforeseen stress arises, he is forced to review and reject his former concept of himself as a generalized other. This awareness means changing not only his relations to himself and the criminal but also his relations to his business partners, his son, and his wife.

In Freudian language, I suppose we could call this stretching the superego, since it is the internalization of external norms. Most of the institutions of society are dedicated to the effecting of such internalization. Hence, the existence of the church, the school, and the most powerful of all educational institutions: advertising. Mead draws no distinctions between types of institutions, for he is more interested in the process of inhibiting than inhabiting. It should be mentioned, however, that the individual's relations with and interactions with such primary institutions as the family and the peer group are much more intense than those in relation to more depersonalized institutions. Any institution is an objective form of action that has as one of its functions the molding of personality. But when one regards the other simply as an other (that is, in terms of status) and regards the other as this other (that is, *this person*), the distance of the relationship is diminished; and its intensity is increased.

One example of this would be fighting. Desmond Morris points out that the outcome of fighting within most species is not death but defeat.[23] When conflict arises over matters of territory, hierarchy, or family, animals of the same species clash. But the fighting of other animals is confined to their bodies. Man's use of tools and his symbolic systems provide him with greater amplification of displacement possibilities, but they also provide him with greater distance. Hence, while animals of another species fight, they are always close enough to react to the signal system of the other. Defeat is achieved and life is preserved. But man, through his ability to extend distance and through the sophistication of his weaponry, can remove himself from the bodily context and hence the species context. He is thus able to become the species that kills its own kind, though he can so distance this act as to make it completely impersonal. The Texan riding the bomb down in *Dr. Strangelove* is absurd precisely because his personal fervor has no place in modern warfare. From a B-52, those are not towns but targets, and those are not people but dots. Thus man may indulge in unlimited and indiscriminate destruction, for his media of fighting so extend his body as to depersonalize it. Technology is ever willing to supply new modes of inhuman obliteration, as for example the napalm America has used in Vietnam. War, then, becomes depersonalized slaughter; and one can take the wry thought that with increasingly distant and ferocious mechanisms such as rockets and H-bombs, man is slowly working toward a political millennium: Soon we shall all be able to share the ultimate democracy of anonymous death.

Even at the level of the generalized other, that is, at the level of the social-symbolic person, Mead realizes that there is some subjective content involved. Being basically committed to an objectivist position, however, he usually refers to this as "adopting the attitude of the other." In one passage, however, he reveals greater sensitivity when he admits that in learning a new language one not only learns words but, more importantly, learns the attitudes of the users of that language and their life style. He realizes that you cannot convey a language as a pure abstraction but must become clothed in it; and hence he says, "A person learns a new language and, as we say, gets a new soul."[24] Beyond attitude, of course, there is sympathy, which Mead acknowledges, though he resists taking it in its fundamental sense of feeling-one-with. I believe that Mead really means not sympathy but empathy. There is no direct participation of the self in the other at this level except as a self, and that self must still be kept apart and reflective. But at most what is involved is the tension between the self as a self and the self in relation to the generalized other, not the basic participation directly in the rhythm of the other. Basic participation can occur in life and does, but it is below the level of self-consciousness. Yet at the level of self-consciousness, the tension between the self-as-object and self-as-generalized-other produces what we normally call "personality."

The Stoics called this the "persona," or mask. We still use it on the programs for stage productions and even occasionally in films, when we list the persons involved as the "dramatis personae." Such a listing identifies the individual with the mask he is to assume, and the mask is defined by the gaze of the other. Alfred Hitchcock has almost made a career of bypassing or using the gaze of the other. The whole theme of *Rear Window* is based on this relation, and some of the most memorable shots in *Strangers on a Train* were reflections in a girl's glasses. These reflections were so unnerving to the murderer that he almost strangled an innocent girl. Many Hitchcock villains also wear glasses, and this underlines their menace. One reason glasses appear frightening is because they magnify the gaze.

During rehearsal, the stage actor is in much the same situation as the motion-picture actor; that is, he must construct a persona for himself, not in terms of an actual audience, but in terms of what the part calls for and his own conception of the generalized other. At this stage, if the actor acts, his acting is highly artificial and stilted for the simple reason that he is being abstractly symbolic. This type of acting was often used in the old silents; and, though it was inappropriate to the film medium even there, the audience was so fascinated at seeing movement that anything went. Such acting, of course, is much too calculated today even for the stage. However, Mead evidently considered this to be the only mode of acting.

> It is only the actor who uses bodily expression as a means of looking as he wants others to feel. He gets a response which reveals to him how he looks by continually using a mirror. He registers anger, he registers love, he registers this, that, or the other attitude, and he examines himself in a glass to see how he does so. When he later makes use of the gesture it is present as a mental image.[25]

Mead seems to confine this description primarily to facial gesture, and he admits that it does not apply adequately to vocal gesture.

> There is, further, a whole set of values given in speech which are not of symbolic character. The actor is conscious of these values; that is, if he assumes a certain attitude he is, as we say, aware that this attitude represents grief. If it does he is able to respond to his own gesture in some sense as his audience does. It is not a natural situation; one is not an actor all of the time.[26]

Involved here, of course, is what is "not of a symbolic character" that the actor is aware of and utilizes and also how he gets closer to a "natural situation."

Ingmar Bergman's early films are theatrical in the sense that they are filled with people deciding to "act" in a certain mode in order, deliberately, to produce expected results in the other. In keeping with this theatrical stance, the films are filled with close-ups of such things as make-up, mirrors, and theatrical props. In fact, *The Magician* had as its Swedish title *Ansiktet,* which means *The Face.* One viewing of the film, however, convinces that the title should have been *The Mask.* This fascination with the theatrical, the deliberate and self-conscious creation of illusion, also accounts for Fellini's inclusion of magicians, clowns, and the use of heavy pancake make-up, for example, on the mentalist in *The Nights of Cabiria* and the mind reader in *8½.* Such acting as Mead describes, then, is used even in film. But if it is not used for a specific purpose, as, for example, a metaphor of illusion, it is misused, and we say that actor overacts and is too calculating. Both the screen and the modern theatre demand a more natural mode of acting due to two factors: the warping of context and the gaze of the other.

Had Mead applied his basic philosophic principle of relativity to the situation of the actor, he would have understood why acting is not as deliberate and self-conscious an attitude as he describes. This is especially true in film. Pudovkin conclusively proved how the cutting and juxtaposition of different shots could change an audience's interpretation of the actor's expression. Perhaps the most down-to-earth example of this, if true, is Hedy Lamarr's admission that the "extreme love" she was supposed to portray in *Ecstasy* was really caused by the director sticking pins in her derriere. The camera captures the expression, but the context determines what the expression means.

The stage actor does not have as much control over the context as the film director has. But he has an advantage over the screen actor which cannot be matched and that is his ability to respond to a live audience. He can adjust his gestures and intonations to the rhythm of the audience and to its particular circumstance. This is why plays vary from city to city (actors *assume,* not always with proper justification, that the audience will be more sophisticated in New York) and from performance to performance. Advances in technology also have a bearing, particularly the spot microphone and the kind of space to be used, for example, in-the-round. It was unobservant of Mead to miss the fact that our voices do not sound the same to us as they do to others. Since the technical amplification of pitch, volume, and so forth, is more controlled in film, the film actor tends to talk more in his normal voice, although even here there may be a disparity between his voice as he hears it and as we hear it. Whether on stage or on screen, the actor has become aware of expressive quality. Due to advances in technology, he can utilize more subtle means of expressive quality, hence the lower pitch, the decreased gesture, and the more natural mode of acting. He must not so much strive for effect as relax into it.[27]

Jean-Paul Sartre has made much of the stare of the other and being caught with your subjectivity showing. Due to his recurrent paranoia, he interprets this to mean that human relations are basically ones of war involving an unending fight for dominance. Had he paid more attention to the communicative process, however, he need not have been so frightened. Of course, there is a frightening thing about the stare. Perhaps because, as Morris says, it is immediately interpreted as hostility. In normal conversation, however, we do not look at each other constantly but shift our eyes from one thing to another and then back to the other. If someone does stare at us constantly, we search for a different response. But we don't trust anyone who won't look us in the eyes. Hence, normal conversation is a mixture of fixture on the other with the eyes, wandering, and returning. When one views the other as abstract, that is, not as a concrete person, the situation can become unnerving and one of battle and fear. This may have been Sartre's trouble: he just had trouble recognizing the concrete individuality of the other.

Anyone who has talked in public is familiar with the constriction in the throat, the dryness of the mouth, and the other symptoms that we call "stage fright." One can even perceive a felt difference in teaching the class of another person, since the unfamiliar class is not "my" class, that is, it is not individuated but is a "strange class." Poor teachers, of course, escape by staring out the window. Good teachers overcome the massed stare by either falling so in love with their subject that it takes possession of them (as E. E. Cummings has said, "A professor is a predicate in love with his subject") or by talking directly to individuals or both. When the abstract situation is made concrete the fear evaporates. When one treats himself and others as individuals, he has slipped into trust. I say "slips into," for what was originally willed becomes one's basic address, attitude, way of being-with-the-others. One ceases to be *before* them and becomes *with* them. This is one reason why a first class is so important, for if the instructor is with them then, he will be accepted and forgiven almost anything during the semester.

Some people are so self-conscious and so up-tight that they cannot be with it. "Being with it" here means being able to coalesce and move with the rhythm of the situation, much as a jazz musician improvises. Basically, that is what good teaching is: planned improvisation. There is a sense in which Louis Armstrong was right when he said, "Baby, if I got to tell ya, you ain't never gonna know." But some people cannot perceive and they cannot be told. Hence, they try to work on their fear externally and *tell* themselves to relax. Nothing could be more futile. It is like trying to grasp a handful of water. The more one tries to order himself, the more his self as an object emerges, and the tighter his grip becomes. Some people become simply mute with such fright. There are others, however, who escape into the familiar. One may, of course, hold his hands over his eyes, but this is much too clumsy. Another technique is for the speaker to put on dark glasses and thus recede from the stare of his audience. By far the most familiar escape, however, is for the speaker to begin rocking on his feet to the rhythm of his own respiration or heartbeat and to use recurrent clearings-of-the-throat and such pat phrases as "it seems to me," "I would like to suggest," and "on the other hand." Such phrases are not merely transitional devices; they are forms of defense against the massed stare of the others.

I have noticed that this is also true of accents. When I taught in Texas, I often talked to students on an individual basis. Even when they were addressed as individuals in class, they usually showed merely a trace of accent. After all, in class seated *among* the others, few others could look at them directly nor could they catch the stare of those behind them. But invariably, when a student had to stand in front of a class and make a verbal report, he would slip into an accent so thick that you could smell magnolias and see the honey dripping from the clauses. This was not a calculated effect but merely a slipping into a previous, more simple, more familiar, and hence safe mode of behavior. By escaping into accent, they felt more at home.

The force of the stare can also become evident in the transference to objects. This is what we normally refer to as "mike-fright" or "camera-shy." If one concentrates on the device before him instead of on the audience and the individuals in the audience, the normal anxiety of a performance is amplified by the sum of his imagination. I remember experiencing this vividly once when talking to a crowd. The words were flowing well until I noticed the red bulb on a TV camera. My eyes immediately began to swim, and I had difficulty reading the speech. What happened here was that an infinite and unknown generalized other had suddenly invaded my given situation. I was cut off from their response; in fact, the audience became an abstract "they." This is one problem the screen actor can have that does not afflict the stage actor. The stage actor can constantly, like the teacher, read his perform-ance in the faces and the vocal expressions of the others. He may misread them, of course, but at least the response is before him. The film actor has the advantage that editing may make his movement of an eyebrow more important than his soliloquy and carry the scene, but he has the great disadvantage that he is speaking to an unknown and unknowable mass. The camera, not a person, is his audience. No doubt this is why directors spend so much time on reassurance, for the anxiety level and hence the blink level of the film actor may reach fever pitch.

Another difficulty for the film actor at the level of the generalized other is really a function of the bigness of the film industry. It was in the past and still is dependent on large audiences to recoup the enormous financial investments. This is increas-ingly true of the stage also, but the stage has not gone into the manufacturing of a deliberate persona with either the intensity or the success of the film industry. In films, this was the star system, which is dying out due to structural changes in the industry itself and the growing sophistication of the audiences. Most audiences now want actors; and, although at this point a good deal of acting is simply bone structure and camera angle, there is a general drift away from the contrived star. There are genuine stars still, such as Frank Sinatra and Elizabeth Taylor, but the old-time, manufactured or, perhaps, maxfactored, product is dying out.

What happens in the star system, essentially, is that a person is turned into a thing. The thing he or she was turned into may not have had any real relevance to himself as a person and rarely had any relation to the individual as an I. The results sold tickets, for the creatures (one cannot call them human) created with make-up, lighting, editing, ballyhoo, and "created situations" were larger than life, more glamorous, and all too inhuman. The actor himself usually found one of three ways to relate himself to this fictitious creature deliberately contrived by press agents for the delectation of the generalized other. One way of relating was simply to ignore one's image as much as possible. This was the road to sanity, and Humphrey Bogart, James Cagney, and a few others took this road. Some, like Paul Newman, found themselves living up to the image or repeating themselves, and so they quit acting for awhile. The more tragic courses were the other two roads: identifica-tion and rejection. Some actors began to believe their own publicity. They were aware of the disparity between themselves and the created image but then tried to become what they conceived the generalized other expected them to be. This was the road taken by John Barrymore, Errol Flynn, Jayne Mansfield, and Ava Gardner. Perhaps it is an enjoyable form of suicide, but it is suicide all the same.

Those of us who do not live lives as public as those of movie stars and who need not try to hold on to concepts of the self as a me that are as artificially contrived, can still fall into the same traps as the star. If one accepts his me as myself and as I, then life becomes a process of continuous striving and ultimate failure, for it is utterly impossible for us to be what we and others define as proper goals. Externally viewed, attempting to live up to the expectations of others may appear as high-minded idealism, although it is actually more misguided than high-minded. Internally viewed, it is suicide. One is attempting to transform himself into an object. The normal teen-age response to this is rebellion; but such rebellion is merely inverted idealism. It is playing the game of the other but this time by negative rules. Such rebellion still assumes that the game is both meaningful and real. But, of course, it is only a game. One cannot win a game by striving; it is only by relaxing into the game and playing it for itself, by giving up on the concept of winning either by identification or by rejection, that one can truly win. It is not merely that one ought or ought not to justify one's existence. One cannot. He exists. Existence cannot be proven or justified. It is not the case that each of us should try to be an individual; we are born individuals. There is nothing else we can be. We can be and become, but we cannot *will* to become. Hence the futility of striving to be anything else. One is himself when he coalesces with himself and moves with his own rhythm. What others make of that is their problem.

So far, I have been at the level of the me and, while accepting Mead's basic description of its nature, have added a slight shift in meaning so that the me is not merely the product of the other, whether generalized other or particular other, but is the function of the tension between the myself and the me. It should be apparent that the me is our self-conscious character. Another way of saying it is that our me is the self as a function of the expectation of the other and of the self when regarded as other. Mead sums it up this way:

> The "me" is a conventional, habitual individual. It is always there. It has to have those habits, those responses which everybody has; otherwise the individual could not be a member of the community.[28]

He realizes that there is a difference of nuance with each me, not merely because each occupies a different stance with respect to society, but because there is expressive power with the individual.

> But an individual is constantly reacting to such an organized community in the way of expressing himself, not necessarily asserting himself in the offensive

Plate 1

The two trends of the
motion picture were evi-
dent from the beginning
—fantasy in Méliès'
Voyage to the Moon and
concurrent realism in
William S. Porter's **The
Great Train Robbery**.

Plate 2

Courtesy of The Museum of Modern Art / Film Stills Archive

In Sarah Bernhardt's **Queen Elizabeth** the camera fell to the stage —and it was a primitive stage.

D. W. Griffith freed the camera from the stage. He moved it out into the open and into its own (**Intolerance**).

Plate 3

The painter's cinema reached its high point in German Expressionism —**The Cabinet of Doctor Caligari**.

Courtesy of The Museum of Modern Art / Film Stills Archive

The Russian film has seldom equaled and never surpassed the compact lyricism of **Potemkin**.

Plate 4

Leni Reifenstahl's
Triumph of the Will
demonstrated the emo-
tional impact and filmic
importance of editing.

Camera angle and fluid
movement were used by
Orson Welles (**Citizen
Kane**) to express the-
matic development.

Courtesy of The Museum of Modern Art / Film Stills Archive

Courtesy of Janus Films

Plate 5

The documentary, besides being factual, often makes strong personal statements. Flaherty's **Man of Aran**.

Courtesy of Janus Films

Courtesy of Audio Film Center, Inc.

The film with a thin social conscience often suffers by being sentimental and moralistic (**Ballad of a Soldier**). The characters are consequently depthless.

Plate 6

Courtesy of The Museum of Modern Art / Film Stills Archive

Lord of the Flies failed to find adequate visual equivalents for the novelist's technique.

Tom Jones successfully adapted the novel. Its schizophrenic form was unified by progressive color drainage.

Courtesy of United Artists Corporation

Plate 7

Antonioni often uses things as expressive of human relationships (**L'Avventura**).

Courtesy of Janus Films

Courtesy of Audio Film Center, Inc.

Until she can exorcise her past, the actress (Emmanuelle Riva) of **Hiroshima Mon Amour** cannot move successfully with her present.

Plate 8

Both **Wild Strawberries** and **Rashomon** demonstrate that human reality is always more complex than we assume it to be.

Plate 9

A motion picture is not a series of stills (**Winter Light**).

Courtesy of Janus Films

Courtesy of United Artists Corporation

Although the people danced, the film did not. **West Side Story** was smothered by color, production values, and false realism.

Plate 10

In **Hud**, Alma (Patricia Neal) insists on being treated as what she is — a person and hence a center of value.

Courtesy of Paramount Pictures Corporation

The slaughtering scene from **Hud**. In the loneliness of the new West, men are united only by the community of death.

Plate 11

Lumet's **The Pawn-broker** was a fine film, but it suffered from theatricality. There were very few codas in its emotional intensity.

Courtesy of Commonwealth United Entertainment, Inc.

Courtesy of Audio Film Center, Inc.

Buñuel's **Viridiana** exhibited masterful economy. It was conceived and executed in cinematic, not theatrical, terms.

Plate 12

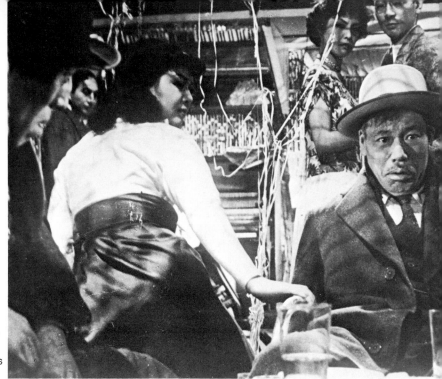

Besides being a great
action director, Kuro-
sawa may be the most
philosophical—certainly
the most existential—
of all modern film artists
(Ikiru).

Courtesy of Toho International

Courtesy of The Museum of Modern Art / Film Stills Archive

**Occurrence at Owl
Creek Bridge** suggests
that the short story or
narrative poem could be
used more as bases for
fine films.

Plate 13

External form: **The Graduate**.

Internal form: **8½**.

Stills printed by permission of Avco Embassy Pictures Corp.

Plate 14

Juliet of the Spirits demonstrates that the personal film is not confined to autobiography.

Courtesy of Rizzoli Film S.P.A.

Extension of theme beyond plot. Juliet's spirits depart assuring her they are friends.

Plate 15

The personal film: **The Four Hundred Blows** tenderly reveals the warping of a young boy's personality.

Courtesy of Janus Films

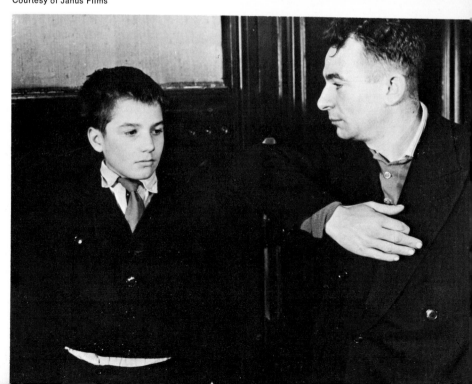

Plate 16

Anger's **Scorpio Rising** is one of the few underground films with a tension between plot and theme.

Courtesy of Kenneth Anger

© 1966 Metro-Goldwyn-Mayer Inc.

The artist's girl and the nameless photographer fail to communicate. Nevertheless, **Blow-Up** with its search for new values may be the **Citizen Kane** of the sixties.

sense but expressing himself, *being himself* in such cooperative process as belongs to any community. The attitudes involved are gathered from the group, but the individual in whom they are organized has the opportunity of giving them an expression which perhaps has never taken place before.[29]

There is no "perhaps" about it. Each of us is a different expressive center of synthesis; and one may take comfort in the thought that, for better or for worse, the universe has had it as far as he is concerned.

Now, what Mead is moving toward here, of course, is subjectivity and its status in reality. He sums this up in the word "I" and feels that while the me provides the form for the I, the I provides the expressive energy that animates the form. But under the concept of the I Mead identifies two things: the I as object and the I as synergic subject. Hence, his discussion of the I is not as clear as it might be. I shall therefore, for the purpose of analysis, split this I. I shall refer to the I-as-object as the myself and reserve the word I for the I-as-subject. It is quite obvious that Mead confuses the two, for he speaks of the artist as being the most unconventional person, much like an impulsive person in whom "the structure of the 'me' does not there determine the expression of the 'I'" and here what he means by the I is the I-as-subject. On the other hand, he states that the "'I' appears in our experience in memory. It is only after we have acted that we know what we have done; it is only after we have spoken that we know what we have said";[30] and here he obviously means the I-as-object. This confusion leads him to put too much stress on self-consciousness and to assume that all habits are by their very nature social. But if I am to keep the discussion clear, I must use some different terms. Hence, I shall refer to the level of consciousness as the "myself" or the "I-as-object" and to the level of awareness or, if one prefers, prehension as the "I" or the "I-as-subject."

Due to his principle of relativity, Mead admits that, although each individual is a kind of monad that reflects the social process as a whole, it is still the case that each individual is individual, for he has a unique place within the whole, a unique perspective and standpoint relative to the whole. When we add to this the recognition of the expressive energy of the individual, we can see that the individual's place is not merely *this* place, it is his place, that is, an embodied presence, which brings qualitative differentiation to the spatial metaphor. This qualitative synergic system we refer to as expressing our body image or as our impalpable body of individuated habits.

I have already noted that Mead's total objectivism brings him to overlook the self-reflective character of the body and to confuse people with things. It also leads him to be unaware of the body image as such.

> The parts of the body are quite distinguishable from the self. We can lose parts of the body without any serious invasion of the self. The mere ability to experience different parts of the body is not different from the experience of a table. The table presents a different feel from what the hand does when one hand feels another, but it is an experience of something with which we come definitely into contact. The body does not experience itself as a whole, in the sense in which the self in some way enters the experience of the self.[31]

Mead is correct when he states that the eye can see the foot, but he is incorrect in assuming that it is the eye alone that sees; that is, that the relation is merely an external one in which one organ registers the impression of another. He is further incorrect in asserting that we have no experience of the body as a whole or that the body parts can be lost without a change in the total self.

As Marcel has pointed out, it is not the same thing to say "this car belongs to me," "this nose belongs to me," and "I belong to me." It is problematic whether one can belong to himself at all in the sense of elementary possession. But there is also a difference between my car and my nose. My nose is an immediate part of me, unlike my car, which may become, but is not initially, an extension of my bodily schema. In short, my nose is me in a way that my car cannot be, for it is an element in the constitution of the whole of my body schema and not something acquired or initially apart from me and my body.

Furthermore, while it is quite true that we cannot see our bodies as a whole, it is nevertheless the case that we still have a consciousness of what they are like, even without mirrors. If a person is shown photographs of parts, for example, of hands, he has great difficulty trying to determine which hand is his own. Yet of all parts, these should be the most easily identifiable, since the hands are, for the most part, before our eyes almost constantly. Yet no one has difficulty picking out that which never appears in direct perception: his body moving as a whole. Each has no difficulty recognizing motion pictures of himself, and, in fact, it is easier for us to recognize moving shadows of ourselves than to pick out from a group of still photographs our much more substantial hands. Mead has fallen into classical psychology and has assumed that parts precede wholes. But what is in fact constantly given in experience is a tension of figure and background, or parts-and-wholes. Though we have no direct perception of the body as such, the schema of the body is the horizon within which all perception takes place, and we have an awareness of it that is lived directly. For this reason, also, any loss of a part will change the body schema as a whole. Merleau-Ponty's analyses of phantom limbs, anosognosia, and other phenomena all show that when a part is altered the body-image is altered and hence experience as a whole becomes warped.[32] Our body parts are not mere *partes extra partes* but are elements of a whole, and these elements are intimately engaged with each other and engaged in the structure of the whole. If the body image is the sieve for the selective being of the world-before-me, then the self is definitely altered and experience as a whole is altered should the structure of the body-image or any part of it suffer alteration.

The body-image mediates my consciousness of the world; and this mediation is basically ambiguous, for it both allows me to open up unto the world and at the same time restricts the range of my opening-up. Furthermore, it provides me with a refuge and with an excuse. For the self is not always conscious. Consciousness is an intermittent phenomenon. Not only do we have the phenomenon of speech, but during waking hours there is a waxing and waning of awareness. Sometimes I call myself forth, sometimes I am called forth by others. When I call myself forth in imagination, I am regarding myself as an other and thus am regarding the myself and not the I. If the imagination is turned forward, we call it imagination proper, for then the myself is inhabiting future possibilities. If, on the other hand, the imagination is turned backward, it is memory, for then the myself is being shaped and is reshaping past events. Mead is quite right in insisting that most such awareness is retrospection, but the I that is thus known is the I-as-object, or the myself.

We usually refer to the myself, then, when we speak of an ego, for there is a strong tendency to identify the self with the withdrawal from the self-as-merely-other or the generalized other. Furthermore, since the myself has its impalpable body of habitual patternings, it exhibits a stability, which appears attractive. I am thus able to persuade myself that I have a self and that this self endures through time. Since endurance as an identifiable thing is an ideal, I tend to acquiesce in the belief that this self-as-object-to-itself is "my" ego, it is "my" I. Notice the possessive. We have a tendency to assimilate the ego under the grasping mode and to say *my* ego, as though the ego were something that could be held and, preeminently, controlled. A reflection upon lived experience will show that there is nothing to control and nobody to control it, but the illusion persists. Thus though there are some who become anxious because they are not living up to their me, that is, the conceived characteristics that one assumes are demanded by the generalized other, the more basic state of anxiety is the effort to try to live up to the ego or the self-conceived-as-object. Such a struggle can lead to a persistent sense of failure, for any man is greater than any concept he can conceive. In living himself, he goes beyond his static conceptualizations.

This urge to identify the self with the myself brings many people to deduce their lives instead of live them. They are always (in imagination and actually) getting-ready-to do this or that, but spend so much time getting-ready-to that they never live. This identification with the self as stable object brings the sense of loss, as though time were a passing away over which one had no control and as if life were in the end merely a carnival of phony tinsel that is constantly on the verge of evaporating. But fundamentally, life is in the living of it, and there is no other time to be in but now. If one were to stand outside, where would he stand?

This same false identity exhausts much of the energy of the lived self. For the self now becomes engaged in trying to justify or to just defy itself. In either case, it is taking the ego as real and again is merely playing the game affirmatively or negatively. But it no longer is a game, for it becomes serious. Thus, the whole force of the selfhood game is thrown into attempting to build walls against the others, the self-as-object, and the world. The belief is that by separating oneself, security will be achieved. What is not perceived is that by building walls, one is making the self closed and incapable of seeing. It is not by looking that we see, but rather by relaxing into our vision. It is not by striving to be that we are, but rather by sliding into our rhythmic being. Ethically, the meaning of this is simple. Since there is nowhere to hide, why hide? But emotionally, we have difficulty trying to assimilate such an insight, for we feel that safety occurs only *inside*. Fortunately, the self as a living being keeps escaping through this straitjacket of the self-as-conceived. It escapes forth in our unintentional gestures, which we cannot wholly suppress and which express who we are and reveal our pose to the world as merely a pose. It escapes in our tones. It displays itself overtly when we play and when we accomplish the fortuitous. We reveal who we are when we do what we don't have to do.

This who that we are is the I. But it is not a who in any substantial sense of being a separate and separable entity, either apart from the other levels of the self or apart from its milieu and its world. It is the rhythmic patterning of circumstance, which sings its own melody. In a fundamental sense, it is nonexistent, if by "existence" one means a self that is stable and sure and known. This is the self as lived and not the self as known. It is the self that, unaware of itself, colors its world. It is a self that has an awareness of the self as an ongoing phenomenon but not as a conscious object. The I is the self as living. It is that self that one can find if he merely sits quietly doing nothing in the lonely hours of the night and begins to rock slightly with the rhythm of his breathing. In this type of experience, it is really irrelevant whether one says "I am breathing." In fact, the experience is more like "it is now breathing me." It is the self that expresses itself when the golf ball is struck with the maximum rightness of grace or when we throw the basketball and walk away, for we know it will go through the hoop. It is the self known only to intuition, the self that leans this way or that against possibilities. It is the self that is frightening precisely because it is so amorphous and ever so possible. It is the self to which we constantly hope to flee but seldom achieve. It is the self of direct, active feeling of being-one-with-oneself and with the world. Perhaps its best analogy is to tone. If we are to believe one of the world's great religions, in the beginning was the word, but not the word *as word*. On the contrary, the word *as sound*. The object that the Great God Shiva holds in his upper right hand is not a concept but a drum. And with the beating of the Great Cosmic Drum, the rhythm of existence breathed itself forth. No wonder the Hindu word for the ego is not the self-as-object, but "aham" which is literally the sound of exhaling. In the beginning was the rhythm.

That this self-as-subject of the true I, as distinguished from the myself, existed was apparent to Mead even though he had woven himself into an objectivist position. It was evident to him because it was a given phenomenon of behavior. Hence, he recognized that the I reacts to the self even though it is not in the limelight and that the separation of the I from the me is not only not fictitious, but reveals an I that is "something that is never calculable." This uncalculable, unpredictable level of the self must be acknowledged, for it is evident in overt behavior. It reveals itself not merely in unconscious gesture and tone, but in the relief of letting-go, the direct participation in the being of the other, unconscious imitation, astonishment at the self, and the invisibility of the familiar.

While we have seen that there is a strong drive for the self to escape into the self and to build walls against the other and, in times of stress, to escape into the familiar, we have also noted that each individual is a synthesis of ambiguities. Hence, it should not surprise us that there is also a strong drive in us to let-go, to be-with others, and to share their being directly. Marcel is not the only one aware of this drive. Mead also acknowledges it:

> I have referred to the situation in which a person can sit down with a friend and say just what he is thinking about someone else. There is a satisfaction in letting one's self go in this way. The sort of thing that under other circumstances you would not say and would not even let yourself think is now naturally uttered. If you get into a group which thinks as you do then one can go to lengths which may surprise the person himself.[33]

Mead is, of course, much too self-conscious here and he is still thinking in terms of communication. But he is aiming for something more fundamental than communication; it is the direct I-Thou relationship. It is basically a communion. Such a communion presupposes great trust, and this is one reason why deep friendships are so rare, for they demand that the friend have the strength of his weaknesses, that he can put up with us, be with us even when we are not at our best. This drive to immediate sharing is also, no doubt, the impulse in modern society to supplant religion with sex, for the sexual relation is one in which there can be an immediate sharing of the being of the other. As E. E. Cummings has remarked, "I am through you so I."

Mead also recognizes participation when he states that "the principle which I have suggested as basic to human social organization is that of communication involving participation in the other."[34] Again, of course, he remains at the external and objective level and does not see the reality of true subjective sharing, a subjective sharing that is analogous to the film experience. That such sharing does occur even at the level of an audience, is shown by unconscious imitation. One can tell which classes many students are taking simply by listening to them talk and watching them move. It is not the content that is important, but the way of expressing. When one does so attend, he will find the phrasings and the characteristic rhythms and intonations of his colleagues emerging. Such imitation is really simple unconscious assimilation and is often an embarrassment to the student when pointed out. Almost all of us walk taller when leaving a Western.

Similarly, couples who have been married for a long time often express each other's thoughts before they are vocalized and assume the same stance to the world as their mates. In very long marriages, they even tend to look alike, as well as behave in the same rhythms and modes. There is nothing mysterious or mystic then, in the direct participation in the being of the other. We move in and out of each other's being. It is a normal, observable phenomenon, though its occurrence, like that of good fortune, may be rare. Its occurrence in the film experience is common.

Another indication of the reality of the living self-as-object is the phenomenon of astonishment. Since we are never fully aware of who we are, we often astonish ourselves by our own deeds and surprise ourselves by the revelation of hitherto unknown possibilities. Others can tell us many things about ourselves that we are unaware of; and, though we may astonish them, we can also astonish ourselves. If one goes back and reads something he wrote at an earlier stage in life, he has the situation in which he can confront himself as an other. Usually, what one feels is embarrassment, and he wonders how he could ever have written anything so immature and gauche. But, even here, one will run across a phrasing here, a line there, that is astonishing. That past person who I was then is, in a sense, as dead as Marcus Aurelius, and yet I am astonished by some of the things he wrote and pleased by some of the insights he had. To those who have the strength to be open, this capacity for self-astonishment can become a common thing in the present, and not merely a reflection on past life. Hence, the artist and the mystic can become a locus for marvelous accidents, which surprise both their audiences and themselves.

Another indication of direct participation is the increasing invisibility of the familiar. The more we get to know a person, the less he is a visible object to us. Once we have reached the perspective where we are sharing his being-with him as distinguished from only being-beside him, it takes a true effort of abstraction to see him at all. We thus have the strange circumstance—we can give quite accurate descriptions of people whom we know slightly, but we find it very difficult to describe our most intimate friends. It is not merely that we know them so well that their complexity overwhelms us with the inability to verbalize their appearance. It is that in part, of course, but more fundamentally it is because their appearance has disappeared. We do not abstract ourselves from them far enough to constitute them as visible objects. One may note a similar phenomenon with close friends. With slight friends, one has difficulty starting a conversation; and, no matter how great the good will, the conversation runs out of content in a few minutes or, at best, hours. With deep friends, however, time and space become irrelevant. One begins a conversation almost where he left it the last time, and it can continue indefinitely. It does not become exhausted. Again, one is participating in the being of the other and not regarding him as an other but as a co-participant in the mutuality of the self.

Now, it is precisely in this area of the self-as-subject that the poet moves. This is one reason that he is such a valuable and such a dangerous friend. On the one hand, he is open to the possibilities of himself and others, for he is acutely sensitive to his milieu and to its nuances of meaning. On the other hand, he cannot be counted on, in the sense that neither he nor the other knows which possibility he will choose next and sometimes the choices he makes are offensive. Yet without risk, there is no gain. Even a turtle can't cross a room without sticking its neck out. In *Wild Strawberries,* even Borg became.

The difficulty in much modern art, of course, and the great failing of Durgnat's book on film, is the inability to differentiate between expression and self-expression. Young people go through a poetic phase; but, unlike true poets, they grow out of it. That is, they go through a stage in which they are acutely sensitive. But accompanying this sensitivity is a large factor of incoherence. This is true also of some artists, and they constantly mistake their symptoms for their work. Thomas Wolfe's "wild goat-cry to the universe" is real. It is a real expression of Wolfe's frustrations. But it is not an artistic expression. It is simply self-expression in a fairly inarticulate form. The mark of an artist is that he feels things deeply, but feeling is not enough. He must also be able to shape that feeling into an objective expressive form, which speaks apart from himself. Thus, the poet will be marked by sensitivity; but, if he is a true poet, he will also be marked by the capacity for brutal choice. To create is to shape, not merely to vent. No one goes to hear a baby cry, but one does go to hear a symphony. The artist, then, must shape his sensitivity so that it answers to and arouses reverberations in a wider world than that of his own subjective feelings. He must learn to transform those subjective intensities into the objective tuning forks of society. He must, beginning with his own subjectivity, so shape it as to reveal contents of emotional range and depth that go beyond what he felt or even conceived himself to be feeling and may not have had in mind in the first place. In fact, if he is truly an artist, he will rarely have had them in mind, since the process of shaping is the process of articulating and becoming clear about what we feel. In this sense, the work of art and the artist himself become emergents from the process of articulation. To articulate a feeling is to be freed from it.

If the artist is successful, he will so shape his object that it will provide the spectator with a horizon on not merely his world but a common expressive world. If it is a visual object, it will teach him to see in a new way; if an audible object, to hear. If a motion picture, both. Mead himself had a passing awareness of this possibility of the motion picture:

> The possibilities in our nature, those sorts of energy which William James took so much pleasure in indicating, are possibilities of the self that lie beyond our own immediate presentation. We do not know just what they are. They are in a certain sense the most fascinating contents that we can contemplate, so far as we can get hold of them. We get a great deal more of our enjoyment of romance, of moving pictures, of art, in setting free, at least in imagination, capacities which belong to ourselves, or which we want to belong to ourselves. . . . The possibilities of the "I" belong to that which is actually going on, taking place, and it is in some sense the most fascinating part of our experience. It is there that novelty arises and it is there that our most important values are located. It is the realization in some sense of this self that we are continually seeking.[35]

It is precisely to this level of the self that the motion picture can appeal. It is also this level which, above all arts, movies have the capacity to reveal. The motion picture can drive directly toward and record our ways-of-being-in-the-world, and hence it is more concerned with us as beings than as personae. The motion picture does not provide us with a mere "redemption of physical reality"; it provides us with other voices, other worlds to be in. It is not primarily a representation, but a presentation. It presents us with an illusory world both livid and lived. It presents us man alive in the concrete circumstance of his being-in-the-world.

Notes

1. Desmond Morris, *The Naked Ape* (New York: McGraw-Hill, 1967), p. 133.

2. Maurice Merleau-Ponty, *The Phenomenology of Perception* (New York: Humanities Press, 1962), p. 169.

3. Merleau-Ponty, p. 170.

4. Gabriel Marcel, *Creative Fidelity* (New York: Farrar, Straus & Giroux, 1964), p. 17.

5. Marcel, p. 16.

6. Marcel, p. 17.

7. Merleau-Ponty, *Phenomenology,* p. 165.

8. Those interested in the complexity, flexibility, and variability of animal aptitudes might read Konrad Lorenz. The great distinction between man and other animals, as Lorenz sees it, is the symbolic-social situation: culture. See *King Solomon's Ring* (Crowell, 1952), *Evolution and Modification of Behavior* (University of Chicago, 1965), and *On Aggression* (Harcourt, Brace & World, 1966).

9. Maurice Merleau-Ponty, *The Structure of Behavior* (Boston: Beacon Press, 1963), p. 181.

10. Marcel, *Creative Fidelity,* p. 20.

11. In film, the camera is the ground for any objects appearing at all. Since the spectator identifies with the camera, it becomes his "virtual body" or "temporary habitation."

12. Marcel, *Creative Fidelity,* pp. 27–28.

13. Marcel, p. 28.

14. This increased tension is true even of ants. They will take much greater risks going home than moving away from the home place.

15. George H. Mead, *Mind, Self and Society* (Chicago: University of Chicago Press, 1934), p. 136. He says, for example: "The mere ability to experience different parts of the body is not different from the experience of a table," but, of course, it is.

16. Mead, p. 330.

17. Mead, p. 329.

18. Mead, p. 78.

19. Mead, p. 247.

20. Mead, p. 69.

21. Mead, p. 77.

22. Mead, p. 90.

23. Morris, *The Naked Ape,* p. 146ff.

24. Mead, *Mind, Self and Society,* p. 283.

25. Mead, pp. 65–66.

26. Mead, pp. 197–198.

27. Miss Mahdhur Jaffre told me that she much prefers film acting to the stage. She said the projection necessary for the stage invariably left her hoarse.
28. Mead, *Mind, Self and Society,* p. 197.
29. Mead, pp. 197–198. Italics added.
30. Mead, p. 196.
31. Mead, p. 136.
32. Merleau-Ponty, *Phenomenology,* p. 98ff.
33. Mead, *Mind, Self and Society,* p. 213.
34. Mead, p. 253.
35. Mead, p. 204.

6

The Personal World

Beginning with man's incarnate condition, we have seen that he can and does extend himself into his world through the processes of appropriation, assimilation, and extension. We have also examined man's levels of awareness of himself. We have discovered that man's condition is one of basic ambivalence and ambiguity. But this ambiguity does not entail vagueness or incoherence. On the contrary, it is a function of man's peculiar intimacy with his existence, the existence of others, and the existence of the world. We must now turn to that common world, for it is a common one even though partially constituted by the self. We should not be surprised if we find that it also is ambiguous—it is both hypothetical and given. Again, I shall try to keep this account brief. But one should not underestimate its difficulty. As Merleau-Ponty has said, "Nothing is more difficult than to give an account of what we see." Let us begin with a genetic approach to the increasing articulation of the patterning process. This means that we will begin with those "various vague beings": children.

Now, a hypothetical world is a world based on hypothesis, and a hypothesis is an implicit belief, a way of leaning toward. Since the child's world is primarily a perceptual one and the adult's world is more clearly a conceptual one, we will have to put aside or bracket some of our conceptual presuppositions. One, of course, is that children and adults see the same world and that they see it in the same way. This is false. For the child, seeing may be believing, but the opposite tends to be true of adults. With adults, believing is seeing, for the adult lives in a symbolic world the child has not yet come to inhabit. We find again, then, that we will be discussing a process of emergent articulation from a world that is basically perceptual and affective to a world that is conceptual and effective. But the effectiveness of the adult world is itself ambiguous, for what it gains in utility, it loses in vividness. The world the adult inhabits also inhibits his ability to feel and to perceive directly. Perhaps this is one reason why films can exert such a strong force on the adult; they allow him to return to a perceptual-aural level of vivid, implicit belief, where the appearance seems to carry its own numinous validation.

Before we turn to that first world, we will also have to put aside some of the assumptions we adults usually make, which we believe apply uniformly to these two different worlds. The normal assumption of adults is that what we perceive is reality. Not only do we share this blind faith contrary to most of our empirical experience of others, but we also believe that our perceptions are veridical and true. We adhere tenaciously to the latter corollary, since we assume that perception is essentially passive (it's something that happens to us), pure, clear, and adequate. The latter beliefs are the precipitates of British Empiricism; and we hold them to be true, in spite of the fact that we have never met anyone with a simple idea in

Hume's sense nor has any of us ever experienced a simple idea except in abstraction. Such an experiential observation does not bother the stimulus-response psychologist, however, since he is too busy studying mythical sense-data and their supposed synaptic correlates to notice that even his white mice are more complex

ng that just happens to us. It is not passive. Like all their environment before they react to it. Perceiving r Koestler puts it:

> nfirmed that perception is "something the organism
> h happens to the organism"; that responses enter at
> chy into the processing of stimuli; and that motor
> yze the input long before it has achieved its full status

ago that the infant is surrounded by a "blooming, ensation sans organization," but no normal adult is n. If he were, it would not remain confusion. It would cit meaning from it or read meaning into it; we would lective synthesis. This activity of the individual at the ng that it has led Arnheim to state that "vision is a n mind," and he goes on to add an analogy to thought: Perceiving achieves, at the sensory level, what in the realm of reasoning is known as understanding."[2] Even with the greatest relaxation of tension and attention, it would seem that there is no such thing as passive sight. Patterning takes place in perception. "Eyesight is insight."

Even if we set aside the dynamic power of the unconscious, there is, on the conscious level, no such thing as an absolute stimulus to perception. To use Koestler's language, which is somewhat too artificially scientific, any inputs that aspire to be stimuli are screened before they reach the realizing consciousness. Our intentions, our attitudes, and our expectations determine what will be a stimulus and what will not. Hence, in order *to be* a stimulus, the input must be anticipated, filtered, processed, abstracted, distorted, interpreted, resynthesized, recognized, and expressed. All this activity is subject to the resident grid-work, or symbolic system, that has gradually been built into the human adult by past experience and education. This means, of course, that our perceptions cannot be "clear, pure, adequate, simple, veridical and (hence) necessarily true." It also means that the world of the adult is a world different from that of the child.

Probably the most brilliant work that has ever been done with children has been that of Jean Piaget. Let me remind you of how he describes the child's view of the world. First of all, he asserts that a child has a "protoplasmic consciousness"; that is, the child makes no sharp separation between his ego and the world. For him, the self *is* the world because the self is the center of the expressive forces that move through, surround, and impinge upon him. Secondly, children are optical realists. For them, things *are* what they *appear to be*. Thus, visual links become causal links, and the child has a stronger sense of magic than of logic. But, as Arnheim has pointed out, we must be careful about this word "realism." We should not confuse it with the supposed realism of Renaissance painting with its intellectually fixed perspective opening onto a closed, self-contained world. Children, like the American Indian, the Egyptians, and Picasso, "draw the baby in the mother's belly" and make no artificial distinctions of inner/outer. There are not only no such sharp separations for children, but their sense of perspective is quite different from Renaissance realism.

One may wonder why children and primitives draw "so funny" and may be puzzled by their "odd" uses of perspective. In fact, the tendency on the part of the adult is to make a judgment and to say that the child's drawing is wrong or that it is distorted. It comes as a shock, then, to realize that children draw the way they do "precisely because they draw what they see."[3] One explanation for this is the relative ineffectiveness of distance as a factor in the perceptual processes of adults but its strong influence in the perceptivity of children. Distance helps adults rationalize; it helps children see. We have already seen in the hand experiment that though the images on the retina differ in size, we do not see the hands as of different sizes. Children, like the motion-picture camera, do see them as of different sizes; they both register the projective distortions of distance, for their grid systems are not yet developed enough to correct what they see. The same thing may be said of the child's awareness of space.

Adults often complain that the child is disoriented, but it would be simpler to say that orientation is of no particular importance to the child. He has not yet learned, as Whitehead claims adults do, that simple location is a fundamental and necessary way of approaching his world. Children's reading does not seem to be impaired significantly when the page is turned at a ninety-degree angle, and their drawings show little indication of unified space. As Arnheim states: "The children will spontaneously draw upside-down figures or turn the paper freely without minding the changing orientation. A unified spatial framework develops only gradually."[4] I have tried this with my youngest child and found that it makes no difference to her whether her drawing is right-side up or upside down. I used to be puzzled by the fact that my children could stand in front of me and read a story or see a picture almost as well as I could, though from their point of view it was upside down. It would seem that the most important thing to the child is rhythm and force and that conceptual spatialization occurs later. Arnheim claims that "orientation apparently begins to play a role in the sixth year of life" but that its force is still not so strong as to impair sideways reading even at the age of eleven. Both distance and orientation are strong shaping factors in the perceptions of adults. It would seem, then, that the title *I Am a Camera* would apply only if the main character were a child. One film in which the camera consistently took the child's point of view was *The Fallen Idol*.

Adults also tend to say that children are anthropocentric and that hence, when a child, or a poet, talks about the moon "rattling like angry candy," the child-poet is projecting his fantasies into the world. Such a description is not merely condescending, it is inaccurate. To the child and the poet, everything is animate, but that does not mean that he thereby assumes it has a resident soul. He has not yet, as the adult, become differentiated enough to become schizophrenic. Morris has shown that the humanness of animal identification comes late and is preceded by identification with expressive quality.[5] What this does mean is that the child is oriented toward forces, expressive qualities, and that these are emergent from his direct perception of happenings. That the child is oriented toward happenings is shown in his use of words. Arnheim has discussed the fact that the child first learns nouns:

> It would be erroneous to conclude from this that the child is more interested in objects than in happenings. Rather do these nouns represent "one-word sentences" that stand for questions, demands, and reports at a stage at which the verbal statement has not yet been differentiated into several different words. Person, object, and action are still represented as an undivided entity through one word.[6]

The learning of language later becomes the learning of syntax, that is, ways of becoming more articulate and specific. When it comes to nouns, it is truly surprising how abstract we become as adults. Hence, we define a pronoun as "that which stands for a noun" when we know that they can stand for noun phrases or even entire situations so that it would really be more accurate to say that a pronoun is that which "sometimes functions as a noun or noun-phrase." But the point here is the child's basic orientation toward happenings, toward events and situations, as expressed in his use of language. The same may be said of motion.

In the drawings of children, the vertical-horizontal axis is the first dominant. In fact, as we have seen previously, they usually start with the most simple of forms, the circle. They avoid the oblique. This may be because they have as yet an undeveloped sense of proper perspective or it may be because oblique lines are stronger and more forceful. At any rate, their early drawings make "no distinction between a running person and one standing at rest." But children, like dogs and cats, are fascinated by sheer movement. Hence, they strive to try to portray movement and to overcome the simple ambiguity of the early drawing. Thus "children grope for higher stages of differentiation because they are dissatisfied with the limitations of the lower ones,"[7] and they finally achieve the drawings of movement by the embodiment of force in lines. Since the child is oriented toward happenings and motion, if he is a camera, the camera the child is most like is the motion-picture camera. Perhaps it might be better, then, not to talk about the optical realism of the child, but of his basic *perceptualism*. "To the young mind, things are what they look like, sound like, move like, or smell like."[8]

Now, the fact that children are oriented toward motion and happenings means that they are oriented toward forces, and this explains why they are oriented toward expression. The tone of voice one uses with a child is much more important than what one says. When one smacks a child on the bottom, the first thing the child does is to inspect the face of the adult. If the child perceives humor on the face, it will be "the funniest thing Daddy ever did" and he will laugh. If, on the contrary, the child perceives anger and resentment, the smack will be followed by a Niagara of tears. The assimilation and recognition of expressive quality is direct and is not confined to children. Shout at a dog that you love him, and he will cringe. Nor is this priority of expressive character or "physiognomic properties" something that should come to us as a surprise. On the contrary, argues Arnheim, who states:

> Our senses are not self-contained recording devices operating for their own sake. They have been developed by the organism as an aid in properly reacting to the environment. The organism is primarily interested in the forces that are active around it—their place, strength, direction. Hostility and friendliness are attributes of forces. And the perceived impact of forces makes for what we call expression.[9]

What is true for the organism is also true in art: Expression is given in perception. That this is also true of children is shown by the phenomenon of tickling.

If one tickles himself, he will not laugh. Laughter-producing tickling must be done by another. This is not some unfathomable mystery of human nature but results from the fact that tickling depends upon a situation of ambiguity; it is a bi-sociative response. Hence, a tickle must be seen as an attack upon the person tickled, but at the same time it must be seen not to be a real attack. The illusion of attack brings the laughter. If the child does not see that it is a *mock* attack, it will squirm to try to extricate itself. The laughter of tickling, therefore, depends upon trust in the "reality" of the illusion and is perhaps the first "willing suspension of disbelief" that we undergo as children. This may be our first access to the illusions of stage and film. At any rate, one thing is apparent: The response of laughter is dependent upon the perception of the falsity of the attack; it must be seen as an attack that is not an attack. The only way this can be seen by the child, just as peek-a-boo and other such "threats" can be seen, is by the child being open and receptive, trusting, toward the expressive qualities involved. "Children laugh fifteen times more often when tickled by their mothers than by strangers."[10]

We shall return to the bi-sociative attitude later, particularly in our discussions of dreams and motion pictures. But the point to note here is that the orthodox wisdom in psychology is for the most part false. Children do not depend upon learning and incorporate clues from their situation, which they then decipher and project into things or people. On the contrary, expression is a function of structure, whether that structure happens to be tonal or visual. The "message" is seen on the face of it; and it is seen for just what it is. This may well be why the disingenuousness of children is so direct, and they are often so accurate. My college students were quite unable to "see" an abstract painting I brought before them except through the lenses of their concepts. Hence, they gave me the most intricate and extravagant interpretations of what the painting "was about." My children took one look at the painting and said, "It's birds." The title of the painting: Paul Zelanski's *I Smile at Birds*.

Of course the students "saw" many things my children did not, such as balance, texture, and depth; hence, it is not true to say that adult perception is "corrupt." It is much more complex and, in some senses—nay, in all senses—more articulated and restricted. What the adult gains in clarity, he loses in feeling. But even we adults can slip into the attitude and the vision of the child in the case of objects of great expressive power, for here we are twisted from our preconceptions and forced to see. This is what I have called in film the "power of the camera to elicit the visibility of the seen." With luck, we may see what the child sees and more. For besides seeing the equi-valence of qualitative structures, we are also capable of knowing what they mean; that is, we can relate them to other symbolic contexts. The immediacy of expressive quality, however, is there from the beginning. Arnheim, too, rejects the orthodox wisdom in this regard. He sees the willow as weeping, and he states:

> Particularly Wertheimer asserted that the perception of expression is much too immediate and compelling to be explainable merely as a product of learning. When we watch a dancer, the sadness or happiness of the mood seems

to be directly inherent in the movements themselves. Wertheimer concluded that this was true because formal factors of the dance reproduced identical factors of mood.[11]

Our participations in coexistence are much more intimate than we normally assume; and, when we reflect upon the qualitative analogical identity of patterns, we see them as expressive. We are once again "as little children."

My two-year-old and I are watching *Wild Kingdom*. The image of a coyote comes across the screen. She says, "Dog." Somewhat later, the image of a bobcat comes across the screen. She says, "Kitty." There has been no verbal overlay to identify the different species, simply the recording of the images of a hunting coyote and a hunting bobcat. What am I to make of this experience? Must I go back and read Plato? The answer is Yes. Besides immediate qualitative assimilation, an element of remembering or anamnesis is involved in awareness. The third term, form, does not come from some mythical heaven as Plato humorously speculated, but it does come from somewhere. Where does it come from? From perception. Children do not really see particulars, individuals. Every male on the television screen is "Daddy," every female is "Mommy." What the child does see is "daddy-ness" and "momminess." The over-all structural features are the primary data of perception, not isolated qualities or individuated structure. It is difficult to know what to call these entities, but perhaps one might refer to them as "vague forms" or as "perceptual concepts," for they appear to perform the same functions at the perceptual level that concepts do at the intellectual level. A sense of form, then, is not a late development of abstraction but is an early way of coming to terms with one's being-in-the-world. "The young child sees 'doggishness' before he is able to distinguish one dog from another."

But form, even for the child at the level of perception, is not a bare "given." It is something that is recognized in the sense that it is literally *re-cognized*. That is, the imagination of the child is brought into play to help constitute the form, for the subject—say the image of what is to me this coyote and to my daughter, "doggie" —does not provide a form adequate to represent it. Hence, the child must participate in the constitution of the form, not in the McLuhan sense of putting a whirl of dots together, but in the sense of trying to express adequately that limited moving mass which it sees. When it comes to attempting to draw the "doggie," the search for adequate form becomes even more active. As Arnheim puts it:

> Imagination is indispensable, because a subject itself does not offer the form needed to represent it. Form must be invented; and since no form invented by someone else will fit an artist's own experience, he himself has to do the

inventing. An impressive example can be found in the drawings of children. When children start to experiment with shape and color, they are faced with the job of inventing a way in which the objects of their experiences can be represented in the given medium. Occasionally they are helped by watching other children's work, but essentially they are on their own. The wealth of original solutions they produce is all the more remarkable because their subject matter is most elementary.[12]

It would seem, then, that the movement from the presentational to the representational level of perception calls for a greater commitment on the part of the child and a greater activity in a search for modes to constitute expressive form. The form that the child will settle for is the one that appears to him to be the most expressive of life or "lively."

Now, the perception of liveliness or of life qualities is not dependent upon the assumption of a basic split between an inner secret life and external appearance. It does depend on being able to perceive that there are different orders of behavior and on the ability to recognize these orders as constituting a hierarchy. In agreement with the "opinions of children," Arnheim attempts to sketch this hierarchy of increasing complexity in behavior patterns:

> I cite first the difference between what moves and what does not move. Second, flexible movement, which involves internal change, is at a higher level of complexity than the mere displacement of rigid objects or parts of objects. Third, an object that mobilizes its own power and determines its own course is higher than one that is moved and steered—that is, passively pushed, pulled, repelled, attracted—by an external agent. Fourth, among the "active" objects there is a distinction between those that move merely by an internal impulse and others whose behavior is influenced by the existence of external centers of reference.[13]

This description would fit quite well with Merleau-Ponty's levels of the physical order, the vital order, and the human order or, if one wishes, the syncretic mode of behavior, the amovable, and the symbolic modes. In all three descriptive attempts, we have movement away from rigidity to greater and greater flexibility and openness to the world. One might say, then, that expression is the aspiration of perception. Expression is neither thought nor thing, it is behavior. This may help us to understand why the mad, careening cars of the Keystone Cops appear so human. They move as if they behave, as if they were acting in terms of external centers of reference.

Even in the adult world we probably have at best a blur-to-blur correspondence in our perceptions. With children, this "fuzziness" is intensified due to three facts:

(1) children normally remember not by articulated abstractions, as adults do, but by vivid images; (2) they have a less advanced symbolic system through which to filter their percepts; and (3) they have a different value system, that is, different standards of relevance. It is interesting to note in partial confirmation of these points that eidetic imagery is a normal mode of consciousness for children (90 percent or better) before puberty, and the ability to reproject an image in whole and detail is abnormal (10 percent or less) in adults. In Koestler's stilted scientific language: "Pictorial memory, as we say, belongs to a phylogenetically and ontogenetically earlier level of the mnemic hierarchy."[14] We seem to remember things in two ways, either as abstract schemata or as vivid close-ups. The vivid close-ups are nonlogical constructs of emotional significance whose retention is based on affective force and quality. In this sense, also, the child appears to be like the motion-picture camera, for his memories tend to be of the close-up variety.

In our discussions of the body and its world and the descriptions of the constitutive activity of society in the construction of the self, we saw the process of standards of relevance being built into the structure of the individual through behavior patterns. These styles of behavior and standards of relevance become, at the intellectual level, concepts; and such ideas become the conceptual presuppositions of adult perceptions. They become the grid-work through which adult percepts are filtered. Knowledge demands concepts that are applicable to many contexts, and hence the first step in knowledge is ignorance. That is, we must learn to ignore the individual differences of things, we must dis-regard with our regard those peculiar ways in which the singular object is constituted. The adult demands and expects a unified, meaningful world. We cannot even remember meaningless phrases unless we import meaning into them. Meaning is the glue that holds together our adult perceptual constructs. Hence, in the adult, concepts and percepts are inextricably mixed and fused. We are given objects-in-aspects, which we constitute as wholes in a foreground with a background of meaning. We come out of this process "seeing" an inferential construct, which retains its constancy regardless of angle, distance, or size. Hence, the adult eye can soon collapse into the TV screen and see the images of normal size. To the child, they are images of little people.

While children live in a world of vivid images, adults live in a world of shadows; but the shadows among which they live are shadows saturated with meaning. Once the percepts have been filtered by the various levels of symbolic relevance in the adult, the percepts themselves have become articulated and pregnant with meaning. Now, meaning is the grasping of the relevance of function, and relevance is a function of the patterned expectations of the individual in relation to the given contexts. The learning process would thus seem to be the acquiring of new patterns of relevance, which would allow the individual to go from perceptions of gross differences to perceptions of fine differences. What one learns as an undergraduate is almost entirely negated in his graduate studies, for he sees that what had been regarded as simple is really much more complex. There is a kind of uncovering, then, in learning, for the covert becomes overt and more and more articulations emerge as relevant from the background. But the horizon of this process must be a horizon of generosity. If the individual becomes fixated at a given level of abstraction or a given mode of patterning, he ceases to learn and ceases to grow. Perhaps this is why one goes to art museums, reads poetry, or watches motion pictures. For artists are the skin divers of the mind, and the treasures they bring up from the deeps are new modes of articulation, new standards of relevance. They expand our storehouses of symbolic meaning. They remind us of the universal in the particular. The artist expresses this sensing of the universal in the particular through the use of metaphor. In so doing, he expands our ways of seeing, hearing, and experiencing; and this stretching to new horizons of relevance is what keeps us going, for man has a desire to know, to feel, and to see, which is as strong as any other drive. Maybe one reason for art is that it keeps us alive.

But this learning from the arts is not a matter of telling. It is seldom a matter of statements at all. It is a direct participation in a different value system. Certainly, it is not a matter of stimulus-response conditioning. I have always been amazed that anyone could be impressed by Pavlov's dogs being able to salivate at the sound of a bell, though some amazement is perhaps justified. What is not justified is taking this as an indication of learning. The puzzling thing about Pavlov's dogs is not that they salivated on sound but why they were so incredibly dumb. Why did it take so long for them to learn? The answer seems to be that an ape will use a branch as a tool before he uses a stick or a box. The branch is a natural extension of his situation. The stupidity of Pavlov's dogs, then, may be attributed to the fact that learning is not a simple stimulus-response process and that Pavlov had to destroy the entire value system and natural attitudes of the dogs. With sufficient electrical shocks, he was able to reduce their behavior to a pathological phenomenon: stimulus-response. Fortunately, due to the lead of Konrad Lorenz and others, the study of animals is moving out of the artificial, abstract situations of the laboratory and zoo and into the world where the animal lives.

Pliny knew a long time ago that the mind is the real instrument of sight and observation. Although in theory we should be able to see one hundred and eighty degrees, in practice focal vision "subtends an angle of only about four degrees, less than the angle of the point of a pin, out of the total field."[15] Since we are aware of more than four degrees, however, our eyes must move. This they in fact do. There is no such thing as passive vision. We scan constantly and "finger" the world with our eyes. Seeing is exploring based on expectation and anticipation. Even complex skills have hierarchic structures that express the value-orientations of the individual. No matter how you try to disguise your handwriting, an expert can discover your own particular mode of gesture. If the normal writing hand is damaged or destroyed, within a few months the writing with the other hand becomes indistinguishable from the previous writing. As Koestler says, "the signature is in the brain." This individuated activity of selective receptivity is one of the major differences between the adult eye and the camera. To a large extent, vision is not a physical process. It is a mode of behavior.

Both Arnheim and Koestler have contrasted the camera eye with the human eye. Arnheim states:

> There has been a tendency among scientists to describe the experience of vision in analogy to the physical process. As far as seeing is concerned, the mind was assumed to perform much like a photographic camera. But, if, instead of assuming things, scientists observe the facts with an unprejudiced mind, they discover that vision is anything but a mechanical recording device. First of all, vision is not mere passive reception. The world of images does not simply imprint itself upon a faithfully sensitive organ. Rather, in looking at an object, we reach out for it. With an invisible finger we move through the space around us, go out to the distant places where things are found, touch them, catch them, scan their surfaces, trace their borders, explore their texture. It is an eminently active occupation.[16]

And he adds:

> Vision, then, differs from what the photographic camera does by being active exploration rather than passive recording. Vision is highly selective, not only in the sense of concentrating on what attracts the attention, but also in its way of dealing with any one object. The camera will register all detail with equal faithfulness, but vision will not.[17]

Koestler adds to this:

> What we perceive in vision is not the camera-image on the retina but the "inferential construct" of people and objects which preserve their constant shape and size regardless of angle and distance. The eye may be a camera, but

immediately behind its lens there is a series of compensating, correcting, and retouching devices—the perceptual matrices of skilled vision.[18]

And these matrices are the developments of experience and knowledge. Thus it is that trained vision can see more than naive vision, for the critic has a wider range of relevant symbolic matrices from which to choose and a wider range of contexts into which he can place the object before him. Of course, the matrices of either the man of trained vision or the naive perceiver may inhibit his ability to perceive; and the more he looks, the less he sees. Hence, he must learn not to strive, but to relax into his gaze and explore the field. Sometimes a couple of martinis can improve a critic's receptivity. His eye, no longer being innocent, may attend too closely to techniques and ignore the whole. Hence, he will be unable to relax and enjoy. But nobody should go to a movie to count the cuts, pans, and fades. The first thing that any work of art asks of us is surrender.

The artist, then, invites us to participate in his search for new standards of relevance; and, insofar as we participate with him in this work, we become accessories after the image. The camera, left to its own devices, cannot institute this search. It is for this reason that I have argued the importance of the director, for he uses the camera as a tool to express the theme, tension, conflict, and ultimate revelation of his quest. For those who have become fixated and have ceased to grow, he may have to provide a strong bi-sociative emotional shock to start them on their journey. Some may refuse to take the trip. (This can be taken literally, by the way. Some of my students returned again and again to see *Juliet of the Spirits*. When I asked them why, they replied it was cheaper than LSD.) The search of the director, then, is really the human search; it is the quest for self-transcendence. Many people make this trip every night. As Koestler states it, "Dreaming is for the aesthetically underprivileged the equivalent of artistic experience, his only means of self-transcendence, of breaking away from the trivial plane and creating his own mythology."[19] Since there is a long history of regarding the motion picture as a form of dreaming (Hollis Alpert calls his book *The Dream and the Dreamers,* Hollywood is called a "dream factory," and numerous theatres are named "dreamland"), let us now turn to that strange bi-sociative experience: the dream.

Dreams have always been fascinating to men because of their vividness and their intrinsic ambiguities. Perhaps one of the first things one notices about dreams is their bi-sociative character, which is expressed in the experience of the individual as a sense of psychic bi-presence. One is both in his dream and not in his dream at the same time. This ambiguity is further expressed in the relation of possession, that is, it is both one's own dream and not his own dream. One feels that the dream is in his head but that it also is not in his head. As children, we tend to regard not-being-in-one's-head as of more import than the being-in-one's head. Hence, children and primitives tend to believe that in dreaming they actually go out of themselves to live a mythic world and return to themselves as they awake. The dream is initially interpreted as a "going outside" and is thought to be, in some sense, external. Joseph Campbell summarizes the phenomenon in this way:

> The enigma of the dream, for example, is at first interpreted as in no sense mental: it is external to the dreamer, even though invisible to others. And the memory of the dream is confused with ordinary memories, so that the two worlds are mixed.[20]

It would seem, then, that we are initially possessed in the old sense of demons or witchcraft—that is, the dream is not considered to be a possession of ours, but we are possessed by it.

Campbell then goes on to quote an interview by Piaget and to add his own comments:

> A little boy of five years and six months was asked, "Is the dream in your head?" and he answered, "I am in the dream, it is not in my head. When you dream you don't know you are in bed. You know you are walking: you are in the dream. You are in bed, but you don't know you are." Even at the age of seven or eight, when dreams can be recognized as arising in the head instead of coming from outside—from the moon, from the night, from the lights in the room or in the street or from the sky—they are still regarded as in some way external.[21]

As one grows, however, the dream comes to be interpreted more and more as being a subjective experience and the intensity of possession in the sense of property relation becomes increasingly determined. This means that as one grows he tends to identify the I with the dream. Hence, adults are very chary about telling their dreams to one another, as if the dream would somehow reveal too much of them. Even with one's close friends or one's spouse, one is reluctant to express the *entire* content of a dream, not merely because dreams seem to be disturbing, but also because most of us have read Freud and tend to take him too literally. Another result of this wary attitude is a sharp intensification of the sense of ownership. Hence, one insists that the dream is *my* dream and is no one else's. Though we may be ashamed or frightened of the dream content, we are very proud of the creative activity involved in having produced this brain child. One simple way to verify this is merely to steal another's dream. If a friend tells you his dream and you tell it to another friend as though it were your dream, your first friend will cease to be a friend. You have hurt him more deeply than by striking his body; you have stolen his dream. Somehow we still seem to believe that "he who takes my dream takes my life." We regard such an act as a direct violation of our being.

That a man *is* his dreams is true. But that a man *is not* his dreams is also true. If we were to say what a man truly *is,* we would have to return again to the concept of expression and say that a man is his expression in all of its modes. The dream is, in part, an expression of the self, not because it reveals the "true images of the self," but because the dream can reveal the ways in which the images *are had.* That is, the importance of the dream is not primarily its content, but the way in which it reveals how we relate ourselves to that content, our address, our style of imaging. The dream content itself consists of wishes, unfulfilled possibilities, emotional rhythms and crises, images of past experiences, and the prehensions of present experiences all fused together into an ambiguous, sequential jumble. Trying to sort out the various portions and to interpret their symbolic meanings may be fun, but it may or may not be revelatory of the individual as a living being. What will be revelatory, however, is the way in which these elements are synthesized into one fluid whole.

Campbell reproduces a child's drawing and then quotes the child's commentary on his drawing of his dream. It is one of the most charming and revealing passages written on dreams that I know:

> "I dreamt that the devil wanted to boil me," said a little fellow of seven, explaining a picture that he had drawn. . . . On the left was the child himself, in bed. "That's me," he said. "It was specially my eyes that stayed there—to see." In the center was the devil. And on the right of the picture was the little boy again, standing in his nightshirt in front of the devil who was about to boil him. "I was there twice over," he said in explanation. "When I was in bed I was really there, and then when I was in my dream I was with the devil, and I was really there too."
>
> The reader will not need to be told that we have here a type of logic that is not precisely that of Aristotle, but familiar enough in fairy tale and myth, where the miracle of bi-presence is possible.[22]

Campbell's choice of the phrase "a little fellow of seven" is already reminiscent of film, for "little fellow" is a sentimental phrase that has been collapsed into the complex simplicity of Chaplin. But the passage is much more strikingly like the experience of watching a film than such minor phrases. The whole feel of it is like experiencing a film, for in the experience of film, we are "there twice over" and when we are "with it" we are "really there" and we are "really in the theatre too." And it is 'specially our eyes that stay there—to see.

As we grow older, of course, our impalpable body of individuated habits and our persona begin to exert greater and greater force, not merely on our overt, but also on our covert, behavior, that is, our dream. Hence, as we grow up, while we tend to internalize the locus of the dream and to be highly possessive of it, we at the same time tend to regard ourselves as dis-inhabiting our dreams. We have a weaker sense of being in them. This sometimes reaches the point with those who have extremely strong superegos that they will thus alter the dream in mid-course, change the characters or the plot as though they were directing a motion picture. They don't like the direction of the dream, so they take over the direction itself. One then not only produces the content, he also produces the form of the dream and may rearrange the content to fit the form. Not all of us do this, of course, but all of us do restructure the dream in the telling of it and even in the remembering of it, for dreams must be reconstructed backward. We dream them forward, but remember them backward and then must remember them forward again. The principle of simplicity enters here, and we usually forget, that is, suppress, the secondary details (which may be the most interesting ones) and remember only the vivid high points. If one reads much film criticism, he finds the same type of telling going on. The critic remembers certain striking scenes or sequences, but it is very difficult, perhaps impossible, for him to translate the entire flow of sights and sounds into verbal equivalents. This may also explain why there are so many mistakes in film criticism and reporting.

There is probably no more sensitive, perceptive, and intelligent book of film criticism, at least of the modern film, than John Russell Taylor's *Cinema Eye, Cinema Ear*. Taylor knows films, he knows what he sees, and he knows how to say it well. Yet even he makes mistakes. For example, he tells us that the hero in *North by Northwest,* Cary Grant, "finds himself alone in the depths of the country, far from cover, with a pest-spraying helicopter spraying him with bullets instead."[23] Taylor correctly recalls the terror and the exposedness of the sequence, but the unexpected weapon of vengeance was not a helicopter—it was a biplane. Taylor makes two such mistakes in his discussion of the complex film *8½*. He asserts that the mind-reading occult is an old woman, when in fact the woman was merely the transmitter. The mind reader is a man and an important (in the sense of emotional importance, not status) friend of Guido's—a trickster out of his past with whom he partially identifies. An even more revealing mistake is his description of Guido's encounter with the dream cardinal when he states, "The dream cardinal produces only the oracular assurance that nothing is possible with the church."[24] The cardinal in fact quotes Origen and says that salvation is impossible *outside* the church. This is quite different. But the point here is that, though Taylor is incorrectly reporting the facts, he is *also correctly reporting*. What he is reporting correctly is the *emotional meaning* of the encounter. The literal meaning to Guido and the audience is that he must return to the church, but its emotional meaning is that return to the church would be futile, it would be of no help to his tortured soul. One critic in discussing *8½* went so far as to interchange Anouk Aimée and Sandra Milo, which means, in effect, mixing up the wife and the mistress. That tells us something about him. The fact that I cannot remember which critic it was, tells us something about me. Again, the importance is not the content, but the way in which the content is had or forgotten.

Dreams are what they seem to be; and, again, they are not what they seem to be. Like motion pictures, there is always an emotional beyond from which the images flow and into which they recede. This ambiguity of the dream image and the dream sequence along with its pointing beyond to deeper levels of meaning is both general and particular. The general ambiguity is the same that we find in myth and art and is a function of ambivalence; there are vivid values pointing both ways. Hence in myth, A is A and B is B, but A is at the same time and also B and B is at the same time and also A. There is an identity-in-difference, which does not provoke indifference but on the contrary stirs us to the depths of our being.

Koestler states that "while dreaming we *constantly bisociate in a passive way*."[25] It is doubtful that dreaming is as passive and uncreative as Koestler assumes. He is correct, of course, about the bi-sociation and the process of dreaming involving the emergence of similarities of form regardless of function. He is most helpful in describing some of the modes of patterning in dreams: the *pun,* the *optical pun,* the *phenomenon of displacement,* the *concretization* of the abstract, the use of concrete images as *symbols* for unverbalized concepts, *condensation,* the unearthing of *hidden analogies,* and *impersonalization* (being at the same time, oneself and something else). These characteristics could also be descriptions of film. One need only reflect on the purchased prop in *Blow-Up,* and he will find that it "means" in all of these dimensions and categories—and perhaps more.

Nor is Koestler unaware of the strong similarity between dreaming, day-dreaming, and film. He constantly uses film as an analogue when discussing the dream process. In describing James Thurber's Walter Mitty, he states:

> He lives, like the spectator in front of the screen, on two different levels, simultaneously or in quick alternations—by mental quantum-jumps, as it were. If he settles for a single level then either the illusion ceases to function—or it grows into hallucinatory delusion.[26]

Again he contrasts the two experiences in this manner:

> He [the dreamer] is the spectator passively watching the sequence of images on one level, which he actively produces at another; he is the cinema operator who works the projection machine, and the audience at the same time. But while the spectacle on the screen is visible, the operator is not. He operates in complete darkness, and there is a good reason for it: the production is frequently childish, obscene, confusing, an affront to logic and common sense.[27]

Koestler's metaphor is striking and contains much truth, but again I shall have to demur from his mechanistic horizon. The projectionist should not symbolize the unconscious. The projectionist is merely an extension of the machine; and his task is a simple mechanical one of turning it on and seeing that the speed adjustments are correct, that the volume is at proper pitch, and that the arcs don't burn out. On the contrary, the *director* should be placed in the metaphor as the embodiment of the unconscious, for it is he who picks the images, their intensities, their sequences, their rhythms, and their contexts. The film thus becomes a gesture of the director, for it reveals the ways in which he had his images, just as the dream reveals the way the individual's wishes and memories are had.

It is not really accurate to say that the dream is irrational. Such a way of putting it is also a way of putting it down and saying that the dream is "irresponsible and not-to-be-identified-with-the-self." Nor is it quite correct to say that it is nonrational, though this comes closer to its nature. Koestler uses the term "prerational," which is even closer to the right description, but it unfortunately posits an unnecessary temporal and logical priority for the dream over more overt behavior. The dream may have the appearance of chaos, but it is not chaos; it has its own structure and order. Like a film, it may be discontinuous or continuous; it can reverse time processes or collapse them into each other, for its temporality is fluid. The dream is *par excellence* an example of the aesthetic principle of relativity. So it is difficult to try to find a phrase that captures its phenomenal essence. Perhaps the best would be to say that it is structured by emotional necessity; its theme calls what it needs, and it appears. That there are both psychic and biological necessities for dreams is shown by the experiments in which dreaming was interrupted, and the dreamers then dreamed twice as much on succeeding nights to try to catch up. A person without a dream is truly at a loss.

Freud was very much impressed by the obscurity of the dream, perhaps in the same way that Sartre was impressed by people's failure to communicate. Hence, although Freud's brilliant pioneering has changed our entire mental horizon and we must note, as we did before, his true genius, we must also note that his attitude toward dreams is basically negative.

> "The dream," wrote Freud, "neglects in a most conspicuous manner the logical category of opposition and contradiction. The concept 'No' does not seem to exist in the dream. It likes to compress opposites into a unity, or to represent them as one. It takes the further liberty of representing any given entity by its emotional opposite, so that *a priori* one never knows whether a reversible entity is thought of in the dream with a plus or minus sign."[28]

Of course, Freud was brilliant enough to perceive that the emotional opposite is also the emotional identity and hence the intense ambiguity of our most intimate relationships. Koestler is very struck by this ambiguity and especially by the shifts (like motion-picture cuts) that it makes possible with unnerving suddenness. Hence, he likens the sudden shift of emotional level and context to the shifting reversibility of figure and background that takes place in the visual perception of deliberately ambiguous objects. But back to Freud. I wish to comment on two ideas here: Freud's attribution of obscurity to dreams and the true insight he had into the shifting concept of identity.

Freud's approach to the dream is that it is the function of the dream to hide one's true intentions. Hence, the best way to discern what a person believes his dream means is to ask him what he thinks it means, then negate his answer. From a Freudian point of view, then, a dream never really means what it seems to mean. The true meaning is always the opposite, hence the dream's alleged obscurity. In contrast, Jung has maintained, according to Arnheim, "that symbols reveal rather than veil the message."

> When Freud speaks of the "dream-facade," he is really speaking not of the dream itself but of its obscurity, and in so doing is projecting upon the dream his own lack of understanding. We say that the dream has a false front only because we fail to see into it.[29]

Jung's language concerning Freud here is a bit sharp, but if we are to take the dream as a symbol, there seems to be no alternative but to side with Jung. The function of all symbols is to express, and to express not merely their content but, by the way in which they are used, the behavior of the symbol user. Hence, what the interpretation of a dream boils down to basically is patience. One must have the patience to follow the emotional thread through its various twistings and turnings, through its gestures toward self-hiding and withdrawal (on this Freud was right), until one reaches its partial articulation. If the articulation is merely intellectual, it will probably have little effect on behavior but will merely be an exercise in skillful trickery. If, on the other hand, the revelation of the articulation is taken to heart, becomes an emotional commitment, then its shock can change the rhythm of patterning. That emotion has such power is shown by the phenomenon of organ speech and the fact that we "just can't get over" some emotional experiences. In the first case, we have displaced expression; in the second, we are cut off from possibilities, a way of being with the world. In the second case, we become fixated and say we have an emotional block. If Spinoza was correct, nothing can move an emotion but an emotion, in which case emotional revelation is the only method of removing the block and regaining access to the flexible world.

In a choice of how to inspect a dream, whether from the viewpoint of Freud or that of Jung, then, I lean toward the side of Jung. Jung's theory is more on the objective side of things, in the sense that he believes the dream to be a gesture revelatory of behavior.

> As far, then, as my observations go, I have not discovered in the unconscious anything like a personality comparable to the conscious ego. But, although a definite alter ego seems not to exist (except in the rare cases of dual personality), there are at least *traces of personalities* in the manifestations of the unconscious. A simple example is the dream, in which a variety of real and imaginary people enact the dream thoughts. In nearly all important cases of dissociation the manifestations of the unconscious assume a distinctive character. The unconscious *personates*.[30]

This is quite in accord with our saying that the unconscious is the director of the film, not merely the projectionist. Another way of stating this choice is in terms of optimism. The unconscious and its contents *can* be frightening but they *need not* be so. Freud's attitude is an authoritarian-Calvinistic one: The unconscious is necessarily *bad;* man is infected by an ineradicable and necessary evil. But the unconscious as such is simply the possible. Its possibilities may be frightening and, on the other hand, some of its possibilities may not be frightening. In fact, if we are frightened, it is more like anxiety than fright, for the feeling is nonfocal; we don't *know* what the force is which we feel to be threatening. Hence, if we are afraid, we are anxious concerning the possible, for we discern that there is no crime that we do not have the capacity to commit. This does not mean that man is inherently evil, however. Nor does it mean that he is inherently good. All it means is that he is basically possible.

The dream makes no artificial distinctions between the factual and the fictive.

Like the other processes of the unconscious, it primarily consists of picture-strip thinking; hence, its closeness not merely to art but the art of the film is obvious. Rudolf Arnheim is quite sensitive to this relationship of dreams to art in general when he states:

> During sleep the human mind seems to descend to the more elementary level at which life situations are described not by abstract concepts but by significant images. We cannot but admire the creative imagination awakened by sleep in all of us. It is this dormant power of picture language on which the artist also draws for his inventions.[31]

The relationship between the unconscious and the expressive art work was noticed, of course, by Freud himself, and he gave us some sketchy accounts of some bad novels. This same relationship is the basis of the aesthetic theories of Sir Herbert Read and Christopher Caudwell. It is interesting to note in passing that Caudwell, though claiming to be a neo-Freudian, consistently inverts the Freudian metaphors. Hence, he talks about the unconscious as "the white radiance of the self," and so on. But what we are concerned with here is not the general relationship of dreaming to artistic expression, but to the film. Hence, the significant phrase in the quotation from Arnheim is "picture language." This is precisely what the director is attempting in film: to express an emotional theme through picture-language in both senses of that ambiguity.

Were we not so warped by our Aristotelian heritage, we would not insist so stridently upon all-or-none thinking. Since we do incorporate this heritage, however, we usually insist that an image must either be a complete illusion or that it "assumes a mere 'meaning' based on convention":

> Actually, all images are experienced as literally "being"—to some extent— the thing they represent. Instead of foolishly assuming that the child who uses a stick for a doll is the victim of an illusion, we ought to realize that there is nothing unusual in an object being a piece of wood and a baby at the same time.[32]

As Arnheim has pointed out, the American Indians were truly disturbed that the artist who sketched the buffalo was diminishing the herds and hence reducing the food supply. But they did not, thereby, stab the page on which the artist sketched nor did they try to eat it.

> The bisons were real and unreal at the same time. Partial identification of the image with the real object is the rule rather than the exception, not only in

children and primitives, but in man's reactions to all effigies whether they be in dreams, churches, movie theatres, photographic albums, or art museums.[33]

This tendency to identify is stronger in dreams and in the experience of the film than it is in art museums because not merely the objects are given but also their "behavior" in their milieu. The danger, here, of course, is that of underdistancing. If the film merely becomes an excuse to send one into a reverie of his own, he will miss the film and become entrapped in his own creations. Such a process will "lead away from the meaning of the work rather than elucidating it." We do not pay to dream; we do pay to see films (obviously, this sentence is meant literally). Though the film has many characteristics of the dream and engages our participation on the basis of these similarities, it is the film that is the object of attention. Hence, if one regards films as some form of dreaming, he must regard them as *provoked* dreams, objective dreams, dreams that money can buy. A film is a dream whose gesture is not ours.

The other insight that Freud had strikes right to the heart of the difference between science and art. I have called it "the shifting nature of identity," but perhaps it would be better to call it "the difference between identity and comparability." Both art and science are productive of understanding. If all art can do is to titillate the senses and massage the ego, if all it can do is to reproduce nature either by "redeeming physical reality" or by capturing the fugitive moment in a frozen analogy, then art is simply of no importance and is basically a waste of time. But art is not a waste of time. Aristotle was not talking nonsense when he said that the poets are more valuable than historians, for they come closer to the truth of things as they happen. Historians, like brokers, are men who argue over the rights of priorities, but poets somehow transmit to us not merely the event but its feel. As Arnheim has said, "Art's reputation must be due to the fact that it helps man to understand the work and himself, and presents to his eyes what he understood and believes to be true."[34] Art presents us the universal in its concrete circumstance for our perceptive appraisal. In this way, it brings understanding, though the understanding brought is shaped by its mode; the message is carried by the emotions, not primarily by the intellect. Whether one calls this "the process of psychic bi-presence," "empathy," "communion," "participation," or "coexistence" is irrelevant. All these words strike for the same core. And the difference of science is that its mode of presentation is different.

The dominant mode of science is quantitative; the dominant mood of art is qualitative. Hence, the scientist achieves understanding by disregarding by his regard the differences of things and places emphasis upon their similarities. Science seeks the common. A scientific law is the reduction of individuality to a common set of shared characters. Such an approach is perfectly valid from an abstract point of view—and extremely useful. Science does not so much consist of looking as of overlooking. By reduction and by eliminating negligible differences, it is able to quantify phenomena and place them in the same abstract order. There is an identity of indiscernibles. But the artist is concerned with discernibles. To him, they make all the difference, both in himself and his world. Hence, his stance is qualitative rather than quantitative, and his drive and "message" are to reveal the differences in identities. Arnheim states:

> The mature work of art succeeds in subjecting everything to a dominant law of structure. In doing so, it does not distort the variety of existing things into uniformity. On the contrary, it clarifies their differences by making them all comparable.[35]

There is a sense, then, in which the scientist and the artist work different banks of the stream of experience, one being concerned with the individual as instanced in the universal, the other directed toward the revelation of the universal in the particular. Both drive for understanding: one intellectual, the other emotional. The scientist is trying to get his ideas clear; the artist is trying to give his feelings form. Since, either way, muddy water settles, they can both provide us with clarity in different ways.

Let me turn to a specific example of the ambiguous identity of films and dreams: color. Some of my friends claim they dream only in color. Some assert that they never dream in color, and others dream in color sometimes and sometimes not. Though there is probably no objective way to determine whether dreams are in color or not, the answer seems to be that they are in an indeterminate realm, which is neither colored nor noncolored. I know that this isn't logical, but that doesn't bother me. The determining factor in images, whether of imagination or of dreaming, seems to be their intensity. If I imagine my cattle, I may "see" them in the mind's eye as neutral in color, but if the "image in the mind's eye" becomes sufficiently vivid, they "are" white and red. I find myself incapable, regardless of the intensity of the image, of imaging them as Angus. Subjectively, then, it would seem that increased intensity brings color to the images, and decreased intensity drains it away. I observe the same kind of phenomenon when I attempt to remember a film.

On seeing *Dr. Strangelove* the second time on 16 mm., I was shocked to perceive that it was *not* in color. I had remembered it vividly in color, beginning with a *silver* superplane jockeying for sustenance in a *blue* sky surrounded by *white* clouds and with the ironic overlay of "Try a Little Tenderness" on the audio. I was wrong. The film had been in black and white. But the impact of the film, its images, had been so vivid and so intense that the eye had remembered it in color. Was it a *red* turn-signal blinking in *Who's Afraid of Virginia Woolf?* On the other hand, the opening sequence of the stroll on the campus and the "Bergin" soliloquy were definitely *gray*. Hence, it must not have been in color. There are some films, of course, like *Lord Jim*, for which we have to remember that they were in color if we remember them at all, since the film itself was so pallid that the photography was the only thing worth remembering. Then there are directors who deliberately play with this ambiguity of remembrance, like Antonioni. At least the first half of *Blow-Up*, a color film, is concerned visually with exhausting the possibilities of black and white through the various tones of gray and purple.

The experiencing of a film, is, of course, different from its remembrance. When we watch a film, we watch it not merely with the mind's eye but with the body's eye. In the experiencing, both perception and imagination are involved directly. Cognition usually occurs later. And since perception is conjoined with imagination while watching a film, we have no doubt about whether it is in color or not. We *see* whether it is. But in remembering (literally re-putting-together), it is different, for the situation then becomes more ambivalent and ambiguous. One person who evidently has such a difficulty even when viewing a film is Jean-Paul Sartre. Though his theory of the imagination is fascinating, he ends by collapsing the body's eye into the mind's eye. Perhaps this difference is due in part to the fact that Sartre is emphasizing absence, while we are attempting to emphasize presence. One thing is certain: For Sartre, all aesthetic objects are primarily objects of imagination, not of vision.

Sartre thus defines art as inherently unreal. "We can at once formulate the law that the work of art is an unreality,"[36] he states; and he adds, "the esthetic object is something unreal." He thus posits an absolute split between the realm of the imagination and the real world. Objects of imagination alone can be beautiful, never the world; and access to aesthetic objects is gained only through intuition of an image which does not consist of real colors, and the like, but *visits,* from time to time, certain synthetically constructed material objects. He thus denies that there can be any *objectification* of the imaginary, since these two different worlds are split, absolutely. Thus, in discussing a certain red used by Henri Matisse, he declares that the rug was chosen for the red, to justify the red, and not the red for the rug; and this particular red can be enjoyed only by grasping its fleeciness, as "the *red of the rug,* and therefore, unreal." The word "of" is therefore positive for Sartre only in relation to an image and not in relation to the painting. In relation to the painting, it asserts a negation. We are meeting here the same type of argument one finds in the writings of Ortega y Gasset. The argument runs thus: To form is to stylize, to stylize is to deform, to deform is to negate reality, and (for Ortega) to negate reality is to dehumanize. But it is quite possible, as we have argued, that to form may be to elicit, to articulate, and not merely to negate. Some art does consist of images and representational form. But some art also consists of presentational immediacy and here the emphasis is not upon imagination, but on perception. Sartre tries to reduce all art to the status of literature, that is, to the realization of imaginary worlds.

Sartre has defined an image:

> So our conclusion is that the image is an act which envisions an absent or non-existent object as a body, by means of a physical or mental content which is present only as an "analogical representative" of the object envisioned.[37]

One might be tempted to state on this basis that Sartre is merely a pure Idealist and that his theory should be classified with that of Croce and others. And, at times, this would seem almost to be correct, for, like Croce, Sartre defines art negatively and believes it is no more subject to moral judgment than a triangle or a square. Ironically, however, the real intention behind Sartre's aesthetic theory is not aesthetic but an intensity of moral fervor. He desperately wants us to assume our responsibilities with respect to the creation of aesthetic objects. But Sartre is not a pure Idealist, for he adds, "The specifications are determined by the material, since the informing intention remains the same." Hence, though he is arguing that the aesthetic object is an imaginary object, the reason I imagine *this* imaginary object is because I am regarding this specific artifact.

Somehow, the image emerges from the physical artifact. The "somehow," of course, is not a mystery. The image emerges because my mind becomes active when it is presented with the artifact that embodies the directions to the construction of its image. In the description of this process, by the way, Sartre makes his normal error of overstating his case and drawing too sharp distinctions. Hence, he states that the imagination is active and participates in helping create the aesthetic object (true in most instances), but he also states that "perceptual consciousness appears to itself as passive."[38] Now, while it is true that the process of perception appears to consciousness as if it were passive, as if consciousness were hallucinated by objects, the process is not what it appears to be. It involves, as we have seen, a direct inherence in the world and an active synthesizing of objects-in-profiles. Sartre here as elsewhere tends to identify consciousness with self-consciousness and self-consciousness with a negation of mere existence. Whether one is conscious of his active, creative attitudes in constituting objects is beside the point. Experience and reflection show that we do in fact shape what we see. Hence, the distinction of activity/passivity is not absolute but relative. Furthermore, it is conditional. The "pole" which comes to the foreground and is emphasized will depend upon the object before the body's eye and the body's ear. If the object demands but weakly that its will be done, the imaginative activity of the spectator will have a wider field of activity. If the object exhibits strong organic unity, the spectator's imagination will be comparatively passive, though it must still *follow* the directions of the art work.

At stake here is the nature of the affective-cognitive synthesis and the status of a transcendent ego. I agree with Sartre that this synthesis is the ground of image consciousness. One can thus say that feeling is the body of consciousness and consciousness is the use of feeling. Besides use, it has no body. But Sartre would not agree with this last assertion. He adamantly assumes a transcendent ego that is apart from and not a part of its inherence in the world. Consequently, he insists on negation and states that we must remember *"the essential characteristic of the mental image: it is a certain way an object has of being absent within its very presence."*[39] This emphasis upon negativity and separation is also expressed in his description of the four forms by which imagination can posit its objects: "This act can assume four forms and no more: it can posit the object as non-existent, or as absent, or as existing elsewhere; it can also 'neutralize' itself, that is, not posit its object as existing."[40] Notice, however, that only two of these acts are negative. The fourth is a suspension of belief or an "epoche," while the third alone is positive. Even it, however, negates the actual and present existence of its object.

While I would deny the existence of any transcendent or substantial ego, one must agree with Sartre that there is a negativity involved in imaginative and aesthetic experience. This negativity allows a bi-sociative response, for it is the "willing suspension of disbelief." But the suspension of disbelief is also the acceptance of the perceptual object before us. If we return to the concrete instance of the film, then, and ask which of these four categories of positioning it would fit, the answer would seem to be the third; that is, the film is an object that appears as existing elsewhere. While the positional act of the spectator does negate his natural standpoint, it also allows him to be-with the presence of the film. This being-with the film we have termed "excarnation," for it is like our inherence in the world but at the same time unlike it. But this does not demand that we assume a transcendent ego. It merely demands that we describe a different mode of experiencing. A film is a kind of excarnate, immediate, perpetual elsewhere.

Sartre also establishes several different levels or types of images. These levels go from the most embodied to the level of the least embodied, that is, to those illusions such as faces seen in a fire, and then to hypnagogic images, which have no physical analogue at all. The various levels of images he describes are (1) portraits, (2) signs, (3) pantomime, (4) abstract line drawings, (5) sheer appearances (such as the face in the flames or ink blots), and (6) hypnagogic illusions. While many films include various of these levels, it is obvious that the basic nature of the film is in the first level. Since films are moving photographs, the majority of them are in the same category as the portrait, though some experimental films, such as *The Gondola Eye,* attempt to be expressive almost exclusively at the level of sheer appearances. A great film director includes many levels, and the difficulty of most experimental film is that exclusive confinement brings exclusive communication, almost a contradiction in terms. For there to be communication, and especially communion and participation, there must be common ground, not merely an exclusive vantage point.

Quite rightly, Sartre is emphasizing the creativity of the spectator as well as that of the artist, and he is arguing the ideality of the aesthetic object. There can be no doubt that many aesthetic objects do attain ideal status and exist most vividly as images so that the contemplation of them becomes a kind of induced dream. This is generally true of representational art, such as literature, and quite true of the experience of many films. Of course, the key word here is "induced," since the consciousness of the moviegoer is not totally absorbed and hence lost in his own creation (as in dream) but in the creation of another. Nor with the critical eye, is it totally absorbed, though the danger of psychic underdistancing in film is much greater than it is in other arts.

Sartre's analysis of the experience of the actor is particularly rewarding. It resolves (or, rather, dissolves) many of the so-called problems of the relation of the actor to his roles. The two dangers of the actor are either that he so lives his role that he loses control or that he is under such strong control that his acting becomes "hammy" or stilted. The Method, of course, says that one must *live* his role. Another approach emphasizes self-consciousness and the shaping of the external image, a kind of continuing schizoid attitude with a utilitarian goal. Sartre synthesizes these two points of view. The artist does indeed use his body as a tool and in this sense is "other" than his body. But he also lives his body. Sartre combines these two:

> He uses all his feelings, all his strength, all his gestures as analogues of the feelings and conduct of Hamlet. But by this very fact he takes the reality away

from them. *He lives completely in an unreal way.* . . . It is not the character who becomes real in the actor, it is the actor who *becomes unreal* in his character.[41]

Thus, a girl may cease to apprehend her own stage fright as an object and turn it into an analogue of Ophelia's timidity. The actor may cry real tears, which are his tears, but he and the audience will experience them as the tears of Hamlet insofar as they are turned into an analogue. Since I have argued previously that film acting differs fundamentally from stage acting, the difference from this point of view would be "Who creates the analogue?" The answer in film is, of course, the director. The film actor cries real tears, reveals himself in his fugitive gestures, which cannot be hidden, and the director cuts the recordings of these to build the "unreal" character of Fred C. Dobbs. An example of such nonacting transformed into acting by directional brilliance is John Cassavetes' *Faces.*

But as creative and as helpful as Sartre's theory of aesthetics is on these points, we must still put his main thesis aside, for it is not the case that an aesthetic object must necessarily appear only in the mode of intuition nor is it the case that all aesthetic objects are and can only be images. Sartre cannot reconcile himself to having a body. Hence, though he specifically talks about communication being based on incarnation (for example, "The original has the ontological primacy. But it becomes incarnated, it enters into the image"[42]), he forgets this insight when it comes to writing a theory about art. Hence, he ends by arguing that he does not actually hear the performance of the Seventh Symphony. He states, "I do not hear it actually, I listen to it in the imaginary," and he goes on to conclude that reality is not and can never be beautiful.

Eugene Kaelin, I believe, is correct when he says that Sartre's problem is not really with "aesthetic object" in the phrase "the aesthetic object" but with the "the."[43] That is, Sartre has started and ended with a particular art with which he is most familiar: literature. In literature, it is usually the case that the work does consist of an imaginatively constructed image. But Sartre has then gone on to overgeneralize the case of literature to include all the other arts in much the same way that Clive Bell overgeneralizes painting to apply to all other arts and claims they must exhibit "significant form." This overgeneralization has two effects for Sartre: It weakens his plays and restricts his aesthetic theory. One merely has to see or even read *No Exit* or *The Flies,* and one is immediately struck by their narrative strength and dramatic thinness. They lack the emotional texture and depth needed for the best plays. In aesthetic theory, Sartre's insistence on intuition of the image restricts him to talking about only representational works. Works that consist of presentational form alone are perceptual objects and, by their structure, do not intend anything beyond their sensuous surface. Hence, Sartre cannot speak of them.

Granted that man alive is an incomplete, an open, unity, yet he is a unity nevertheless. Not merely is intuition involved in the apprehending and appreciation of aesthetic objects, but perception, cognition, imagination, and some of the motor properties of the body proper may well be involved. Feeling and emotion are also involved. Hence, while it is true that some aesthetic objects involve the recognition of a representational image, it does not follow that all of them do. All aesthetic objects involve perception, but the imagination may or may not become fully activated. Sartre may hear Beethoven's symphony only with his imagination, but the rest of us hear the symphony with our ears and with all that that "with" involves.

While Sartre tries to reduce all art to the imagination, Kracauer, in his discussion of fantasy, rules out the possibility of film appearing in the imaginative mode with any legitimacy. Though he admits that this trend in film was one of the first uses with Méliès and that it has continued to be used as a film form, Kracauer maintains that "since it lies outside the area of physical existence, it seems to be as unmanageable as the past in terms of the cinematic approach."[44] Hence, he quotes with disapproval René Clair, who denied that film should try to limit itself to so narrow a basis as an aesthetics of realism. Kracauer then goes on to add:

> A number of critics even go so far as to contend that "the true import of the cinema is the realm of dreams." The opinion of these extremists finds some support in the undeniable fact that, due to its specific techniques, film is better equipped than the other representational media to render visible things that have been imagined.[45]

But, Kracauer concludes, film makers who insist on such freedom are truly violating the nature of film medium, they are "blind . . . to the restrictions imposed on the formative tendency by the peculiarities of the medium."

Now, there are certain practical difficulties in accepting Kracauer's judgment on this point. One would either have to forbid film makers to produce fantasies and include dream sequences in "true" films, or one might allow them to make such things, but would have to deny that they are films. This means we would have to reject *The Cabinet of Doctor Caligari, Dracula, The Wizard of Oz, Beauty and the Beast,* and innumerable other fine films. It would also mean that we would have to excise drastically such films as *Los Olvidados, Subida al Cielo, Medium Cool, Midnight Cowboy,* and *Wild Strawberries* and reduce *8½* to a film about a middle-aged director taking a few steam baths. Naturally, all drawn motion pictures such as *Snow White and the Seven Dwarfs, Fantasia, Mr. Bug Goes to Town,* and

The Yellow Submarine would have to be eliminated, as well as all cartoons. It is interesting that in his entire book on film, Kracauer never discusses the cartoon. It is doubtful that he never saw any; it's just that (presumably) he did not consider them to be films.

The acceptance of Sartre's premises would confine us either to films with a strong narrative line or to fantasies. The acceptance of Kracauer's perspective would rule them out. As distressing as this might be, it could be done if there were some compelling reason for it. Of course, there is no such compelling reason. As a matter of fact, there are good reasons for emphasizing the close relationships between imaginary worlds and those of the film. There are even good reasons for emphasizing the similarity to dreams. This emphasis is exactly that used by Susanne K. Langer in one of the shortest but most perceptive reflections ever written on the film medium.

The horizon of Mrs. Langer's thought is that of Whitehead and Cassirer, but she modifies the sharp distinctions of Cassirer concerning symbols and extends the word "symbol" to include that of aesthetic expression. Hence, she defines art as "the creation of forms symbolic of human feeling."[46] This initial definition, however, is much too general and vague; and, as her thought develops, she specifies and articulates the definition so that its meaning becomes clear. In a later work, she states, "A work of art is an expressive form created for our perception through sense or imagination, and what it expresses is human feeling."[47] This definition is a great step forward in articulation because it tells us not only what an art object is but also how it comes to be and at what level of human awareness it is designed to function, that is, the level of perception. Now, there are static forms and dynamic forms. Artistic form is "congruent with dynamic form" because its function is to make perceivable something that is dynamic, that is, human feeling. Not only is the work of art a dynamic form, it is a dynamic expressive form. Import inheres in it. Mrs. Langer defines expressive form:

> An expressive form is any perceptible or imaginable whole that exhibits relationships of parts, or points, or even qualities or aspects within the whole, so that it may be taken to represent some other whole whose elements have analogous relations.[48]

Another way of saying it more simply is that a work of art is a primary metaphor. Since metaphor precedes institution, the poets *are* the true creators of language, and the language they create is the language of articulated feeling. Discursive form is a later use of metaphorical form. What the expressive form expresses is man's inner life, "the stream of direct experience, life as it feels in the living." It should be immediately apparent how close this is to my assertions that what film does is present us the way being-in-the-world feels. But it is not enough for the artist merely to present his feelings or just any feelings. What articulation means is formed, structured feeling raised to the level of a percept. Hence, expression is not *self*-expression, "it is neither a confessional nor a frozen tantrum; it is a developed metaphor."[49]

The differences between Susanne K. Langer's theory of aesthetics and that of Sartre are extensive. The first great difference is that she says, "imagination or sense"; and the "or" is inclusive, not exclusive. Furthermore, she emphasizes the perceptual character of the art work: It is created to be seen, to be heard, to be touched with the body's eyes and ears as well as the mind's. Their theories differ on the meaning of intuition and many other aspects, but basically the difference is reducible to the difference between import and purport. For Sartre, a work of art is significant because of its purport, the meaning that it conveys. Hence, the painted canvas is, for him, a diving board or an excuse. It is a jumping-off point to an image. For Mrs. Langer, a work of art "has"—better, "embodies"—import. It does not primarily profess meaning, it *contains it*. Thus, she is concerned with the weight, texture, and articulation of meaning, whereas Sartre argues its negative insubstantiality. Mrs. Langer's theory emphasizes presence; Sartre's theory emphasizes absence. But surely, if one were to speak only of imagination and to de-emphasize the role of sensation, as Sartre does, it still would not follow that he has given us the primary meaning of "imagination." Its primary meaning is positive.

D. W. Gotshalk defines imagination positively when he states, "By 'imagination' is meant the ability to connect the absent with the present . . . the ability to apprehend as if present in an object for perception something only suggested but not literally present."[50] This definition is in perfect accord with the stance taken by Mrs. Langer when she states, "The dynamic form of feeling is seen *in* the picture, not through it mediately; feeling itself seems to be in the picture."[51] A work of art is, then, a "living form"; it does not primarily *connote* feeling but *contains* it as organically articulated for perception. The reason for the quotes around "living form" and Gotshalk's "only suggested" is not because Mrs. Langer and Gotshalk are excessively careful (that is, pedantic) professors, but because when they use these phrases they wish to indicate that they are using precise metaphors. A work of art is an illusion or an apparition breathed forth from or emergent from a created body. Like living, working in an art medium is a process of increasing articulation and differentiation, a growth toward maturity. And also like life, the "success or failure" of the work is always on the edge.

Every cell in the human body is "perpetually breaking down and perpetually being replaced" and the "whole vast system is in unceasing flux." Since the body is like an army company with new recruits coming in and old recruits going out—all of them initially other than and unfamiliar with the rules—we tend to identify permanence with the *person,* that is, the rhythmic patterning that provides the functional identity through change. Hence, the self is thought of as a kind of vital form; but, unlike Epicurus' gods, it runs out of replacements and is subject to decay and death. Like the person, the work of art is a vital form; it is dynamic; and what holds dynamic form together, whether in the body or in a work of art, is the reciprocity of rhythm. Both works of art and the body consist of elements, not mere parts. They consist of semi-independent centers of mutually enhancing activities. The aesthetic object inheres in the painting. Yet it somehow emerges for our perceptive appraisal. Hence, the work of art as a symbol is a peculiar symbol since it does not point beyond itself but primarily substantiates itself, that is, gives itself substance; and the "idea" it contains "remains bound up in the form that makes it conceivable,"[52] for the simple reason that its conceivability is implicated in its perceivability. The apparency of import—that is, its ability to appear and to be apparent—is a function of the articulation of the materials.

It should be obvious that the theory of film toward which I have been developing is, to use her phrase, "congruent with" the theory of art advanced by Mrs. Langer. We should therefore take seriously her assertions concerning film and the strong resemblance she perceives between film and the dream. At the end of her major work, *Feeling and Form,* she has an appendix entitled "A Note on the Film"—an appendix, I might add, which is so incisive that it should not be excised. It is inflammatory only in the sense of insight, not in the sense of heat.

Mrs. Langer recognizes that film is a new art, a new mode of poetic expression, and that it became an art when the moving of the camera was introduced. Camera movement allowed the film to become other than the mere recording of stage performances and brought with it another characteristic of film: the fact that its form is closer to narrative than it is to drama. As she states it: "The screen is not a stage, and what is created in the conception and realization of a film is not a play."[53] But it does not suffice, though Croce or Sartre might have us think so, merely to define an art mode negatively. It must be described positively. Hence, Mrs. Langer goes on to define film's primary illusion, the mode in which the illusion presents itself, and its secondary illusion.

Primary illusion is a basic or key concept in Mrs. Langer's aesthetics. By "primary illusion" she does not mean what the artist conceives first. That is usually the "commanding form" or what, in film, I have called "theme." Nor is primary illusion that which the artist makes first. "Primary illusion" means the necessary condition that defines an art. Thus the primary illusion of painting is plastic, or virtual, space. "It is what is *always* created in a work of pictorial art."[54] What then, does she choose as the primary illusion of film, that is, its necessary condition? *Virtual history.* Now, she had already described the novel (or, as she prefers to call it, prose fiction) as a form of virtual history. Since a film, on the face of it, is not a novel, the mode in which it presents virtual history must be of fundamental importance. It is. What is this mode? It is, says Dr. Langer, the *dream mode.* Concerning film, she writes:

> It makes the primary illusion—virtual history—in its own mode. This is, essentially, the *dream mode.* I do not mean that it copies dream, or puts one into a daydream. Not at all; no more than literature invokes memory, or makes us believe *we* are remembering. An art is a mode of appearance. Fiction is "like" memory. . . . Drama is "like" action. . . . Cinema is "like" dream in the mode of its presentation: it creates a virtual present, an order of direct apparition."[55]

Film is not dream, then; but, to echo Hamlet, it is very like it. In what ways is it very like it?

Mrs. Langer continues:

> This aesthetic peculiarity, this relation to the things perceived [the equal immediacy or authenticity of everything in a dream], characterizes the *dream mode:* it is this that the moving picture takes over, and whereby it creates a virtual present. In its relation to the images, actions, events, that constitute the story, the camera is in the place of the dreamer.[56]

Movies *are* like dreams. They have the same elasticity of time and space, the same sense of immediacy, and the same haunting vividness whereby objects are united, not by causal or spatial contiguity or relations, but by the same feeling matrix. Furthermore, some of them are in black and white and some of them are in color. She then goes on to describe the camera as not being in the picture and says of the camera, "It is the mind's eye and nothing more." This assertion seems questionable. If it is the function of media to extend the body and thereby to negate the natural standpoint, then the camera becomes the virtual eye of the body and thereby assimilates its virtual stance and address. The eye of the spectator, his bodily eye, identifies with the shifting perspectives of the camera—just as the ear identifies with the traveling mike.

The motion picture, then, is a poetic structure that has a matrix or commanding form from which it evolves and which it articulates. This is what I have termed "theme." It does not portray things so much as present them, and it does not primarily present things going on but "the dimension in which they go on—a *virtual* creative imagination; for it *seems* one's own creation, direct visionary experience, a 'dreamt reality.' "[57] This seeming helps to explain the extremely forceful vivid impact of the film and its voyeuristic appeal as well as its apparent omniscience. But the spectator does not create the film, though he does help re-create it, following the lead of the director. Hence, the film is also unlike the dream. It is unlike the dream in several important respects.

In the first place, there is absence of control. The spectator is not able to alter the movement or direction of the film; but, at least on some occasions, as we have seen, he *can* re-direct his dream. In the second place, consciousness is usually submerged in the dream, and the dream rules by fascination. But the film director rules us by making us accomplices. A third difference is the presence and absence of his majesty, the ego. I am always in my dream, and in fact, am usually at the center of it. But I am not in the film. I do identify with the camera perspective, and I may or may not identify with a major character. But *my* ego is not the central agent of the film. I am always *there* in the dream and sometimes, though not always, *with* the film. The illusion of omnipotence, then, is just that: an illusion. Another difference is in time span. Though we now know that dreams take longer than we formerly believed, they do not last as long as most films nor are they so clearly articulated and organic. Hence, they are more formless and less structured than films. They lack the perceptive tension between texture and depth, though dreams do display surface and depth. One more difference is in the nature of the space involved. While things may suddenly appear in dreams and take on unusual aspects or meanings just as they do in film, in the dream I seem equidistant from all things. The space of a film is fluid, but it does have a defined frame. Furthermore, no matter how much the camera shifts, tilts, dollies, and so on, the camera still has a definite, though variable, position.

This last characteristic of film, its space, Dr. Langer calls its "secondary illusion," for she says *"its space comes and goes,"*[58] a phrase reminiscent of Whitehead's remark about color that "it haunts time like a spirit; it comes when it is wanted." Dreams also are not oriented in any total space; they lack horizon. This variability of motion-picture space brings Mrs. Langer to deny that the motion picture is a plastic medium. This denial is no doubt shocking to those painters who create films and to those who think of films in painterly terms, but I believe her intuition here is exact and correct. A plastic medium usually involves three dimensions and modeling. Furthermore, the very word "plastic" carries with it a connotation of fixity, as plaster, which becomes set. But the space of film is not plastic; it is elastic. It is characterized by being expansive, resilient, easily changeable, and flexible, even though it recovers to its home base of the frame. Further, the word "elastic" carries with it a connotation of buoyancy, drive, and élan, which is perfectly suitable to film quality. Dr. Langer does not call film space elastic; but, in denying that it is plastic, she points out that its lack of plasticity provides its omnivorous quality.

That the film is omnivorous is true. It is able to assimilate and transform pantomime, the stage, music, drawing, painting, dancing, natural objects, and many other elements. Of course, the presence of music in film is another difference from the dream. The film is an audible-visible synthesis. Just as it is the function of painting to make the feel of lived space visible and the function of music to make the feel of lived time audible, so it is the function of film to make the feel of lived space-time perceptual. It does this by subjectifying the world and objectifying the expressive rhythms of the subject, that is, the actors and director. Thus, in his films, we know not merely what Fellini thinks about the world, but we see with our eyes and hear with our ears what he understands concerning how he feels about his world. The same is true of any other director who has evolved an identifiable style and mode of presentation.

The ability to assimilate so many things makes film a particularly difficult and expensive art to practice well. It is a kind of true omnibus art. It also means that many devices must be used to try to bring about emotional convergence, for it is "the continuity of emotion which holds it together while its visions roam through space and time."[59] Through the synthesis of texture, light/shadow, sound, color, and movement, film can condense into a felt unity and thus touch a basic function not normally appealed to in art directly: synaesthetic sensations. If we are to hold that man is a unity, as we have, then his senses must be a unity or must exhibit a unity prior to their articulation and differentiations. Mere contiguity of these elements would not be enough to explain their vivid impact. Film may appeal to a "primary layer of sense experience which precedes its division among the separate senses."[60] Intelligence can supply only an apparent communication between sense modalities; hence, it claims that such unity is either an accident, a convention, or a fiction. But, as Merleau-Ponty argues, synaesthetic perception is not the exception. In the natural standpoint, *it is the rule.*[61]

We fail to realize this, he says, because science has altered our center of gravity (in both senses of gravity) for experience. Science has taught us to unlearn "how to see, hear, and generally speaking, feel." We are taught to construct our body image as the physicist, the biologist, or Arthur Koestler tells us we ought to conceive it and then to deduce from this construct what we ought to see, ought to hear, and ought to feel. As I have said, most men do not live their lives, they deduce them. But if we put science aside—bracket it, if you will—and return to natural perception, we will find that the senses "intercommunicate by opening onto the thing." We will find that each sense modulates the thing and that the senses "communicate through their significant core." We will find that our bodies are "the fabric into which all objects are woven" and that the significance, the expressive value of qualities, is "the ground of the antepredicative unity of the perceived world."[62] Thus things grip our bodies before we have symbols or concepts by which to intellectualize them, and their qualities are pregnant with reference to each other. As Merleau-Ponty states, "The senses translate each other without any need of an interpreter, and are mutually comprehensible without the intervention of any idea."[63]

If the camera negates the natural standpoint and becomes our virtual body, then the experience that film engenders is a synaesthetic experience. In describing the object, the motion picture, not the subject, as we have here been doing, Professor Langer comes to the same type of conclusion:

> Like dream, it enthralls and commingles all the senses; its basic abstraction —direct apparition—is made not only by visual means, though these are paramount, but by words, which punctuate vision, and music that supports the unity of this shifting "world."[64]

I am sure that her use of the word "paramount" was not intended as a pun, but its bi-sociative meaning is peculiarly apt. Our discussion of perceiving, conceiving, imagining, and dreaming, then, has led us to the conclusion that film is a type of synaesthetic experience that is much like the dream. It provides an "immediate experience," a phrase that became the very title of Warshow's book.[65] As a final description of this immediate experience, I could do no better than to quote Professor Langer's closing words:

> The "dreamed reality" on the screen can move forward and backward because it is really an eternal and ubiquitous virtual present. The action of the dream goes inexorably forward because it creates a future, a Destiny; the dream mode is an endless Now.[66]

Notes

1. Arthur Koestler, *The Act of Creation* (New York: Macmillan, 1964), p. 535.

2. Rudolf Arnheim, *Art and Visual Perception* (Berkeley: University of California Press, 1957), p. 31.

3. Arnheim, p. 131. In his essay "The Gap between Intuition and Expression," Joyce Cary has a delightful description of a young child drawing the expressive force of a swan and an older one "corrupted by concepts" stating it doesn't look like a swan at all. The older child then draws a purely conventional "Christmas-card swan." Cary says: ". . . give a child the name of a bird, it loses the bird. It never *sees* the bird again but only a sparrow, a thrush, a swan . . ." Joyce Cary, "The Gap between Intuition and Expression," in *A Modern Book of Aesthetics,* ed. by Melvin Rader (New York: Holt, Rinehart and Winston, 1960), p. 111.

4. Arnheim, p. 69.

5. Desmond Morris, *The Naked Ape* (New York: McGraw-Hill, 1967), p. 230ff.

6. Arnheim, *Art and Visual Perception*, p. 140.

7. Arnheim, p. 150.

8. Arnheim, p. 128.

9. Arnheim, p. 365. The perception of hostility, confidence, or fear is so evident in humans that Konrad Lorenz defines dogs and other mammals as "the animals which think with their noses."

10. Koestler, *The Act of Creation*, p. 80. If you wish to verify this, tickle the next stranger you meet on an elevator.

11. Arnheim, *Art and Visual Perception*, p. 363.

12. Arnheim, p. 114.

13. Arnheim, p. 327.

14. Koestler, *The Act of Creation*, p. 531.

15. Koestler, p. 158.

16. Arnheim, *Art and Visual Perception*, p. 28.

17. Arnheim, p. 28.

18. Koestler, *The Act of Creation*, p. 527.

19. Koestler, p. 360.

20. Joseph Campbell, *The Masks of God: Primitive Mythology* (New York: Viking Press, 1959), p. 79. Campbell is summarizing the investigations of Jean Piaget. See Piaget, *The Child's Conception of the World* (Totowa, N.J.: Littlefield, Adams, 1960), pp. 92–96.

21. Campbell, p. 79. See also Piaget, pp. 96–97.

22. Campbell, pp. 79–80.

23. John Russell Taylor, *Cinema Eye, Cinema Ear* (New York: Hill & Wang, 1964), p. 196.

24. Taylor, p. 48.

25. Koestler, *The Act of Creation*, p. 178.

26. Koestler, p. 179.

27. Koestler, p. 180.

28. Freud as quoted in Koestler, p. 191.

29. Jung as quoted in Arnheim, *Art and Visual Perception,* p. 374.

30. Carl G. Jung, *The Integration of Personality,* trans. by Stanley Dell (London: Routledge & Kegan Paul Ltd.), 1956, p. 16.

31. Arnheim, *Art and Visual Perception,* p. 374.

32. Arnheim, p. 94.

33. Arnheim, p. 94. Whether this magical collapsing of meaning into bisociative presence is a function of the collective unconscious, as Jung maintains, is unclear. Nevertheless, there is something primitive in us, something that perceives forces intensely. The line between the original and aboriginal is not as clear as we normally assume. Such fusing may explain what I have termed the "irrationally right" image.

34. Arnheim, p. 374.

35. Arnheim, p. 374.

36. Jean-Paul Sartre, *The Psychology of the Imagination* (New York: Philosophical Library, 1948), p. 274.

37. Sartre, p. 26.

38. Sartre, p. 18.

39. Sartre, p. 104.

40. Sartre, p. 16.

41. Sartre, p. 278.

42. Sartre, p. 32.

43. Eugene Kaelin, *An Existentialist Aesthetic* (Madison: University of Wisconsin Press, 1962), p. 80.

44. Siegfried Kracauer, *Theory of Film: The Redemption of Physical Reality* (Fair Lawn, N.J.: Oxford University Press, 1960), p. 82.

45. Kracauer, p. 83.

46. Susanne K. Langer, *Feeling and Form* (New York: Scribner's, 1953), p. 40.

47. Susanne K. Langer, *Problems of Art* (New York: Scribner's, 1957), p. 15.

48. Langer, *Problems of Art,* p. 20.

49. Langer, p. 26.

50. D. W. Gotshalk, *Art and the Social Order* (Chicago: University of Chicago Press, 1947), p. 18.

51. Langer, *Problems of Art,* p. 34.

52. Langer, p. 67.

53. Langer, *Feeling and Form,* p. 411.

54. Langer, *Problems of Art,* p. 35.

55. Langer, *Feeling and Form,* p. 412.

56. Langer, p. 413.

57. Langer, p. 414.

58. Langer, p. 415.

59. Langer, p. 414.

60. Maurice Merleau-Ponty, *The Phenomenology of Perception* (New York: Humanities Press, 1962), p. 227.
61. Merleau-Ponty, p. 229.
62. Merleau-Ponty, p. 235.
63. Merleau-Ponty, p. 235.
64. Langer, *Feeling and Form,* p. 414.
65. Robert Warshow, *The Immediate Experience* (Garden City, N.Y.: Double-day, 1964).
66. Langer, *Feeling and Form,* p. 415.

7

The Film World

The short review of psychology was a necessary step in order to structure the horizon. Without a horizon, one cannot determine very well what is in the foreground. In fact, there can *be* no foreground nor any knowledge of awareness at all unless there is the emergence from context of a "this" which is not a "that." How such an emergence takes place has been accounted for in three major types of psychological theory: the idealist, the empiricist, and the existentialist. For the idealist, the determining function is mind, and the basic principles are those of identity and internality. Hence, for the idealist, mind creates the world—ultimately, out of itself. But the idealist is so enchanted by the whole that though he may be able to see, he cannot find adequate status for, the individual. The idealist cannot see the trees for the forest. Empirical psychology starts with simple sense data impinging on the organs. For the empiricist, the determining function is the stimulus-response of neural synapses, and the basic principles are difference and externality. Hence, for the empiricist, a stream of sensations impinge on and interact with organs—ultimately, there is no mind. But the empiricist is so enchanted by the parts and their supposed causal relationships that though he may be able to see, he cannot find adequate status for, the whole. The empiricist cannot see the forest for the trees.

Existential psychology starts with behavior and the body incarnate in its concrete circumstance. For the existentialist, the determining function is the stance, or value-attitude, one takes toward the world forming before him, and the basic principles are situation and articulation. Hence, for the existentialist, man acts on the world before he reacts to it; and, through the mutual dialectic of behavior/world, the self and the world emerge with greater and greater definition—ultimately, mind is not a new kind of thing but a new level of organizing. The word "organizing" is used in both senses of that ambiguity: (1) in the sense of patterning, that is, eliciting or creating form, and (2) transforming into an organ, or tool, which solidifies action opening onto a certain aspect of the world. But the existentialist is so concerned with ambiguity, nuance, and action, that though he may be able to envision, he cannot find any status for, perfection. Neither the individual nor the context from which he emerges is a complete whole. Both display structure and unity, but both are incomplete totalities. The existentialist cannot see the intervals for the trees.

Now, I have been taking the position of existential psychology, not merely because I see it as a middle position between two extremes but because I believe it is impossible for there to be a value-free psychology. There is no one more nervous than a psychologist. He is a man. And if he is a man alive, it is not possible for him to abstract himself totally from his situation. Whether committed or not, he is doomed to intrude upon his data. But I side with existential psychology for another reason: It is closer to life as it is in the living of it. While it is a spin-off from Gestalt psychology, the existential psychology, particularly of Merleau-Ponty, avoids the simple one-to-one correspondences of most Gestalt theories. It strives to describe the phenomena of experience in the experiencing of them. Insofar as it attempts to explain, of course, it is constructing rational structure and attempting to give a reasoned account of what we feel. Such an enterprise is very close to art, for the artist also is trying to articulate the life of feeling through the creation of perceptual objects. Insofar, then, as we are describing the perceptual process, we are analogously describing the creative process of the artist. His techniques of patterning are more powerful and precise, and his use of techniques is often much more conscious and self-conscious. But the processes of coming-to-awareness and creating-a-work-of-art are basically congruent. There is no reason to believe that "putting a film in the can" is any different. A purely realistic approach to film theory thus seems to me to be inaccurate and restrictive. As Dr. Langer has said: "There is no sense in trying to *convey reality* pure and simple. Even experience itself cannot do that."[1]

The artist also starts with the awareness of a gestalt that is incited in him through perception, imagination, thought, or intuition; and he proceeds to try to articulate this excitement into an original, unique whole. His aim is not an abstract constructed unity such as the counters of language become—whether the language of words or the language of mathematics. What he tries to create is an embodiment, "an organic differentiation of an original whole," and his method is thus nonsystematic. Discursive symbolism, such as science or mathematics, may have a common base with art. If so, that common base is metaphor. But they differ both in method and in direction. Yet a strange thing happens in both. The more science abstracts from the concrete situation, the more it talks about nothing in particular. But the more it talks about nothing in particular, the more it talks about everything in general. An inverse process occurs in art. The more the artist succeeds in moving away from the what of things to their thisness, the more concrete his work becomes. When he achieves the break from "this kind of thing" to *this thing* it turns out that he is also expressing the universal in its concrete instance.

A poem, for example, is built of words but it does not consist of them. A poem is not a discursive statement, though it may contain discursive statements. But the statements it contains are subordinate to and function for the poem. A poem is an intentional structure and what it intends is its own expressive quality. It does assert something, but what it asserts primarily is itself. It is not an actual statement about life, but a formed expression of life. Hence, the assertion of a poem is no more a cognitive statement than the pears in a painting are a snack. What the poet's life was like may be interesting, but it is not necessarily relevant—at least not to the poem. It is the poem that makes the poet interesting, not vice versa. What *is* relevant to the poem is how the poem works. Thus, John Ciardi's question "How Does a Poem Mean?" is a very meaningful one. A poem is not words, but it is what it does with words, what it *invests them with*. And, as S. Alexander was fond of saying, the words used may or may not be enchanting. But if it is a poem, they will be enchanted. Likewise, a motion picture is not photographs but what it does with them, how it enhances them.

With poetry or film, of course, we are talking about a high-powered activity. But the same type of thing happens in more prosaic circumstances. For example, when I began this book, I was suffused with a general excitement about our dual awareness of space and the meanings that this might have as an approach to film. My first projected title was "Reflections on the Screen." But, the more I wrote, the more my perspective began to take shape, and the title became "Remembrances of Things Present"; that is, time became an emergent factor. As my stance developed, the title changed again, for I was forced to think about form and to hunt for words to express my attitudes toward it. Since the most appropriate words seemed to be "situation, articulation, revelation," the title then became "Excarnation." The publishers, however, have decided that "excarnation" is too esoteric. Hence, I am back to the precise ambiguity of "Reflections on the Screen." The point is this: in doing what we do, we discover what we are doing.

In the beginning (we use that phrase because we have to use *some* phrase, even though there is no literal beginning), then, there are feeling-tone and the conscious and unconscious levels, along with a general synaesthetic synthesis of the field. There is an awareness of general, over-all structural features but no sharp distinctions of this from that. Things blur into each other. Then through the dialectic interaction of self/world, certain structures become outstanding; that is, they stand out from their contexts due to vividness or articulation or both. These structures are given names, and the choice of names is originally indifferent to which sense modalities they belong to. All that we ask is that they convey the feeling-tones involved and express the perceived emerging aspects of structure. Asking itself, by the way, is a kind of formulating or articulating, since a question is a feeling leaning against a possibility. What the answer does is rule out certain possibilities and point to a few as relevant. At any rate, feeling-tone may become expressed in words. As Professor Langer points out, a study of Western language development would show that *black* and *blakk,* Norwegian for white, have a cognate in *blanc* and *blank* and a probable root meaning in *bleak.* She states:

The original reference of adjectives especially appears to have been primarily
to feeling tones, and hence, quite freely and naturally, to any sense qualities that
helped the conception of them.[2]

As was said, Adam saw the animals before he named them.

But Adam's seeing was already an abstraction from the situation in the sense that
he had focused on one modality: sight. Sight itself involved certain perceptual
concepts, such as "doggishness," and a group of privileged percepts; for example,
trees are more important to both men and dogs than are the intervals. With the
movement to naming, then, we are already at a higher level of abstraction. We have
not only become aware of and helped constitute structure, we have broken it down
and located it. Goethe had observed, "Ersheinung und entzweien sind synonym,"
which Rudolf Arnheim interprets to mean "What comes into appearance must
segregate in order to appear."[3] To see in ordinary life means to follow the
outstanding, or at least, minimal clues. To see is to orient. Colleges have orientation
programs so that students will be able to find their way around the landscape of the
college and the inscape of the mind. To orient is to become and to be located.

Now, one of the most common phenomena of the motion-picture experience is a
feeling of disorientation. One feels disoriented in entering the theatre but even more
so when he finds himself thrown again into the now unfamiliar world. It takes some
time for the film to drain away from our bodies and for the outside world to take on
its normal appearance, an appearance that is considerably less sharp and vivid. We
feel lost when we leave the theatre; and, if we stop to try to recall *where* we were in
the theatre, we find that it is difficult to remember. Isn't this strange? As Whitehead
has remarked in another context,[4] when we have a feeling of disorientation and
lostness we immediately ask the question "Where am I?" But, as he further points
out, the question is absurd. We *know* where we are. But the question is not
therefore meaningless. What we mean is *"Where are all the other things?"*

I suggest that we feel disoriented when leaving a film because we cannot find the
other things. We had difficulty orienting ourselves in the theatre, and this difficulty
carries over as a sense of lostness when we emerge. The striking change of light is
disorienting, of course; but there is something more close than that—our whole
bodies are disoriented. In the theatre, we sit in the flickering dark, unaware of our
actual surroundings and the relation of our bodies to them. As a further complica-
tion, the primary object upon which we concentrate does not help us fix our
position, for the position of a moving picture is infinitely variable. It may be
almost entirely in two dimensions and half-dimensions, as in *Henry V,* or it may be
in an infinite number of perspectives and shifting dimensions as in *Citizen Kane.*

We do not see shadows moving on a strictly delimited screen; we see a variable apparition moving in elastic space. Even if the film were shot with a fixed focus and a fixed camera position, we would have difficulty orienting ourselves. Our eyes identify with the viewpoint of the camera, and we cannot fix our own position relative to the film because it is a moving, constantly shifting, phenomenon. A film is a gesture without horizon.

Our ordinary experience is constructed within a double sense of space: the sense of the relation of things to things, and the sense of the relations of our bodies in this complex. We see *through* our eyes. Our ordinary experience is filtered by our bodily position, and its stance is a *privileged* position. My body is not in space in the same sense in which other things are in space. It inhabits space and is the center of the space it radiates. My body is a constant here. In our experience of the motion picture, however, we lose this primary stance of the body. We relinquish our bodily perspective through identification with the viewpoint of the camera, and we come close to pure perception. The position of our body or its attitude toward the object before us is irrelevant and unknown. This is why we have a feeling of disorientation while in the theatre and a sense of lostness when we emerge. It is because we literally *were* lost *in the experience.* The normal withness of our body is dislocated, for the camera vantage becomes our virtual posture. The motion-picture experience is an experience of excarnation.

There is a direct analogue here between what happens to us as spectators and what happens to the actor. He also has his bodily location disrupted, for his initial stance is to the studio and its sets; but he must learn in film to alter it and address the camera. There is also an analogue to film form itself, for the primary implication of theme is the alteration, through such devices as plot, accident, and event, of stance. Film provides us with the initial posture of its characters. The development of the film is the progressive articulation of that posture. The articulation ends by revealing the resultant altered address of the main characters in relation to their lived world.

Before the beginning of the film, we can and do locate ourselves in the theatre space; and we settle into our seats. But once the apparition has begun to take shape and tone and movement, it becomes our temporary abode. Under certain circumstances, of course, we slip back into our seats. If, for example, it is a bad or dull film, we will become aware of the bodily static reaching us from our derrieres, or the popcorn chewing of our neighbors. Or the film itself may force us suddenly back into place for some specific purpose as in *Tom Jones* or *The Great Train Robbery.* Here, by a sudden shift, we are forced to realize that we have *been taken in;* and the emotional result is one of amusement as a result of embarrassment. One can be taken in, of course, in other ways, as one is by the intricate plotting of symbolism in *The Magician,* only to find at the end that it was all a farce. Here the result is anger. But I am not talking about this sense of "taken in."

Even the worst film can become our temporary abode, and we may be unable to tear ourselves away from it simply because we wish to see how much worse it can get. But it has one thing going for it: the camera. The medium of the motion-picture camera, by negating our natural standpoint and the primacy of position, captures not merely our imagination but also our bodily eye. It presents us with a new position in an intangible but perceptual space. We see what the camera chooses for us to see; our attention follows our vision. This is one reason for the immediacy of the film experience. Another reason is motion.

Motion per se has the strongest visual appeal to attention, as if the moving object draws the eye to it and holds it by fascination. If one regards the behavior of other animals, his dog, say, he will find that while the dog exhibits sudden spurts and flurries of activity, the greatest part of its day is spent simply lying and looking at the world before it. Being less compulsively active than his master and not at all concerned with profit and loss, the dog can afford to coincide with his living and "while." But if one introduces a moving object into his field of vision, the dog's eyes will immediately follow the course of its movement. If the movement is one of abstract regularity, such as a swinging ball on a string, his eyes will move back and forth in the same rhythm. If the movement is characteristic of some natural object within his field, say a rabbit, he will prick up his ears and tense his muscles. His body will become set to pursue. As Arnheim has observed:

> Young kittens seem completely at the mercy of any moving thing as though their eyes were tied to it. Human beings are similarly attracted by movement; I need only to mention the effectiveness of mobile advertising.[5]

Though it is romantic to believe that the music played by the Hindu charms the savage soul of the cobra, experiments have shown that the snake will move in rhythmic response to a soundless moving stick. The movement of the flute charms him, not its sound. Human beings are more complex than dogs or cobras, but there is no reason to believe that we do not react in the same ways to motion. In fact, experience shows that we do. Motion as such draws our eyes forth and rivets them to its sway. Reflect for a moment on the soothingness of watching the regular movements of the ocean waves or the delightful relaxed mindlessness of watching waves roll to shore or dancing flames in the fireplace. Or think of the average family with all eyes glued to the TV screen.

Motion is one of the prime characteristics of happenings, and happenings attract us. This intuition is no doubt the basis for the almost continual dancing and jerking of the teen-age rock band. It will no longer do for the band to remain sedately seated. The music must be so amplified that it blasts through the body and the musicians also move in the "big beat." The bodies of the audience are not only permeated by the sound, but their primary object of vision, the band, is also in continual motion. A happening, of course, includes other types of change, such as qualitative alteration. Thus, the colored lights on the band change, just as the color of the apple changes as it ripens or the color of the leaves change to their last flamboyance before the death of winter. For something to be a happening, then, it must involve motion and also qualitative displacement, which takes place within an observable time span. Hence, it is easier to see the lobster turning red in the boiling water than the apple or the leaf turning red on the tree. The phenomenon in the apple and the leaf, of course, can be captured by time-lapse photography and then speeded up. But what is needed here is the compression of process. Arnheim sums it up:

> In other words, what distinguishes the experience of happenings from that of things is not that it involves the perception of passing time, but that we witness an organized sequence in which phases follow each other meaningfully in a one-dimensional order. When the event is disorganized or incomprehensible, the sequence breaks down into mere succession. It loses its main characteristic; and even the succession lasts only as long as its elements are being squeezed through the gorge of the immediate presence. Beyond that point they lie scrambled in disorder. No bond of time connects them, because time cannot create order. It is order that creates time.[6]

This connects with our assertion that the ultimate difference between function and substance is lapse. When the lapse extends beyond the perceivable, we call the object a thing. When the lapse is restricted and compressed, we say that it is a happening. No doubt this is one reason why inferior directors think that fast movement is good in itself, since it tends to hold a film together. But sheer movement and its acceleration are not enough. There must also be direction, and direction can be made coherent only by the addition of depth. One characteristic of organic form, then, must be that it requires both tension and compression. Tension is unitary and continuous, while compression and expansion are discontinuous and sporadic. But the compressions and expansions are such that they must refer to and be involved in the basic tensional line of development, before the form is said to attain unity or to express meaning. This description of organic form, I believe, would apply as well to Buckminster Fuller's geodesic domes as it would to film or the life process of animals. Applied to film, it means that film form is always dual. There is the background movement of developing tension, which I call "theme," and the foreground discontinuous processes of expansion and compression, which I shall call "plot" or "event." When these are synthesized into a moving whole, they constitute expressive meaning, and the film is said to have "organic form."

Any object or image in motion immediately engages our eyes and our attention, forcing the stable surroundings into the status of background. But the motion picture is not merely an indeterminate *something* in motion; it is a perceived event in motion. As Arnheim states:

> Whatever the psychological causes of the wish to make likenesses may be, it will suffice here to point out that making images of events is more important than depicting objects in their static shapes and colors because the fundamental biological reaction is that of reacting to happenings, not that of contemplating objects.[7]

He puts this point even more forcefully when he asserts:

> The motion picture in itself is an event: it looks different every moment, whereas there is no such temporal progress in a painting or in sculpture. Motion being one of its outstanding properties, the film is required by aesthetic law to use and interpret motion.[8]

What we see on the screen, then, is very much like what we see in our everyday living-in-the-world. What we are aware of are images of things, people, relations, in all their multiplicity of qualities and in motion. On the screen (or, rather, in front of it), we are aware of an apparition of immediate presence—to which we give prereflective assent. The assent is not willed. And one reason for this is the immediate impact of motion. But, as we have seen, motion itself is not enough. There must also be depth.

Now, the prime element that adds depth to tensional development is plot, that is, the changing qualitative relations of people to each other and to their milieu. But if we put plot aside, temporarily, and turn simply to the perceptive process, we find within the perceptive process itself elements of depth already present. For this reason, our assent is not willed and our attention follows vision. Of course, in viewing a film, the spectator is subliminally helping to reconstitute the motion. The projector is so timed that it exploits the time-lag of the eye; hence, through a defect of lapse, we are already prereflectively engaged in re-creating the movement of the film before us. In an eighty-minute film there will be about fifty minutes of pictures. The rest is darkness. The image is not in the eye of the beholder; his perceptions are part of the image perceived. But if we put aside this subliminal cooperation also, there are still factors operative in the visual field that help to constitute depth.

One such factor is hierarchy. Time and again I have emphasized the foreground/background relationship and the emergence of objects as things. But these synthesized-aspects-in-profile, which we call "things," are themselves ordered. The relationships of dependence are already present in the visual field. Thus, one sees the flea as attached to the dog; he does not see the dog as attached to the flea.

> The dancer is a part of the stage setting, not the stage setting the outer rim of the dancer. In other words, quite apart from motion, the spontaneous organization of the field assigns to certain objects the role of framework, on which others depend. The field represents a complex hierarchy of such dependences."[9]

When we add to this elementary perception of hierarchy and dependence the fact that motion is perceived as the displacement of things in relation to each other, that is, the perception of relativity, we can see depth and meaning coming into the very formation of the visual field. When one is driving a car, he sees the road as static and the near ground as moving. But if one shifts his vision, he can see the car eating up the road or, with another shift, he can see the far horizon moving with him and the intermediate ground falling away. Any one of these events is perfectly compatible with our retinal images, but we chose one stance and not the other. The perception of motion, then, depends also upon fixation.

That which seems stationary to me is that which I have chosen as the temporary abode of my eyes. But this choosing is not a matter of my articulating intellectual hypotheses. On the contrary, it is a function of my posture to the perceived world. Merleau-Ponty has said:

> Movement and rest distribute themselves in our surroundings not according to the hypotheses which our intelligence is pleased to construct but according to the way we settle ourselves in the world and the position our bodies assume in it.[10]

When I look at the tower outlined against the cloud, the clouds are scudding lazily along the sky; when I fixate the clouds, the tower seems to vibrate and fall. It is the figure, the looked-at object which I engage and to which I anchor myself, that "will always seem fixed, and I cannot take this meaning away from it except by looking elsewhere." Perception of relative motion is not a kind of incipient science depending on how I use my mind. On the contrary, it is dependent on where my eyes adhere. That to which my eyes adhere and toward which I assume a posture remains static, and it is the other that moves. Man is not a mere spectator of the world; but, on the other hand, he does not construct it out of whole cloth from his understanding. He is a "being thrown into the world and attached to it by a natural bond."[11]

Now, it is precisely this natural bond, the stance of the natural standpoint, that is suspended or negated in the experiencing of film. This is what is meant by saying that the film is a gesture without horizon. It is without horizon with respect to our bodily address. Of course, the apparition has its own internal and variable horizons, and they are established by the vantage point of the camera. When the vantage point of the camera shifts, the "fixated" objects change, and the hierarchies of dependence, the horizon, and the directions of relative motions also change. Hence, by merely moving the camera without any additional change, the director can add visual depth to his film. It is not the same thing, in spite of Kracauer, to walk down a street and to watch a film in which an invisible camera dollies or tracks down a street. In the latter case, we are not inhabiting the street; the street encounters us. We are not moving in it; it is moving in on us, for we have allowed the camera to assume our natural standpoint. Most of the illusions of *Laterna Magica* were based on this assumption. The director can thus use the technique of the moving camera to create the other half-dimension of film and to give the apparition "body" as it emerges from the two-dimensional screen. Arnheim states:

> The pioneers of the motion pictures were quick to discover that a "travel-ing" camera obtains more depth. The same effect is observed if we watch the landscape from a moving train or car. The apparent movement of objects varies in proportion to distance. It is fastest at close quarters, comes to a standstill along the horizon line, and increases again in the opposite direction. Objects above the horizon, such as buildings on a hill, clouds, or the sun, will travel with the observer, whereas everything between the horizon and the foreground speeds backward. In this way motion applies a consistent distortion of relative location to the entire visual world.[12]

If we realize, then, that the perceptual field before us in film includes the natural attractiveness of motion, the relativity and hierarchy of the field with fixation as its base, and camera movement as an additional depth factor, we may begin to understand why the motion picture has such a strong sense of immediacy and impact just at the level of a flow of images. And the way in which motion is presented will already structure meaning into the situation.

Let's return to a concrete example we used before. In *Blow-Up,* Hemmings participates in the antique-shop sequence; then, as he is driving away, he calls his secretary and gives orders to buy the place "because the queers and the poodles are already moving in." To the attentive viewer, these instructions are an affront. Not because of their content but because they are *redundant.* Antonioni does here what he seldom does: he makes a mistake of overstatement. At the beginning of the sequence, Hemmings sees the two boys with their pretty hair and their poodles walking down the street. Antonioni shoots the whole scene from an off-angle. Hence, the frame is oblique and the movements of the figures through it are diagonal. Visually, this is exactly right, for visually homosexuals are oblique, they are elliptical, they do not fit into the straight coordinates of "straight" society. Hence, they are deviates. By his camera movements and his use of angles, Antonioni has already told us that the men are homosexual; thus, his verbal gloss later is superfluous. As soon as the two men turn the corner, the camera takes Hemmings' position and rights itself. Many such examples could be chosen from film, but the point is that the meaning of the situation is already written on the face of the image by the use of the camera.

But the mobile framework of a film exhibits itself not merely in space; it is also mobile in time. Hence, if the duration of a shot is increased, its density will be increased. As R. Leenhardt has reported, a short shot of a smiling face will mean an amused smile; whereas, if the shot is extended in lapse, the face will be seen as indifferent; and, if it is further extended, the face will appear sorrowful.[13] The density of lapse functions, up to a point, as intensity of expression. The task of the director is to choose the proper rhythm for any sequence and for the film as a whole. By "proper rhythm" Leenhardt means "a certain order of shots and a certain duration for each . . . so that taken together they produce the desired impression with maximum effectiveness." Reflection on such thoughts led Merleau-Ponty to state, "Let us say right off that a film is not a sum total of images but a temporal *gestalt.*"[14] Film is a flexible space-time continuum that can be condensed into an emotional and visual organic unity. "Film is more than a variation of the immobile image, obtained by multiplication: it is fundamentally new and different."[15] Hence, films are not normally composed of alternating still shots, and they are fundamentally different from paintings and sculpture. If we reflect for a moment on the differences between motion and fixation, this will be evident.

When motion is stopped, one is struck by the embarrassing duration of fixity. When Tom's pratfall into the water is suddenly transformed into a still, we laugh, which is what we are supposed to do in *Tom Jones.* The reason is not merely because the stop motion breaks up the assumed sequence, but the stop shot arrests his fall. When a dancer runs across the stage and stops, she is not at rest but arrested, for the momentum of her movement seems to have come up against some invisible force. The same is true of Tom, and since we know there is no such force here, the sudden stop arrests our attention and amuses us. As the shot is prolonged, another factor, that of the embarrassment of fixity, comes in.

A work which intends "to show the fleeting moment," the "transitory gesture," and which fixes it in a static pose, not only "fails to render any activity at all" but infuses into the arrested gesture an uncomfortable duration. The extreme example, as Arnheim says, is the representation of "the winking eye in commercial posters"; that is, we see one eye open and one closed, but we see no movement. This sudden arresting of the momentum of the film in both time and space can have at the end of the film a strong effect of moving the spectator from sheer vision into the realm of contemplation.

Think, for example, of the parting shots in *La Strada,* in which we leave Zampano shaking with grief but essentially immobile, or of the large close-up of the boy's face at the end of *The Four Hundred Blows.* In the latter case, we have complete arresting, as we almost have at the end of the madcap pace of *Breathless.* In *La Strada,* though there is camera movement, notice that it is appropriate to the contemplative mode—the camera draws away from Zampano. Now, in film sequences, the sequence long-shot–close-shot is the analogue of iambs in poetry, and it speeds the visuals up. The sequence close-shot–long-shot slows the visuals down and is the analogue of trochaic rhythm. Since the rhythm is slowed, we are induced to contemplate. The same thing happens at the end of *Blow-Up;* we have a long track back from Hemmings standing in the patchwork grass. This draw-back not only brings us to think about his situation, to which he has finally committed himself, but also makes a visual pun. The visual theme of the film had been that in close-up everything turns out to be some form of disaster—murder or noncommunication or poverty. But the grass and the trees seen in close-up in the park are incredibly green and lush. Hence, we feel that "nature is beautiful, only man is vile." But in the closing back-track, Hemmings has abandoned and then picked up his camera, has joined the fictional game of the clowns, and now the park looks like an old, rotted horse's hide. Hence, we are given the view that "only man, no matter how silly or insane, is beautiful and nature is vile." Then he simply disappears. Again, what we have is expressive assertion by sheer camera movement and without any verbal statements. Any verbal statement would be superfluous.

Now, when we contemplate the function of fixity and gravity and weight in film as compared with painting or sculpture, a fundamental distinction emerges between the elastic and the plastic arts. The relation of motion and rest appears to be inverted. Rodin's *Walking Man* has no head or arms and is arrested to a heavy bronze base. The very increase of this resistance to his motion and the incompleteness of the over-all body adds dynamism to the figure. The massive legs are literally striving to overcome the great weight of the pedestal. As gravitational impetus increases in the plastic arts, then, the conflict of forces makes the apparition appear to be undergoing a great struggle for movement. Contemplate for a minute the late works of Michelangelo, in which the figures are struggling to release themselves from the rock. But when gesture is portrayed in a drawing, as in the case of the winking ad, the result is not a sense of motion but an embarrassing fixity. Just the opposite seems to be true in dance and in the film. When gravity and weight are increased, apparent motion is decreased. When gravity and weight decrease, apparent movement accelerates.

The acceleration of motion does change the qualitative impact of the images and this is no doubt why inferior film makers speed things up. They hope we won't have time to stop and think of the poor quality of their work. Just as duration can affect expression, so the rate of change can also affect expressive quality. If cars move at a normal speed down a filmed street, we have simple displacement from one place to another. If the film is speeded up, however, as it is in the old comedies, the cars suddenly become berserk forces, expressive monsters. The same holds for the distance traversed. Hence, a dancer on a large stage appears to move more heavily and more slowly than on a small stage, and a film projected on a normal screen appears to be "soft" and "slow" when it is expanded to cinerama proportions.

Deceleration of the movement of the images has the same effect as using the larger screen: It enhances the dreamlike quality of the sequence and puts it in the mode of contemplation. Think, for example, of the remembrance sequences in *The Pawnbroker,* in which the children float down through the fields in slow motion. A very striking use of such changes of pace is in *The Seven Samurai.* The death blows come with such sudden swiftness that one can hardly see the sword; but the dying is in extra-slow motion, giving an added "punch" to death. When an entire film is slowed down, however, as is *Accident* or *Le Bonheur,* the effect is not so much one of romanticism as of turgidity. Acceleration and deceleration of image flow, then, alter the pictorial and emotional quality of film and such techniques, to be effective, must fit into the over-all structural pattern of movement and must have a purpose to fulfill within the moving whole. A film that does not unify its motions, either through contrast or synthesis, is "dead."

We thus discover another principle of organic form: permeation. Not only must there be a unifying tension that evolves throughout the film and constitutes its emotional horizon, but also the subordinate compressions and expansions must be relevant to and enhanced by their relations with their background. Any work of art that is alive is organized around a major dynamic theme, and this theme must reverberate or permeate to the smallest elements (for example, costumes and individuate gestures) of the work, establishing their comparability and emotional identity without negating their individuate status. This means that an organic form has different levels, and elements of the same type must belong to the same level of order. Otherwise, they do not fit.

Examples of this violation of unitary hierarchy are easily found in many of the films of Walt Disney. When he confined his films to abstract line drawings of humanized animals, the films were consistent within their given patterns. But when he mixed drawings of human beings with those of animals as in *Snow White and the Seven Dwarfs,* the humans could not emerge from their line-drawing context and appeared stiff and unnatural, that is, inhuman. And they *were* inhuman, for they were organized on the same plane as the more simplified animal drawings. An even more striking malformation is found in *Mary Poppins.* The film as a whole is delightful, and one can even accept the Norman Rockwell kids with their clean-scrubbed and carefully placed freckles. But in the sequences where people are mixed with dancing line-drawings of penguins or rabbits waving their derrieres (no one, I think, has ever done a study on the assumed amusement Disney found in the waving rears of animals),[16] we have an uneasy clash of two levels of abstraction. Disney tried to segue this fault (and one could think of it in geological terms) by moving the sequence into a fantasy of runaway merry-go-round horses. This almost worked. But not quite. At least it was a step forward. The usual Disney technique was to try to gap these discordant image levels by a resort to sentimentality, a device that is understandably human but inartistic. It denotes a failure of artistic power, either in terms of what is felt or what is articulated or both.

I am not saying that fantasy is not a proper mode of film presentation. It is. And it can be one of the most delightful of all modes. But I am insisting that the apparent world that the film creates be consistent artistically within itself. One is almost tempted to say that it should be logical, although what is involved here is more than mere class resemblance. What is involved is the necessity of valuational reverberation and mutual interaction that enhance, but do not destroy, hierarchic levels. This fusion of quality with the retention of structural integrity is what we have termed "authenticity." Film form that violates it appears to be phony and the spectator feels, quite rightly, that he has been had.

A notable example of the failure of expressive synthesis is Alfred Hitchcock's use of music in *Psycho.* Visually, the film is a pastiche and looks as though it were a committee job done by Charles Addams, Orson Welles, and Jean Cocteau (the old mansion, the swinging light bulb, the ominous cop with shades). I suppose one could also throw in Marcel Duchamp for the Nude Descending a Shower. But the use of music in this film is most offensive. Instead of weaving the music into his theme and using it to heighten or counterpoint, ironically, the visuals—as for example, the wild merry-go-round at the end of *Strangers on a Train* blares "Ain't We Got Fun?"—Hitchcock applies the music like a brickbat. Thus, as Norman comes barreling down the stairs at the detective, the music screams out of nowhere. The sudden shock of sound certainly scares the audience, but it feels that it has been acoustically had. A more authentic and appropriate use of the scream occurs in *High and Low*. Kurosawa uses the whistle of the train to punctuate Gondo's existential act. In this context, it is appropriate, for Gondo is throwing the ransom out the window of the train. Opening the window allows the sound naturally to come in.

A fine contrast to Hitchcock's use of music in *Psycho* would be Satyajit Ray's use of similar sounds in *Pather Panchali* and *The World of Apu*. In *Panchali,* there is the masterful background music of Ravi Shankar's sitar, which is skillfully woven into the emotional themes—most delicately and notably in the waterbug ballet sequence. But we are concerned here with similar sounds or "screams," and a comparison with the waterbug sequence would be unfair. When the idealistic and inept father returns home from the city, he carries presents for the family. The music rises in anticipation of his joy at being able, finally, to provide some things for his wife and children. The music continues to rise as he holds out the sari he has brought for the daughter, and suddenly the wife confronts him with the girl's death. The sitar rises to a high pitch, the mother and father pitch their heads in anguish, and it is not clear whether they are screaming, the music is screaming, or both. Here the natural progression of musical pattern and human gesture has been fused into one intense meaning. Ray does the same thing with the screech of a train in *Apu*. Here the new wife rises from the bed and begins to make breakfast. We have a beautiful visual mixture of the smoke arising from her charcoal mixing with the smoke from the passing train—one smoke connoting the tenderness of open concern, and the other the brutal indifference of the mechanical milieu that will eventually grind away at Apu. The shriek of the train announces the dawn and the mingling of the two smokes. Again, in both the audio and the visual, everything fits.

One of the most memorable systems of images condensed into this kind of synaesthetic unity can be found in the opening sequence of *The Magician*. Here we begin with the camera in a dense fog in the forest. One can feel the density of the scene, with its ghostly shapes and evanescent light. We hear horses and the creaking of a wagon, but the horses' hooves sound muffled as though they were treading on cotton. This adds to the soft texture and ghostly menace of the visuals. Then we see the horses looming up, and they are moving in slow motion. Suddenly the ghastly stillness is cut by a shriek. In this sequence, Bergman has brilliantly fused the sound, distorted naturalism, with the motion, distorted naturalism, with the visuals, distorted naturalism. All the various levels work together to constitute the same expressive quality and to render the forest a place of gloom and foreboding.

Many more such examples could be cited from various films, but the main point is clear: There is a definite difference, not merely a felt difference but a perceived one, between mere sequence and synthesis. One is mechanical, the other organic. Either may be remembered because it is so striking. In the first situation, the juxtaposition of qualitative elements is so inappropriate that they stand out; and the cleavage is, in this case, unattractive. In the second situation, we remember the organic and synaesthetic scene because of its unified impact. Everything is appropriate to everything else, connected not merely externally and logically but also by an inner bond. Everything fits and contributes to the whole, while being enhanced by it. The parts have become elements, and the elements *belong*. There is a kind of mutual internal longing of the elements, which call forth the evocative echo in each other and reinforce the rhythm of the whole. Movement, then, does not mean merely gross visual displacement or only qualitative change, but it also intends transition and mirroring of emotional substance from one image to another. Such synthesis must be seen to be felt or known or believed, and this is one reason that films are difficult to abstract and remember discursively. They do not leave relics like mollusks or poets. Being a moving phenomenon, they are so tied to the present that we must re-view them in order to review them. A motion picture is delibly written in the presentness of the present.

Poets and mollusks leave behind the remains, the skeletons, the artifacts, which are expressive of the living rhythms that prompted them forth. The moving abode of the snail is a rhythmic construction formed from the excretions of chalk liquefied into paste and shaped by the living movements of the snail's body. The over-all tensional rhythmic patterning of its life with the various points of conflict, compression, expansion, and resolution, become constitutive of the nuances of shape in its self-created architecture. The shell of a snail is the articulated fixation of its life encounters.

Thus nature is alive to our eyes partly because its shapes are fossils of the events that give rise to them. The past history is not merely inferred intellectually from clues, but directly experienced as forces and tensions present and active in visible shapes.[17]

Nor is there any great difference with human beings, except that our abodes, our bodies, are less rigid than that of the snail. On the human body also are written the glow of exercise and the grooves and shallows of past griefs. Not only does everybody have the face he deserves after thirty-five, he has the body he deserves. And his body is a walking history of his past.

The poet, of course, has a body like the snail and like other people. But he excarnates in another form also—he writes marks on paper. But a poem is not what is printed on a page. What is printed on a page is the occasion for a poem, the remembrance of a poem, as E. E. Cummings has put it, which the reader must rebuild in order—and in the order demanded by the poet in the poem—to reexperience it. Thus the poet leaves us a fixated skeleton of an articulated feeling-rhythm that "is" the poem. The reader must reconstitute the aural poem from visual clues. He must discover it before he can participate in it. What appeals first to the eyes are fixated marks; but, as the eye and ear begin to function, the poem emerges, with the aid of imagination, from its written remains. All the poet asks of us is that we become active and then yield to his poem. All we ask of the poet and the chambered nautilus is that they bring to us, through the structure of their remains, the beyond from which their shapes emerged. And we ask that they not merely echo that beyond but also articulate it into a this.

This distinction of fixation and remembrance points to one of the differences between literary works and films. What works on the screen does so by providing us, not with a fixated skeleton, but with a fluid body of sensory qualities. The appeal to the senses of the literary work is indirect, but the film engages us at once by exploiting the persistence of vision. This means that the apparition in film is *before* us and is more concrete than the world of a poem or the world of a novel. Literary works are inherently more abstract than films. All art involves abstraction, but the literary work emerges at a different imaginative level. In fact, this very presentness of the film hampers the appeal to past experience or to imaginative construction. This is why symbols in film may be missed until the second or third viewing. Fellini's shots of the religious procession in *La Strada,* for example, when he shoots through a butcher's window past a hanging pig, may not register the first time one sees the film; but when the film is re-viewed, one can catch the visual comments and nuances. In first viewing, one is swept up in the sheer movement of the film itself. Though few would refuse to see a play of *Hamlet* again on the grounds that they "had seen it already," this is the normal response to the suggestion to re-view a film. It is precisely the film that ought to be seen twice—the first time to grasp the over-all tensional development of the theme and plots and the second time to see how these are articulated in the subordinate elements.

In matters of this type, I believe it is safer to quote poets than philosophers. Therefore, let me refer the reader to Robert Frost's "Carpe Diem," in which he sings:

> The present
> Is too much for the senses,
> Too crowding, too confusing—
> Too present to imagine.[18]

Now, the motion picture, as we have said, is deliberately written in the present; that is, so written that we can act on it—but we have to be quick. It does not call upon our imagination or memory to bring forth things that are absent. It excites us, instead, to unite with that which is present. For this reason, the experiencing of a film is often referred to as subjective and the illusion itself as having the appearance of an objective dream. In order to experience a motion picture, we need to be able to see and to hear and to feel. It does not make the demands on our imaginations that a poem or a novel or even a painting does. In this regard, a spectator of a film is much more passive. But, though his imagination is not called upon so forcefully, his eyes and ears are more active. His imagination does come into play, but only as a result of being enjoyed in the event, not as its cause. This relative passivity of the imagination is a result of the givenness of the film.

Naturally, the film creator who understands his work uses various techniques, such as montage, double printing, double exposures, close-ups, and jump-cuts, when they are appropriate to his articulation of the theme, in order to emphasize the presentness of the medium and to exploit the visibility of the images recorded. Compression into the present alone gives his film the beginnings of organic form. But compression is not enough. Richard Lester's pastiche advertising style was appropriate and effective in *The Running, Jumping, Standing Still Film* and in *A Hard Day's Night* since both films had no depth dimensions to develop but were sheer expressions of high spirits. The same technique was inappropriate to and almost ruined *The Knack,* which does have a deeper tensional theme; but that theme was violated by the surface agitation of the overly swift images and jump-cuts. Syntax in film, as in poetry, should be not merely adequate to but also expressive of theme. This might be called the "principle of relevance of technique." Let us turn to a comparison of painting and films to see how this works.

At first thought, it would seem that a painting is an instantaneous whole given all at once. But we have learned from our excursion into psychology that our eyes are not passive but constantly sweep the field with their gaze. And just as in music that which is on the left of the staff signifies what comes before and that which is on the right indicates that which comes after, so also in the painting (which is a record in pigment and canvas) are we given embedded temporal clues. Eisenstein has noted this:

> And then we realize that an extremely important factor has been ignored, namely, that *the motionless whole of a picture and its parts do not enter the perception simultaneously.* . . .
>
> The art of plastic composition consists in leading the spectator's attention through the exact sequence prescribed by the author of the composition.[19]

Thus the perception of a painting, like the perception of a film, is a process. But the difference is this: In the painting, the time element is dependent on recorded clues, whereas, in the film, time is a fluid element immediately presented. Hence, the brush strokes on canvas are symbolic of time relationships; they indicate or represent them through the medium of forces. But time in films is not primarily represented; it is presented. Even if it is past time, such as in the historical film or a memory sequence, it is presented as if in the present.

Now, no one who has seen a painting can deny that lines move or that colors vibrate. Yet the movement in a painting is not the same as the movement in a film. Why? Because like the relations to the poem, the novel, and the mollusk, the film and the painting exist at different levels of abstraction. The movement in a painting must emerge, if it does at all, on the level of the imagination and memory. One must synthesize and hold the whole and then articulate the parts. But in film, the whole is never given all at once. Like a symphony or a dance, the form of the whole cannot be grasped *as* a whole until the entire film has been perceived. Painting is prospective; film, retrospective. The movement in painting depends upon the remembrance of things absent. The movement of a film is given; it consists of the remembrance of things present.

One might say that the temporal factor is on the horizon of the painting, and it must be worked on by the eyes and the imagination before it emerges into the foreground. But the temporal factor in film is already the moving figure before us and can be seen as a patterned whole only when it is grasped as background in retrospection. In the perception of painting, the gaze precedes the glimpse; in the perception of film, the glimpse precedes the gaze. If we can see, remember (literally re-member, that is, put back together again), and imagine, we can then see the movement in a painting. If we see no such tension or movement in the painting, then either it is dead and lifeless, or we don't know how to see. But in a film we do not need to reconstruct clues; the movement is immediately given. In a motion picture we do not perceive because we remember, we remember because we perceive.

The influences of painting on film have been tremendous. One can "see" El Greco throughout Cocteau's *Beauty and the Beast,* and the majestic float up into the clouds at the end is a filmic version of Mary's bodily ascension. But compositional elements must be transformed in order to be relevant to screen rhythms. Like music, they should either be fused with the moving structure of the film gesture, or they should enhance by reinforcing contrasts. For film is essentially an elastic, and not a plastic, medium. Its space is a different space from that of the canvas and a different one from the world we normally inhabit. One contemporary work of genius is a good example of using pictorial framing and composition as powerful elements: *Rashomon.* But notice that Kurosawa emphasizes the purely compositional shot only when it is aesthetically relevant, that is, in the court scenes. In the court scenes he wants maximum stability and balance to go with the sedateness of justice, but the forest sequences are all movement and the fragile terror of sunlight flashing on leaves. Kurosawa uses framing to enhance stability and the measured slowness of justice.

Another instance of enhancement, this time through contrast, is in *The Graduate.* Nichols shoots the emergence-toward-the-water scene through the frame of the scuba mask. This gives us an ironic contrast to and revelation of the catatonia of the main character by enhancing the absurdity of the external, expectant middle-class people dutifully watching the cumbersome birthday boy flap his way to the pool. It also gives us a feeling of claustrophobia, as does the opening tunnel in *8½,* and is an ironic comment on the boy's relations with these adults—they won't let him breathe. Except artificially, of course, in an artificial antiseptic womb (pool). One finds a similar kind of wry comment in one framing of a sequence in Bergman's *The Silence.* We see the screen split into two arches, and then as the camera dollies back we realize that the boy is looking through a door. We are looking through the door with him. The irony comes in with the focus on the object of his fascination: a wild painting of satyric rape. We suddenly realize that the framing being used, and being used on us, is the traditional split canvas that dominates the thousands of portrayals of the annunciation of Mary, but the "angel" the boy is viewing is violent sexual assault. Both of these boys have strange baptisms into life.

The purely compositional film, or the painter's cinema, reached its peak between 1920 and 1925 in Germany with *The Cabinet of Doctor Caligari* and *Siegfried.* Carl Dreyer revived this style in Denmark with *The Passion of Joan of Arc, Day of Wrath,* and other works. Composition tended to be the dominant element in the silent screen. But the film has rightly moved away from this style toward its true nature, the rhythm of motion. The addition of sound was not merely a new technical advance but the incorporation of a new dimension and an essential change in structure (or rather one should say "form," since the movement was away from structure as such and toward rhythmic synaesthesia). This rhythm may be pure jazz on film, ragged and angular in its neurotic cutting and music, as in *Breathless;* or it may be the slow measure of inner resolution, as in *The World of Apu* or *L'Avventura.*

There is a prevalent prejudice among American directors that a pan is sissy, whereas a cut is masculine. This erroneous belief may be due as much to the frenetic pace of American life and music as it is to the (again, erroneous) belief that adherence to the principle of compressed quantity will by itself provide the illusion of life. *Ikiru* is a long film; and, during almost half of it, the main character is dead. Yet its rhythms are appropriate to its theme. *Shane* should move slowly, since it is not an action picture but an aesthetic contemplation of the Western myth. Since it is thrown into the contemplative mode, it should be spare in visuals (which it is—what a dreary town!) and in compression of incident. To put it briefly, it is as right that *Shane* should be stately as that *Breathless* should be frenetic. Not only does shot follow plot and plot follow theme, but also the compression or expansion of sequence should embody and express theme.

Let me briefly compare two recent films from this point of view. One is a triumph, the other a disaster. Recently, in *Winter Light,* Bergman has attempted, and failed, to revive Dreyer's style. In cinematic technique, *Lolita* is a far superior film to *Winter Light.* Although it is almost two hours long, *Lolita,* like *The Graduate* or *King and Country,* appears to last only about ten minutes. Art should be eternal; there is no need for it to be everlasting. *Winter Light* seems to last forever; it is static. It is static because it is composed of a *sequence* of shots that are brilliantly framed but still. But a film is not a sequence of pictures to be taken down and hung in a frame. *Lolita* has a smooth, unified rhythm; its scenes are not parts of a sequence but are contributing elements constituting and having their own meaning enhanced by a moving whole. The same is true of *Dr. Strangelove.* Notice that Kubrick uses the jerky hand-held camera and grainy texture only when it is aesthetically relevant, when he wishes to get a newsreel quality in the attack on the airfield. Kubrick thus demonstrates a surer cinematic sense than Bergman. *Lolita* and *Dr. Strangelove* have attained James Agee's standard of excellence in film, a standard that Agee did not state but always used: earned immediacy.

Thus, framing, like symbolism, may be used in film; and it is often used effectively and successfully to express depth elements. But the film is primarily a mode of presentation, not representation; thus, the representational elements should be kept subordinate to the moving rhythm of the theme. Painting defines and elicits movement through being; film elicits and defines being through movement. The existential ground of film is change, and it reveals permanence only through the echoing and reechoing of pattern. Because of this essential movement, the film is more accurately comparable to music or dance than to painting. For film, when successful, is a rhythmic whole moving in time. Like dance, the film displays an over-all theme that is articulated through support and contrast of various phases. But the essential difference between painting on the one hand and dance or film on the other, is not that one is oriented to space and the others are embodied in time. The significant thing, as Arnheim has pointed out, is how these factors are handled and hence how they appear.

> The essential difference between the two kinds of artistic media is not that one is based on time and the other on space, but that the sequence in which the parts are related to each other is prescribed by the work itself in the dance or play whereas it is not in a work of painting or architecture. The order of our perceptions is not a part of the composition when we look at sculpture or painting, whereas it is when we look at a dance.[20]

To say that the order of our perceptions is thus *prescribed* is to say that they are *pre-written,* and in film the language in which they are pre-written is an aural-visual synthesis presented for immediate perception. As Merleau-Ponty has said, "A movie is not thought; it is perceived."

Several times I have described the motion picture as a gesture. I have said that it is an immediate gesture, that it is a gesture without horizon, and, in my discussion of drama, that it is a gesture without response, for the flow of images on the screen is supremely indifferent, unlike the actor, to audience response. Film, then, has the appearance of a *given* gesture. But it remains to be said what is meant by "gesture," whose gesture film is, and what its direction portends. Since dance is also gesture, an examination of these points will help us to see some of the differences between dance and film. One difference, of course, is immediately apparent. Whereas both dance and film convert sheer measure into distance, that is, they humanize space, the dancer is immediately inhabiting actual space that is shared by the audience. In film, of course, the actor is inhabiting the actual space only of the location or the set, but in the film his image appears in the frame of a fluid and intangible space. In the experiencing of dance, the spectator inhabits a space that is tangential to and relevant to the one being shaped by the dancer. In experiencing film, one inhabits filmic space or takes it as his temporary abode only insofar as his eye collapses into the camera viewpoint and permits it to become his virtual stance.

Most simply stated, a gesture is a vital movement. Professor Langer has pointed out that "gesture" means an *expressive movement* but that "expressive movement" can itself mean either (1) self-expressive, "i.e., symptomatic of existing subjective conditions" or (2) logically expressive, "i.e., symbolic of a concept that may or may not refer to factually given conditions" or both.[21] If all we mean by calling film form "gesture" is that it is "expressive form," we are not saying very much, since all form is expressive insofar as it is fine art and exhibits dynamic shape. Hence, to say that a film is inexpressive is to say that it is inarticulate, that is, a poor film. Now, certainly I do mean this, but I mean more than this. I also mean that a film is logically expressive, that is, referential, since every film tells a story. But I mean more than this. I mean that a film is an expressive movement that is self-expressive, but I do not thereby intend the subjectivity Susanne Langer does when she then translates "self-expressive" into "symptomatic." They are not merely symptomatic, because types of behavior, styles, ways of meeting the world are not hidden behind one's natural gestures—they are revealed through them. A gesture, then, is an expressive movement. What it expresses is the meaning imminent in the situation, which it presupposes and to which it contributes closure.

Let us turn to the example of speech. As Kaelin has stated, "effective speech does not presuppose any thought."[22] After all, if speaking is merely using words, that is, discursive utterance, then there would be no need to speak since all the words are there in the language; and there would also be nothing to say. Words are the vehicles of speech, but one must not confuse the vehicles and the passengers. And words, like thoughts, are *had* by us only insofar as we have used them, that is, expressed them. Words function as closures for perceptual processes. Hence, when I say, "That is a dog," the word "dog" completes the process of synthesizing the aspects-in-profile before me by naming or pronouncement. But "the physical act of expressing the thought does not *translate* a pre-existent ideal entity; the expression merely completes the thought process."[23] Hence, Adam had to see the animals before he named them, but he had to name them before he could know them. Utterance is more discovery, then, than it is reportage. It is closure and disclosure.

Now, a film, like a poem, is a novel utterance; but, unlike a poem, its vehicle is composed not so much of words as of moving sights and sounds. These moving sights and sounds are gestures expressive of the intentional structure of the apparition before us. They may also be symptomatic of the director's attitudes toward these moving images, but that is not their primary reference. In fact, Jean-Luc Godard makes the same error that Mary McCarthy does in literature: He keeps telling us how smart he is. But we don't go to see *him;* we go to see films. Godard confuses self-expression with expression and thus comes out with a kind of armpit or narcissistic aesthetic filled with inside jokes and irrelevant intrusions of the self into the object. The film is a gesture, then, in the sense that it presents for perception a style of living, a posture and approach, imminent in the flow of images before us. Its mode is one of coexistence and in so far as we "get with" the film, we understand its gesture, just as we find ourselves as subjective beings thrown into a world where we learn who we are from the gaze of others.

The instance of Godard brings up the problem of style and its relation to film. Godard's influence on François Truffaut alone would be enough to make us wary of him, for one can perceive an unwarranted and irresponsible incursion into false subjectivity in *Shoot the Piano Player* that is not present in *The Four Hundred Blows.* Put briefly, the mistake is taking "show biz" to be equivalent to the world and the self in itself as a fascinating object of regard. Truffaut, in *Shoot the Piano Player,* and Godard, in *Band of Outsiders,* made amateur films. The difficulty was that they had the wrong object of love: themselves. Like the directors of most amateur and underground films, they wallowed in the sentimental belief that what they happened to feel was of cosmic import. But there is no trick in feeling. Anyone can and does feel. The difficulty is in articulating feeling so that it may be a meaningful object for perception and understanding. While it is quite true that an artist cannot divorce himself from his style—he *is* his style—it does not follow that style is its own articulation and justification. Style is revealed *through* use; it is not self-reflective use. Hence, the theory that style should function as a simple mirror of the self is misleading. The self does not make the film important, but the film brings value to the self. Creative activity is as much a self-creation as object-creation. But the purpose is to construct the object, and the self-creative part of it is a subsidiary precipitate.

An opposite point of view is represented by Sartre and Albert Camus. Both express the belief that the best style is invisible. Sartre, of course, is taking the position that there is no difference between a symbol and a sign. It is characteristic of him to collapse the one into the other and to think of poets as men who "refuse to utilize" language because they pay attention to words instead of what the words intend. Camus is a bit more subtle; hence, while still maintaining the value of invisible style, he moves away from the Sartrean rigidity to the position that the "purpose of the novel is to give style to life's constant 'becoming' and that the novelist does not merely provide wish fulfillment, but enhances life by focusing on 'the legitimate intensification' of its 'possible significance.' "[24] This latter version I hold to be closer to the truth. Style is not a pane of transparent glass through which to see the world, for style is the man and each piece of glass has a different warp and different degrees of transparency. It is as impossible for an artist not to intrude on his data as it is for the psychologist. But the "feel" of this position is correct, namely, that style should be the horizon and not the foreground of the work. The style is a means for viewing the work, not an end in itself.

Style is grace in the expression of power. But grace is visible. Style, at first glance, is not. But as the work is grasped, the style becomes evident. It is not the case that the greater the transparency, the greater the invisibility, the greater the style. But it is the case that the greater the translucency, the greater the style. The function of style is to enlighten the work, to elicit its visibility. Insofar as it does this, of course, style will be in the background and will be partially invisible. And if style is the expression of power, then power must at first glance be partially invisible too, for only then can it become gentle persuasion, only then can reason transform necessity. Thus sweetness precedes light. If it did not, man could never be seduced by art to recognize and thus refuse to be what he is. The position of the artist, then, is a kind of precarious and synthetic idealism with respect to the work. He cannot abandon the world without degenerating into pure emptiness, nothingness, and formalism. He cannot submerge himself in the world, for this would deny his self and would be taking the stance of a distant god who merely enumerates its contents. He thus must discover his own particular mode of embodiment, his voice. But he cannot pursue the creation of a style or his own voice by looking for it. He discovers his voice by working in his medium, by meeting and transforming its demands. Style is thus an emergent from the active function of work; style is the way in which technique is had.

A film as a whole is an analogue of our being-in-the-world, and as such it presents us with the paradox of our existential situation. We are situated and finite, and yet we act and imagine as if we were infinite. Thus, we refuse to give any weight to the reality of our mortality, though, as existent bodies, we have a guaranteed death. Literally, we cannot exist outside our bodies, but these same bodies make us subject to infirmity, decay, and death. Man may not have a given nature; but he does display an inherent optimism with regard to the self, for he constantly mistakes his infirmity for his infinity. But, though we cannot literally get out of the body, we can escape metaphorically. What the film creator can do is to present us with a reality of permeation and an opportunity to participate in that created reality. Insofar as we do participate, the director can "make us *see* the bond between the subject and world, between the subject and others, rather than *explain* it."[25] The motion picture makes manifest to our eyes and ears the inherence of the self in and with the world and the expressions of one through the other. There is no real division between inside and outside in art but an articulation of the continuity of self-and-world.

The gesture of the film is, of course, that of the director as embodied in his use of the camera, microphone, scissors, and so on, and as embodied in the rhythmic whole that is the film. And just as an individual cannot legitimately say that a thought is *his own* until he has expressed it and taken it unto himself symbolically, so the fine director does not fully know whether the film is *his* gesture, *his* style, until he has completed it. The distinction between the film artist and the artisan or hack simply rests on the intentional fallacy. The artisan and hack *know* what they are going to shoot before they shoot it, how they are going to shoot it, and what impact it is intended to have. Since knowledge, as distinguished from felt awareness, is conceptual, they produce a preconceived product for a preconceived audience. And all the responses of this preconceived audience are, like the chrome on cars, either tacked onto or built into the body of the film.

But a fine film creates its own audience in both senses of the word "creates." For the fine film director is initiating a journey of discovery both for himself and his audience. He is a man who has discovered the limits of his loneliness but refuses to relinquish his solitude, though he will share it. Thus, by identifying with the eye of the camera, we can share the situation of the director and his actors and can move with their style, a style that is expressed not so much by the images as by what it invests them with. The gesture of a film, then, is the meaning it contains; and its primary reference is to itself, though it may also have secondary references to its society, its actors, its directors, and so forth. But its primary mode is not one of designation; its primary mode is one of presence.

The complex rhythms of the camera are not merely neutral movements. As Arnheim states:

It can search and hesitate, explore, turn its attention suddenly to see some event or object, leap at its prey. Such complex motions are not neutral. They portray an invisible self, which assumes the active role of a character in the plot. The strivings and reactions of this character are conveyed by a pattern of forces, which become manifest in the motor behavior of the camera.[26]

Film, then, presents us with the poetry of an invisible self. Which self is thus presented will depend on who seizes control of the film. In many cases and in the best films, it will be the director who is in control, for he is fulfilling his function: giving direction. In some cases, it will be the actor. In inferior films, it will be the producer or banker. Sometimes the roles of actor and director are synthesized; but this attempt is usually a failure, since it begins from a perspective of immediate narcissism. Marlon Brando's *One-Eyed Jacks* is a case of such self-indulgence. But whoever this invisible poet happens to be, his insights have informed the film. Insofar as we perceive the resulting expressive form and participate in the world it structures, we also gain insight. Arnheim summed this up beautifully:

> Perception of expression fulfills its spiritual mission only if we experience in it more than the resonance of our own feelings. It permits us to realize that the forces stirring in ourselves are only individual examples of the same forces acting throughout the universe. We are thus enabled to sense our place in the world and the inner unity of that whole.[27]

A film appeals to the individual because he finds in it a "resonance of his own feelings," but it provides him with insight only insofar as it goes on to articulate those feelings and to make them clear to him. This, of course, is a function of all art. If art were not more organized, more clear, and more articulate than life, there would be no excuse for it. Thus, the director can, if he is an artist, lead us from sight to insight.

Now, the dancer uses her actual body to create gestures expressive of a virtual situation. The director uses a virtual eye to reveal the expressive qualities of an actualizing situation. In occidental dance, the whole body is used to create expressive movement; and this means that the dancer must move the locus of her expressive power—its visible locus—away from the head and into her torso. From her torso, this visible center of force then radiates to her legs, arms, hands, neck, and head. As Arnheim has remarked, if we were starfish, this shift of the expressive locus would not be necessary and would cause us no trouble. But we are not. We are people. Thus a tension is established in dance between what we know and what we perceive as the visible center of expressive force.

The director does not need to undergo this shift of expressive locus because he is not *in* the film. The camera becomes his virtual head. It sees as his eyes see or as he directs it to see; and, in our excarnate condition, we see through his eyes. Perhaps this substitution of the camera for the head led Ernest Lindgren[28] and R. E. Jones[29] to confuse the movement on the screen with the spectator's mind. It is neither the spectator's mind nor the director's mind; it is an expressive form that appears to both. I can regard my hand as other than me only insofar as I assume an attitude of schizophrenia and think of my mind as *not* my body. But, of course I am a unity, and my body and mind are one. My mind is my body's expression. However, if one insists on splitting off and separating the mind, I suppose it would be proper to say that the film is an artificial body in which two minds meet or through which they can share the same visions. While it is true that our thoughts dart this way and that and that we have sudden uprushes of memory which "have no respect," it is also true that our eyes behave in the same manner. There is no necessity for interpreting these phenomena as some "mysterious interior." Nor does it clarify matters to say that they spring from the unconscious. The unconscious is no doubt real, but it also is relative. What is unconscious today may be conscious tomorrow, and that tomorrow may revive and recast my yesterdays. Memory is a constant encounter of my past being projected and working itself out in my future.

The movements of the camera could as easily be described as excarnations of the natural gestures of the head and its organs. For example, the cut is much like the normal skipping of the eyes as they move from one area of the gaze to another. When we look out upon the world, we rarely look in continuity. There are gaps in our look. We thus jump from one glimpse to another much as the camera cuts, though our changes of perspective are not nearly so drastic. Another example would be the pan. The pan is like turning the head slowly while holding the gaze steady. The out-focus to in-focus shot is similar to the slipping of binocular into monocular vision or the emergence of the figure from the field. The close-shot is similar to moving the head forward or grasping an object and bringing it to the eyes. Camera movement is not necessarily subjective, though it can be, as for example in the portrayal of vertigo, anxiety, and the like.

Merleau-Ponty seems to believe that camera movement to indicate vertigo is illegitimate if the indication is from the inside.

> If a movie wants to show us someone who is dizzy, it should not attempt to portray the interior landscape of dizziness, as Daquin in *Premier de corde* and Malraux in *Sierra de Terruel* wished to do. We will get a much better sense of dizziness if we see it from the outside, if we contemplate that unbalanced body contorted on a rock or that unsteady step trying to adapt itself to who knows what upheaval of space. For the movies as for modern psychology dizziness, pleasure, grief, love, and hate are ways of behaving.[30]

But Merleau-Ponty is here taking too objective a position. Emotions are also a way of behaving whether they are expressed exteriorly adequately or not. Granted, they may be *magical* modes of behavior (for example, we withdraw into anger and affective disturbance when effective action is cut off from us), but that does not make them any less behavior. Dreaming is also behavior; and some of the most effective scenes have been made of dreams, as we have seen. It has also been effective to present fear and vertigo by a swirling camera such as in the opening sequence of *Ballad of a Soldier* or in *Spellbound*. It is quite legitimate for the camera to become the major character either physically, as in *Ride a Pink Horse,* or psychically, as in the threatening fantasy sequences in *The Lost Weekend* or *David and Lisa*. Granted that David's dreams in the last instance are a bit too pat and lack the intensity they ought to have, they nevertheless contribute to the film. Merleau-Ponty seems here to be confusing emotions with thoughts. At any rate, we follow his general behavioristic stance, as we do that of Mead; but we must insist that dreams also be included in the broad meaning of behavior. It is the function of a film to articulate emotions, and whether it does this by external or internal means, is not important. If it succeeds in bringing emotion to sight and making it an aural-visual object, it may then lead to insight.

Merleau-Ponty also appears misleading in his classification of movie language. Following André Malraux, he distinguishes three types of dialogue. The first is expository dialogue. Expository dialogue functions to describe the situation and to make the action known. Such dialogue is a normal necessity on stage. Think, for example of *Henry V,* which must take us to France by means of language alone. Such language is not only rare in film, as Merleau-Ponty states, but it is almost always irrelevant and inauthentic. In film we are *being shown; we don't need to be told*. This is one reason why the phony "psychologist" at the end of *Psycho* is so offensive. When an artist steps out of his work and refuses to let it speak for itself, he betrays distrust in the clarity of his own voice. This is the truth in saying, "If you want messages, go to Western Union."

The second use of dialogue is tonal. This use of dialogue gives us, presents us directly, with the particular, peculiar, unique accent of each character. On this mode of speech, we must let Merleau-Ponty speak for himself:

> The extravagant or sparing use of words, their richness or emptiness, their precision or affectation reveal the essence of a character more surely than many descriptions. Tonal dialogue rarely occurs in movies, since the visible presence of the actor with his own particular manner of behaving rarely lends itself to it.[31]

But surely, this is precisely the main type of dialogue used in films and utilized in all good films. A motion picture is not a picture *and* words in mere conjunction. It is, on the contrary, a synthetic union of sights with sounds into one rhythmic whole. Merleau-Ponty himself realizes this when he states that "the image is transformed by the proximity of sound." A sound film, in either sense of the word "sound," is not a silent movie with words added. It is the fusion of tonal dialogue with the visual behavior of the actor's image that tells us who he is. This is why dubbed films usually are so incredibly bad. The voices do not fit the visual images and we are given a fat voice with a thin body or an anxious voice with a peaceful scene and a tranquil face. Speaking is an immediate gesture, which expresses the nuances of rhythm that are the being of the person just as much as facial gesture or handwriting. This is why the word "tone" is so marvelously ambiguous. It can mean aural tone, body tone, or muscle tone, among others. The actor's tonic presence is his mode of being in the film.

The third usage of dialogue is dramatic. The function of dramatic dialogue is to present the confrontation of characters and their mutual interactions through discussion. Merleau-Ponty's assertion that such dialogue is far from continuous in film is true. As Malraux said, films *"break* into dialogue" much as the novelist may break into dialogue after a long narrative passage or people may break into dialogue after stretches of silence. But Merleau-Ponty appears mistaken when he says it is "the movies' principal form of dialogue." The problem is the word "the." Dramatic dialogue is *a* form of film dialogue, as are dramatic silence and tonal dialogue. But this does not make it the main mode. It seems clear that in his classifications of dialogue, Merleau-Ponty is thinking, not of film, but of drama. On the stage, one *has* to talk endlessly, and one must talk dramatically. Neither of these is necessarily the case in film, for the other elements, such as music, color, shape, tone, and texture, can be as expressive as what is said. But in film, what is said is not so important as its context and, particularly, not so important as the *way* in which it is said. It is the manner of speaking that is important. Classification is always inexact and untrue. Perhaps that's why we classify. But if one must choose one of these three types as the major mode of dialogue in film, it would have to be the tonal.

I am simply following the same premise here that I did with another kind of sound: music. Music should not be merely a "stopgap for sonic holes" or a mere "exterior commentary" on the visuals. It should be incorporated into the film, "not juxtaposed to it." It can be used to follow characters, as Fellini follows the "philosopher" in *8½* with her own theme. It can be used to indicate transition and reversal, as he constantly uses it in *8½*. It can be used to heighten the visuals by providing them an aural base and enhancing their texture, as also occurs in *8½*. It should unite "the internal rhythm of the scene" and make it "physically palpable without thereby striving to translate its sentimental, dramatic, or poetic content (Jaubert)."[32] We have already spoken of the violation of this point of view in *Psycho,* and one can certainly find other examples easily. Two which immediately come to mind are the American version of *The Magnificent Seven,* which had a musical theme like all outdoors (well noted by the Marlboro crowd), and *On the Beach,* with its incessantly "Waltzing Matilda." Another example would be the obtrusive blare of "That's the Story of Love" throughout *Guess Who's Coming to Dinner.*

We are brought back, once again, to the problem of subjectivity. It would be better if I did not have to use such words as "subjectivity" and "objectivity," but at the present, there seems to be no other way to talk adequately. But if I return to my somewhat artificial distinctions of the me, the myself, and the I, perhaps I shall be able to clarify the differences intended when stating that Godard utilizes "false subjectivity" or that Merleau-Ponty is taking "too objective a position." That I agree in general with the perspective of phenomenological existentialism is quite obvious. Merleau-Ponty is right when he says that emotion is a "variation in our relations with others and the world which is expressed in our bodily attitude" and that "others are directly manifest to us as behavior."[33] These statements can be seen as true insofar as in our regard of others we relax and do not strive so much to see as to slide into our gaze. But it does not follow from this that an emotion is not an internal fact. Granted that the love visible on this face is not a simple sign of an interior thing or state, it is still an expression of an interior mode of behaving, that is, a rhythm of the I, which is itself a process. An expression must be an articulation, a gesture, a stance *of* something, in much the way that a thought must be *of* something. Granted that our immediate gestures are not self-consciously directed and seldom consciously directed, but they are nevertheless expressive of internal rhythmic patterning. In this sense, life is an art, but it is for the most part an unconscious one. Were this transition from the physiognomy to its patterning force not possible, there could not possibly be any coexistence and permeation. No doubt one reason that Jesus has been able to serve as an ideal for so many years is because there was love written on this face. But it was also because he was an incarnate presence who was utterly permeable.

It has been shown that when subjects are asked to match voices, photographs, handwriting, and silhouettes, the correct matchings greatly outnumber the incorrect ones. Nor is this surprising, for all of these are ways that reveal, not veil, the individual's ways of meeting the world. As Merleau-Ponty states:

> Michelangelo's handwriting is attributed to Raphael in 36 cases, but in 221 instances it is correctly identified, which means that we recognize a certain common structure in each person's voice, face, gestures and bearing and that each person is nothing more nor less than this structure or way of being in the world.[34]

The difficulty comes in the phrase "nothing more nor less than." Merleau-Ponty has fallen into what I have called the "affliction of mereness." Taken literally, his statement is true, for the I is not *a thing* and hence it is *no-thing* "more nor less than"; that is, it is not distinguishable as an otherness-in-contrast-to. Yet the fact that there is an identity of structure implies that there is something expressed through structures. What is this something? It is force. Dylan Thomas called it the "green fuse which drives the flower" and which drives my blood. It is the dynamic patterning of the I, which expresses itself in and through the me and the myself and on into the world. When we say of a person that he has a forceful personality, we certainly do mean that he is integrated, that his unity is manifest in the various hierarchies of his behavior and expression, that he is authentic; but we also mean that this unitary force is a *force*. It is apparent to the eye and the ear and yet is also a presence beyond.

Merleau-Ponty is so anxious to exorcise the "ghost in the machine" that he tends, like Mead, to reduce everything to the me. But this not only de-emphasizes the myself and the I, it terminates in the elimination of the rhythm that is expressed, for it reduces its mode of being to being *as* expressed. But the "for us" is not the only dimension of the self, though it is the most important for practical purposes. There is still that "something beyond," which I do not so much encounter in the other as participate in and, in rare cases, coalesce with and "become." What is love if it is not the demand of the lover that he, as he is, should become the horizon of the being of the beloved? Certainly, it is not the simple and brutal war of sadism/masochism that Sartre portrays from the well of his self-imposed loneliness.

Film, then, can legitimately portray the self-as-other, which is the me, that is, the persona, or the person-for-us. The actor's given image and physiognomy immediately present this aspect. It can also legitimately reveal the myself, that is, the tension between the self as it views itself and the self-as-other. It is illegitimate if it reduces its presentation to the self-as-it-views-itself unrelated to others or as a cardboard front for the I. This is what Godard does. He intrudes himself into the film as he wishes us to believe him to be; and, in this sense, he is lying to us and to himself. Fellini, on the other hand, brilliantly and acidly assesses the myself in all its tricks in *8½* and goes beyond to probe the I in its tensional rhythm with the other levels of emergent patterning, that is, the myself and the me. The overwhelming quality of *8½* is its almost incredible honesty. Here is a man who laughs at himself *seriously* and is unafraid to be permeable. In this sense, *8½* is an essay on the strength of weakness. Thus, the film can and does reach to the I and reveals it through tonal dialogue, unreflective gesture, and the force of presence. Unlike pottery, the self, when broken and repaired, often gains in strength. Hence, those actors who display great presence may at some time have had the levels of their selves severely strained and were then reunited into a more authentic and powerful force. Our position here should now be clear: Every level of the self is a legitimate ground and is, whether one likes it or not, brought to display in film. It is only when one constructs an artificial myself and insists that this *is* the self and that it is the proper object of perception that subjectivity becomes phony.

Perhaps, after all, there is no distinction between what I have been arguing here and the position of Merleau-Ponty except that there is a shift of emphasis. Certainly I agree with him: There is only one reality, life as it is lived. And I agree that the unconscious is not a stable thing, for no one has an impartial past. We are constantly making appointments for ourselves in the future but are never entirely sure who will show up. And the fear that some part of our past that we refuse to accept will meet us in our future sends most of us to the edge. Our future draws out and elicits our past much as theme does in film. Overt marks are not mere signs. They are expressive symbols, but we are placing the emphasis upon the synergic dynamism of those symbols. Descartes posed, in both senses of the word "posed," the problem of whether the world was his dream. Phenomenology displays and elicits the world. But what is to be done with dreams? They also must be included. They are not thereby nothing. And they can be included by broadening the concept of "behavior."

Film, then, is really neither objective nor subjective but a moving synthesis of both. Like a keyhole, it allows us to abandon our bodies, leave them outside the door, and like the voyeur, crawl through the keyhole into another room, another presence. But it also presents us with that presence and allows us to participate in it vicariously. Hence, we are "thrown back" into our bodies emotionally, though not tactilely or spatially. The medium for this excarnate-incarnate tension, I believe, is rhythm. Thus, the film has a high level of infectiousness. Watch people the next time you see them emerging from a motion-picture theatre. If it has been a Western, the small boys will swagger and drawl. They will not merely *imitate* cowboys and Indians; they will carry over the rhythms to the exterior situation. Even adults may mumble a little after viewing Marlon Brando. Why is this? It is because we have been emotionally infected by the film and its rhythms, and we express this infection through our bodily gestures. Our dynamic rhythm has coalesced, for a time, with that of another; and the withness of the body has been altered. This alteration is carried forth temporarily in the way we meet our world. But soon we sense it sliding away and we return to ourselves; that is, we settle into our habitual rhythmic patterning. Even within the experiencing of the film, one can feel the constriction in the chest and the slowed breathing when a shot is held too long and the "deliciously intimate acquiescence when a shot fades at the right moment." The appeal of the film is direct. It is unmediated. We look at a painting, we hear a symphony, we watch a dance, but we find ourselves emotionally *within* the experience of the motion picture.

The power of film is that it enables us not only to see and to hear but also artificially to participate in *coexistence*. It brings us "the actors as they are for us and for themselves," the "simultaneity of lives in the same world." Just as the director must exploit the complicity of sounds and sights through their common rhythms, so he also exploits the complicity of the audience with his rhythms. He cannot do this through the use of an actual shared space and a response to response as can the stage actor. But he can do this by constructing an apparition so forceful that it brings each individual in the audience to create a theatre of his own. Thus, the response of the spectator is through a direct awareness of the phenomenon before him, and the response of his neighbor, if noticed, is usually ignored. We do not normally see the motion picture *together*. There is a felt difference between being in the audience at a play or ballet and being in the audience watching a film. We are *members* of the audience at a play; we are *individuals* in a movie house watching a film. And yet the infectiousness is so great, the self-abandonment so total that one of my most sensitive friends usually refuses to go to the serious movies because, as he says, he just can't *"take"* it.

Film comedy would seem to be an exception to this description, for if few others laugh in the movies, our laughter may be diminished. The same is felt to be true of TV, hence the presence of "canned laughter," which is about as genuine as a parrot's grunt. But this lack, I think, is due to the degeneration of the comedy as a film form. Most film comedies (for example, those of Bob Hope, *et al.*) are not really filmed comedies; they are visual radio or, more accurately, radio that had been incidentally recorded on film. Hence, they are closer to phonograph records than to film. But visual movie comedy (such as that of Chaplin, Lloyd, Laurel and Hardy, *et al.*) wrenches our laughter from us in spite of ourselves, regardless of the response of the rest of the audience. The same is true of those few films that successfully unite sight and sound into mutually enhancing film comedy. One example would be the work of W. C. Fields, whose surrealistic imagination was able to synthesize the absurd of all realms in *The Face on the Barroom Floor* and *The Bank Dick*. Another would be the bitter but balanced laughter of Billy Wilder in *The Apartment* and *Some Like It Hot*. In his later films, however, Wilder is getting just that; he is turning to the shout and away from his true synaesthetic genius. Regard, for example, *One, Two, Three* in which he mistook speed and volume for synthesis.

But a motion picture is not a recording. If it were, it could, in principle, be perfect. Given enough time and money, one could simply keep shooting, splicing, and cutting until he had recorded an object with no flaws. But though a movie is more precise, more formed, and more highly articulated than our everyday living-in-the-world, it is not purely artificial. It also is subject to accident—if none other, then time. One could not, for example, continue to photograph Sir John Gielgud over a span of fifty years, for the simple reason that there would come a point where his image would be indistinguishable from that of Tallulah Bankhead. Of course, there is a serious point here, and that is unity. In the sense that both display internal organization of a complete whole, the film is closer to the radio play than to the phonograph record. The phonograph record usually consists of several songs, which are merely externally related no matter how perfectly reproduced; and if such a mélange is comparable to film, it would be comparable to the episodic films such as *Boccaccio 70* or *The Seven Deadly Sins,* neither of which holds together. The omnibus film is usually a disaster, as is the episodic film, such as *Tales of Manhattan.* On occasion, when a genius tries it, as in *La Ronde,* the style and tone are strong enough to hold the whole together and synthesize it into unity. Usually, however, too many cooks end with froth.

No doubt, the fact that we as spectators are not welded into an integrated group, an audience, when watching a film but remain individuals related directly to the powerful but indifferent shapes before us, is another reason why the experiencing of a motion picture is referred to as a subjective experience. Movies *move*. This is meant in both senses of that ambiguity, namely, that they consist of moving pictures and moving sounds fused into one moving whole. It also means that they move us, the spectators, emotionally, and hence provide us with a *moving* experience. They are able so immediately to infect our emotions and move us in the second sense because they move in the first sense. It is not the function of a film to transmit ideas, though the theme can usually be summarized in a few ideas. It is the function of a film to incorporate its meaning into its rhythm "just as the meaning of a gesture may immediately be read in that gesture" and primarily to mean itself. Ideas or "prosaic facts" are merely the raw materials of film, they are "only there to give the creator an opportunity to seek out their palpable symbols and to trace their visible and sonorous monogram."[35]

One may well wonder why a philosopher should concern himself with film at all. One reason, of course, is that to philosophy, nothing is irrelevant. Another is that film can be and should be considered a legitimate art form. Hence, as a human enterprise it is subject to critical evaluation. But perhaps the best reason has been given by Merleau-Ponty:

Therefore, if philosophy is in harmony with the cinema, if thought and technical effort are heading in the same direction, it is because the philosopher and the moviemaker share a certain way of being, a certain view of the world which belongs to a generation.[36]

And if one asks, "Which generation is this that we share?" the answer is: the Now generation.

In my discussion of the film world, I have attempted to clarify its organic form and to place the emphasis upon one direction of quality: immediacy. Hence, I have said that a film is an expressive gesture that is immediately given. Since it is immediately given, it is experienced at a lower level of abstraction than is a painting or a literary work. And I have indicated a canon of judgment that is grounded on the basis of its appeal: the coherence of thematic rhythm, earned immediacy, or the synaesthetic unity of sight and sound. This means, then, that a film is not to be judged primarily as a translation. It is not primarily a translation of a play; it is not primarily a translation of a book; it is not a translation of anything. It is a unique, multifaceted synthesis moving in time, an object, if you will, that exists at its own level of abstraction—a level different from that of other art works. Although it may be compared with other art works, it should therefore be judged by its own criteria, not by the criteria of an alien medium. The most constructive way to approach films would be to compare films with films.

My argument has been woven from many strands and perhaps no one of them runs through the whole cord. Yet I have endeavored to stay close to those characteristics of the motion-picture experience that are verifiable by anyone who reflects upon his experience and his perceptions. The impact of presence, authenticity of illusion, the displacement of the body of the spectator, emotional infectiousness, the fusion of psychic levels, the disjunctive relations of the audience, and the individuate identification with the viewpoint of the camera by the eye of the spectator—all these are to be discovered in the experience itself. And since our experience *of* things tells us something about those things, namely, they are such things as can be experienced in this way, I have outlined a perspective for understanding the film. The old newsreels did not lie. They claimed to be the eyes and the ears of the world. They were.

Notes

1. Susanne K. Langer, *Problems of Art* (New York: Scribner's, 1957), p. 93.
2. Langer, p. 171.
3. Goethe as quoted in Rudolf Arnheim, *Art and Visual Perception* (Berkeley: University of California Press, 1957), p. 50.

4. Alfred N. Whitehead, *Process and Reality* (New York: Harper & Row, 1957), p. 259.

5. Arnheim, *Art and Visual Perception,* p. 304.

6. Arnheim, p. 306. Those who think metaphysically on such matters might recall the words of a man who tried to avoid metaphysics at all costs and nevertheless talked it. Buddha said, "The world is this Being that Becomes."

7. Rudolf Arnheim, *Film as Art* (Berkeley: University of California Press, 1964), p. 161.

8. Arnheim, p. 181.

9. Arnheim, *Art and Visual Perception,* p. 311.

10. Maurice Merleau-Ponty, *Sense and Non-Sense* (Evanston, Ill.: Northwestern University Press, 1964), p. 52.

11. Merleau-Ponty, p. 53.

12. Arnheim, *Art and Visual Perception,* p. 225. The arrested train in the old thrillers with the split-second rescue of the heroine may also have provided us a thrill because the train was the mechanistic image of the fire-breathing dragon. Such changes in the visual field often initiate deep reverberations in the unconscious.

13. Merleau-Ponty, *Sense and Non-Sense,* p. 54. Perhaps the most famous compression of lapse (which also used change of costume, make-up, and so forth) is the brilliant breakfast sequence used by Welles in *Citizen Kane.*

14. Merleau-Ponty, p. 54.

15. Arnheim, *Film As Art,* p. 180.

16. Such a study has now been done. See Richard Schickel's *The Disney Version* (New York: Avon Books, 1969).

17. Arnheim, *Art and Visual Perception,* p. 351.

18. Robert Frost, *Complete Poems of Robert Frost* (New York: Holt, Rinehart and Winston, 1949), p. 448.

19. Sergei Eisenstein, *Film Form and the Film Sense* (New York: Meridian, 1957), p. 148.

20. Arnheim, *Art and Visual Perception,* p. 307.

21. Susanne K. Langer, *Feeling and Form* (New York: Scribner's, 1953), p. 180.

22. Eugene Kaelin, *An Existentialist Aesthetic* (Madison: University of Wisconsin Press, 1962), p. 283.

23. Kaelin, p. 284.

24. Camus as quoted in Hazel E. Barnes, *Humanistic Existentialism* (Lincoln: University of Nebraska Press, 1959), pp. 36–37.

25. Merleau-Ponty, *Sense and Non-Sense,* p. 58.

26. Arnheim, *Art and Visual Perception,* p. 328.

27. Arnheim, p. 328.

28. Ernest Lindgren, *The Art of Film* (New York: Macmillan, 1952), p. 92.

29. R. E. Jones, *The Dramatic Imagination* (New York: Duell, Sloan & Pearce, 1941), pp. 17–18.

30. Merleau-Ponty, *Sense and Non-Sense,* p. 58.
31. Merleau-Ponty, p. 56.
32. Merleau-Ponty, p. 56.
33. Merleau-Ponty, p. 53.
34. Merleau-Ponty, p. 53.
35. Merleau-Ponty, p. 57.
36. Merleau-Ponty, p. 59.

8

Film Form:
Situation, Articulation, Revelation

Situation

The opening sequence of a film may start at the beginning, the middle, or the end. It may be an explosion of images and sounds in montage, a slow movement of poetic development, or a middle-length establishing of the milieu. In fine films, the opening sequence usually is short, condensed, and fairly swift. It establishes its own time-space relationships. It is always symbolic no matter how "realistic" the situation initially presented. The opening sequence is symbolic in two senses: in the sense that it includes concrete image-symbols, which will later recur, and in the sense that the sequence itself presents a moving symbol of the whole. The opening shots are striking and unusual, often enigmatic.

The presentation of the initial situation is not a dramatic exposition, though it presents the environment and includes a statement of the over-all theme. It is not an overture, yet it includes nascent nuances of all of the rhythms that will be articulated later. Hence, it establishes the over-all tone and mood. Everything is both itself and something else. For the function of the initial presentation of situation is not to explain but to establish form. Hence, the initial incidents are not incidental. As we have seen, film form is dual and dynamic. It consists of background thematic tensional development and foreground "figures," that is, compressions and conflicts. The theme exposed but not explained runs throughout the film, and the function of the foreground compressions and conflicts is to expand and deepen the tensional rhythm of the theme. Development becomes envelopment as the elaboration of momentum increases. The opening sequence must be moving. It ends with a cut, a fade, a pan, a rhythmic shift, or a change of elements.

The titles and credits of the film should come before or after the initial sequence, but not during it. In the older movies of the 1930s, 1940s and 1950s, the titles almost invariably came before the first movement of the theme. It is now fashionable to move their place in the whole. But when the titles are shown over the first sequence, they distract both the eye and the attention. Since the function of the initial movement is to engage the eye immediately and hence to engage the attention, the titles and credits should either precede the initial statement or should be used as a coda to mark its end, as in *The Pawnbroker*. A word should also be said about naming. In the old days, when the moviegoing public was enormous and consistent and the studios had stables of stars, the use of names to indicate the cast was adequate. With motion-picture attendance becoming a more infrequent, sporadic, and selective affair, along with the demise of the studio system and the importation of foreign films, names are insufficient to provide identification. Since what is provided the spectator is more concrete than a name—that is, the visible and sonorous shape of the actor—it is best to label the characters with their images accompanied by names. After all, the actor as a persona is not so important as his face and gestures, particularly these images as shaped by context. Since such images might become confused with the first movement, it is proper that the identification of the cast come at the end of the film and that this identification be by image, not by name alone.

The primary movement, or tensional development, of a film is indicated by some concrete embodiment of ongoing force. It may be an actual journey, which becomes the horizon and hence the moving thread on which the foreground is strung. An actual journey is often used as such a device, as, for example, in *La Strada, Wild Strawberries, The Seventh Seal, Two for the Road,* and *Tom Jones.* Or the journey that is initiated in the first sequence may be a movement of social forces, which then precipitate an actual trek in space, time, or an intensified social movement, as in *The Grapes of Wrath, High Noon,* and *Potemkin.* The journey may or may not have a goal. It often has no goal but is sheer movement, as in *The Wild One.* Or the journey involved may be a movement into the interior of the character and the development of his inner landscape, as in *Ulysses, The Pawnbroker,* and *Hiroshima Mon Amour.* A motion picture, then, involves a movement initiated in the first sequence, which may often be a journey. This journey can be an actual spatial-temporal one, a geographic journey, a social movement, a sociological journey, a movement into the depth of character, a psychological journey, or a combination of all of them. The opening sequence should clearly establish the limits of the journey, its milieu, and the things involved, for things will often be as important as characters. The one overriding quality demanded by the presentation of the initial situation is economy. For the function of the beginning situation is to initiate movement and to pose, but not ex-pose, character and plot. Articulation comes later. Hence, the first sequence should be directed primarily toward the presentation of person (as image), motion, mood, and condition. Psychologically, situation is anticipation.

Since film is as equally concerned with inscape as with landscape, the symbolic character of the initial movement is often presented in overtly symbolic form, that is, in dream. Hence, *Wild Strawberries, The Pawnbroker, 8½,* and other such films begin in the interior of the main character. On the other hand, the initial situation may be a virtual dream symbol concerned with the main character and his milieu, as in *The Graduate, Who's Afraid of Virginia Woolf, Viridiana,* and *Last Year at Marienbad.* The important point is that the initial situation should not merely present the emergence of the main character or characters from their natural/social environment but should also convey their symbolic import with relation to the form as a whole. Since our first impressions of characters are in terms of swift images, these impressions are necessarily external and fairly superficial. It takes time to develop the nuances of their depths, and the temporal development of the thematic form of the whole articulates these nuances, which move us in and out of the characters to reveal who they are. We begin with the glimpse, which turns into the gaze.

If the ensuing incidents are at a constant high pitch, as they tend to be in *The Pawnbroker,* we are turned to the daze, for the constant impact of vivid images is so intense, with so few changes of rhythm, that we become fascinated but we cannot "lean back" into our gaze and move with the rhythm. Sheer intensity of image is one mode of unity, but like compression into time of quantity, it is an inferior mode. We need time to come to a comprehension of compression. Unless there is room in the rhythm to breathe, the visual/aural monogram becomes mere impact. The eye and ear are drunk with dazzle, and film fails to bring experience whole into the human heart. One flaw of *The Pawnbroker* is that it has few "lows." It is simply high drama mixed with fascination. But it is not necessary for valleys to scream because mountains have altitude. Since the initial situation is symbolic, it also presents a philosophic perspective and value structure in the way in which the images are handled. This handling of value structure is the normal function of the director, and the way in which things are shown will reveal his stance. Hence, Sidney Lumet reveals his social concerns and his basically theatrical biases in the example just cited.

Each of Tony Richardson's films is an attempt at unity with a schizophrenic style. In some instances, the split of styles falls apart, as in *The Loved One.* In *The Loved One,* there is an uneasy clash—which turns into a chasm—between ironic social portrayal and slapstick. The film falls apart from lack of unity. This duality, however, works most effectively in *Tom Jones.* Here Richardson engages our approval of the boisterous, romping, open, unself-conscious characters and we think, "It would really be great to live in such a bawdy time with none of my current hang-ups." But as soon as he has engaged our admiration and identification, he cuts to the close-ups of a horse being whipped, a stag having its throat slit, a squire in the mud, a corpse being prepared for burial, a mother suckling her child in a dungeon, and we feel, "These people are brutal fascists; thank God I didn't live at that time." This ambivalent shifting back and forth of value systems and audience identification in *Tom Jones* increases the pressure of the film. Since laughter is the explosive release of pressure, the laughter is thereby increased.

The rhythm of the value shifts, then, is one unifying factor in *Tom Jones.* Another unifying factor is the use of color. The film begins in an incredible green.

Everything is shot through a filter and is greener than green. As the characters move closer and closer to the city, however, the color more and more drains from the film. By the time Tom and his companions reach London, the scenes are almost sheer black and white, with the use of much grey. Their quality becomes Hogarthian. We have already mentioned the use of other elements in this film to increase pressure and release laughter, for example, the use of stop photography as Tom falls, the use of blocked framing in the holding of the hat over the camera, the turning of Tom to the audience. Sound, of course, is also used to intensify these sequences, as is movement. The chase through the inn uses speed-up in the manner of the Keystone Cops. A similar sequence is used in the capture scene of the boy in *8½* before the priests punish him for visiting La Saraghina.

Color is often used as a change from one level of film to another. The most notable case, of course, is the end of the opening sequence of *The Wizard of Oz* and the beginning of the articulation. The same device is utilized at the end of *La Belle Americaine*. In *Oz,* of course, color is framed on both sides by black and white. *High and Low* displays an even more unusual use of color—a one-shot use. When the pink smoke rises from the chimneys in the context of a grey city we laugh —and the laughter is appropriate. The absurd device (colored powder in the ransom cases) of the police has absurdly worked (to help locate the killer). But more normal uses of color are to provide unity or to express tonal nuance. In both *Red Desert* and *A Man and a Woman,* color is used to express interior states. Thus the warmth or coldness of Anouk Aimée's remembrances of her husband is revealed through the intensity of the color. The coldness of the race-driver's remembrances of his wife are also so expressed in bleak white.

There are some brilliant devices in *A Man and a Woman,* most notably the romp of the dog on the beach and the warped Giacometti shots of the man walking in fog. But the film story itself is shallow and the images are often exotic with no meaning beyond their impact. Hence, we have a shot of the race/cut/camel's feet/cut/race/ cut/camel's legs/cut/race/cut/camels/cut/race/cut/Aimée being a script girl on a camel picture. This intercutting is exotic; the images are exotic; but there is no depth meaning to the sequence. We have been dazzled simply to be shown that she is working on some Arabic film while he is driving a car. This is the use of virtuoso technique for no purpose and hence weakens the film. In some cases, of course, this technique trips the film. In the opening sequence, for example, the camera movement is from inside to outside the car. From the inside it is raining hard, and the windshield wipers are going furiously. The outside shots show no rain, and the wipers are static. This leads one to expect that the entire film will be a fantasy or a flashback, but then normal time resumes. In this instance, bad editing and poor use of technique vitiate the film. The same thing occurs at the end of *The Pawnbroker*. Steiger mutilates his left hand on the spike, but in the long shot that ends the film he is walking disconsolately examining his right hand. If the switch of hands is symbolic, then it should be more clear. What it looks like is bad editing.

Color can also be used to follow characters, as can music, and to establish a motif for them. Or color can be used as a transition, that is, as what used to be mysteriously referred to as "continuity." Hence, in *Juliet of the Spirits,* red is used to symbolize sex and excitement. Juliet goes to the party in a red dress, she throws her gloves (a gauntlet?) on the white expanse of the bed prior to the thwarted Hindu seduction, and the red becomes the flames of the child-martyr being lifted toward heaven in the ensuing fantasy sequence.

Sometimes color is used just for its sheer appeal, as for example, when Antonioni holds a shot of a blue building in *Blow-Up* simply because it is such a striking blue. As we have noted, he plays with black and white and color throughout this film. He even includes visual puns with color. The romp with the mod girls is in purple paper, which could be "purple passion"—which it is not, since it is of no consequent depth—or that they are "in violet"—which they certainly are not, except in the sense of the innocence of ignorance. He also uses textural puns; and has the artist's girl, the only one who deliberately and deeply cares for Hemmings, dressed in a net dress during their crucial scene of noncommunication. It is not that he "sees through her" but that she is "caught in the net" of her habits, as is he; hence, like mute fish, they travel on.

The function of color, of course, is to quality space; that is, to expand or contract space by giving it hue, texture, gradation, pitch, and vibrancy. The addition of color to film greatly expands the director's problems of control. Not only is it difficult for him to determine exactly what the resultant hues and their intensities will be, but also it means an expansion in technical facilities and in cost of production. This means that control tends to slip away from him into either accident or added pressure from producers, technicians, and others. There is also the temptation to fall into color as an excuse to carry the expressive force of scene. But, as we saw in our discussion of dream, the important quality of the dream image may be its intensity, and the intense image may well be remembered in "color." Hence, the swift cut to the Siamese dancers in *La Dolce Vita* may be remembered as being in gold, though it is actually black and white. In fact, most of *La Dolce Vita* may be "remembered" in color, with the exception of the Steiner episode, the religious bit, the suicide attempt, and the tower climb, which are definitely black and white mixed with greys. The reason memory makes this mistake is because the images are so baroque, so overwhelming, and so florid, that one tends to think them in color. So far, American directors have tended to use color as an excuse for intensity, and the most masterful uses of color are, at this point, to be found among the Japanese and Italian directors. The full meaning and import of color as a unitary and depth factor has not yet been grasped by most film makers.

While we are thinking of *La Dolce Vita,* by the way, let us note that John Howard Lawson mistakes the premise of the film and its thematic development. He criticizes Fellini for introducing a complex narrative into the first sequence of the film.[1] This is probably because Lawson will not accept a purely symbolic initiation as a beginning. The film can and should be criticized, for it suffers from lack of unity plus some internal incoherence. Steiner needs no reason to commit suicide other than the short despondent talk in the bedroom with Marcello, but he does need some indication of why he must so hate his wife. Otherwise, there is no justification for his killing his children also and leaving his wife destitute. There are other episodes in the film that do not "hold"—for example, the religious scene is a disaster compared to the analogous ones in *The Nights of Cabiria* and *La Strada,* and Fellini shows himself to have an incomplete grasp of his film. But the main failing is one of form. While *La Dolce Vita* deepens on a second and third viewing, Marcello's degeneration is not striking enough to hold the whole together. He is a bum at the start and a bum at the end. The film seldom attains the lyricism of its opening sequence with Christ the Worker being carried over the buildings and the bikinis.

The sequence between Marcello and Maddelena, however, is properly the beginning of the articulation of the film and not its initial statement. This is shown by the cut to the Siamese dancers, which is abrupt, and the fact that the entire episode is a contrast to the desperation of Emma who is on the edge waiting for Marcello. The unity of this sequence with the rest of the thematic development is further emphasized when Marcello is at a loss to find a place to bed the film star and he calls Maddelena to ask if they can come there to visit, then realizes what a stupid ploy this is. The Maddelena sequence is dramatic narration, but it is a development intended to amplify the beginning sequence and not to be an integral portion of it. Lawson would have been more accurate had he chosen to direct his criticisms at *The Pawnbroker.*

The Pawnbroker begins in dream and then cuts to suburban wrangle as exposition of situation. That suburbia is intended as part of the opening sequence is shown by the fact that it is then followed by the titles. It is further demonstrated by the fact that this family never again appears in the film except in a conversational reference by the gangster. Lumet made a powerful film, an almost excruciating one, in *The Pawnbroker,* but its beginning is really half in dramatic terms, not in filmic terms, in spite of the beautiful textures and slow motion of the dream sequence. The suburban sequence is stated and then dropped from context. This tends to flaw the form. Of course, it leads us to see that the pawnbroker is isolated and apart from the values of his dense and phony family, and in that sense it sets the situation. But it is conceived in dramatic, not cinematic, shape. We are *told* it; we do not *experience* it.

The difference between telling and seeing here may be subtle, but it is crucial. Take the example of another stage director who has become a film director: Mike Nichols. In *The Graduate,* the function of the opening sequence, which is quite long, is to reveal and to satirize upper-middle-class values. But it functions also to establish the ongoing action and movement, which continue after the boy calls the woman for their first encounter. The beginning sequence starts with his withdrawal, which is symbolic of his character, for he is not merely a graduate from college but is going to be a graduate from subjectivity, incoherence, and incompetence into life. We are also given the water and fish symbols that recur throughout the film, as well as exterior views of most of the main characters—all except the daughter, who, however, is brought in by dialogue and portrait. Hence, the opening sequence of *The Graduate,* which goes from the tropical fish catatonia of the beginning through taking Mrs. Robinson home and up to the first telephone call, includes elements that will occur and recur throughout the film to bring depth to symbol, theme, and character.

The same may be said for the much more economic and marvelous simplicity of *Viridiana.* Here we are given a short sequence with Viridiana leaving the cloister. We have a cut to a child's feet as they jump rope. We have the feet of the uncle and Viridiana. We have the uncle playing his organ—a direct visual statement of his problem and of Viridiana praying—a direct visual statement of her problem. Buñuel has, with masterful economy and in a short span, established the initial situation, and there are no irrelevant details. The large tree will recur later in the film, the house will play an important part, and the rope will recur as the device the uncle uses to hang himself. The phallic nature of the rope handles is later echoed in the milking of the cow. The rope also recurs as the belt used by the bum who rapes Viridiana, and we see its handles banging against her. One may not like Buñuel's theme or his acid statement; but his film is conceived and executed as film, not as a novel or as a drama. Art is the attempt to capture difficult unity. Luis Buñuel, whatever else he may be, is an artist. And a film artist. One can find even his most commercial products, such as *Subida al Cielo,* filmically exciting.

These reflections are not meant to downgrade *The Pawnbroker.* A few flaws do not constitute a disaster. It is a good film. Lumet uses his actors well and gets maximum performance from all of them—with the exception of a fine, dignified man, Juano Hernandez, who is turned into a sentimental caricature of a stumble-bum philosopher. But the other characters are fine and are shot with the proper menace when appropriate; for example, our introduction to the big hood is from a low-angle shot that emphasizes the menacing flare of his nostrils and his aggressive jaw. The two-bit hood touching the nipples of strong-man pictures with his gun is particularly filmic and reveals his character through seen gesture. And Lumet's use of his other techniques are good. The traveling el as a transitional device is a bit stagy; but the flash-shots of memory, which Lumet carefully interweaves with the ongoing articulation, are like electrical jolts to the nervous system of the audience. Hence, the memories of the rings and fences are intercut with the pregnant girl trying to pawn her glass ring, the cattle car and the death of the son with the subway ride, the soliciting prostitute with the wife-officer memory. Hence, the transitions and jumps from the realistic articulation and the memory sequences fuse and enhance the basic theme, which is the problem of whether a dead man can come alive before he dies. He does, of course, just as Professor Borg does in *Wild Strawberries,* though Lumet does not follow this revelation with ironic commentary as Bergman does.

As we have said, the initial sequence may come at the beginning, the middle, or the end of the film. In actual time, of course, it always necessarily comes at the beginning. And in the most ordinary and most simple films, the progressive film time and the "actual" time usually coincide. But this can also be true of more complex films. If one thinks of the form of films and attempts to visualize them, both *La Dolce Vita* and *Wild Strawberries* display the same spiral form, which returns on itself at different levels of perspective. Both *Shane* and *The Virgin Spring* have the form of clear, cool arcs. Shane comes out of nowhere, the "action" proceeds, and he rides off into the sterile horizon. The same form is less detached and is stuffed full of Nordic and Christian symbols in *The Virgin Spring,* as it is rammed full of sexual ones in *A View from the Bridge.* Bergman, however, reverses the visual form on us through dialogue at the end of *The Virgin Spring.* Throughout the film, we see the theme as the developing, inevitable tension of the Nordic/Christian tension of the father and his abandonment of the "Christian" sword. He takes a sauna and uses the pig-sticker of Odin to reinforce this inevitable progression. But we are still bothered by the priggishness of the daughter. We grasp the father's wrath, but we feel that it may be simply excessive. At the end, however, when he and the wife walk toward the spring where he will build his "church of atonement" he says to the wife: "I forgive *you.*" Suddenly we understand that the full force of his wrath was not against the rapists alone but also against the phony veneer of fanatic Christianity displayed by his wife. She has been so "insane" in her false Christianity that she has even enjoyed the suffering of pushing her fingernails into her palms and pretending her pure Christian devotion. But subjectively, she still has not banished the Nordic blood gods. She cannot help herself and *goes to watch* the slaughter. At the end, then, we understand that the father was at least honest in his wrath and open in his allegiance. It came and he expressed it. But the wife, in her false purity and her actual voyeurism, is the one who is in most need of redemption, not the husband. He knows it, and she knows that he knows it. This twist at the end does not modify the visual arc of the form, but it casts it into a different emotional context.

In some films, the initial sequence is in close proximity, almost juxtaposed, to the end. Hence, the film begins near the end and the rest of the film is built in flashbacks or in straight progression after an initial flashback. This type of form is found in *Citizen Kane,* which begins with the explosion of newsreel images and then goes to the reporter's attempt to reconstruct Kane's life. There has been much argument over the rosebud symbol. Personally, I feel that it is not adequate to carry the whole, but Welles's intuition is correct: namely, that film is concerned not primarily with intellectual but with emotional meaning. We know at the very outset of the film that Kane is dead. There is no conceptual problem of how he will end. The problem is: "What meaning, what emotional import, what depth, did his life have and why should we be interested in it?" The same type of form is found in *Ballad of a Soldier* and *Lolita.* In both films, we are given the initial situation and then tension and articulation are built back to that situation. The opening sequence of *Lolita,* by the way, is probably one of the most brilliant sequences of surrealistic comedy since W. C. Fields playing his zither with mittens. The difference between *Lolita* and *Ballad of a Soldier,* on the one hand, and *Citizen Kane,* on the other, of course, is that the initial situations are repeated at the ends of these films, where in *Kane* the first sequence is never repeated and we get the first part of the flashback, the sled, in the closing shot. This form of close proximity of the initial situation to the final revelation is a particularly filmic form; and when it appears on stage, as, for example, in *Death of a Salesman,* the play appears to be more filmic than dramatic. This is a basically filmic form, since its shape is to coalesce the film-time into the present as a fluid amplification of past-future.

An interesting attempt has been used by Jack Clayton to employ a different form of construction in *The Pumpkin Eater.* We begin with Jo wandering—like the smoke of her cigarette—aimlessly around the house. She hears sounds. She flees to the white garage and cringes in a catatonic state. We don't know what the signposts of where-when are. As the film develops, we find that we are in the middle of it and that the time is expanding in both directions from the center with the future interacting with the past. Even on second and third viewing, it is a difficult form to grasp intellectually. But it is an interesting experiment. If it can be done clearly, it may well become a major new film form. It is not that other films do not begin in the middle—they do—but few others have warped their time-space relationships in this way. That is, when they begin in the middle, they then jump to straight progressions or flashbacks alternating with forward progressions. *Cleo from Five to Seven,* of course, attempts to duplicate real time. In *8½,* Fellini's base is a constricted present from which radiate dream time, memory time, imaginary time, fantasy time, and all the nuances between, creating an organic, pulsing form that is perfectly suited to his content and the various levels of aspects he intends to reveal.

The fact that so many films have the form of reminiscence in one way or another is significant. The film may itself be an effort either to exorcise certain memories, as in *Hiroshima Mon Amour, A Man and a Woman,* and *The Pawnbroker,* or to establish them, as in *Last Year at Marienbad* or *Persona.* One could draw up a very long list of such examples. The point is that such films are not accidental at all but are legitimate attempts to bring form to the elastic character of film time and space without rigidifying it. Though memory has the initial aspect of the past, it is forced to be presented in the present. Hence the enchantment with memory in film is not of a settled past, but a remembrance in a fluid present. And since this fluid present is itself pregnant with its future and is moving into it, it recasts the shape of its past. As we have remarked, the stream-of-consciousness novel may bring us to imagine in this all-at-onceness way, but such a method in the novel is a style. In film, it is the essential nature of the medium.

Articulation

Landscape is, of course, important. One cannot produce or reproduce on stage the vast exterior settings that are commonplace in films. Nor can one invest things with either human or unusual import on stage in the way that the camera can. A chair on the stage is merely part of the set. If not utilized, it simply sinks into the horizon and becomes part of the scene. But the moving camera can invest the chair or any other object with figure status and, by choice of angle, lighting, rhythm, and the like, also can invest it with emotional import. Thus, an actor could merely use a cigarette lighter to light his way or his cigarette on stage, but Hitchcock can use a lighter as both a concrete symbol of the transference of guilt and menace and as a stalling device in the progress of articulation of movement as he brilliantly does in *Strangers on a Train.* An actor on stage can wear his glasses, take them off, or gesture with them. But Hitchcock can use them to amplify the gaze, to reflect murder, and to increase anxiety. Film form warps space just as it warps time; and the purpose of this warping is to invest situations, people, and things with intensified and unexpected values.

There is a sense in which film annihilates both ordinary space and ordinary time. This is what I have meant by "bodily displacement" and by stating that a film must establish its own time-space matrix in its initial sequence. The annihilation of "ordinary" space-time, especially time, has led some observers, notably Gilbert Seldes and Alain Robbe-Grillet, to claim that the time of film is mental time. If by "mental time" is meant the rhythm of the emotions and not some kind of accent of a substantial ghost, I would agree. Our sense of time in life is dual, as is our sense of space. Our body's time is the ground of our being and our mortality. But its progression, just as the stance of the self, is seldom noticed. It is that by means of which we see. Hence, time experienced is a fluid duration, which is similar to film time. Sometimes it drags for apparent aeons, and at others it evaporates into nothing. We know that the body has certain set times; for example, the heart beats about seventy-two times a minute and the breathing has its own rhythms. But these set times are merely the horizon, the ground for our lived durations, which may be sporadic and intense, languid, or filled with gaps and caesuras.

The same may be said of film, though in film time is a function of thematic unity. It is the over-all design that determines the basic rhythms of the temporal flow. Hence, time is a function of organic, dynamic structure, and structure is not the result of time. One can have simultaneous time in film, as D. W. Griffith has in *Intolerance*. One can slow down time in film in the dream sequence or in other types of slow motion or in the use of close-ups. Time can be stopped in arrested motion. Or it can be accelerated, as in the speed-up Keystone Cops chases or in the condensed time sequence of breakfast in *Citizen Kane,* in which the monotony of marriage is compressed into a few dry moments by simply holding the distance of the shot and changing the costumes, the props, and the make-up of the characters. But time, by itself, cannot create unity. Hence, *Intolerance* really consists of four films that are concurrent. It is not that the four episodes are unconnected by a base of actual time that makes them fall into four episodes, but that the symbol used to try to unify them—time rocking in its endless cradle—is shallowly conceived and incapable of creating an organic relationship. It would be quite possible, however, by interacting emotional rhythms, to make the four episodes into one rhythmic whole, provided that one could construct them in a horizon of tensional progression.

Motion is given in film. This motion provides the unity and impulse of the initial situation—a unity that must be elaborated to become the emotional pulse of the whole. Thus, movement becomes flow. As John Dewey has said, flow is *from* something *to* something. That is, form becomes dynamic through growth. Since it is in seeing that we see and in hearing that we hear, the whole can become engaged through cumulative development. This development, when properly articulated, becomes envelopment. Though motion is given, emotion must be generated. Immediacy must be earned. Unless immediacy is earned, emotion cannot work as the functional cement of qualitative identity. Such failure results in the merely typic and engenders recognition but not participation. Re-creation degenerates to recreation. Such failure results in non-art.

Visually, the over-all structure of a film could be described as the movement from the glimpse into the gaze and then into vision. As we said, the function of the initial phase is to state the theme and to pose but not ex-pose the major characters and rhythms. The function of the second phase of articulation is to explore these unrealized relationships, to make the covert overt—to elicit new aspects of the theme and to render them unhidden. This movement is not merely the addition of foreground incident—as we have said, the accidents and incidents are never incidental—but has the function of acting as variations on the basic theme. Thus, the foreground events (whether of story, plot, action, or whatever), are all relevant to and supportive of the horizon-theme, just as they are emergent from and enhanced by it. This means that the foreground compressions and extensions are internally related to the ongoing tension of the whole, and they function by adding increasing emotional depth and range to the form of the whole. The events are the echoing in the concrete instance of the over-all rhythmic movement. But they also add depth to that echoing through their reverberation. Thus the "tone" of the film is deepened and intensified until the final phase of revelation.

This movement of film structure is fluid, but, amazingly, many films can be analyzed into five different modes or levels of movement. Eisenstein has done this for *Potemkin* and describes the movement of the theme in five stages with theatrical headings.[2] Both *La Strada* and *The Nights of Cabiria* can be analyzed into five stages. The task is more difficult with the overblown *La Dolce Vita* since it consists of about ten episodes, though one could squeeze all of them into the five categories of blood (father), love (Emma), society (socialites, actors, Maddelena, Steiner), religion (opening sequence, Steiner-Bach, "miracle"), and work (reporting, idealistic novel-writing). The very difficulty of so classifying *La Dolce Vita* results from its opulence and hazy form and indicates that the classification itself does not always work. And, of course, it doesn't. Nor is there any magic meaning to the number five. Yet it is significant that many films can adequately be analyzed in terms of fives, whereas plays usually fall into threes, the middle of the three being the obligatory scene—a scene that is absent from film.

John Howard Lawson has correctly seen that the main difference between film and drama is that suspense is the fundamental mode of drama while tension is the fundamental mode of film. Fine film is not centered on plot. Plot is an element in film that is utilized to enhance and move theme. That is, plot is a subordinate phase in the over-all composition of film. Suspense is a function of a specific event that is partially foreseen. Hence, one is in suspense for the obligatory scene in drama and its inevitable resolution. Tension is pervasive and constant; it usually progresses from a known situation. As Lawson says, "In general, the plot is expressed in suspense, while the theme is developed through mounting tensions"; and he adds an important point: "Both are aspects of the human experience which is the heart and meaning of the story."[3] Though the initiation of tension is known, its resolution is not evident; and, since suspense has an end which is only partially foreseen, both film and drama share the search for the unobviously inevitable. One wonders, for example, how Kurosawa can possibly increase the tension of *The Seven Samurai* after the next to last encounter with the bandits—there seems no more *to do*. Then, in a stroke of genius, he shoots the final battle in the rain. Mud is splashing everywhere, and the hand-held camera is almost crushed by the charging, frantic horses. Here is the inclusion of the unobviously inevitable. Tension and suspense may coalesce, as they do in the so-called suspense films of Hitchcock and others. But they also can be discussed separately.

Luchino Visconti, for example, as far as I am concerned, is an overrated director since he has little sense of thematic tension. *La Terra Trema* is a long, slow bore; and, though it has some striking visual shots—such as the women, like rocks, waiting out the storm for their men—it builds no tension but simply slodges along. The same may be said for *Rocco and His Brothers* or *The Leopard*. Not only is *Rocco* dependent upon plot almost entirely for its development, but also it is restricted by cardboard characters. Again we have some striking visual sequences (for example, the pursuit on the roof of Milan Cathedral), but the tension of the film does not build. Rocco is so incredibly saintly and Simone so simplistically "bad" that one feels he is watching a contrivance. *Rocco* is pure plot. If *Rocco* is a cartoon, it fails to be funny.

The compressions and expansions that form variations on the theme and constitute the articulation can be either internal or external. If they are internal, they take the form of dream, reminiscence, imagination, intuitive vision, or memory. If external, they take such forms as action and plot. Only the latter form of movement is deemed legitimate by Lawson. Hence, he argues that films with a theme of alienation, such as *Hiroshima Mon Amour, Last Year at Marienbad, L'Avventura, L'Eclisse,* and *La Notte,* are flawed in form because they try to extend their development beyond the climax of the film.[4] This breaks form, he claims, and hence is an inevitable flaw in their structure. There are two answers to his objection. One is that the articulation of theme *should* extend beyond the climax of plot. The other answer involves discerning why Lawson comes to this conclusion. The answer is obvious: He confuses the source and the meaning of human emotions. Therefore, Lawson states that Antonioni is revealing that "feeling is atrophied when it is cut off from its source and meaning—outside ourselves." Now, from what we have said, we would agree that the meaning of feeling and emotion is outside ourselves. We would agree that its source is sometimes outside ourselves, but not always. Hence, we conclude that the source and the meaning are not to be identified by common and consistent locus and that the film of alienation is a valid form, since it proceeds to articulate depth by internal movement toward source and then to return to external manifestation and meaning. Such movement does not go beyond the form of the whole and is legitimate.

   Lawson's understanding and grasp of film form, however, is profound. His five-fold analysis of Chaplin's *The Gold Rush* cannot be improved upon; it can only be quoted:

> Each section has a distinctive mood and tempo that suggest a musical pattern: Part 2 (beginning the progression)—*scherzo;* Part 3—*allegro;* Part 4—*adagio;* Part 5 begins slowly and develops to a furious *presto.* This design has a dynamic development which does not depend on suspense, and which has more scope and imagination than the plot. We can look at *The Gold Rush* in two ways, as a plot, and as variations on a theme. These two aspects can be examined separately. They develop in different ways yet they are fused together as the sum-total of the tramp's experience. The dialectical conflict and unity between them creates the form of the film. We cannot identify the story with the plot. On the contrary, the thematic pattern gives the story its full scope and meaning."[5]

The same type of analysis would apply to Chaplin's *Modern Times* and also to *City Lights,* though *City Lights* has two plot lines and is more dependent upon plot development. It is also more dependent upon sentimentality and the emotional cop-out. It is not enough that the girl be poor, she must also be blind and must *also* be a flower girl. Chaplin seems to have a weakness for professional destitutes. The point to be seen, however, is that Chaplin is a genius of film form and well understood that the theme extends and interacts with plot in such a way that plot becomes an element of dialectical rhythm within theme. If we turn to a more current example, we can find the same kind of structure. *The Graduate,* like *Monsieur Verdoux,* is a sustained attack on middle-class materialistic values. Unlike *Verdoux,* however, it does not argue from an abstract premise, that is, the equation of business-war-death. Notice, by the way, that Chaplin has a crippled wife in *Verdoux,* just as he has a crippled paramour in *Limelight.* These plot devices show that in spite of his genius and grasp of film form he is unsure of his ability of expression; hence he pleads with his audience for identification. This is a constant feature of the films of Jerry Lewis, who is often erroneously compared to Chaplin. Mike Nichols is more self-assured and hence does not lower himself to spastic identification or the puppy-dog syndrome. He is cool not cute.

The Graduate can also be analyzed into five phases or rhythms of movement, which provide the tensional theme. The theme of the film, of course, is included in the title. Ben is a graduate from college, but this is only incidental. The theme is his graduation from affective to effective being. Hence, the rhythm of the film is built around his thematic emergence from subjectivity into life via sex and an active rejection of parental values. This theme is stated vividly in the opening sequence, Phase One. We begin with Ben withdrawn into his small cloister—the room itself is indicative of his parents' value structures, everything in the house is organized for others—communing with his mute tropical fish. His father urges him to join the party, which is ostensibly a celebration in Ben's honor. With diffidence, he joins and endures the sincere but still phony plaudits of the crowd. He is clued in to the ultimate mystery of the universe: plastics. And he flees back to his room.

Mrs. Robinson seduces him out of his catatonia on the excuse of a ride home. He takes her home and is nearly bedded at once. The conversation is brilliant in this sequence, for Ben is incoherently forthright while Mrs. Robinson is coolly ambivalent: she says exactly the opposite of what she intends. Naturally, Ben, being simple, is confused. This introduces the subordinate theme: the superior emotional maturity of the American female. Ben is rescued by the return of the husband. Mr. Robinson is an overgrown, boozy boy who either can't hear Ben's request for bourbon or is simply insensitive to others' requests. His character underscores the secondary theme and we see him as another Ben who, like Peter Pan, never grew up, but in Mr. Robinson's case it's because people ceased to believe in him. During Phase One, the daughter is introduced both by dialogue and portrait.

Phase Two begins with Ben calling Mrs. Robinson on the phone in the hope that she may turn him down. He finds her voraciously eager to comply; hence, he heads to the hotel to engage in various mix-ups with the desk clerk, a party, and so on. His naiveté and incoherence are painful. While he is acutely sensitive internally, he is externally unobservant. He even leaves Mrs. Robinson to pay for the drinks while he goes to secure a room. The bare, joyless room and the black lingerie are reminiscent of Roberto Rossellini's *Open City,* perhaps a visual pun on Nichol's part. Ben touches her breast and flees. He'd just as soon call the whole thing off. Here we have a fusion of the two themes. His intensified ineffectiveness and her cool maturity. In spite of himself, Ben is seduced. Throughout Phase Two, he is basically passive. His beer can is erect, but Ben still cannot take the initiative. He tries ineptly by insisting on conversation and pushing it to the point of pain. Desire reconciles the dispute, though Mrs. Robinson takes off her hose with the air that she is really suffering a fool. This verbal dispute sets the stage for Phase Three, because Ben is made to bind his future: that is, to promise not to have anything to do with Elaine. The scuba-diving sequence, already discussed, comes in this phase, as do several shots of Ben lolling on a water mattress—prone again with shades—while his father tries to urge him into the world of work. There is also a short scene in which the mother tries to dig out his romance and both parents intensify their efforts to try to get Ben and Elaine together. He is finally forced into taking her out.

Phase Three is the sequence with the humiliation of Elaine. Ben takes her to the crummiest dive he can find and sits as close to the stage as possible. The water symbolism is changed to liquor. He crassly insults Elaine and makes comparisons between her and the stripper. She flees and cries. Ben melts with compassion. They go to a drive-in and talk and eat. Here they are like any other teen-agers. But they have become intrigued with each other. Ben starts to take her home and they swerve hilariously to the hotel at Elaine's suggestion to have a drink. Ben confesses an affair in the abstract. He tries to date Elaine again. Mrs. Robinson tears into him. Ben decides to reveal all and both run dripping wet into the house. Elaine doesn't need to be told; she can see. She is shattered. Ben leaves, disconsolate. Mrs. Robinson cringes in the hall—wet and bereft as a whipped bitch. Thus Phase Three goes from humiliation to reconciliation to revelation. In this process, which is agonizing for Ben, he is forced to make three decisions: (1) he will drop Mrs. Robinson, (2) he will tell all to Elaine, and (3) he will pursue and win her. Ben is beginning to graduate into the world, to move out of his internal affectivity. That he is not entirely out of it, however, is amusingly shown when he announces to his parents that he is going to marry Elaine. They become excited and immediately start to put the social wheels in gear; then he announces that he hasn't told *her* yet.

Phase Four consists of the Berkeley pursuit sequence. Elaine is much too lovely a girl not to have competition for her hand and other adjacent parts, so Ben must try to show himself a better alternative than Carl. This phase also begins internally with Ben sitting by the fountain (now dried up) at Berkeley and merely waiting for glimpses of Elaine. After glimpsing her a couple of times and mooning in a dreamy way about her, he finally pursues her as she gets on a bus. He incoherently tries to make it seem like an "accident." He rides with her to the zoo (another of Nichol's ironic comments), where she meets Carl and they both cut Ben dead. But Ben persists and she comes to see him. Ben visually is becoming persistently more eager and active, as, for example, in the library scene. He wants Elaine, but she wants something more important to her: a husband. Pair-bonding is more basic than sex. She takes her time. Again, the secondary theme of greater maturity of the female is woven with the primary theme of Ben's emergence from subjectivity. Elaine's father intervenes, announces he is divorcing his wife (though it should probably be the other way around), and forbids Ben to marry Elaine. She is whisked off by her parents to marry Carl, a solid pre-med student who inhabits a fraternity peopled by young goats.

Phase Five consists of Ben's frantic efforts to track Elaine down. He races to her house, back to Berkeley, ferrets out the information of the wedding, and rushes to the town where it is to take place. He rips up a telephone book trying to locate the church, then runs out of gas. But he doesn't need fluid any longer to go. He falls back into his old habits as a racer and runs on his own. He breathlessly arrives at the church and clambers into the clerestory.

The shot of Ben pounding on the glass of the clerestory while the wedding is being concluded below has erroneously been interpreted as a Christ symbol meant to elicit sympathy for Ben. No doubt Nichols has read *A Portrait of the Artist as a Young Man;* but, whereas Joyce uses the image for a Christ symbol, Nichols uses it as a parody of the Christ symbol. Ben's arms are too high for the cross and he is beating on the glass like a furious ape. Somehow, he manages to get down to the wedding party and begins to drag Elaine away. But sheer force won't do. Mrs. Robinson says, "It's too late." The decision is Elaine's. She looks at Carl, the respectable people, and the frantic Ben. She replies, "Not for me." By the intensity of his emergence, Ben has convinced her to reject her parental obedience and choose him. He picks up the cross and uses it as a sword to waylay the wedding party. Ben and Elaine rush to the door, which he jams with the cross, making exit impossible. The church stands as a sanctified, antiseptic symbol, which blocks living in this given world. They clamber onto a bus, the symbol of the beginning of his pursuit, and ride away under the puzzled stares of the populace. Love, like a bus, is a common carrier. We have the feeling that, though they have started in an uncommon way (her marriage will have to be annulled) on a common conveyance, Ben and Elaine, while they will join the plastic world, will never identify with its swimming pools and spangles. We feel that they might "live happily ever after." We know, of course, that such a thing can happen only in fairy tales and films. In life, nobody lives happily ever after.

The fine Simon and Garfunkel score—including "God Bless You, Mrs. Robinson," "Scarborough Fair," "The Sounds of Silence"—occurs and recurs throughout the film to help sustain and articulate the visuals. The score complements the images and actions. Sometimes it provides lyrical aural ground for the visuals, sometimes it complements by ironic contrast. It is never obtrusive. The plot, which the moralistic find objectionable or unreal—though life can easily verify anything more fantastic than fiction—is subordinate to the theme. At certain key points, the plot and theme coincide vividly, for example, in the revelation scene of Ben, Elaine, and Mrs. Robinson, which has been preceded by Mrs. Robinson's deep fury. Her fury is not merely that of a woman betrayed or of a woman forced to realize her age by younger competition. It runs deeper than that. And even deeper than the fear of exposure (which she is strong enough to take and surpass). The point is that she is a mother. (I intend that in its original sense though Nichols may not. Think of Ben's *role*.) The same coalescence is evident in the direct confrontation at the wedding when Elaine rejects her mother's values, bitterly pointing to her age and failures.

The visuals and the music are utilized to instantiate or "concretize" the basic thematic rhythm, and the plot is used as foreground "punch" to emphasize the major and minor themes. Phase One, with the establishment of theme, character, and plot, is *scherzo;* Phase Two, in which Ben is essentially drifting and passive, is *largo;* Phase Three is a short *allegro,* almost an *allegretto,* and may well be criticized as being too short for Ben to fall in love, if we overlook his still intense subjectivity and his inability to value Elaine as a person as distinguished from a sexual object; Phase Four, with the emergence of Ben as an effective suitor, is *andante;* and Phase Five, which begins slowly, builds to a furious *presto.* The order of rhythms differs here from *The Gold Rush,* but the structure is basically identical. Phases One and Two are tied together by job anxiety and the presence of Ben's parents. His parents also tie together the end of Phase Two and the beginning of Phase Three. Having served their plot and thematic function, they drop out. Phases One and Five are tied together by Mrs. Robinson as mother, Two and Three by Mrs. Robinson as sex partner. One and Four are tied together by Elaine's father as a decision-force, though both he and Mrs. Robinson appear shortly in Phase Two to contrast her cool with his shallowness and Ben's guilt. The same symbols run throughout the film and their appropriateness is determined by thematic emergence. I have already mentioned the water-beer-liquor-gasoline imagery. The same holds true of Ben's graduation present: the car. It is an absolute presupposition for his mobility in Phases One, Two, and Three; he finds it unnecessary in Phase Four and uses the bus; and he discards it in Phase Five. He is on his own.

It is no accident that *The Graduate* is extremely popular with young people. They perceive quite clearly how it rejects the property-owning, up-tight value systems of affluent America. Nichols brilliantly uses his Nichols-and-May technique to transform ordinary adult conversations into fatuous nonsense. Ben's father, his mother, and their guests are particularly hilarious. It is to be hoped that the full import of the film will not be lost on the young, however; namely, Nichols' acid view of the fraternity boobs and his wry critique of Ben's incredible ineptitude, incoherence, and subjectivity. If one insists that *The Graduate* must have a message, it has another message for the young, which they ought not to misread: Grow up!—meaning "emerge from your cosmic paranoia and engage yourself in the world."

Let us turn to another film of quite different "objective" form, *8½*, and see how another master of film, Frederico Fellini, articulates his theme. *The Graduate,* after all, is a comedy; hence, its depth themes are always kept subordinate to its surface movement. *8½* is a serious film, in which the surface images are precipitates of its depth movements.

Pauline Kael entitles her critique of *8½* "Confessions of a Movie Director."[6] She objects that the film is simply narcissistic fluff (which means she does not intend to take it seriously) and that it is incomprehensible (which means that she is unwilling to work). Her main argument, however, insofar as she talks about the film at all, is that Fellini has presented us with a phony Freudian autobiography, which should be of little interest to anyone. Certainly, it is of no interest to her and so she uses her "review" to express her ennui evoked by an army of unspecified "mute, inglorious Miltons." In other words, she accuses Fellini of suffering from closed-circuit vision. She then abandons him to help "save" society—no doubt a noble cause for a modern Joan of arch.

It is true that *8½* is autobiography—or, more accurately, autophotography—but it is puzzling that anyone, especially a critic, should argue that *therefore* it is unacceptable as art. One need not be a rhapsodic advocate of the *auteur* theory to maintain, and quite rightly, that many great works of art are in part autobiographical. This is particularly true of poetry. This may be another one of the meanings of "authenticity"; namely, that the poet, unlike the rest of us, is unafraid to reveal his value attitudes and biases. He does not hide but discloses his closures. Hence, he is able to free himself of them by embodying his attitudes in his work, thus making them meaningful both for us and himself. He is a man who has the courage of his uncertainties. If eccentricity is to be valued anywhere, it certainly should be valued in art. To rule out a work because one considers inclusion of personal values a disvalue would eliminate a great deal of what we normally call "fine works of art." But *8½* is more than eccentric and personal in that sense. In fact, its significance lies in the honesty with which Fellini has been able to objectify his personal preferences and hence render them expressively valid through form.

We have already pointed to the difference between expression and self-expression. It should be added that it is as false to assume that the inclusion of personal elements in a work is a disvalue as it is to thereby assume that it is a necessary value. In either case, it is inevitable. The artist cannot keep part of himself out of his work; and the significant thing, then, is how he includes, how he excarnates, how he transforms. The coherence, the consistency, the rigor, the toughness, the honesty, and the depth of *8½* as an objective work bring me to regard Fellini with awe. Like any artist, of course, Fellini makes mistakes. Think of *La Dolce Vita. 8½*'s greatness lies, not in the inclusion of personal elements, but in the fact that Fellini has so objectified these characteristics as to make them applicable, by extension, not only to all creative persons, but to man alive. In art, the universal always comes from the particular and is embodied in it. This drive for the universal is the justification of *8½*.

The argument that *8½* is incomprehensible says more about the critic who makes the charge than about the object before him. Admittedly, *8½* is a difficult film. It demands disciplined vision and hard work on the part of the spectator. But difficulty is not the same as obscurity. To confuse the two is to make a common error: mistaking the mystical for the mysterious. The mysterious is opaque, vague, amorphous, and incoherent. It may puzzle or excite wonder. But, in any case, the ultimate ground of the mysterious is ignorance. The mysterious may be something seen, but it is uncertainly seen through a glass darkly and not face to face. The mystical *is* seen face to face; it is direct encounter. The ultimate ground of the mystical is knowledge. Granted, the knowledge involved is not discursive and is rarely rational. It is intuitive knowledge. But knowledge nevertheless. Fellini has shaped on celluloid this intuitive insight into his own character and, by extension, into the condition of man and the meaning of his life. His vision is difficult, but not vague. *8½* is intensely mystical, but it is not mysterious.

Externally, the structure of *8½* appears as complex as that of *The Graduate* appears simple. But just as *The Graduate* revealed an inner thematic rhythm that was complex, so *8½* reveals an inner thematic core that is simple. The theme is grounded inside the major character, Guido Anselmi, and the various levels of its development radiate from the center of his being as the arms of the starfish. The spectator sees the world as Guido sees it in various levels and gradations of possibility. Level One is the level of realism; and, on this plane, Guido is a somewhat commercial director at a health spa suffering from nervous exhaustion. He is trying to pull himself together in this last resort while constantly being circled by others who are making demands on him in a dry time. His producer, his wife, his mistress, the press, aspiring actresses, and others, all are trying to get something from him. His writer acts as a cold, intellectual, excessively verbalized guide through the Dante-esque hell of the spa. Guido is not merely empty; he is torn. And in his symbolic suicide at the end, he sees how simple life could have been. The form of the film is a spiral of many levels returning on itself with progressive evolution to mystic insight and newborn personal unity. Guido emerges with a new stance toward himself, others, and his world.

Level Two is an intermediate level between fantasy and reality. This level determines the tone of *8½*, which is as strongly masculine as *Juliet of the Spirits* is feminine. But it is not a real masculine tone. The women in the film are portrayed from a masculine point of view, but it is Fellini's simplistic Italian point of view: the perspective of Either/Or. Fellini has said, "Woman is mother, sister, saint, and virtue and, on the other side, is a whore, vice, corruption, and sin." These attitudes are expressed visually by dressing Claudia in pure white and La Saraghina in black. Notice that the wife is dressed in a white masculine blouse with black-rimmed glasses and black skirt, while the mistress is dressed in black with white cuffs and a white hat (she assures us in one Freudian line that it is real fur). At this tensional level between almost-reality and almost-fantasy, Fellini allows his imagination concerning costume full freedom. Hence, we have the women of the spa wearing fantastic hats and almost surrealistic clothing as they circle around the central source of healing water. He also plays here with contrasts of black and white and their fusion in polka dots. Whether a woman is a saint or a whore, Fellini loves her; and he loves to dress her as a fantastic doll. But it would be a mistake to think that this is what he is saying women *are;* what this level is asserting is that this is how Fellini views them. By extension, it is saying that men who share his mode of imagination view them in the same simplistic terms. This level is the expression of a perspective, a stance, a posture, not a metaphysical description. The second level then might be called "filtered reality."

Level Three is the level of imagination and fantasy. Here we have Guido's incredible visions of the harem sequence, in which he views himself as master of all womankind. The opening sequence of the film begins at this level. There is no sound; Guido is trapped in a claustrophobic tunnel. There is a pan to the left, and we see a husband sitting in the back of the adjacent car nagging his wife/cut/ people like pigs jammed into a bus with their arms dangling out of the sweltering interior. Guido sweats profusely; he opens the top of the car and soars free. Here we have the escape-sexual-flying theme repeated by grandfather in *Juliet*. But there is a rope tied to his ankle (compare the rope in Juliet's first vision when she drags in the Turkish invaders and death). This is no simple Freudian umbilical cord. It is a much more complex tie to concrete existence. Like a kite, Guido is pulled down to earth by his counsel/cut/ Guido is lying under some black covers. He raises his head, and the blanket forms a nun's hood. I have used the term "Guido" here, since this is who it turns out to be, but up to this point the spectator only sees "a man." Finally, we get a shot of him from above. And, as he enters the enormous white bathroom, we get a close-up, and the music comes up. We realize that "a man" was Guido, and that the initial sequence has been concluded by tying in to Level One.

Level Four is the level of memory, a level that is sometimes fused with Level Three. For example, when Guido is remembering the burial of his father symbolically, he sees himself lowering his father into the ground; and he turns to kiss his mother, who dissolves into his wife in a jump-cut. Sometimes the memory sequences are mixed with Level Two, as when he is discussing or, rather, listening to his father complain about his poor funereal settings, and the producer comes in to assure appropriate sumptuousness. Sometimes the memory sequences are "straight," as when the mystic phrase "Asa Nisi Masa" sends Guido back to the child-Guido being bathed in the wine vat and toweled up to bed with the other children to stare at an ancestral portrait. Or, again, in the punishment sequence, in which the sadistic and queer teaching assistant puts the child-Guido's food on the floor and he is forced to wear a dunce cap and "vergogni" (shame) written on his back.

Level Five is the level of mystic vision. The film concludes on this level, after Guido has gone through the press conference, has symbolically tried to escape (his mother's voice comes in here saying, "Guido, you wretched boy, where are you going now?"), has committed suicide in fantasy, has endured a torrent of the writer's words in reality. Suddenly a variation of the *La Strada* march occurs, with musicians appearing from nowhere led by the child-Guido. Guido realizes that he cannot do anything without the others and that it is right to love and accept everyone. He realizes that all of this confusion is *him*. There is no inner/outer split between himself and his world. He joins the dance of life, and the lights go out on the set.

These various levels are not always clearly separated as Guido moves through this catalog of life and infirmity, for we find the same people emerging in different levels. Claudia, for example, appears at Level Two as a water girl, at Level Three as a solicitous nurse and as a woman fixing an ideal supper in a Di Chirico alley, and at Level One as an actress who is genuinely interested in being in Guido's projected film. Though they are not clearly separated, however, they are clearly distinguished. As Guido moves in tensional rhythm from one level to another, the transitions are marked by changes of music, silence, natural sounds, pans, fades, and cuts. Sometimes the transitions are by gesture, as when Guido lowers the newspaper and "sees" Carla and Luisa making friends and dancing. Like the poet and the mollusk, Fellini constructs the form from the inside out. He ex-poses Guido and himself visually and aurally to our perceptive participation.

The theme of *8½* is the *Ulysses* theme, which we find in Joyce, *Wild Strawberries,* most of Antonioni, and others: the difficulty, if not impossibility, of emotional commitment in the modern world. It is an arid theme of alienation, but it is made more concrete in this particular film and rendered in a mode that some may find absurd. *8½*'s specification of the theme is male pregnancy. Like most pregnancies, it begins in illusion and ends in reality.

One need not be an extreme devotee of Freud to arrive at such an interpretation. All he has to do is to be able to hear and see. Think, for example, of the beginning and the ending symbols of the film: the claustrophobic tunnel and the rocket, both of which, like the many bronzed war heroes in our parks, are determinedly going nowhere. Objectively, given a short lapse, the period of gestation has the appearance of nothing going on. Internally, it is like Marshall McLuhan's universe: Everything is happening all-at-once. Even more internally, there is a smooth, undirectional, and goal-oriented patterning. This is the nature of *8½*. In fact, the title may even refer to pregnancy, but if it does, it is not a premature birth. On the contrary, it is the objective expression of a mature poet.

Another meaning of the title is Fellini's wry arithmetic. By his computations, he had made seven feature films and two episodes. That only adds up to 7½, so he includes the process and product of this one to make 8½. This might be called Russell-Whiteheadean addition, or the Pirandello approach. Thus, *8½* is a film about making a film which, like Luigi Pirandello's plays, keeps sliding back and forth from various levels of illusion to reality. And like Pirandello, Fellini is saying, *"It is all reality,* every bit of it." Unlike Pirandello, however, for Fellini there are not merely the levels of imagination and reality but also various levels or ways of meeting the world. Fellini's viewpoint is quite clear: Man is not merely objective; he is also the stuff of dreams, illusions, fantasies, and memories. We *are* such things. And because we are such things, we are not things at all, but people.

8½ retains the social conscience but not the social consciousness of the neo-realist movement and the warmth, but it has less of the moralizing tone and less dependence on bad dialogue, which were evident in *La Dolce Vita*. It incorporates the standard Fellini symbols and sequences. As noted, the "good" women are in white, the "bad" in basic black. La Saraghina is the whore of *La Strada,* the friend in *The Nights of Cabiria,* and La Bomba Atomica. Carla is a combination of these and the movie star of *Dolce Vita.* There are the symbols of flying, of the rope, of the band of musicians suddenly coming from nowhere (*La Strada, Cabiria*)—Fellini's expression of the optimism of accident—and the final affirmation of life. There is also a religious sequence in which the cardinal mentions other birds (albatrosses) and warns of life outside the church (*Dolce Vita, Cabiria, La Strada*). *8½* includes within its form, then, not merely its own theme, but it sums up and reworks the symbolism and sequences of earlier Fellini films.

8½ is also related to other films and forms a condensed history of film in itself. Fellini has said that he doesn't watch films much. He is not telling the whole truth. This film has elements from many others. The moon rocket could be from Méliès, the complex gantry with people streaming down it from D. W. Griffith, the rush of the train from Porter, the Keystone Cops chase on the beach, the final dance, not of death as in Bergman's *The Seventh Seal* or of decadent skeletons as in *Rules of the Game,* but of life. Fellini uses visual elements from many of the films he has absorbed whether he is conscious of it or not. The difference between plagiarism and creativity is transformation into depth. Fellini takes up and transforms these elements by his handling into a new whole and gives us a history of film in general. Robert Gessner has classified fifteen different types of motion in the film. *8½* uses every one of these, ending with the double reverse motion in the dance of life. The sheer technical brilliance Fellini displays in interweaving these elements leaves one feeling that there is no more to be said on film.

The relation of the artist to his techniques is an analogue of the relation of our living to our bodies. Technique is the artist's expressive tool just as our bodies are our expressive tools of our living. But though we can and often do use our bodies to excarnate, we also use them as a refuge and an excuse. The same may be said of the artist. Sometimes he may use technical proficiency as a refuge and an excuse for lack of depth meaning and expressive power. This is particularly true of Salvador Dali in painting and Claude Lelouch in film. The same could be said of *Dear John.* In general, *Dear John* is a good film, with some warm human qualities and a sharp understanding of the ways of women. The cutting is so rapid and so frequent, however, that the time-sense becomes disjointed. This would be no failing, but it becomes disjointed for no *apparent* reason, that is, no reason that appears to the eye. Hence the use of cuts here becomes excessive and tricky and hides the refusal of the director, or his inability, to render greater thematic depth. Fellini's technique does not betray him; he *uses* it to express and reveal.

With the exception of *I Vitelloni,* Fellini's other films have suffered from lack of unitary form. Each was built of episodes and, usually, of five episodes. *La Strada* had the illusion of strong form because it was set in a mythic reality that was neither real nor unreal, and the main characters were strong. Furthermore, its tensional horizon was tied together by a journey through this presented "reality." In *La Dolce Vita,* the main character, Marcello, is too weak to carry the narrative line alone; hence, the spectator has the sense of having seen a series of episodes externally strung like beads without a string, not a unified film. *8½* solves the problem of unity by taking us inside the skin of Guido. The objective occurrences are not now mere sequences or "bits," but are events which he, Guido, is happening. Fellini has found a middle, or phenomenological, position for his form. While portraying alienation, he has avoided the subjective aestheticism of *Last Year at Marienbad* and the early objective, almost scientific, positivism of Antonioni. Fellini has achieved the *personal* film with a personal form. This form is perfectly adapted to the treatment of autobiographical materials but is not confined to them, as is evidenced by *Juliet of the Spirits.* This form allows Fellini to use elastic time, fantasy, reality, and accident and to weave them all into one forceful rhythm. What it gains in rhythm, it loses in plot—at least, plot as normally conceived. While it provides the possibility of evolutionary and emergent unity, it also allows him to leave his form open at the end, to include, as he puts it, "mistakes." Fellini has said: "Movies should have mistakes in them, like life, like people." This form is a particularly filmic form of the 1960s, and it allows Fellini to improvise from an emotional perspective. This is absolutely necessary, for Fellini is a poet; and a poet's task is to transform accident into inevitability. And nothing can be transformed until it is first accepted. The images then, and even the external sequences, are precipitates of the underlying emotional rhythm.

The use of such a form puts tremendous pressure on the central actor. He not only has to be able to express with the slightest nuance and gesture, but he must also know what he is expressing and why. Hence, he must be able to enter a kind of spiritual symbiosis with the director. Fellini was very fortunate and very shrewd in picking Mastroianni for the main part. For Guido must reveal a man who is being born into a new life, a new posture. Such a man can be described in many ways. In Bishop Fulton J. Sheen's words, he is the "twice born," in Eric Berne's words, "the autonomous man," in Norman O. Brown's words, "the polymorphously perverse body," or, in the words of Erich Fromm, "the man who is completely born." Guido is compulsively indecisive. He views himself as an other; he doesn't know if he is only partly fake or all fake; but, in his hierophantic vision at the end, he comes to a stunning insight: *Life is no problem.* As Fellini put it: "When we make too many problems, we lose ourselves. It is only when Guido gives up on his problem that he's saved." Marcello Mastroianni, in an incredible job of sensitive acting, embodies and excarnates Guido for our vision.

We have already spoken of music and its relations to the image. Sound, of course, can be music; it can be natural sound; it can be voice. All these are used as tonal variations and can be used to enhance the unity of the film. *A Man and a Woman* had such an overwhelming musical theme that one tends to read more into the visuals than is actually there. The simplicity of the musical themes in *The Nights of Cabiria* and *La Strada* adds affective unity to the films. As Fellini has grown, his use of music has become more complex and he has tended to follow each character with a musical theme, as well as using sound as an aural base for his visuals. Perhaps the high point in an attempt to synthesize sight and sound from a visual point of view occurs in *Alexander Nevsky,* in which Eisenstein deliberately tries to match the position of the notes on the scale with the elevation of his visual shots. But such an abstract matching is only a step toward legitimate unity. The unity of sight and sound comes through common rhythms, in which the visuals and the aurals amplify and modify each other's appearance. This is admittedly a difficult task and is one reason why fine sound films are so difficult to make. The factors to be synthesized are so many and so complex. Only a director who begins with a strong grasp of his over-all thematic rhythm can hope to synthesize his individual sounds and shots in such a way as to make the various incidents and plots coalesce with the theme.

We have now examined briefly two examples of modern film making from the perspective of the articulation of form. One is an external form, *The Graduate,* and the other, an internal form, *8½*. Both reveal that film development is the cumulative emergence of character and theme through the progressive changes and articulations of pace, mood, tone, and incident. Both show that plot becomes subordinate to theme and is used to illuminate theme. At the same time, plot develops its own tensional relations to the theme itself. Film establishes its own time; but its claim on the elements, like its claim on our lives, varies. Though sheer compression in either time and space is not enough for film form, it can add to the tension of the whole. Since the essence of film form is the coherence of thematic rhythm, the function of the articulation is to clarify and explore, to ex-pose the theme, while increasing the momentum and pressure toward the final revelation. Its function is not to solve or dissolve the theme, but to unravel and reveal.

Revelation

Everybody knew what was going to happen in Greek tragedy (they did not all go off to the beach and have a picnic). Hence, the Greeks were not concerned with what happened; they were vitally concerned with why it happened and what its meaning would portend. The articulation of import, or denouement, in Greek tragedy is thus long and involved. Its purpose was understanding. Modern plays have short denouements, perhaps because modern audiences lack attention, are impatient, or simply do not wish to understand. Hence, the endings of most modern dramas are relatively short and swift. The structure and form are focused on what happens and not on its why. Like the modern play, the revelation sequence, or denouement, of film is usually short. But this is not because of a pragmatic concession to spectator impatience. It is a function of film form itself. Since film is concerned with what is happening as distinguished from what has happened, it keeps happening right up to the end. The structure of the revelation sequence, then, should be such that it allows a summation of the events but at the same time allows them to expand into a larger context of meaning. Its purpose is comprehension.

The revelation sequence, then, has a purpose—literally and figuratively folding prehensions together—comprehension. It accomplishes this goal by performing two functions. One function is to end the plot. As the plot is concluded, the various elements, events, rhythms, and subrhythms are echoed. The second function is to extend the theme beyond plot closure. This extension of theme beyond plot is not a prophecy. Its function is not to assure us that everybody really did live happily ever after or that they all went to the beach and held an eternal picnic. It must point to future possibilities, but, more importantly, it must reveal *how they are to be met.* The extension of theme, then, has as its primary function the revelation of stance. It reveals a new or altered posture on the part of the main characters and the emergent manner in which they will now shape their being-in-the-world. Film form, then, is both open and closed. With respect to plot, it is closed. With respect to theme, it is only a partial closure indicating a way of meeting the world beyond. This closed/open duality, when handled properly, moves the spectator from vision to envisioning, from emotional engagement to contemplation, from sight to insight.

John Howard Lawson has an eloquent description of the end of film, which he terms the climax.

> The climax concludes *what happened* in a particular system of events; it is also a judgment on *why* it happens, *what* it means and *how* it affects our lives and conduct. The *why, what* and *how* are embodied in every part of the story; the end refers back to every part and summarizes the total result. Since the climax is the key to the story, it reveals the creator's purpose—or his confusion

or lack of purpose—in the sharpest form. The limitations of the modern film are most evident in the climax.[7]

What Lawson says before the last sentence is partially true. What he says in the last sentence is only minimally true, for he is getting ready to launch another round of drum beating for social realism. We have seen in Chapter 4 on socialist realism, however, that Lawson's attempt to ground the validity of *Potemkin* on the external conditions of the revolution is simply illegitimate. A fine film does not have its value dependent upon such external circumstances. Its primary function is aesthetic, that is, to provide man with a perceptive experience; and any other function, whether religious, social, educational, or whatever, must be subservient to that primary purpose. Lawson's love of the mass at the expense of the individual has again led him partially astray.

The revelation sequence of film should display for us *what* has been happening, *why* it has been happening, *what* it means, but not necessarily *how* it affects the spectators' lives and conduct. It should present how it affects the characters' lives and conduct in their world, and most importantly, it should reveal *who they now are* and *how they will be*. At the end of *8½,* Fellini presents us with who Guido now is and how he will meet his world. True, Fellini is also presenting an aesthetic standard for life, but the primary function is the revelation of Guido. The plot of *The Graduate* ends in Ben's furious assault and Elaine's decision. The rest is the extension of theme, which presents us with who Elaine and Ben now are and their new stance, their new mode of meeting and coping. But Nichols is not saying, "Go ye forth and do likewise." The pragmatic injunction is an inference, not a necessary condition, and certainly not the goal of the film. The goal of the film is to develop and to articulate, as well as possible, these two people in their given and changing world—their dialectical interactions and transformations through that process and their resultant perspective and posture. Their new posture is the meaning of the film.

The word "end" is marvelously ambiguous: (1) It may mean cessation or a full stop; (2) it may also convey a telic meaning, fulfillment. Life guarantees us an eternal stop; it seldom provides us with fulfillment. But life, experience, existence, whatever one wishes to call it, is a leaky sieve. Art, however, is clarified fulfillment. Hence, the superiority of art to life and its raison d'être. Poor films, like life, simply stop. Fine films, unlike life, are not a mere constant undergoing. On the contrary, they embody anticipation, cumulation, and consummation. Plot culminates; theme consummates. The spectator is thus thrown into the reflective mode and left to engage the whole in retrospective imagination. He is moved from the glimpse to the gaze to the vision. And in the vision, he can envision the whole. If the artist does not perfect a new vision, he has produced a film, but not a work of art. But fine film is an organic whole, that is, a work of art. Its last phase is thus telic fulfillment, disclosure, and discovery. Just as it is the function of initiation to pose purport, so it is the function of revelation to disclose import.

There is no difficulty in finding films with flawed forms. The majority of them are flawed, but so are the majority of paintings and novels. But the film with a poor ending is not the one that refuses to incite social change or world revolution. It is the film that pulls an emotional cop-out. This usually takes the form of extraneous sentimentality and the attempt to carry plot beyond theme instead of theme beyond plot. *Alfie* was a rollicking comedy until it suddenly acquired a Catholic conscience in the middle, after which its form became schizoid. It still could have been saved, however, if plot had not been extended beyond its theme. There are two places it could have ended but did not: (1) when the American woman turns to Alfie and says, "You're too old," or (2) when Alfie threw the flowers into the river. The theme and tone of the film are acid and dry, but the extension of the end back to a resurgence of the beginning vitiates the form and sentimentalizes it. The same thing happens in *The Americanization of Emily*. Here we are given a surprising and telling portrait and theme of a soldier who is a card-carrying coward and detests war. The plot, the tone, and the other characters admirably enhance this theme. Then at the end, the director decides to take it all back and cry, "King's X! I didn't *really* mean it." *Emily* (its new name) could and should have ended (1) when his friend says of the photograph, "Well, there's our first hero," or (2) when the general turned and exclaimed, "My God, you didn't follow my orders while I was in that condition?" Instead, we find that good old James Garner never did die; and, though the attempt is made to make the ending funny, the laughter is phony and forced. Again, theme has been sacrificed to plot and (presumed) box-office acceptance.

Juliet of the Spirits is a particularly relevant example of the dialectic of film form and of the extension of theme beyond plot into a context of larger meaning. The plot of the film consists of Juliet's relations with her husband, Giorgio, with her friends and family, with his friends (for example, Val, Susy, Jose); and the structure of the plot is that Giorgio is involved in adultery. Juliet has to decide what to do about it. But this is not her main problem. Her main problem is the theme; namely, how can she come to be a whole woman, how can she enjoy being a girl. The culmination of the plot comes when Giorgio actually leaves her for another woman. This crisis throws Juliet into her last series of visions, in which she understands the weakness of her virtue, the "teachings" of Susy, Jose, grandfather,

Bhisma-Iris, and others. Juliet rebels against her mother and frees the spirit child. Her "bad" visions disappear. She has become reconciled to her mortal femininity and has accepted her finite body. She walks forth into the sunlight. Whether she divorces Giorgio or whether they are reconciled is unimportant. What is important is that Juliet has attained a new stance, a new wholeness and integrity, a new mode of being-in-the-world. She walks forth into the sunlight as the voices assure her they are her true friends. This is the way revelation should be handled. Theme extends beyond and encloses plot.

There are many ways in which a film may end, but its aesthetic structure is complete when it resolves plot and slightly extends theme. The end may be stated at the beginning, as in the framing story. Both *The Cabinet of Doctor Caligari* and *Rashomon* end by returning to the initial statement and extending it. The end may be an almost complete repeat of the first sequence with only minor differences, as in *Lolita*. Or the end may be a partial repeat of an earlier situation and sequence. This may involve a return to a former place or time or both but with an altered stance on the part of the main characters. *Treasure of the Sierra Madre, The World of Apu, Nothing but a Man,* all display this form of partial recurrence and altered stance. The exact technique used for the ending may be dolly-back (*Blow-Up, La Strada*), a zoom close-up (*The Four Hundred Blows, Breathless*), a speed-up (*Strangers on a Train, The Graduate*), stop-photography directed at the audience (*The Great Train Robbery*), or other techniques. But the point here is not the technique used, but the manner in which it is used. It should be utilized to throw the audience, and hence the apparition, into the contemplative mode.

I have already discussed the common character of revelation. It is always magical but not always religious. Nevertheless, the fervent are usually unable to distinguish one from the other. Being fervent, they mistake intensity for clarity, motion for emotion, emotion for imagination. Thus the young—whether in years, mind, or heart—insist that revelation is to be found in the avant-garde or underground film rather than in such "commercial" products as *Juliet of the Spirits, Persona, Rashomon,* and *Ikiru.* Their shout consequently becomes "If you want revelation, look at the underground films!" My advice is—Don't. This negative advice springs not from a puritan moral distaste (though the subject matter is often raw) nor from technical incapacity (though that is usually the case) but from the defective form of the underground film. The underground film is essentially presentational patterning. It thus normally lacks the dyadic tension that is necessary for fine film and the precondition for articulate revelation. The "pure film" is usually stunning—in which case it is shallow—or shocking—in which case it is inchoate. Revelation without articulation is mute; articulation without revelation is disorder.

At its most subjective level, the avant-garde film or the film of "pure cinema" corresponds to the hypnagogic illusion, for it presents a flow of images that have little or no external counterparts in either lived or scientifically assumed reality. Most avant-garde films share the rejection of story or narrative meaning altogether. Perhaps the most articulate and eloquent spokesmen for this point of view have been Maya Deren and Hans Richter. Jonas Mekas is forceful, but no one would dare accuse him of being coherent and only on occasion of being intelligible. The argument of the avant-garde movie maker is freedom. He insists that he must be free from convention and from commercial standards. The notable thing about his freedom so conceived is its negativity. He wishes to be free *from* and hence his films are often an open attack on given values. While he regards this as daring, he fails to see that he is still playing the social game; the only difference is that he is playing it negatively. The rationalization for his stance is that he must be freed from the fetters of convention so that he may present new visions and new techniques. Yet, if the spectator but reflects upon his experiences of underground films, avant-garde films, or "pure cinema" films, the overwhelming feeling he has is that if he has seen one of them, he has seen them all. Were they truly successful in providing new visions, one might be able to distinguish one film from another or even to remember their names, but the striking feature of such films is usually their monotonous sameness. As for the discovery of new techniques, this is highly questionable. On occasion there are different approaches used, but for the most part the technique is amateurish and incompetent.

I am speaking now of avant-garde film at its worst, of course, and not at its best. The avant-garde film maker, like the adolescent, is either unable or unwilling or both to distinguish between the intensity of his feelings and their objective expression. Because he feels that he feels things deeply and exquisitely, he therefore assumes that what he has to say and how he says it will also be deep and exquisite. At its worst, this is a type of subjective idealism bordering on paranoia. At its best, it can become an attempt to objectify the rhythms of life in external visual-aural shape. The difficulty of this articulation, however, is built into the basic stance of most avant-garde film: defective form. The aim of the pure cinema is to create sheer design. Design in this context means either (1) subjective intensity—hence the heavy emphasis upon homosexuality, necrophilia, fetishism, and other such deviations, that is, raw content—or (2) abstract visual-aural patternings. In Case One, the emphasis is upon foreground incident and the film becomes episodic with little or no thematic tension. In Case Two, the theme itself becomes the entire content; and there is little foreground incident, merely a moving mural, a sheer presentation that seldom achieves depth of import. In both cases at their most subjective, there is no story; hence, no depth meaning or unifying tension can be established between theme and event.

The avant-garde film of sheer events is the most normal mode of its appearance. Its structure is episodic; its content is raw. It is subject to overstatement, for, in spite of his bravado, the director is unsure of his voice. Often the content and its handling is highly repetitive. One wonders, after watching a series of such films, if it is possible for an avant-garde film maker to avoid the images of, for example, the atom bomb, the nude, the toilet, and guts, or the underexposed and overexposed shots. What is a supposed cry of self-expression is often a dreary exercise in meaningless cliché. *To Hollywood with Love, Unsere Afrikareise, Chumlum, Relativity, Prelude: Dog Star Man, Schmeerguntz,* and *Cosmic Ray* are all examples of this type of strong but disorganized and often overlengthy content. Kenneth Anger's *Fireworks* might also be included in the list..

It must be admitted, however, that Anger's films show great visual sensitivity and a strong grasp of form. Hence, they display unity, a quality often missing from the avant-garde episodic. The interplay of sight and sound in *Scorpio Rising* is an example of how film can become fine film. Anger reveals both the objective and subjective meanings of the various phases of the development of his theme. Hence, there is mechanical proficiency contrasted to femininity, unconventionality (pot, for example) and intellectual dwarfism (TV, Brando, comics), simplicity and childishness, showing off among contemporaries and narcissism, camaraderie and homosexuality, brutality and consecration, competition and death. These contrasts are enhanced by such elements as the cuts to the child and the toy and the scenes from *The King of Kings,* and the music works as both underlay and as ironic contrast to the visuals. Thus the song "Blue Velvet" indicates the feminine streak at the beginning and the other songs, "Wind Me Up," "I Will Follow Him," and "Point of No Return" add acid aural comment to the visuals. This music is not only woven in with the visuals but exhibits intensive progression and cumulation when regarded on its own. Both the aurals and the visuals interact, then, and reveal the theme of brutality and homosexuality, while at the same time moving toward the final revelation of death. Jules Dassin has handled some of the same themes in *Chant d'Amour* and transformed it into a poetic, coherent unity, almost a filmic ballet. At its worst, then, the avant-garde film of subjective intent degenerates into pornography or episodic incoherence. At its best, it can rise to short, lyrical statements of "outlaw" themes.

The grandfather of this mode of film is, of course, *The Andalusian Dog* by Luis Buñuel and Salvador Dali, a film that looks curiously tame and dated in present viewing. Buñuel has never completely moved away from this surrealistic beginning;

but, in his more mature films, as I have noted, he utilizes the surrealistic image and the dream sequence as integral elements to articulate his over-all form. The avant-garde episodic is usually a short film, no longer than a cartoon. Of late, however, the public has been subjected to longer versions, such as Andy Warhol's *Empire State, Sleep,* and *The Chelsea Girls.* On the commercial plane, one might also include the various *Mondo* films, *Private Property,* and *The Savage Eye.* Despite their presumed sensitivity, most of these films have in common the erasing of the distinctions between people and things. Their approach is curiously external, with people viewed as if they were objects. This may be due to the strong element of voyeurism in the avant-garde episodic.

The avant-garde film of design as moving pattern or thematic foreground had its ancestor in the early films of Man Ray. Here the emphasis is not upon raw content, but upon aesthetic preciousness. Since such films usually lack the storied image, they are even more difficult to remember and to separate than the avant-garde episodic. Here technical proficiency is at a much higher level and is often used with bewildering fluency. Thus, one is subjected not merely to double printing, but triple, quadruple, and, I understand, in *The Gondola Eye,* eight superimposed shots. The latter film is a good example of the type. It consists of a long series of fluid visual images woven together with avant-garde clicks, drum beats, and music. While I was viewing it, the only part that came alive was the short wedding sequence, in which wedding and death were briefly identified. The rest of the film seemed to dissolve into a sheer flow of bobbing boats, arches, and lapping waters. Later, in a television interview, Ian Hugo, its director, said that the wedding sequence had originally been a separate film entitled *Venice Etude No. 2,* which he finally decided to incorporate into *The Gondola Eye.* This explains its superior unity.

Such films can, on occasion, discover striking images. In *The Gondola Eye,* there are several repetitions of one shot through an irregular opening in a wall which assumes the status of a mask of death. This image finds an echo in the La Saraghina sequence in *8½,* in which Fellini's camera moves in on a gap in her house with splintered bamboo and the sea beyond. The same may be said of Maya Deren's *Meshes of the Afternoon.* The enigmatic, mirror-faced clothed figure finds its echo in the faceless stranger in the first dream sequence of *Wild Strawberries,* the figure of the chess-playing Death in *The Seventh Seal,* the first "realist" shots of Guido in *8½,* and the nuns in the martyr sequence and other visions of *Juliet of the Spirits.* Whether Mr. Hugo or Miss Deren had any influence on Bergman or Fellini is doubtful. It is more likely that the same images occurred because they wished to say the same things. *Meshes of the Afternoon* is a fascinating, though highly repetitive, expression of what it feels like to commit suicide.

Again, at the commercial level, one could include such films as Ben Hecht's *Spectre of the Rose,* Cocteau's *Blood of a Poet* and *Eternal Return.* At a more sophisticated level, one might also see Bergman's *Persona* and Resnais's *Last Year at Marienbad.* Experiencing *Marienbad* is like going through a combination of psychoanalysis and shock treatment. And if one needed any confirmation of the impact of the motion picture on superficial levels of the appearance of behavior patterns, that is, style, *Marienbad* had as strong an effect as *It Happened One Night.* In the latter film, Clark Gable, single-chestedly almost ruined the undershirt industry. We are still surrounded by millions of *Marienbad* hair styles, even though the film will probably never have a wide popular appeal. *Marienbad* almost stands as an end-point of aestheticizing subjectivity and preciousness in the commercial film. Its appeal is thus restricted to the highly intellectual. As an exercise in creative decor, it made architecture more interesting than people.

The usual conditions of the two modes of avant-garde cinema should now be evident: design as episodic subjective impressions and design as thematic formalism. But, as I have argued throughout this book, subjectivity is not to be opposed to the world; the difficulty is in externalizing it, embodying it meaningfully into situational contexts. For only insofar as intent is expressed and completed in the world of gesture, behavior, and thing, can it attain either closure or clarity. We live, as I have said, outside. Whatever the individual hang-ups of the underground film makers may be, they are *their* problems. One might even agree that they are or were born into a mess, as Mekas complains: "The new American artist cannot be blamed for the fact that his art is a mess: he was born into that mess. He is doing everything he can to get out of that mess."[8] But this appeal to pity will not even hold the water of tearful sympathy. For the avant-garde film maker is asking me as a spectator to watch his film; and, for the most part, I have less inclination to watch bad films than to read bad poetry. It is doubtful that he is "doing everything he can to get out of that mess" or, if he is, *what* he is doing and *how* he is doing it is often inept. One must judge the object before him, and the object before one in the theatre is the film, not the artist.

There is a saying among the Japanese: "The baby sparrow cries for its supper; the Samurai carries a toothpick." The difference is discipline. When it comes to the artist, particularly the film artist, there is probably nothing more difficult of attainment because all discipline for the artist must be self-discipline. He must learn to make form before he learns to break form. Spontaneity has its own ground in the impalpable body of the mastery of the materials and the rules. One can dive from a tree or a rock, but the graceful dive comes from the mastery of the high board. One must therefore agree with both Langer and Arnheim that the significance of art lies not in self-expression but in objective expressive form. Arnheim states this view succinctly:

> It will be evident that what is advocated here is not the so-called "self-expres-sion." The method of self-expression plays down, or even annihilates, the function of the theme to be represented. It recommends a passive, "projective" pouring-out of what is felt inside. On the contrary, the method discussed here requires active, disciplined concentration of all organizing powers upon the expression that is localized in the object of representation.[9]

In both art and life the same appears to be true: The only way to achieve controlled power is through disciplined work. Accidents occur in film as they occur in life, but what is done with them depends on the effective transformative power of the director.

The avant-garde film of thematic foreground displays greater discipline and control than the episodic-type design. It displays greater rhythmic unity, though it lacks narrative depth and sometimes even lacks any discernible "events." But it is in the nature of artistic form that it is a vehicle, an articulate expression of meaning. Hence, form "always points to something beyond itself" and "the character of the meaning and its relation to the visible form intended to express it help to determine the degree of simplicity of the whole work."[10] If the spectator cannot experience the intention in the work, as distinguished from the artist's intention, there is no way he may participate in the work.

Art, as I have said, is the search for difficult simplicity. The thematic avant-garde film too often settles for the easy simplicity of the fuzzy image or the fluid grace of flow. It may sometimes be fascinating, as the ebb and flow of the tides are fascinating, or the spreading of an oil-slick on a puddle. At its highest level of fascination, the thematic avant-garde film may well shade over into another order: the illusion that has some substantial base. But its lack of story and its resultant half-form make it shallow. This may be why it normally avoids the most difficult of all expressive forms: dyadic tension. It may also be why it tends to collapse people into things. Ultimately, the thematic "pure film" fails "to master the abundance of existence" and instead it "escapes to the poverty of abstinence."[11] Abstinence may make the heart, and other vital organs, grow fonder, but it is no basis for a full-bodied artistic form. Abstinence rarely achieves revelation.

Just as revelation is seldom found in the underground film because it is inarticu-late, so revelation fails to occur in the average commercial film since the director has no vision to reveal. He is a craftsman; and his task is to produce a carefully constructed—and often painfully constricted—mass dream. The old mythic forms are still being produced, but the B and C films no longer hold the attraction for the mass audiences they did in the past. The musical, the horse opera, the soap opera, the gangster, science fiction, and horror films are either converted into blockbusters and saddled with opulent "production values" or are fading away as phantom myths. Part of this is due to the decline of the studio system. But it is also a function of the modern audience. People no longer go to films for escape. They will not go to watch anything. They attend films to watch something and to have something to talk about afterward. If they wish to watch anything or to escape, they turn on the TV set. Whether the director likes it or not, then, he is being forced to become an artist. He can no longer succeed with a simple gangster film but is forced by audience demand to produce something meaningful, for example, *Bonnie and Clyde*. This new type of film I shall call the "existential film" or the "personal film." It is a film that is both objective and subjective, a film that displays cumulative development toward revelation. It is a film that exemplifies the philosophic theory advanced in this book.

The philosophic perspective of this book is existential in the sense that it places the emphasis upon man as the finite creator of meaning. But it is a humanistic or a communal form of existentialism, for it recognizes that mind is from the outset social as well as individual. Furthermore, it recognizes that although we are cut off from others conceptually, we are not necessarily cut off emotionally. It asserts that men can communicate and that they can communicate affectively, hence effectively, insofar as they participate in common experience. The person-to-person relationship is rare, but it is direct and unmediated. It is a form of sharing or communion. And communion is possible when the self is rendered permeable and shares its being-to-the-world. This attitude, and I must call it an attitude instead of a fully-developed philosophy, I believe is characteristic of the new film.

These films do not present everything to us as given and resolved. They often make heavy demands on the spectator, both emotionally and intellectually. They demand that we keep up with them; but, at their best, they *allow* us to keep up with them and, in fact, indicate how we should go about it. These films, says Penelope Houston, "are more spontaneous . . . more inclined to snatch at the fleeting moment:"

> They relish ambiguity, the kind of Pirandellian situations in which characters are always going in search of their own identities, are not even entirely sure where life ends and film begins; they are based on a knowledge of the cinema's past which enables them to use quotation and allusion, to work within the frame of reference necessary to the creators if sometimes perplexing the audience;

they look as though the people making them enjoyed what they were doing: and they admit their own imperfections.[12]

If such films become too internal, they create a specialized audience; but, as we saw with *The Graduate* and *Dr. Strangelove,* this is not a necessary consequence of the approach. Most people may see *Blow-Up* for the wrong reasons, but this does not prevent *Blow-Up* from presenting meaning at both the commercial and artistic levels.

Truffaut's film *The Four Hundred Blows* is a fine example of this perspective. Whereas we are always conscious of the camera in Godard's films and of the trickery thereby involved and while Bergman often uses the camera to dissect character, Truffaut makes us forget the camera by using it, like Renoir, to present people directly. Truffaut is concerned with presenting social reality immediately but always from a personal perspective. It is not France as a whole to which we react in *The Four Hundred Blows,* nor is it the social inequities of bourgeois society, but the given reality of a twelve-year-old boy: *his* France. Truffaut sacrifices direct messages and ideological preachments for depth, and his film is one of intense personal feeling—not merely the feeling and posture of the boy to his world but also of the director toward that posture. The perspective of *The Four Hundred Blows* is the unique, accidental, concrete situation of a small boy undergoing the warping of his personality and his world. The film is intensely personal, yet it presents us with his emergent posture and thematic indication of how he will meet his future.

The same kind of analysis could be given *Pather Panchali; The World of Apu* (*Aparajito* doesn't quite make it); *Wild Strawberries; Divorce, Italian Style; Il Posto; This Sporting Life; Saturday Night and Sunday Morning;* and many, many others. I have discussed many others throughout this book. The only Russian film of later years I would include, however, would be *The Lady with the Little Dog;* and I would exclude *Ballad of a Soldier, Cranes Are Flying,* and *The Forty-ninth* as merely signal gestures. The personal films are less formal, less intellectual, more emotional and direct. They are also more hopeful, though this is not by any means a necessary condition. It is a usual one, however, since most of them consist of a humanistic affirmation of life. They present man as the perpetual beginner who may end in tragedy and yet who develops a new and stronger posture in his stance. Motion pictures cannot help but be objective. Their locations are conditions of their situations and often active participants in it. Yet these directors are adding to things the dimensions of their values as perceived and attempting to adduce in us a sameness of vision.

Penelope Houston has said of the personal directors:

They are more interested in the way things look and feel and sound than in what they signify in general terms; more interested in mood than in narrative; more concerned with how people behave and give themselves away in action than with how they may choose to see themselves. They are asking from their actors not the great neon-blazing star turns but performances which break through the hard professional surface.[13]

This is true. The personal director does not demand that the actor assume a role or play a part. He asks only that the actor be what he is and do what he can. Since nothing is more difficult than honesty, he is asking a great deal, perhaps more than most professional actors can give. The personal director is requesting that the actor share with him in an adventure in self-discovery and revelation.

But he is also asking the audience to share in that same process, for he also is engaged. He is trying to find his artistic limits, his strengths, and his meanings; and, in so doing, he does not hide his weaknesses. This may all sound like a series of emotional strip-teases, but it isn't. All that is being said is that the personal director is concerned with visceral themes and that he is attempting to be as honest with them and with himself as possible. If he can do that, he will also be honest with us. But he doesn't direct in this way *because* he wishes to be honest with "the audience." On the contrary, he directs in this way because he wants to create a significant expressive form and to excarnate his value system. He knows how the theme feels before he shoots the scene, but he does not fully know what film he has until the cutting and scoring is done. As Huineng said: "A hand is no-hand until it plucks a rose; a mind is no-mind until it expresses itself." In order to do this, of course, the director must be open to his work. As Fellini said: "You have to get to know this new creature who is emerging; you have to try to like it."[14]

The personal director, then, is on a voyage of self-discovery; and, if successful, he holds his rebellious crew together and, like Columbus, presents us with a new world to be in. This is the step beyond neo-realism. It is the step into emergent contexts of wider meaning. To the perceptive moviegoer, the adventure can also be a self-disclosing experience. It may even be a civilizing one if it is true that man is composed of both aggressive and participatory emotions, for the major thrust of the rest of our institutions is to foster and intensify our aggression, not our participation. The director cannot be totally honest. Only God could be that. But one does ask that he be as honest as he can. And if he is honest, his film will be a revelation to him and to us.

The result of this approach, of course, is that every film will have its personal signature written across the face of its individuate monogram. That this is true of most European directors and has been for some time is quite obvious to those who watch films. Though the tendency of the studio system was to suppress personal style, it still occurred in America in such films as *David and Lisa, The Little Fugitive,* and *Nothing but a Man.* The personal film has long been a mode of the documentary and is evident in, for example, *The Quiet One, The River,* and *Man of Aran.* Nor should it be thought that the personal film can arise in America only outside the studio or in the documentary. The good Hustons (such as *Treasure of Sierra Madre, Beat the Devil,* and *The Maltese Falcon*) were studio, as well as the less admirable films. *Sunset Boulevard* is a magnificent achievement, which could not have been made in any other country or by any director other than Billy Wilder, who was in complete control. The same things may be said for Stanley Kubrick, who stamps every film with his character, humor, and rhythm. Americans may be ashamed to call some of their films art or even reluctant to see Martin Ritt—a boy from Brooklyn who made a film about cowboys (*Hud*)—as an artist, but an artist he is—and there are many more. The hopeful thing is that their talents will no longer be as subject to precensorship and studio control as in the past and that the American film can speak boldly more freely in the future than it has in the past.

It should be obvious that the personal film is the most compatible with my general theory of perception and film form. It is a theory that has its glimmerings in a remark of Fellini: "The human eye sees things as the human eye, with all its weight of sentiment, ideas, the past. . . . The camera doesn't work like that; it performs a purely mathematical function."[15] But the point is that with the better directors the camera does work like that. It selects, it emphasizes, it creates a living human milieu. It constructs, by inclusion and elision, an effective and affective form that is a moving analogue of our being-in-the-world. This means that the director must exercise great care about his film, but about one thing he can be careless. He need not be anxious that his personal style or voice will not come through. Nor need he try to impose such a conceived style on the work. Insofar as he is honest with his work and with himself, both its authenticity and his will be written all over the film. This has always been true of the great directors, and it will be true of the future ones.

When we watch a film, we do not see shadows moving on a screen any more than when we look at a painting we see fragments of canvas spotted by pigments. What we see in both cases is a visible form, an apparition. This apparition emerges from its created context; and, in the case of the film, it is also aural. But though it is an apparition, it is a real appearance. In this sense, it is like a rainbow, which exists only for perception. Susanne K. Langer has a beautiful description of the status of a work of art, the mirror image, and the rainbow:

It is not unreal: where it confronts you, you really perceive it, you don't dream or imagine that you do. The image in a mirror is a virtual image. A rainbow is a virtual object. It seems to stand on the earth or in the clouds, but it really "stands" nowhere; it is only visible, not tangible. Yet it is a real rainbow, produced by moisture and light for any normal eye looking at it from the right place. We don't just dream that we see it. If, however, we believe it to have the ordinary properties of a physical thing, we are mistaken; it is an appearance, a virtual object, a sun-created image.[16]

Of course we have discovered that the mirror-image of my head is less than half the size of my actual head. Still, the eye sees the virtual image as "being the same size" for the eye's activity is "corrected" by the matrix of the mind. One should also add this to Professor Langer's description of the rainbow. It is not merely a sun-created image, but a sun-and-eye-created image. For we know that the rainbow is "really" a continuum; there is nothing else it could be. Yet we see it as bands of distinct colors, which shade at their "edges" and yet retain emergent individuate identity.

Like the rainbow, the film does not "stand" anywhere. It is constituted not by moisture and light but by sound and sight. It is a visible-aural object but intangible —one which inhabits a created space-time that is nontangential to our natural standpoint—a kind of perpetual elsewhere that enters the presence of immediate experience. The film does not have the ordinary properties of a physical thing. It is a projector-amplifier-eye-ear-created image; a visual and sonorous monogram that emerges for perceptive engagement. And as with the rainbow, we return again and again to perceive it with the ever-reborn hope that this time, at the end of it, we will find treasure.

Motion pictures, like dreams or rainbows, are true myths that we tell ourselves so that we may try to come to grips with what life means in the living of it. Motion pictures, when understood, end in revelation.

Notes

1. John Howard Lawson, *Film: The Creative Process* (New York: Hill & Wang, 1967), pp. 329–330.
2. Sergei Eisenstein, *Notes of a Film Director* (London: Lawrence & Wishart, 1959), pp. 59–61.
3. Lawson, *Film,* p. 338.
4. Lawson, pp. 340–341.
5. Lawson, p. 335.
6. Pauline Kael, "Confessions of a Movie Director," *I Lost it at the Movies* (Boston: Atlantic–Little, Brown, 1965), pp. 261–267.
7. Lawson, *Film,* p. 350.

8. Jonas Mekas, "Notes on the New American Cinema," in *Film: A Montage of Theories,* ed. by Richard Dyer MacCann (New York: Dutton, 1966), pp. 183–184.

9. Rudolf Arnheim, *Art and Visual Perception* (Berkeley: University of California Press, 1957), p. 366.

10. Arnheim, p. 42.

11. Arnheim, p. 38.

12. Penelope Houston, *The Contemporary Cinema* (Baltimore: Penguin Books, 1963), pp. 183–184.

13. Houston, p. 192.

14. Federico Fellini, "The Road Beyond Neorealism" in MacCann, *Film: A Montage of Theories,* p. 383.

15. Federico Fellini, *Juliet of the Spirits* (New York: Ballantine, 1966), p. 36.

16. Susanne K. Langer, *Problems of Art* (New York: Scribner's, 1957), p. 5.

Bibliography

Agee, James, *Agee on Film*. Boston: Beacon Press, 1966. A collection of the movie reviews of America's best film critic.

Alpert, Hollis, *The Dream and the Dreamers*. New York: Macmillan, 1962. Occasional essays which are often not worth the effort of reading.

Arnheim, Rudolf, *Art and Visual Perception*. Berkeley: University of California Press, 1957. A theoretically exciting and scientifically sound investigation of aesthetic perception written in clear and forceful language.

——, *Film as Art*. Berkeley: University of California Press, 1964. A reprint of an early and still important theory of film and the film experience.

Balázs, Béla, *Theory of the Film*. New York: Roy Publishers, 1952. A theory of film based upon the concept that emotion is the core of photography and film.

Barnes, Hazel E., *Humanistic Existentialism*. Lincoln: University of Nebraska Press, 1959. A fine survey of existentialist literature with the emphasis upon Sartre and Camus.

Battestin, Martin C., "Osborne's *Tom Jones:* Adapting a Classic," *Man and the Movies,* edited by W. R. Robinson. Baton Rouge: Louisiana State University Press, 1967. The most perceptive essay in an uneven anthology.

Bluestone, George, *Novels into Film*. Baltimore: Johns Hopkins Press, 1957. The standard work on film and novels. It includes a general theory and analysis of specific novels that became films.

Campbell, Joseph, *The Masks of God: Primitive Mythology*. New York: Viking Press, 1959. The first and most impressive work in Campbell's four-volume investigation of comparative mythology.

Crist, Judith, *The Private Eye, the Cowboy and the Very Naked Girl*. New York: Holt, Rinehart and Winston, 1968. A chronological series of reviews of contemporary films. Well written from a moral point of view.

Durgnat, Raymond, *Films and Feelings*. Cambridge, Mass.: The M.I.T. Press, 1967. An uneven examination of film, weakened by two flaws: (1) overconcentration on science fiction and (2) an inability to distinguish self-expression from artistic expression.

Eisenstein, Sergei, *Film Form and the Film Sense.* New York: Meridian, 1957. The basic explication of Eisenstein's theory of montage—a theory based on formal analogues and intellectual correspondences.

——, *Notes of a Film Director,* London: Lawrence & Wishart, 1959. Advances the theory that visual conflict is the essence of film theory.

Fellini, Federico, *Juliet of the Spirits.* New York: Ballantine, 1966. Contains a long interview with Fellini plus two scripts (shooting and actual) of the film.

Gotshalk, D. W., *Art and the Social Order.* Chicago: University of Chicago Press, 1947. A clear and concise theory of aesthetics based upon the principles of four-dimensional analysis and interdimensional integrity.

Houston, Penelope, *The Contemporary Cinema.* Baltimore: Penguin Books, 1963. A lively and readable account of the films of the late 1950s and early 1960s.

Kael, Pauline, *I Lost it at the Movies.* Boston: Atlantic–Little, Brown, 1965. Acid essays ostensibly about films—actually, a series of sociological reflections.

——, "It's Only a Movie," in *Film Study in Higher Education,* edited by David C. Stewart. Washington, D.C.: American Council on Education, 1966. An essay warning that academic study will be the death of film. The anthology as a whole is not worth the effort.

——, *Kiss Kiss Bang Bang.* New York: Bantam Books, 1969. More pop sociology by the self-acknowledged mistress of the ad hominem. Caustic and lively reading.

Kaelin, Eugene, *An Existentialist Aesthetic.* Madison: University of Wisconsin Press, 1962. Advances a theory of the tension between texture and depth as the essence of aesthetics, while providing an assessment of the writings of Alain, Sartre, and Merleau-Ponty.

Kennedy, Margaret, "The Mechanized Muse," in *Film: An Anthology,* edited by Daniel Talbot. New York: Simon and Schuster, 1959. A standard essay in a standard anthology.

Knight, Arthur, *The Liveliest Art.* New York: Macmillan, 1957. The liveliest history of the movies yet written and an invaluable historical source.

Koestler, Arthur, *The Act of Creation.* New York: Macmillan, 1964. A survey of current psychology written in barbarous "scientific" language. Worth the effort of reading but it does take effort.

Kracauer, Siegfried, *From Caligari to Hitler.* Princeton, N.J.: Princeton University Press, 1947. Advances the theory that the German film expresses the unconscious of pre-Hitler times. A useful historical account of German Expressionism.

——, *Theory of Film: The Redemption of Physical Reality.* Fair Lawn, N.J.:

Oxford University Press, 1960. The most turgid theory of film yet written, which attempts to make the photograph the essence of film.

Langer, Susanne K., *Feeling and Form*. New York: Scribner's, 1953. Professor Langer's major work in aesthetics. A good book, which often suffers from pedantry.

——, *Problems of Art*. New York: Scribner's, 1957. A series of clear, concise essays that express the essence of Langer's theories on aesthetics unhampered by extensive qualifications.

Lawson, John H., *Film: The Creative Process*. New York: Hill & Wang, 1967. A fine and forceful book on film theory unfortunately biased by Russophilia.

Lorenz, Konrad, *Evolution and Modification of Behavior*. Chicago: University of Chicago Press, 1965. Presents the theoretical basis of Lorenz' ethology: the injunctive definition. The argument is that "innate" and "learned" are not mutually exclusive concepts but that both must be used in explaining levels of behavior.

——, *King Solomon's Ring*. New York: Crowell, 1952. A witty and urbane series of essays on animal behavior.

——, *On Aggression*. New York: Harcourt, Brace & World, 1966. A survey of animal behavior patterns plus speculation that the "higher values" of human society are based upon transformation of aggression.

Macdonald, Dwight, *Against the American Grain*. New York: Vintage Press, 1962. A series of sharp essays on contemporary mass culture by a longtime film critic.

Marcel, Gabriel, *Creative Fidelity*. New York: Farrar, Straus, & Giroux, 1964. A series of situtional analyses, which investigate the I-Thou relationship as a paradigm of personal encounter.

——, "Possibilités et Limites de l'Art Cinématographique," *Revue Internationale de Filmologie*, Vol. 5, Nos. 18–19 (July-December 1954). A modern dramatist looks at film and analyzes it brilliantly.

McLuhan, Marshall, *Understanding Media: The Extensions of Man*. New York: McGraw-Hill, 1964. A series of random intuitions concerning mass culture, lacking logical coherence and consistency. A very witty book but weakened by an atomistic and outmoded psychology.

Mead, George H., *Mind, Self and Society*. Chicago: University of Chicago Press, 1934. Mead's major work on the emergence of personality from the web of social interaction.

Mekas, Jonas, "Notes on the New American Cinema," in *Film: A Montage of Theories,* edited by Richard Dyer MacCann. New York: Dutton, 1966. An inchoate essay embodied in a useful anthology.

Merleau-Ponty, Maurice, *The Phenomenology of Perception*. New York: Humanities Press, 1962. The major work in phenomenological psychology, which builds upon the previous *Structure of Behavior*.

Merleau-Ponty, *Sense and Non-sense*. Evanston, Ill.: Northwestern University Press, 1964. Occasional essays on politics and art, including an important reflection on film.

———, *The Structure of Behavior*. Boston: Beacon Press, 1963. Merleau-Ponty's survey of Gestalt and stimulus-response psychology, which advances the theory of levels of behavior.

Morris, Desmond, *The Naked Ape*. New York: McGraw-Hill, 1967. Personal opinions of a reputable zoologist.

Prall, D. W., *Aesthetic Analysis*. New York: Crowell, 1936. An articulation and application of the basic stance taken in his earlier *Aesthetic Judgment*. Prall's attempt is to establish a science of the immediate by demonstrating that apprehension of aesthetic surface is a function of structure.

———, *Aesthetic Judgment*. New York: Crowell, 1929. The argument of this book is that the aesthetic object is an emergent from a transaction between the observer and the observed. The qualitative import of the object is a function of the structural articulations of the materials.

Pudovkin, V. I., *Film Technique and Film Acting*. New York: Grove Press, 1960. The major written work of one of Russia's film giants. Pudovkin differs from Eisenstein by placing more emphasis on the emotional and personal meaning of montage.

Richie, Donald, *The Films of Kurosawa*. Berkeley: University of California Press, 1965. An invaluable analysis of Kurosawa's films. The writing is visual and profound.

Sartre, Jean-Paul, *The Psychology of the Imagination*. New York: Philosophical Library, 1948. Sartre's most important work on aesthetics, which is weakened by an overgeneralization of the literary experience.

Schickel, Richard, *The Disney Version*. New York: Avon Books, 1969. Disney fans may not be enchanted, but they should be. A gentle and perceptive study of Disney's corporate creativity and anal fixation.

Scott, Nathan A., Jr., "The New Mystique of *L'Actuelle:* A View of Cinema in Its Relation to Our Period-Style," in *Man and the Movies,* edited by W. R. Robinson. Baton Rouge: Louisiana State University Press, 1967. A sprightly essay in an uneven anthology.

Solmi, Angelo, *Fellini,* trans. by E. Greenwood. London: Merlin Press, 1967. A book about Fellini and his works, which tends to degenerate into gossip.

Spottiswoode, Raymond, *A Grammar of the Film*. Berkeley: University of California Press, 1965. A dull technical book.

Stephenson, Ralf, and J. R. Debrix, *The Cinema as Art*. Baltimore: Penguin Books, 1965. A tight, concise, and important contribution to film theory.

Taylor, John Russell, *Cinema Eye, Cinema Ear*. New York: Hill & Wang, 1964. A perceptive and sensitive appraisal of the works of several major directors. Taylor knows what he sees and writes about it beautifully.

Tyler, Parker, *Classics of the Foreign Film*. New York: Citadel Press, 1962. This work contains some odd choices of "classics" and many pretty pictures. The written text is high-grade gossip.

Warshow, Robert, *The Immediate Experience*. Garden City, N.Y.: Doubleday, 1962. One of America's best film critics writes and thinks seriously about film and film genres.

Whitehead, Alfred N., *Process and Reality*. New York: Harper & Row, 1957. Metaphysics in the grand manner.

Index

von Sternberg, Josef, 4
von Stroheim, Erich, 4, 15

Wages of Fear, The, 98
Waiting for Lefty, 92
Walking Man, 212
Warhol, Andy, 78, 272
War Lover, The, 99
Warshow, Robert, 194
Welles, Orson, 213, 248
West Side Story, 119
Whitehead, Alfred North, 124, 133, 188, 192, 203
Who's Afraid of Virginia Woolf?, 75, 78, 182, 241
Wilde, Oscar, 74, 82
Wilder, Billy, 233, 278
Wilder, Thornton, 10–11
Wild Kingdom, 166

Wild One, The, 140, 241
Wild Strawberries, 38, 108, 113–117, 155, 187, 241, 247, 262, 272, 276
Williams, Tennessee, 75
Winter Light, 7, 75, 115, 220
Withness, 130–131, 134
Wizard of Oz, The, 187, 243
Wolfe, Thomas, 155
Wood, Grant, 92
World of Apu, 80, 102, 214, 220, 269, 276
Wrap-around screen, 26
Writing, 41–42

Yellow Submarine, The, 188
Young and the Damned, The, 38

Zelanski, Paul, 165
Zero for Conduct, 38, 98